THE REIGN OF KING COVENANT

BY THE SAME AUTHOR

FICTION

The Phoenix and the Laurel
Thunder on St. Paul's Day
The Lady of the House
The Sealed Knot
Dark Conspiracy
Fortress in the Forth
Parcel of Rogues
Longon Goes to Heaven
His Fight is Ours
Gin and Bitters
He Stooped to Conquer
England for Sale
You Can't Run Away
Sir Devil-May-Care
Come to the March
Prelude to Kingship
King's Critic
Be Valiant Still
Undaunted

BIOGRAPHY

Puritan, Rake and Squire
Titus Oates
King James the Last

FOR YOUNGER READERS

Desperate Battle
The Escape of the Prince
The Escape of the King

The high & mighty Monarch CHARLES by y grace of God King of Great Brittaine France & Ireland Defender of the Fayth. etc.

EDYNBURGH

Co: v. Dalen sculp:

King Charles I at the time of his Scottish coronation

THE REIGN OF
KING COVENANT

by

JANE LANE

(Elaine Kidner Dakers)

Illustrated

ROBERT HALE LIMITED
63 Old Brompton Road, London S.W.7

FIRST PUBLISHED 1956

PRINTED IN GREAT BRITAIN BY
NORTHUMBERLAND PRESS LIMITED
GATESHEAD ON TYNE

To

W. L. LLOYD-JONES

In admiration of his skill, and in gratitude
for all his kindness to "Geordie"

CONTENTS

FOREWORD   *Page* 11

PROLOGUE *"Our Own Native-born Sovereign"* 1633 *Page* 13

PART ONE

THE BEGINNING OF THE TROUBLES
1633–1638
Page 21

PART TWO

KING CAMPBELL
1638–1644
Page 63

INTERLUDE

THE CHALLENGE OF MONTROSE
1644–1645
Page 125

PART THREE

THE SELLING OF THE KING
1645–1647
Page 149

PART FOUR

THE STRUGGLE FOR POWER:
Argyll *versus* Hamilton
1647–1648
Page 179

7

PART FIVE

ALLY TURNS ENEMY

1649–1651

Page 201

PART SIX

THE BITTER HARVEST OF THE COVENANT

1651–1660

Page 239

EPILOGUE   *The Reckoning*   1660-1661   *Page* 275

REFERENCES AND NOTES   *Page* 293

BIBLIOGRAPHY   *Page* 305

INDEX   *Page* 311

LIST OF ILLUSTRATIONS

1 King Charles I at the time of his Scottish coronation
Frontispiece

Facing page

2 James, Marquis, afterwards Duke, of Hamilton   48

3 Archibald Campbell, 8th Earl, afterwards Marquis, of Argyll   49

4 Archibald Johnston of Wariston   64

5 Rev. Alexander Henderson. Moderator of the General Assembly of 1638   65

6 Alexander Leslie, afterwards Earl of Leven   80

7 George Gordon, 2nd Marquis of Huntly   81

8 View of Edinburgh in the seventeenth century   96

9 Lord Lorn, afterwards 9th Earl of Argyll   97

10 The Marquis of Montrose   128

11 The Marquis of Argyll   129

12 The first part of the Solemn League and Covenant as it was published in England   144

13 Rev. James Guthrie. One of the most fanatical of the Covenanting ministers   145

14 King Charles II in 1650   224

15 Contemporary English satire on Charles II and the Scots   225

16 The crowning of King Charles II at Scone. From a Dutch broadsheet   240

17 General George Monck   241

Acknowledgments

The illustrations above, nos. 9, 10 and 11, are reproduced by permission of the Trustees of the National Galleries of Scotland; the remaining fourteen illustrations are reproduced by permission of the Trustees of the British Museum.

FOREWORD

WHEN some major religious or political struggle terminates in the decisive victory of one side or the other, it is inevitable that thereafter all history will be written from the winning side. Thus it has been since the Revolution of 1688. There have been isolated voices putting forward the case for the losers; but it is scarcely an exaggeration to say that all text-book history, and nearly all historical biography, have been coloured, to say the least of it, by the Whig point of view.

As a consequence of this, certain legends have grown up on the one hand, and certain periods have been neglected on the other. The history of Scotland between the accession of Charles I and the restoration of his son is a case in point. Two vague but picturesque images are evoked in the mind of the average man by the terms "Covenant" and "Covenanters". The first is that of a sort of religious Magna Carta being signed on a flat gravestone (for to the man reared on text-book history 'the Covenant' is always the National one of 1637, never the Solemn League and Covenant of 1643); the second is of helpless old men and interesting maidens saying their prayers in the heather, and being harried by soldiers under the command of Bloody Claverhouse, only for cleaving to the faith of their fathers.

Of the long period when the Covenant was in power, when a Covenanted Kirk was in effect the Government of Scotland, of its consistent attempts to impose its own creed upon England and Ireland, of the persecution of all who would not accept that creed, and of the miseries it brought upon Scotland, of all this very little has been written. My purpose in undertaking the following work has been to present a picture of that period, a picture of the rise, reign, and fall of a theocracy.

The period is particularly rich in diaries, journals, letters, and papers of all kinds, and so far as possible I have drawn from these contemporary sources, quoting freely, especially from the Covenanters themselves. Because the contemporary spelling would prove tedious, and indeed often unintelligible, to the average reader, I have modernized it, and very occasionally I have substituted an English for some archaic Scots word. In the case of proper names, which at the time were spelt in many different ways even by the owners of them, I have selected one spelling and used it throughout.

JANE LANE

"OUR OWN NATIVE-BORN SOVEREIGN"

1633

I

ON Saturday, the thirteenth day of June, in the year sixteen hundred and thirty-three, the little grey town of Edinburgh was *en fête*. For in response to the Scots' repeated and pressing invitations, there had come hither for his Coronation in the Abbey Kirk of Holyrood, the first King of Great Britain to be crowned in Scotland, their own native-born Sovereign, Charles I.

The Scots nobility, resplendent in their robes of scarlet, "doubled with white taffeta and barred with ermine, with hoods thereto belonging", had gone out to meet their King upon the Lang-gait, the rough track which is now Princes' Street. A few of them remembered this man, who was exactly as old as the century, as a weakly little child, taken from the Palace of Dunfermline, his birth-place, by easy stages on the long journey to London, whither, a year previously, his father had ridden to become King James I of England. But nothing remained now of that tongue-tied little cripple save a slight hesitation of speech. The young man who responded to their greetings sat his mettlesome Barbary with the ease acquired from those boyhood days when, by sheer will and courage, he had forced himself to master the art of equitation; and his body, slight, even diminutive, though it was, had strength. The eyes were frank, unshrewd, with a hint of melancholy; the mouth was restrained but smiling between the full, red-brown moustaches and pointed beard.

A small incident marred the decency of this first meeting between King Charles and the great ones of his native land; "there arose a great contest betwixt the elder sons of Earls and the Lords of the Parliament, anent the place of precedency; so that his Majesty was forced to stand still"; his Majesty was forced at last to intervene, and gave a verdict in favour of the earls' sons, bidding Sir James Balfour, Lyon King at Arms, insert the ordinance in his registers, "to be a precedent in matters of the like case in all times coming".[1]

But the great ones' display of ill manners was soon forgotten in Edinburgh's welcome. "For many ages," wrote Balfour, "this kingdom had not seen a more glorious and stately entry, the streets being all railed and sanded; the chief places where he passed were set out with stately triumphal arches, obelisks, pictures, artificial mountains, adorned with choice music, and divers other costly shows." The guns of the Castle, perched up there upon its rock, thundered a salute; and a guard had been ordered to stand on either side of the street, "which shall not budge nor remove, from the time of his Majesty's entering the West Port till he pass forth of the liberty of the said town".

Behind this guard the townsfolk of Edinburgh stood packed as tight as herrings in a barrel, craning to get a view of the procession. First came Scotland's Officers of Estate; the Chancellor, newly created Earl of Kinnoul; the Lord Treasurer, the Earl of Morton; the Lord Privy Seal, the Earl of Haddington; the Secretary, Viscount Stirling; the Treasurer-Depute, Lord Traquair; the Clerk-Register (whose office corresponded to that of the Master of the Rolls in England), Sir John Hay; the Justice Clerk, Sir George Elphinstone; and the King's Advocate, Sir Thomas Hope. Then came the Primate of Scotland, old Archbishop Spottiswoode, followed by his thirteen Bishops; then earls, lords, and knights, all in strict order of precedence; and then the Earl Marischal and the Lord Constable, each with his staff of office.

The cheers redoubled at this point, as the little figure of the King came into view, stately, magnificent, his horse caparisoned with a cloth of crimson velvet embroidered with gold and pearls, the bosses of the bridle set with diamonds, rubies and emeralds, and a "panache" of red and white plumes swaying on the royal head. Immediately behind rode the Master of the Horse, the King's great friend, the young Marquis of Hamilton, leading a "state horse", with a foot-cloth of white satin, "very beautiful to behold".

Then the cheers lessened, as the King's southern entourage began to pass, English nobles and English Bishops, the latter headed by the small, elderly figure of William Laud, Bishop of London, soon to become Archbishop of Canterbury. He was an inconspicuous figure, very plain in his attire; one of his greatest dislikes was to see richly dressed clerics, whom he had nicknamed satirically "the Church Triumphant".[2] Last came the King's English bodyguard, the Gentlemen Pensioners with their gilded partisans, and the Yeomen of the Guard, curious in their Tudor livery of brown velvet bordered with black, with the

Royal Arms embossed on the back and breast of their coats.

Slowly the procession wound its way, through the West Bow, down the Lawnmercat and the High Street to the Netherbow Port which divided the town of Edinburgh from the fashionable suburb of the Canongait. The Provost and his bailies, sweating in furred red robes, presented the keys of the town, and with them a gold basin, "wherein was shaken out of an embroidered purse a thousand golden double angels, as a token of the town of Edinburgh their love and humble service". At the Overbow stood the Town Guard, self-conscious in white satin doublets and black velvet breeks; at the west end of the Tolbooth, the common jail, his Majesty listened to a fourth speech, while admiring the royal pedigree, from the half-mythical Fergus I, "delicately painted".

At the Mercat Cross hard by, his health was drunk by Bacchus, who was perched upon the Cross; and at the Tron, the public weighing machine, "Parnassus Hill was curiously represented, all green with birks, where nine pretty boys, representing the nine nymphs or Muses, were nymph-like clad". And so to the Netherbow Port, the pinnacles of which had been denuded of the rotting heads of malefactors for the occasion, and here a seventh and last speech was delivered. The King must have been somewhat tired by now, yet "the whole orations his Majesty with great pleasure and delight, sitting on horseback as his company did, heard pleasantly, syne rode down the Canongait to his ain palace of Holyroodhouse, where he stayed that night".[3]

What impressions had been made upon him by this, his first adult acquaintance with Edinburgh and her people? It is unlikely that he divined the significance of much that he saw. Of the lessening of the cheers when his English entourage, especially the representatives of the Church of England, passed down the Royal Mile. Of the ungainly height of the "lands", the six or seven storey houses, which testified to the attitude of a people in whom was inbred a fear of English invasion and who still felt themselves more secure when dwelling within the Flodden Wall. Of the strong gates hanging on their hooks beside the black mouths of every wynd which intersected the houses, gates which could be slammed shut when the immemorial cry of "Clear the causeway!" warned the townsfolk that the real rulers of Scotland, a barbaric nobility, each lord with his armed retainers behind him, were indulging ancient feuds in a street fight.

King Charles had been bred in England from his earliest childhood, and it was impossible for him to understand the significance of such things.

II

On Monday, the 17th, Charles went by coach to the Castle where, having been feasted by its Keeper, the old Earl of Mar, he spent the remainder of the day in his private devotions, keeping vigil in preparation for the morrow's sacred ceremony. At eight next morning, the Officers of Estate, with heralds and nobles, having vested themselves in the Great Hall, came to fetch him for his crowning.

In their robes of crimson velvet, with their coronets carried by bare-headed gentlemen, the great ones of Scotland rode before him down the historic Mile. Behind them were carried the Honours, the Crown borne by the Earl of Angus, created Marquis of Douglas the previous night, the Sceptre by the Earl of Rothes, the Sword by the Earl of Buchan. Then came the King, riding under a rich canopy which was upheld by the eldest sons of six earls. Alighting at the Fore Yett, the gate which gave entrance to the courtyard of Holyroodhouse, his Majesty walked to the Abbey Kirk, where he was met by the Primate, the Bishops, and the musicians of the Chapel Royal, and to the accompaniment of the anthem "Behold, O Lord, our protector, and look upon the face of thine anointed", he was escorted into the church.

Here a large stage had been erected, covered with carpets, and having steps leading down to the Communion Table; on this stage was a smaller one supporting a chair of estate, with cushions and footstool of crimson velvet, and a little table on which lay a richly covered Bible. On the north side of the Communion Table stood a pulpit, on the west were seats for the Archbishops and Bishops, and beyond the pulpit a table, covered with green velvet, on which the Honours were placed.

After sermon, Lyon King at Arms, accompanied by the Primate, the Lord Constable, and the Earl Marischal, went to every corner of the stage, crying to the people who packed the church, "I do present unto you King Charles, the rightful heir to the crown and dignity of this realm; this day is by the peers of the kingdom appointed for his coronation, and are you not willing for your King, and to become subject to him and his commandments?" The people answered with a great shout: "God save King Charles!"

Having shown himself to his people, the King approached the
Communion Table, where the several parts of the Coronation
Oath were administered to him by the Archbishop. Would he
swear to "maintain the true religion of Christ now preached and
professed within this realm", rule the people according to the
laws and Constitution, preserve and keep inviolate the privileges
and rights of the Crown of Scotland, grant to the clergy "all
canonical privileges", defend and protect the Bishops "as every
good king ought in his kingdom to defend his bishops, and the
churches under his government"? Laying his hands upon the
Bible, very solemnly the young King answered that all this
he promised, "so help me, God, and by the contents of this
book".

It is most important to note what he promised: to maintain
the Church of Scotland, which had been an Episcopal church,
established so by Act of Parliament, for more than twenty years.
This was "the true religion of Christ now preached and professed within this realm" that King Charles I, in his solemn
Coronation Oath, promised to maintain.

His outer garment being removed, the King was then anointed
by the Archbishop; the Crown was set upon his head by David
Lindsay, Bishop of Brechin, he was invested with the royal
robes, the Sword and the Spurs, the Sceptre was placed in his
anointed hands, and the Archbishop, the Lords Spiritual and
Temporal, and the nobles came to do him homage. Each
repeated the ancient Oath of Allegiance; each made himself
"your man and vassal, to live and die against all manner of
folk whomsoever in your service, so help me, God"; each swore
all subjection and loyalty to "Charles, my dread Sovereign; and
as I wish God to be merciful to me, shall be to your Majesty
true and faithful, and be ever ready to bestow my life, lands, and
what else God hath given me, for the defence of your sacred
crown and person".

The Communion was then administered to Charles, and after
the Blessing, while the guns thundered from the Castle and the
trumpets brazened, he was escorted to Holyroodhouse, the
Bishop of Moray, Great Almoner, flinging among the surging,
acclaiming people gold and silver pieces new-coined for that day.
It was, declared Sir James Balfour, the most magnificent Coronation Scotland had ever seen.

III

On the following Thursday, there took place the picturesque ceremony known as the Riding of the Parliament. The three Estates, the clergy, the nobles, and the burgesses, rode behind their King to the Parliament House in the High Street, Charles wearing the royal robe of purple velvet which had belonged to his great-great-grandfather, James IV, who had fallen at Flodden fighting against the English, the "Auld Enemy". Having opened Parliament, his Majesty returned on foot to Holyroodhouse, and by his brisk walk, so characteristic of his race, "he made his foot-guard to sweat, being as able a footman as was within the town".

From then until the middle of July there were daily festivities, culminating in what must have been a rare sight to see: "After dinner, the Provost, bailies and councillors, each in [each] other's hands, with bare heads, came dancing down the High Street with all sorts of music, trumpets, and drums." But the Estates of Parliament were kept hard at work; no less than thirty-one Acts were passed during eight days' sitting. To only two of these was there any serious opposition; the first was the confirming of an Act of 1617, giving the King the right to ordain what garb should be worn by the clergy; the other was an Act of Ratification of all the Acts concerning religion passed by the King's father, James VI of Scotland and I of England. For the passing of both these Acts there was, however, a majority.

At last, on July 14th, the Parliament having been "ridden" again prior to its rising, King Charles began his long journey to the country which was home to him as his native kingdom could never be, to his adored young wife, to the sturdy toddler who was Prince of Wales, to the baby daughter, Mary, and to that personal rule without a parliament which was bringing England peace and prosperity.

He can have had no misgivings as to the success of this visit for which his fellow-countrymen had begged so often and so hard.[4] Only two things had marred the general harmony of it. The first had happened in connection with the Coronation. In England it was the custom for the Primate to take precedence of all Officers of the Crown; and sending Lyon King at Arms to the Scottish Chancellor, upon whom Charles had just bestowed the earldom of Kinnoul, the King had asked that for this one day old Archbishop Spottiswoode should be given the like precedence in the procession. To this Kinnoul had made the startlingly rude reply that "never a stoled priest in Scotland should set a foot before him, so long as his blood was hot".

The other unpleasantness had come from that section of the ministry which still hankered after Presbyterianism. There had been black looks among them when, at the Coronation, the Bishops had been seen to bow their heads to an image of the Crucified "curiously wrought" in a rich tapestry at the back of the Communion Table, and again when, on the first Sunday of the King's visit, the Bishop of Moray had preached in his rochet and lawn sleeves in the High Kirk of St. Giles.

But these had been small, apparently unimportant things, quickly forgotten in the general atmosphere of welcome and harmony. It was impossible that they should have warned King Charles that his visit to his native land was the too-brilliant sunrise of an era of blood and revolution which, when it ended, would have brought his own head to the scaffold, and laid Scotland's proud sovereignty in the dust.

PART ONE

THE BEGINNING OF
THE TROUBLES
1633-1638

Chapter One

THE Scotland which King Charles had visited in 1633 was
not, in the eyes of foreigners, either important or attractive.
She was the poorest nation in Europe, with a population of
probably less, certainly not more, than a million souls, and with
even her important towns scarcely larger than villages. She was
the butt of English playwrights and ballad-mongers, to whom
her people were only half civilized. A Huguenot visitor in 1600
had been disappointed to find "neither splendid buildings, nor
remarkable antiquities, nor things worthy of special mention",
and seventeen years later another traveller was dismayed by the
absence of flowers in the gardens, and by the scarcity of fruit
and other delicacies.

The uncleanliness of the Scots was remarkable even in that
age, as also was their sloth. Sir William Brereton, who paid a
visit to Scotland in 1634, described the inhabitants as "most
sluttish, nasty, and slothful people". He could never bring himself to enter his lodgings without either holding his nose or
sniffing at some strong-scented herb. The people, he wrote, were
so lazy that they fetched water from the common well only every
other day. "Their houses of office are tubs or firkins placed
upon the end, which they never empty until they be full, so
as the scent thereof annoyeth and offendeth the whole house".
Their pewter pots and pans were never scoured, "they are afraid
it should too much wear and consume them thereby; only sometimes, and that but seldom, they do slightly rub them over with
a filthy dish-clout, dipped in most sluttish filthy water".

This poverty-stricken, slothful state of Scotland had two main
causes. One was the draining of her wealth throughout the long
Wars of Independence, when, under Wallace and Bruce, she had
fought for her sovereignty as a nation against the aggression of

England. She had emerged from that ordeal proudly victorious, but at the price of a perpetual poverty. The other was her oppression by a nobility who, in the peculiar circumstances which had existed after the death of King James V in 1542, had been able to make themselves into dictators. It was a nobility unequalled in greed and hereditary feuds, united only in a resolve to tyrannize over the common people, a nobility who, for many years, had had no central authority to check its rapacity and oppression. For after the death of James V the Monarchy had been represented first by a foreign Queen Regent, then for a brief period by a young Queen, then by a child King, and lastly, since the Union of the Crowns in 1603, by a Sovereign whose Court was in London.

The Scotland over which these nobles lorded it was less a nation than a collection of districts separated from one another by mountains and barren moors, and with but one highway which ran along the east coast. Here were the principal ports, Leith, Dundee, St. Andrews, Aberdeen, and Inverness, the latter a little island of merchants surrounded by wild Highlanders. From these ports went Scotland's few exports, large quantities of wheat, oats, and barley from the fertile district about Edinburgh, hides, salmon, and timber. All along the shores of the Forth, for at least thirty English miles, were salt-works, with their centre at Prestonpans; some of this salt was exported to Holland, but the greater part of it was used for the curing of herrings, the staple food for the poor during the winter months. There was much coal, too, on both sides of the Forth, but the people were too lazy to do more than scratch the surface, and peat and turf remained the most common kinds of fuel.

Oppressed, backward, dirty, and half civilized as she was, Scotland's pride lay in one thing supremely: that, at the cost of her wealth and her best blood, she had retained her national independence against the continual attempts by England to make her a province of that kingdom. John Taylor, the Water Poet, when he went on his "Pennyless Pilgrimage" in 1618, was enormously impressed by the motto inscribed beneath the Royal Arms at Holyroodhouse: *A hundred and six Forefathers have left this to us unconquered.* "I think," he wrote, "few kingdoms or none in the world can truly write the like."

In the first half of the sixteenth century, something in Scotland *had* been conquered, the "Auld Kirk", and the material conditions of the people had suffered severely by its fall. For the monks had been the leaders in agricultural improvement, the discoverers of coal, for long the only ship-owners in the kingdom. They had encouraged the arts and crafts, they had cared for the sick, the insane, and the poor, and they had undertaken the education of the people. Nearly every monastery of importance had had a school within its walls; others were conducted by the monks of some neighbouring monastery. The three Universities of St. Andrews, Glasgow, and Aberdeen, had all been founded by Catholic prelates, the first in 1410, the second in 1451, and the last in 1495. Such benefits to the community had outweighed the abuses and corruptions, great though they were, which had been notorious in the years before the Reformation, and for the reform of which the last Provincial Council of the Auld Kirk, which met in Edinburgh in 1559, had enacted Canons.

The Reformation in Scotland had its own peculiar character. For first it had taken place at a time when the Sovereign was represented only by a Queen Regent, and therefore the enormous wealth of the Auld Kirk, which has been estimated at something between three and four hundred thousand pounds yearly, was seized upon by a clique of greedy nobles who for long had resented the wealth of the Church; "there are few revolutions recorded in history," remarks a modern writer, "where the presence of self-regarding motives is so exceedingly obvious".[1] And secondly the religious spirit behind the Scottish Reformation was not Lutherism but Calvinism, a spirit of violence, hatred and bitter intolerance. Yet its principal dogma had a particular appeal to the Scots. They might be poor, despised, the jest of the playwright and the ballad-monger; but as Calvinists, or Presbyterians, they and they alone were the Elect of God, and the rest of the world was damned.

When the Auld Kirk was destroyed with peculiar violence, no recognizable structure took its place, and the reason for this was the constant feud between the Reformers and the nobility. For with very few exceptions, the nobles, while speaking the language of the new piety, were concerned only in consolidating their enormous new wealth. They had brought down the Auld Kirk; they had not the slightest intention of allowing John Knox's pet ambition to be realized: a new Kirk modelled on Calvin's Geneva, with himself as President of a Consistory, supreme over secular as well as spiritual matters. They were not going to part with any of the Reformation plunder; when Knox pressed the Regent Morton to give at least some of the revenues of the Auld Kirk for the support of the ministry and the endowment of schools, Morton replied that it was indeed "a devout vision", but refused to disgorge.

Yet though Calvinism had been the spirit behind the Scottish Reformation, for a while after that event it seemed probable that the new Scots Kirk would be made conformable to the new Church of England. For the nobles needed the help of Queen Elizabeth in their intrigues against their own Monarchy, and Elizabeth, who detested all varieties of dissenters, made it a condition of her aid that the Scots should embrace the rites, liturgy, and ceremonies of the English Church. "According whereunto, an Ordinance was made by their Reformers, that in all parishes of that Realm the Common Prayer should be read weekly on Sundays and other festival days, with the lessons of the Old and New Testaments, conform to the Order of the Book of Common Prayer of England; it being well known, that for divers years after, they had no other Order for Common Prayer but that which they received from hence."[2]

But apart from the detestation of anything smacking of Popery, a detestation instilled into the people by the Calvinist Reformers, there was the old hatred of England, the old jealousy aroused by the idea of conforming with her in anything, and the rites and Common Prayer of her Church were soon dropped, every minister conducting his services as he pleased and praying extempore. For years there was no one to whom he was answerable; Knox had tried to bring about some sort of order and control by appointing ten "Superintendents", who should preside over synods, plant and displant ministers, and direct Kirk censures; but as the powers of these functionaries remained vague, and no provision was made for their maintenance, the scheme proved quite impracticable.

It was not surprising, therefore, that King James VI, when he attained his majority in the late eighties of the sixteenth century, found his kingdom in a pitiable state. The Crown was bankrupt; the quarrelsome nobles were united in their determination to retain as a class their new power and wealth against King or Kirk; and the ministers, for so long unaccountable to any authority, were preaching sedition and treason.[3] It is essential to understand the power over the people these ministers possessed, and were to possess again.

Since the abolition of most of the old religious festivals at the Reformation, Scotland's means of recreation had been lamentably few. There were no news-sheets; the wretched tracks which connected the country districts with the towns were often impassable; and in these districts there were only the occasional visits of pedlars and mountebanks to break the monotony of wresting a living from the infertile soil. But there was now a brand-new recreation which gained in popularity every year: the Sabbath "exercises", morning and afternoon, in every little mud-walled, straw-thatched kirk.

For first of all there were lengthy sermons which could be criticized and argued over during the ensuing week. The education given to the people by the Auld Kirk, an education in advance of that of the rest of Europe,* had ministered to the disputacious character of the Scots, and since the Reformation theology had been argued everywhere. For those not interested in theology, there were other attractions in going to kirk. The minister served his parishioners as a newsmonger; "nothing passed in the Court or Council," wrote Burnet, "but their pulpits did ring with it". Then there was the unholy delight of seeing certain of one's neighbours sitting on the Stool of Repentance, the raised platform set in some conspicuous place in the kirk, its occupants garbed in sackcloth, doing penance for some fleshly vice. From the pulpit, "the Chair of Verity", would thunder lurid descriptions of hell-fire, appeals to parishioners who sus-pected a neighbour of witchcraft to come forward and denounce her, vivid tales of the wickedness of Papists and Prelatists, spicy gossip about the doings of the great ones of the realm. Lacking any other recreation, it is little wonder, therefore, that the people flocked willingly to their parish kirks, and that their ministers gained an absolute power over them.

Burnet describes these ministers thus: "They were men all of a sort: affected great sublimities in devotion: they poured themselves out in their prayers with a loud voice, and often with many tears. They had but an ordinary proportion of learn-ing among them: something of Hebrew, very little Greek. Books of controversy with the Papists, but above all with the Arminians, was the height of their study. . . . True morality was little studied or esteemed by them. They were generally proud and passionate, insolent and covetous; yet they took much pains among their people to maintain their authority. They affected all the ways of familiarity that were like to gain on them: even in sacred matters they got into a very indecent set of phrases."[4]

All this was bad enough; but when the ministry set itself up as the supreme authority in secular matters, no form of govern-ment could exercise its functions. The first Reformers had set this bad example. "To discipline," had asserted the second Book of Discipline, "must all the Estates within this realm be

---

* An Act of 1494 had imposed a fine of twenty pounds on every substantial freeholder who neglected to send his son and heir to school.

subject, as well Rulers as they that are ruled", and again, "All men, as well Magistrates as inferiors, ought to be subject to the judgment of General Assemblies". In other words, what the Kirk desired was complete theocracy.

In 1582, when ambassadors from France were sent to the Court of King James, and he ordered the magistrates of Edinburgh to feast them, the General Assembly immediately ordained a fast for that same day, and censured the magistrates for obeying the King's order.[5] In 1593, the Kirk enacted that henceforth no Scots merchant should trade with any dominion of the King of Spain; the merchants applied to the King to maintain the liberty of their trade, but he was unable to protect them from the decrees of the Kirk.[6] In a sermon preached in 1596, David Blake of St. Andrews had declared "That all kings were the Devil's brats, that the Devil was in the Court, and in the guiders of it". And in his prayers for the Queen he used these words, "We must pray for her for fashion's sake, but we have no cause, she will never do us any good". He had added for good measure that Queen Elizabeth of England was an atheist, that the Scottish Lords of Session were miscreants and bribers, and the Lords of Secret Council "holly glasses" and cormorants. Another preacher, Walsh, told his parishioners that King James was possessed with seven devils, and that it was lawful to rise up and deprive him of his authority.[7]

Encouraged by Elizabeth of England, whose heir he was, King James, on attaining his majority, endeavoured to curb these petty tyrants, and to give some sort of form to the Scottish Kirk. There was a moderate party in that Kirk, and by its means he succeeded in getting it enacted, in the General Assembly of 1597, that presbyteries should not meddle with anything outside ecclesiastical matters, and that where the King took exception to proceedings in presbyteries as prejudicial either to the State or to private rights, such proceedings should be suspended during the royal pleasure.*

But it was not until he had become King of Great Britain that James was able to bring form out of chaos in the Scottish Kirk. In 1609 the Bishops were restored to their ancient jurisdiction by Act of Parliament; and in the following year, in a General Assembly, it was resolved that the indiction of such Assemblies belonged to the King, and that no such body could be lawful

---

* To give an instance of the Kirk's interference with the daily lives of the King's subjects: it had enacted that the weekly markets, held from the most ancient times on a Monday, should no longer be held upon that day, because folk who came from afar had to travel on the Sabbath.

without the King's licence; that the synods held in each diocese twice a year be "moderated" (that is, presided over) by the Archbishop or Bishop of that diocese; that no sentence of Excommunication be passed without the approbation of the Bishop; that every minister at his ordination swear obedience to the King; and that no minister speak publicly against these enactments. The latter, against which there had been only five dissentients in the Assembly, were ratified by a parliament which met in Edinburgh in 1612, and all Acts inconsistent with them were annulled.

Thus was the Scottish Kirk established as Episcopalian; it remained to curb the extremists, to give decency and order to the services, and to provide for the Kirk's material needs. Canny old King James, who had a life-long experience of Scotland, of the greed of her nobles, the disputaciousness of her people, and the fanaticism of a section of her ministers, felt his way along, tackling first those problems in which he would have the nobles on his side, since they, as much as he, resented the pretensions of the ministry in their claim to interfere in secular matters. In the more isolated districts of Scotland, particularly in the south-west, that sour land of bog and bleak moorland, the home of the old cattle reivers, the ministers continued in a state of rebellion, ordering fasts on their own authority, inveighing in their sermons against Episcopacy, and filling their prayers with supplications to God for its suppression.[8] Here were poverty-stricken, ignorant peasants, who found indeed their only recreation in listening to fiery sermons, and in collecting on the moors for the periodic Communion, the "Holy Fair" of Burns's inimitable poem. Here the Rev. David Dickson's pulpit at Irvine was the focus of attraction to a whole countryside; "the parishioners of Stewarton, who came thither on business, were wrought up to such a pitch by his market-day sermons, that many of them fell down insensible, and had to be carried out of church, from which circumstance the epidemic was known as 'the Stewarton sickness', and its victims as 'the daft people of Stewarton'".[9]

There was set up, therefore, a much-needed Court of High Commission, which took the power from the hands of a rabble of unruly ministers, and made them answerable to ecclesiastical superiors. It enjoined that ministers be properly ordained, and that the Archbishops and Bishops, while they must reside ordinarily in their own cathedral cities, must make progresses from time to time throughout their dioceses to see that due order was kept. Scotland had no cause to complain of these new

Bishops who, with nobles and gentlemen, made up the Court of High Commission. Old Spottiswoode, made Primate in 1615, having his seat at St. Andrews, was gentle, tolerant, and learned. The first Bishop of Edinburgh, William Forbes, who died in 1634, was a man of extraordinary piety and ascetical habits. William Cowper, made Bishop of Galloway in 1612, strove hard to wean the ministers from the old contentions about Church government, asking, " Were it not far better to preach Christ sincerely? "; and the saintly Bishop Forbes of Aberdeen raised the colleges of that University from the most wretched state to one which was the admiration of Europe.

There still remained the lack of Canons for regulating discipline, and the drawing up of Articles of Belief, and a Liturgy. In the General Assembly of 1617, therefore, five Articles were debated: 1. All to kneel when receiving Holy Communion. 2. Private Communion to be administered to the sick. 3. Private baptism to be administered to infants on the point of death, or when they were not in a condition to be carried to the kirk. 4. Children to be confirmed when they were ready to receive this sacrament. 5. Christmas, Good Friday, Easter, Ascension, and Pentecost, to be observed as Church festivals. In England the feasts of the Annunciation, the Purification, the Circumcision, the Holy Innocents, Epiphany, and many other holy days had been observed ever since the Reformation, but knowing the Calvinist spirit of his compatriots, King James did not seek to induce the Scottish Kirk to conform with that of England in this matter.

The Five Articles embodied the rudimentary principles of Protestantism, yet in Scotland there was much wrangling before they were accepted. Some ministers, while ready to accept Confirmation, since Calvin had included it among the elements of Christian doctrine, would have it under another name, since the term smacked of Popery. Others, professing to adhere strictly to the customs of Apostolic times, were offended by the idea of kneeling to receive Communion, though old Spottiswoode drily reminded them that if their quibble were taken to its logical conclusion, they must receive as the Apostles had received the Last Supper, " lying round about the table ". The utter lack of Christian charity which distinguished the zealots was displayed in their opposition to the second and third Articles; the sick were to be denied the consolation of Communion, dying infants the Sacrament of Baptism, because *they* deemed these customs Popish.

But the Articles were accepted by the General Assembly which met at Perth in the following year, 1618, and henceforth were known as the Five Articles of Perth; they were ratified by the Parliament of 1621.* It was a triumph for the moderates, a defeat for the extremists, and each party interpreted certain omens which marked the occasion as suited themselves. When the Articles were made law by the traditional touch of the Sceptre, "an extraordinary great lightning" and three claps of thunder accompanied the ceremony; it was an unmistakable sign of God's wrath, said the zealots; it was a certain sign of His approbation, retorted the moderates, for had not the Law been given on Sinai amid thunder and flames of fire?

Before the debating of the Five Articles, the draft of a Liturgy had been prepared. After his coming to England, King James had been impressed by the contrast between the decency and beauty of the English services and the Sabbath "exercises" of his native kingdom, where "Preachers and Readers and ignorant Schoolmasters prayed in the Church sometimes so ignorantly as it was a shame to all Religion to have the Majesty of God so barbarously spoken unto, sometimes so seditiously that their prayings were plain libels, girding at Sovereignty and Authority; or lies, stuffed with all the false reports in the Kingdom".[10] Accordingly, in the General Assembly at Aberdeen in 1616, there was passed an Act authorizing some of the Bishops to compile a form of public worship, or Book of Common Prayer. This was in the process of being sent up and down between Edinburgh and London, King James "carefully and punctually perusing every passage of it himself", and conferring upon it with the English Bishops, when, in 1625, death overtook him.

Thus it will be seen that his successor, now King Charles I, inherited both a policy and a quarrel; but between the royal father and son there were two vital differences. King James had passed most of his life in Scotland, he had suffered all through his youth from the greed of her nobles who had deposed his mother and had used him as a shield for their oppressions; and his chief object in establishing Episcopacy had been the restoring of the just Prerogatives of the Crown.

King Charles, on the other hand, had no first-hand knowledge of Scotland; and, as Burnet puts it, "what his father began out of policy, was prosecuted by him out of conscience". Charles

* Ironically enough the Covenanters, whom popular tradition has described as men fighting for liberty against an arbitrary king, were to press Charles I to repeal these Articles on his sole authority, notwithstanding that they had been ratified by a parliament.

had grown up in the atmosphere of English Episcopacy; he was
deeply religious; and to him the order and beauty of the Church
of England were the most precious gifts he could bestow upon
her northern neighbour.

Chapter Two

T HERE was one major problem in regard to the Kirk of
   Scotland which King James had failed to solve: that of its
endowment.

At the Reformation, the lands and revenues of the Auld Kirk
had been settled on the Crown by Act of Parliament; but the
peculiar circumstances of the time had enabled the nobility to
share these riches out among themselves. To ensure that their
heirs would inherit such spoils, they had erected the Church
lands into baronies, and were known henceforth as Lords of
Erection. On his visit to Scotland in 1617, King James had
made a somewhat feeble attempt to abolish the Erections; but
finding that this aroused a most dangerous hostility among the
great ones, he had contented himself with naming commissioners
for the settling of yearly allowances upon the starving ministry.
Even this had infuriated the nobles; "'tis not to be imagined
with what zeal they embraced the frugal opinion of that Apostle
who was vexed at the pouring of the perfume upon the head
of Our Saviour".[11]

Full of youthful enthusiasm and courage, King Charles rushed
in where his father, "the wisest fool in Christendom", had
feared to tread. On his accession to the throne, complaints
from ministers and laymen had poured in to him, for both
suffered under the system whereby the wealth of the Auld Kirk
was possessed by the nobility. By the temporalities of the benefices they had annexed, Lords of Erection could command the
services of a vast number of vassals who formerly had held their
lands of the abbots and priors, and they "lorded it with pride
and insolence enough in their several territories". Under the
spiritualities they claimed the tithes intended for the support
of the clergy, which they put into their own pockets, doling out
to the ministers miserable stipends. Moreover they would not
collect the tithes when their vassals sent word that they were
ready, but only when it pleased themselves; and since the vassal

could not cut his nine parts of corn or hay until the tenth, or tithe, had been collected, the abuse very often resulted in his losing the whole of his harvest.

As for the ministry, their financial state was worse than that of beggars, since they were not permitted to beg. Many had neither manse nor glebe, and were driven to keep ale-houses to support their families; more than four hundred parishes were without either minister or reader.[12] The condition of the kirks, too, was deplorable, some of them being " more like sheep-cots than the house of God ". Writing in 1627, a Catholic priest thus described St. Giles, the High Kirk of Edinburgh: " Bare walls and pillars all clad with dust, sweepings and cobwebs, and on every side the restless resorting of people treating of their worldly affairs; some writing and making obligations, contracts, and discharges, others laying counts, or telling over sums of money." Such a sight must have shocked King Charles on his visit in 1633, and horrified Bishop Laud, who was full of zeal for the beautifying of the English churches, and busy with plans for the renovation of St. Paul's.

To Charles there seemed an obvious remedy for this state of affairs. It was an ancient custom for the Kings of Scotland, on attaining their majority, to revoke all grants of Crown property made while they were minors. King James had been too cautious, and too well aware of the power of a turbulent nobility, to take such a step; King Charles was neither; and almost immediately upon his Accession he proposed an Act of Revocation, offering to buy back all the Church lands filched during his father's minority. There was nothing in the least arbitrary or unlawful about this measure; the owners of Church lands were asked, not compelled, to disgorge, and were to be fully compensated; and the object was an excellent one—to give the ministry a living wage, and to free tithe-payers, the vast majority of Scotsmen, from the oppression of the Lords of Erection.

But when Charles sent the Earl of Annandale and Lord Maxwell (afterwards Earl of Nithsdale) to hold a parliament in Edinburgh wherein he hoped that the Act of Revocation would be made law, he found so serious an opposition to it from the class which had benefited by the Reformation pillage that it was obviously unsafe to proceed. The Act was dropped, therefore, but the nobility never forgave or forgot this attempt to deprive them of some of their spoil.

The King was still determined to do something for the ministers and the tithe-payers who had appealed to him in so many

petitions; and accordingly he set up what was called the Tiend
Commission. This enacted that in future the Lords of Erection
were to grant their tenants either a life-lease or at least one of
twenty-one years, instead of the yearly leases under which the
tenants had lacked security and the incentive to build and
plant. Moreover the maximum stipend of the clergy, fixed by
an Act of 1617 at eight hundred merks, was now to become the
minimum, and Charles encouraged the Commissioners to fix
no maximum at all.[13] Both tithe-payers and clergy expressed
profuse gratitude for these measures, acknowledging the King
as "their deliverer from an intolerable bondage, under which
they and their ancestors ever since the reformation of religion
had grievously groaned".[14]

But the nobility of Scotland, insatiable in their greed, and
traditionally impatient of all authority, were now fixed in their
opposition to the King, and from the time of the intended Act
of Revocation onwards they sought to diminish his power. Long
before the fatal year of 1637, two means of doing this were ready
to their hand.

The first was in the common cause they had with the new rich
class created by the Reformation in England; and for the pro-
moting of this common cause—the retention of the wealth of
the Old Religion, and the power which such wealth brings—
very early in King Charles's reign there was drawn up a
"Clandestine Band", subscribed by English and Scottish malcontents, each swearing to assist the other until "they should
draw the King to dispense with divers points of his royal prerogative in such degree as he should not have an arbitrary
government as all his predecessors ever had, conform to the
established laws of both kingdoms", and that the Bishops, who
both in England and in Scotland had a voice in Parliament and
revenues from Church lands, should be abolished "crop and
root". Both James Gordon and John Spalding, reliable historians of the period, refer constantly to this Clandestine Band, and
Clarendon, Nicholas, and Echard mention places where the subscribers to it met to discuss their plans.

The other means by which the privileged classes in Scotland
could obstruct their King lay in the very real and intense hatred
of the common people for Popery on the one hand, and England
on the other. The ruling families took care, therefore, to impress
upon the ministry that the intended Revocation had been but
the prelude to the revoking of all former laws against the Papists,
and that, but for the opposition of godly lords, Popery would
have been re-introduced. Side by side with this, it was impressed

upon the people, those tithe-payers who regarded King Charles as their deliverer from oppression, that all such measures had been suggested by English Bishops, English being the operative word. Thus did the nobles engage both ministers and people in their quarrel with the royal authority, masking the real causes of that opposition under the names of religion and patriotism.[15]

"Wherever the prince is not jealous of underminers," wrote Sir Philip Warwick, "and active to maintain the established government, there will never want spirits given to change who will attempt it, and make religion their shelter for rebellion." Charles I was resolute to maintain the established government; but he was not "jealous of underminers". In the measures he had taken in regard to Scotland, he had acted legally and justly, and for the benefit of the community as a whole. Almost immediately after his visit to Scotland for his Coronation, how-ever, he was given a warning of the depths to which the nobility of that kingdom would stoop in their attempt to undermine his regal authority.

It will be remembered that in the Parliament which had sat during that visit, two Acts had been passed with considerable opposition. Before the King left Scotland, a petition was pre-sented to him for their repeal. It was both insolent and false in its declarations, taking it for granted that the whole of the ecclesiastical settlement made over the years by King James was illegal; and rather naturally Charles refused to receive it.

Scarcely had he left for England than a libellous document was written, in which it was plainly inferred that there had been an intentional miscounting of the votes which had made the two Acts law. The existence of this libel coming to the ears of the Lords of Secret Council (a body similar to the English Privy Council), the matter was investigated, and the author of the libel was found to be a lawyer named Haig. A warrant was got out for his arrest, but he fled; since the investigation had disclosed that a number of the nobility had been his aiders and abettors, it was decided to make an example of one of them, and the per-son chosen was John Elphinstone, Lord Balmerino. He was selected for two reasons; first because a copy of the libel, inter-lined in his handwriting, had been found in his study; and secondly because of all men in Scotland he had the least excuse for intriguing against his King.

For his father, the first Lord Balmerino, who died in 1633, had owed his life and his estates to King James's clemency. Either because he had secret sympathy with Catholicism, or because

C

he wanted to ruin the King his master, old Balmerino, as Secretary of State, had tricked James into signing unawares a complimentary letter to the Pope. Some time later the trick was discovered, Balmerino was tried for high treason, condemned, and sentenced to pay the full penalty. James, however, being "mild beyond measure, some thought beyond policy", not only pardoned the culprit upon his throwing himself upon the royal mercy, but restored him to his estates.

In 1634 history repeated itself in the person of his son. Young Balmerino was indicted for approving and concealing a seditious libel, a capital offence; he was tried by a jury of his peers, found guilty, and condemned; but being heir not only to his father's perfidy but to his knowledge of the Stuarts' mildness, he followed his father's example, and acknowledging his crime, begged for his life. Charles also followed the paternal example; he pardoned Balmerino and restored him to his estates. This news the prisoner received in Edinburgh Castle, and acknowledging the debt he owed to the royal mercy, protested that henceforth his ambition would be to show his gratitude by serving the King to the uttermost of his power. Instead, during the troubles which began in the year 1637, he showed himself one of Charles's most bitter opponents.[16]

The affair of Balmerino, unpleasant though it was, appeared to the King a mere isolated incident. It was not. It was a warning that Scotland was a powder-magazine; the spark which was to light that gunpowder was something which seemed to have no connection with the greed and the intrigues of Scottish nobles, but which in fact was the chance they needed to strike at the very foundations of the royal authority. It was the action of Charles in carrying on his father's work of giving the Scottish Kirk a form: the point at which King James had arrived when death overtook him, the drawing up of a Book of Common Prayer.

Chapter Three

FOUR years previous to his Scottish Coronation, King Charles had sent for the Service Book which had been drawn up by his father; it was brought to London by the Bishop of Ross, examined by the King and a committee of English and Scottish

Bishops, and discarded in favour of the English Prayer Book. On Charles's visit to Scotland, however, it was represented to him by the elder Bishops that, in the mood of militant nationalism which had prevailed in Scotland since the Union of the Crowns, the English Book would arouse resentment; the King, therefore, ordered the Bishops to make yet another fresh start, and to compile a separate Liturgy for Scotland. At the same time a Book of Canons was drawn up.

For hitherto there had been no written collection of the rules of the Kirk government, so that neither clergy nor laity had any certain guide to their powers and duties. The innumerable Acts of General Assemblies had never been printed, and it appeared to the King that it would be acceptable to his Scottish subjects if these Acts were simplified, compressed, and published, so that henceforth "none could be ensnared through ignorance, nor complain that they were overcharged with the multiplicity of them".[17] His hope seemed justified; the Book of Canons was duly published in 1635, and no dislike of it was shown.

But the Service Book, brought up to London again in that same year, was still considered unsatisfactory, and it was not until early in 1637 that a version was approved. At first it was to have been used at Easter; but, in order that all Scotland should be fully informed of its nature, its reading was deferred until late in July. There were many reasons why King Charles was totally unprepared for the furore it created.

First, the Scottish Kirk had been Episcopal now for nearly thirty years, and the Articles of Perth, the establishment of the Bishops, the setting up of the High Commission, and the Book of Canons, all had been accepted quietly save by a fanatical minority. Next, from 1617 onwards, the English Prayer Book had been used constantly in the Chapel Royal at Holyrood, to which service had resorted a large number of Scots of all classes; it had been used in the University of St. Andrews, by the Bishops in ordaining Scottish ministers, and wherever the King had been present at divine service during his visit to Scotland in 1633.

Thirdly, the enormous number of Scots at Court, from great Officers of Estate like the Master of the Horse, the Captain of the Pensioners, the Keeper of the Privy Purse, to the grooms, cupbearers, carvers, and ushers, ever since the Union of the Crowns in 1603 had frequented the Anglican service of their own accord.[18]

Fourthly, the Scottish Service Book was modelled, with slight variations calculated to indulge Scots national pride, on the Liturgy which had been drawn up by the Reformers who had suffered death for their faith in Mary Tudor's day, and who, in Scotland as in England, were honoured as martyrs. There could not be, therefore, to any reasonable man, the least excuse for quarrelling with the Service Book on the grounds that it was "Popish".

Lastly, before the reading of the Book in July, it had been constantly referred to in sermons from Scottish pulpits, not only "without any apparent disgust of the Book, or disgrace offered to the preachers' persons", but with praise and recommendation from ministers who afterwards appeared as its most bitter enemies. All Scotland knew what the Book contained, and the date on which it was to be used for the first time; there was not the least appearance of discontent among either ministers or people. The King had every reason, therefore, for believing that the Book would be received "with great applause".[19]*

But even so, he was both cautious and considerate. Realizing that some of the more fanatical of the ministers might object to the Book, he sent down instructions to the Bishops, signed with his own hand, that they should "proceed with moderation" and not press such portions of the Liturgy which, in their judgment, might be deemed displeasing; and that they should strive to gain the extremists' hearts by time and reason.[20]

On the fatal Sunday morning of July 23rd, the High Kirk of St. Giles was packed to the doors. The King was represented by his Lords of Secret Council; old Archbishop Spottiswoode, recently created Lord Chancellor on the death of Kinnoul, was present, as well as David Lindsay, Bishop of Edinburgh; the Provost and bailies were in their gallery; and the body of the kirk was filled with people of all classes, including a crowd of waiting-women whose duty it was to arrive early at the kirk and keep places for their mistresses. In the custom of the day, these women sat on "creepie-stools", which, after service, were stored in the kirk.

All was decent and orderly until the Dean, James Hanna, began to read from the Service Book. He had not read more than a few of those beautiful sentences when the waiting-women began to clap their hands in derision, and his voice was drowned in curses and outcries. Though unexpected on this occasion, a

---

* An instance of the way in which "popular" history is written is Mr. Morison's statement in his *Life of Wariston* (p. 18) that *months* prior to July, 1637, "the entire nation rose to obtain relief not merely from the Liturgy, but from the incumbus of the whole Episcopal system".

demonstration by such persons was familiar enough in Edinburgh. It was this type of termagant whom King James had christened satirically "the holy sisters"; it was these who had mobbed Queen Mary after her surrender at Carberry, shrieking "Burn the whore!" and flinging filth as she was brought prisoner to her capital; and who had raised a commotion in St. Giles when prayers had been ordered by King James on the news that his mother had been condemned to death in England.

On the present occasion, the Bishop of Edinburgh stepped into the pulpit and appealed to these furies not to profane the House of God; immediately one of them responded by hurling a creepie-stool at him, which fortunately was diverted by someone present. Far from quieting the uproar, his appeals increased it. A gentleman murmuring a response to what the Dean was trying to read, was struck on the face with a Bible by one of these termagants, who cried: "Dost thou say Mass at my lug!" Yells of "False anti-Christian!", "Wolf!", "Beastly belly-god!", "Crafty fox!", were heard above the general din. "He is the son of a witch's breeding and the devil's get!" shrilled a voice, referring to the harmless and learned Bishop Lindsay. "Ill-hanged thief!" bawled another. "If at any time when thou wentest to Court thou hadst been well hanged, thou hadst not been here to be a pest to God's kirk this day!"

The old Archbishop summoned from their gallery the Provost and bailies who, with their officers, thrust this unruly rabble out of the kirk and locked the doors against them. The service continued, but it is unlikely that the remainder of the congregation imbibed any clear idea of what the Book contained, for the rabble hammered at the doors, threw stones at the windows, and continued to bellow out curses.[21]

Not without courage the Bishop of Edinburgh conducted the afternoon service, which passed without incident; but no sooner was he come out of the kirk to go to his lodging than he was set upon by a mob of women. The Earl of Roxburgh hustled him into his own coach, which was pelted with stones by the rabble which ran beside it. It was with great difficulty that the Bishop attained the safety of his lodging, the mob following him and trying to drag him down the stairs by his gown, one woman demanding that he should suffer the fate of Cardinal Beaton, in whose murder John Knox had had a share.

The news of the riots was sent to the King by the Lords of Secret Council, who took care to impress upon him that they had been the work merely of "the rascal multitude", and that all decent people in Scotland thoroughly condemned them. It was a lie, and at least some of the Council knew it was a lie. The riots had been organized.

The breathing-space between the publication of the Service Book and its reading in July, a period intended by the King to prepare Scotland for its favourable reception, had been used by certain persons secretly to incite the rabble to revolt. The evidence for this is ample. Bishop Guthrie, at that time a minister who disapproved of the Book, states definitely that Lord Balmerino and the Lord Advocate, Sir Thomas Hope, together with two extremist ministers, met at the house of a Nicholas Balfour in the Cowgait, and there persuaded some of " the holy sisters " " that they and their adherents should give the first affront to the Book, assuring them that men should afterwards take the business out of their hands ".[22] Both Burnet and James Gordon mention the strong suspicion current at the time that the women had been incited " by many of the better sort ", and Spalding states roundly that the discontented among the nobility ordered the tumult, and that the mob acted "as they were directed". Later events were to lend weight to these statements that the riots were organized.[23]

For the present the Council, each member of which had signed, on June 13th, an order for the use of the Book, wrote the King that though they were ready to command its continued use, the clamours and petitions against it compelled them to seek guidance from his Majesty. The magistrates, who had assured Laud, now Archbishop of Canterbury, that the Book would be readily accepted by " the greatest and best part of our inhabitants ", now wrote in the same strain as the Council, both to Laud and to Lord Stirling, Secretary of State. The King, bewildered by this totally unexpected furore, postponed the use of the Book till September.

His hope that this would allow time for the better instruction of the ignorant was disappointed. It had been instilled into the minds of the mob that the Book was but " the mass in English ", compiled by "Popish-minded" Bishops. All through August, therefore, a witch-hunt was in progress against these unfortunate prelates and all who dared to take their part. Fuel was added to the flame by denunciations from fanatics' pulpits, and by the wide circulation of a most mischievous tract, *A Dispute against the English Popish Ceremonies, obtruded upon the Kirk of Scotland.*

The Bishop of Brechin, in order to avoid lynching, fled the kingdom. The Bishop of Galloway was attacked in Edinburgh, cursed at for a Jesuit because he possessed a crucifix and recommended the same as a pious token of remembrance, and was saved from death only by the Earls of Wigton and Traquair coming to his rescue with their followers. Later the same day Traquair himself was set upon, his hat, cloak, and staff of office snatched from him, and his person nearly trampled to death. The Provost was stoned as he was returning to his own house, and was forced to order his servants to fire over the heads of the mob. A minister who had defended the Book in Glasgow was attacked as he was returning home one dark night, and narrowly escaped with his life. "This tumult was so great, that it was not thought meet to search either the plotters or the actors of it; for numbers of the best quality would have been found guilty."[24]

Moderate ministers like Robert Baillie were astounded by the madness which the Book had provoked. "The whole people," he wrote, "think Popery at the doors; the scandalous pamphlets which come daily new from England, add oil to this flame; no man may speak anything in public for the King's part, except he would have himself marked for a sacrifice to be killed one day. I think our people possessed with a bloody devil, far above anything that ever I could have imagined, though the mass in Latin had been presented." He himself was in fear of his life. "For as well as I have been beloved hitherto by all that have known me," he wrote, "yet I think I may be killed, and my house burnt over my head; for I think it base and wicked to be moved and carried down with the impetuous spirit of a multitude; my judgment cannot be altered by their motion, and so my person and state may be drowned in their violence: I wish my fears may be disappointed."[25]

Brave words; but many a stronger character than Baillie was to be "moved and carried down with the impetuous spirit", not of a multitude, but of nobles, gentlemen, and ministers, banded together to revolt.

Chapter Four

By October there had appeared two very significant and ominous changes in the situation. First, while Edinburgh was still packed with a disorderly mob, certain of the better sort were beginning to besiege the Council with "supplications", and in these they were joined by the magistrates; and secondly the original cause of the uproar, the Service Book (the use of which had again been postponed), was almost forgotten in the outcry against the Bishops.

Sir John Hay, who was both Provost and Clerk-Register, protesting to the Council that he could not keep the multitude in check, a suggestion was made by Sir Thomas Hope, Lord Advocate, himself a bitter Puritan. It was that the "Supplicators" should choose from among themselves certain commissioners to lay the grievances of the rest before the Council. The suggestion was adopted, but on the express condition that the rabble who had flocked into Edinburgh from all the neighbouring districts be sent home, that all rioting should cease, and that the Supplicators meet in small numbers only.

Accordingly four committees were set up, in modern parlance boards, but then termed Green Tables, shortened to the Tables; each had four members and represented respectively the Supplicators among the nobles, the lairds or gentlemen, the burgesses, and the ministers. The Tables had agreed to the Council's conditions in allowing their creation, but had no intention of abiding by them. At Balmerino's lodging they resolved to besiege the Council in the following month "in as great numbers as possibly could be had", wrote Baillie, who by this time was swimming with the tide, that the authorities might be frightened into granting their demands.

That the setting up of the Tables had been a mischievous suggestion immediately became apparent. For to their supplications against the use of the Service Book they now added a demand for the abolition of the Book of Canons (accepted peacefully, it will be remembered, in 1635), the High Commission set up by King James in 1609, and "all other novations"; what was aimed at, it was clear, was a total destruction of the Episcopacy built up so patiently, and without opposition save by the fanatical minority, over so many years. Again, while publicly repudiating the rioters, the Tables demanded that no legal process be taken against these hooligans who had been guilty of the mal-treatment of the King's subjects and the attempted murder of his Bishops, asserting that all they had done had been out of zeal for religion.[26]

Worst of all, it was an open secret that some members of the King's own Council were in sympathy with the malcontents, among them Roxburgh, Privy Seal, who, be it noted, was a Lord of Erection and enjoyed the revenues of the rich Abbey of Kelso and no less than thirty-seven parish kirks; and Hope, the Lord Advocate, whose suggestion of the setting up of the Tables had turned rioters into rebels, rebels who were convening the King's lieges without his permission (a criminal offence), and who, though having no legal authority whatsoever, were beginning to appear as the rivals of the King's authority, aware that by adding a demand for the Bishops' removal to that of the Service Book, they would have the sympathy of the nobles as a class.

Far away in London, the bewildered King listened to reports of these doings. The only solid fact which seemed to emerge was that for some extraordinary reason, the Scots feared a return of Popery. In December, therefore, Charles sent down a Declara-tion, asserting his own detestation of that faith, and his assurance that he had no intention whatsoever of doing anything in the matter of religion which was against the laws of the land. But a particularly mischievous rumour had preceded the Declaration. One of the fanatical ministers had put it about that when Sir James Carmichael, Treasurer-Depute, had been in London just recently, he had heard the King affirm that " he would have the Book through, on all hazards, and would never have a letter of it altered ". The rumour reaching the ears of Carmichael, he indignantly declared that he had affirmed the clean contrary, and that in examining the Book afresh, Charles had marked with his own hand the passages therein which seemed most to incense the Scots, with a view to having them altered. But by that time the rumour had served its turn.[27]

The King's Declaration was ignored; the attitude of the Tables grew more and more insolent and threatening, and that of the Council correspondingly placating. When the Earl of Loudoun demanded that the Tables be heard in accusing the Bishops of a variety of crimes, and the Ministers' Table informed the Council " that the curse of Meroze would fall upon their heads, who were wanting to the Church at such a time ",[28] the only reply of the Lords of Council was respectfully to beg the Tables to have patience while once again they applied to the King. The result of their applications was for Charles to summon one of his principal Officers of Estate, John, Earl of Traquair, to come and give him a personal report upon the whole business.

Traquair returned to Scotland in February, 1638, bringing another Declaration. In this the King took full responsibility for the Service Book, refusing to allow the Bishops to be scapegoats, hoped that in time he would be able to satisfy all misgivings concerning it, pardoned the illegal action of the Tables in convening his lieges without his consent, but discharged all such gatherings in future under pain of treason. He was willing, he said, to accept of their petitions hereafter, providing that neither the matter nor the form of them was prejudicial to the royal authority.

The mistake Charles made was in believing that any such concessions, or any appeal to reason, would move the malcontents; for what he did not know was that the men behind this revolt were the great ones who, ever since his attempted Act of Revocation, had awaited their opportunity. "Let no man think," wrote Andrew Lang, "that Charles Stuart had a possible chance." By instilling into the minds of the people that the Service Book was Popish and of English compilation, these great ones had instigated riots. Under the excuse of stopping the riots, they had set up the Tables; and the Tables had struck the first blow at the Monarchy by demanding the removal of the Bishops. Though the Earl of Rothes was described by Clarendon as "of a pleasant and jovial humour", it was not in jest that he assured Traquair that "if no other order could be had of the Bishops, the noblemen, barons, and burgesses would sit upon them and hang them". Nor was he being "jovial" when he added a veiled threat; he had no desire, he said, to take Traquair's office from him, so long as he remained faithful to what was coming to be called "the Good Cause".[29]*

Though it was not known, or ought not to have been known, to any save the Council what this new Declaration brought by Traquair contained, the Tables sent instructions to the mob, their followers, to come to Stirling to protest against it when it was read on February 20th in that town. Rothes gleefully recorded the response to this summons: "There was twa parts of all Fife at Stirling upon Monday at night and Tuesday in the morning, with a great many from East and West Lothian, and

---

* Traquair himself was to prove a trimmer *par excellence*, and was despised by all parties. Some wit had composed an anagram on his name: "Ho! a very affronted liar." (*Scots Affairs*, I, 31.)

some out of the West, in all about seven or eight hundred in town." No sooner had the royal Declaration been read by a herald, than a "Protestation" was read by a representative of the Tables. Walking home with Rothes afterwards, Roxburgh, a secret sympathizer, expressed a fear that the Marquis of Huntly, the greatest man in the north-east of Scotland and head of the powerful Gordon clan, would oppose the malcontents, but Rothes waved this aside with contempt, declaring that he " would not give a salt citron" for Huntly.

A few days later, when the Declaration was read in Edinburgh, the same mobs packed the town, and the same Protestations followed. A little incident which was to have a most dramatic significance marked the occasion. While representatives of the Tables were reading their Protestation from a scaffold they had erected opposite the Mercat Cross, one of their number, young James Grahame, Earl of Montrose, climbed upon a barrel on the scaffold to cheer and encourage his colleagues. Whereat the merry Rothes cried to him: " James, you will not be at rest until you are lifted up there above the rest in three fathom of rope."[30]

The refusal of the Tables to listen to anything the King had to say without automatically protesting against it, the feebleness or treachery of the Council, and the continued rioting of a mob who were countenanced, even incited thereto, by their betters, all this could have but one end. His fears, wrote Baillie, had been at first for a split in the Kirk, " but now I am affrighted with a bloody civil war ". Such was the atmosphere, and such the situation, in which was drawn up the National Covenant.

From remote times, whenever their interests as a class had induced the nobles of Scotland to lay aside their internecine feuds and unite against the Crown, it had been their custom to draw up " ane band ". It served two purposes; it protected individuals from the royal wrath, and it prevented any of their number from turning king's evidence, because such bands always contained a clause whereby each signatory swore to stand by the rest against all persons whomsoever. Since these included the Sovereign, bands of this nature had been made illegal by the ninth Parliament of Queen Mary, and again by a parliament held by King James in 1585. The National Covenant, since it contained the forbidden clause, was just such a band.

The time-honoured picture of the National Covenant is that of an entire nation flocking to sign their names to a document laid on a flat stone in the Greyfriars' Kirkyard in Edinburgh, a document protesting against the attempt by an arbitrary king to interfere with the national religion. What are the facts?

First of all, this document was of ten large pages, and was couched in language impossible to be understood by the ordinary Scots man or woman of the day; indeed, many of those who signed it were so young or so ignorant that they could not write their names. Next, great opposition to the Covenant was made, not only by the lawyers, who knew that such a band was illegal, but by the ministry.[31] Thirdly, coercion to the point of violence had to be used in collecting the signatures of a great many, both ministers and laymen, as will be seen in a moment. Lastly, the title of the thing deluded many, and was intended so to delude them.

In 1560, a year before Queen Mary came to Scotland to occupy her throne, John Knox had drawn up a "Confession of Faith", which, in the same year, and again in 1567, was ratified by Parliament. It was nothing more or less than a repudiation of Popery. When James VI was a lad of fifteen, a second Confession of Faith, of the same nature as the first, was drawn up, subscribed by the King and Council, and soon afterwards by the whole nation. This was in 1580, 1581, and 1590.

In order to dupe the people into believing that the sole object aimed at was to save the nation from a return to Popery, those who drew up what came to be called the National Covenant— Lord Rothes, a lawyer named Archibald Johnston of Wariston, and two ministers, David Dickson and Alexander Henderson— gave it precisely the same title as the old Confession of Faith. Thus the Covenant first saw the light of day as:

The Confession of Faith, subscribed at first by the King's Majesty and his Household in the year of God 1580. There-after by Persons of all ranks in the year 1581, by Ordinance of the Lords of the Secret Council, and Acts of the General Assembly. Subscribed again, by all sorts of Persons, in the year 1590, by a new Ordinance of Council, at the desire of the General Assembly; with a General Band for the maintenance of the true Religion and the King's person; And now subscribed in the year 1638 by us Noblemen, Gentlemen, Burgesses, Ministers, and Commons, under-subscribing.

The reason for giving the Covenant this title is plain. It was hoped that the people at large would be tricked into believing that it was nothing more or less than the old Confession of Faith directed against Popery, and that, since it included a pledge to defend the King's person, the clause of mutual defence "against all persons whomsoever", would be regarded as innocuous.

That it differed in one vital point from the original Confession of Faith would not be perceived by the common people. In his *Large Declaration* of the following year, King Charles drew attention to this difference. Whereas, he pointed out, in the first three subscribings to the Confession of Faith, either his father's own Act was expressed, or an Ordinance of the Secret Council, equivalent to the royal authority, was obtained, in the subscribing of the document which masqueraded as the Confession of Faith in 1638 neither his own nor his delegated authority was sought or given, nor was there a General Assembly to petition for it. Thus the exacting of a public oath, which was illegal without the King's authority, was done in this February of 1638 without any legal authority whatsoever.*

Even among the adherents of the Tables, there was considerable hesitation in signing this document. When, at two in the afternoon of February 28th, the nobles and lairds of the party assembled in the Greyfriars Kirk, so uneasy were they found to be that, dividing them into two bodies, Rothes and the Rev. Henderson set to work to satisfy their doubts before they could be induced to sign. Next day Rothes and his friends repaired to Taylors' Hall in the Cowgait, where the ministers of the party were awaiting them, and here new persuasions were necessary.

For many of the clergy had been ordained by the Bishops, now to be abolished, and had sworn to maintain the Five Articles of Perth, now to be swept away; moreover these Articles had been enacted by a General Assembly, regarded by those of the Presbyterian persuasion as the highest authority in ecclesiastical matters. But Rothes was ready with his answers. No man, he declared, is tied to a false oath, and since liberty from the yoke of "Popish" bishops was now offered, "they deserve to die in servitude who refuse the offer". To the further objection that all the "novations" complained of had been ratified by Act of Parliament, Rothes replied airily that the Estates of Parliament had not been well informed at the time of the evil of these Acts, and that until such time as another parliament repealed them, the subjects were justified in suspending their obedience to them. As for the fact that only the King could exact a national oath, this, asserted Rothes, was an oath "whereto none would be com-

---

* Even that enthusiastic Covenanting historian, Dr. Cook, admits that this masquerading of the National Covenant under a false name was "a piece of disingenuity which was not necessary to support the cause, and which afforded its enemies some grounds for questioning the integrity of the zealous men by whom it was espoused." (*History of the Church of Scotland*, II, 416.)

pelled, but it was expected all would willingly condescend, and all make their oath to God Almighty".

By the end of that day, March 1st, three hundred ministers had subscribed, and two very ominous ordinances had been made by the Tables: the imposing of a contribution upon all the King's subjects to defray the expense of what amounted to a campaign against him (nominally a voluntary contribution, but those who refused to subscribe to it were to have their names noted, "by which means men's affections could be tried"); and an order that all ministers who refused to sign what was to be called the Covenant should be "exhorted and invited to do otherways", and if they still refused, "to be discountenanced and dishaunted by them all, and all they could persuade".[32]

Copies of this enormous document were then dispatched to every parish in Scotland, with directions to the ministers to see that all their people signed, those unable to write their names to have it done for them by a notary. The names of all who refused were to be "listed". Meanwhile the Tables were to remain in Edinburgh to await the King's answer to this treasonable document; and eight collectors were appointed for each shire to receive the "voluntary" contributions, the people to be taxed according to one dollar the thousand merks of rent. (The nobles took full advantage of the fact that the tax was officially a voluntary one; the contributions of thirty-four of them only amounted to 670 dollars.)

All March and April were spent in collecting signatures. The extremist ministers filled their entire sermons with eulogies upon the Covenant and threats against those who refused to sign it. To them the illegality of the band was nothing; it was a Covenant with the Lord God, and, as Andrew Lang puts it, "nothing was absent from it but the signature of the other high contracting party". Ominous texts were chosen, such as that from II Chronicles, xv, 12: "And they entered into a covenant to seek the Lord God of their fathers with all their heart and all their soul; that whosoever would not seek the Lord God of Israel, should be put to death, whether great or small, man or woman."[33] In the south-west and in Fife, districts always anti-Episcopalian, there was mass hysteria, some signing in their own blood (an ancient custom in the less civilized districts of Scotland.) At one of the Edinburgh kirks a minister made the congregation rise and hold up their hands as they swore to keep the Covenant; "At the which instant of rising up, and then holding up their hands, there raise such a yelloch [sic], such abundance of tears, such a heavenly harmony of sighs and sobs, universally through all the corners of the church, as the like was never seen nor heard of ".[34]

But in other parts there was resistance, and Rothes himself admits that " by threats and terrors" many were compelled to sign against their will. The Tables " proceeded to contumelies and exposing of many to injuries and reproaches, and some were threatened and beaten who durst refuse ".[35] At Inverness, the Provost and two bailies refusing to subscribe, another bailie called up the town drummer and bade him summon the whole town to sign, adding that those who did not would suffer for it. At Elgin the people asked to be allowed to subscribe on the condition that they be permitted to continue kneeling at the Communion, but this was " absolutely refused ".[36] The stoutest resistance came from Aberdeen, where the magistrates one and all refused to sign, " in regard the said commissioners are not come authorized, nor clad with commission from his Majesty, nor Lords of the Privy Council, to exact any such subscriptions, as likewise in regard of his Majesty's proclamation lately published at the Mercat Cross of this burgh . . . prohibiting any such meetings, combinations, or bands amongst his Majesty's subjects ".[37]

In April, a man signing himself " John de Maria " wrote to a correspondent :

" You could not have choosed but laugh to have seen pipers and candlemakers in our town committed to the town jail, by our zealous Master Mayor; and herdsmen and hiremen laid in the stocks up and down the country, and all for refusing to put their hand to the pen, as a thousand have done who cannot write indeed; and yet you would have laughed better to have seen the wives of Edinburgh . . . so many of them as could not subscrive . . . hold up their hands when the *Covenant* (for so they called it) was read, as soldiers do when they pass muster."[38]

But for many it was no laughing matter. An Edinburgh minister, the Rev. David Mitchell, after describing how children not ten years old were made to sign, and how all were termed Papists who dared refuse, wrote of the persecution of those clergy who would not come into line. His Covenanting brethren " have made us so odious, that we dare not go upon the streets. I have been dogged by some gentlemen, and followed with many mumbled threatenings behind my back, and then when in-stairs, swords drawn, and ' if they had the Papist villain, oh! ' " He prophesied very shrewdly and truly that " when all shall be discharged, Service Book, Canons, and High Commission, they will not rest there; there is some other design in their hearts ".[39]

Resistance came also from the Universities*; of the four regents or professors of Edinburgh, two who refused to sign were expelled, and at Glasgow the majority subscribed only under coercion. Throughout Scotland there was uneasiness; tracts for and against the Covenant disturbed the consciences of peaceful folk, " seeing such contrary opinions amongst the clergy of a reformed settled kirk, not knowing whom to believe for salvation of their silly souls, nor whose opinions they should follow in these troublesome times ". The Bishops either had fled or were lying close in their houses in fear of their lives; in the strongholds of fanaticism such as the south-west, opponents of the Covenant among the ministry were beaten and stoned, and Covenanting clergy thrust into their livings by the sole (and legally non-existent) authority of the Tables; laymen who had not subscribed were refused lodging at an inn. Some of the more moderate ministers were tricked into signing by the clause in the Covenant which declared that the compilers of it had neither intention nor desire to attempt anything to the diminution of the King's authority, and would, to the uttermost of their power, stand to the defence of it and of his person.

" I do not only believe," Baillie wrote to his cousin Spang in Holland, " that there is no word in it that makes against the King's full authority, so far as either religion or reason can extend it, or against the office of Bishops, or any power they have by any lawful Assembly or Parliament, or by this write we are obliged to oppose any novation, or anything at all which is not contrary to God's word: not only I believe this, but has professed so much before the whole meeting at Edinburgh, oft both in word and write, without the least appearance of contradiction of any to this hour. . . . If any presently, or hereafter, shall abuse any claims of this write, to overthrow the King's authority, etc. . . . I can make it evident before the world, that the write has no such errors, else would I never have subscribed it."[40]

It was fear of the consequences to himself and his family, and of dividing the Kirk, that later was to prevent Baillie, and many sincere men like him, from withdrawing from the path of revolution upon which the feet of Scotland were set.

---

*In Scotland at this date there were only two Universities, St. Andrews and Aberdeen, which conferred all degrees. Glasgow was termed a university only by courtesy, for long having conferred no degree higher than that of Master of Arts. Edinburgh consisted of only one college.

James, Marquis, afterwards Duke, of Hamilton

Archibald Campbell, 8th Earl, afterwards Marquis, of Argyll

Chapter Five

THOUGH no individual could have stemmed the tide of revolution which rose upon Scotland in 1637, its future course undoubtedly was shaped by the characters and careers of four men: James, third Marquis, and afterwards first Duke, of Hamilton; Lord Lorn, afterwards eighth Earl, afterwards Marquis, of Argyll; James, fifth Earl, afterwards first Marquis, of Montrose; and George, second Marquis of Huntly. It was the first two who were now to take the stage.

Hamilton had been born in 1607, and succeeded his father to the title at the latter's early death in 1625; the second Marquis had been poisoned "by a lady whom he had slighted".[41] Throughout his boyhood young Hamilton was an intimate of the Royal Family, and after the murder of the Duke of Buckingham he received the Duke's post of Master of the Horse and a large share of the love which young King Charles had given to his murdered friend. Except for a brief period of soldiering abroad, Hamilton remained in London, and upon him Charles chiefly relied for advice upon Scottish affairs.

Aware of the touchiness of Scotland's feelings after the Union of the Crowns, King James had taken care that her affairs were never brought before the English Council, but were managed by a small group of Scotsmen at Court, and his son carried on this policy. It was a mark of indulgence to the Stuarts' native land, but its results were far from satisfactory. For while the Scots at Court lost their personal influence over their distant countrymen, and were regarded with contempt or jealousy by the English, in any crisis such as this one of 1638 many of them were honestly torn between the interests of their master and those of their relations and friends at home. Others were plain traitors, intriguing with malcontents both in England and Scotland, while they enjoyed the King's bounty. Such pre-eminently was William Murray, who had been in Charles's service from childhood, and who, with other Grooms of the Bedchamber, picked the King's pockets at night, copying private letters he had received, sending the copies to men of their own ilk in Scotland, and replacing the originals.[42]

Hamilton was of the first group; he was torn between two

49   D

loyalties. His stake in Scotland was great, for his father had got hold of a particularly large portion of the Reformation spoils; and he was near allied both by blood and marriage with those who were now called Covenanters. His mother, a daughter of the Earl of Glencairn, was a hot fanatic; his two sisters were married to Covenanting lords, the Earl of Cassilis and Lord Lindsay of the Byres. On the other hand he seems to have had a sincere love for King Charles, to whom he was bound by an intimate friendship and by many marks of the royal favour. Sir Philip Warwick has left a curiously vivid little picture of Hamilton as a young man:

"I was in the Presence Chamber at Whitehall when, after his father's death, he returned from his travels; and, waiting on the King from Chapel with great observance, and the King using him with great kindness, the eyes of the whole Court were upon the young man. His hair was short, and he wore a little black collot-cap, which was not then usual; and I wondered much that all present, who usually at Court put the best character upon a rising man, generally agreed in this, that the air of his counten-ance had such a cloud upon it that Nature seemed to have impressed *aliquid insigne*; which I often reflected on when his future actions led him first to be suspected, then to be declaimed against. . . . As for myself, I was known to him and ever civilly treated by him: However, I must concur in that general opinion, that naturally he loved to gain his point rather by some ser-pentine winding than by a direct path."[43]

Clarendon speaks of his reserve and "darkness in discourse"; and Burnet, his champion, admits that he was melancholy and lacking in self-confidence; "he was so far from flattering himself with the hopes of great success in any of his undertakings, that he rather apprehended himself under some inauspicious star, that crossed all his attempts, which made him in his latter years long for some secret retirement out of the noise of business". "He was too much a Statesman," wrote Clement Walker, "and too little a Soldier."

But of his physical courage there was no doubt. Sir James Turner, a professional soldier, who later was to fight under his command, bore testimony to this, and indeed had a higher opinion of Hamilton than most of his acquaintance; he was, wrote Turner, "a person of excellent qualities, of a great under-standing, and good expressions, courteous, affable, humane; so merciful that he was a bad justiciary . . . one of the best masters to vassals and tenants that our kingdom afforded". It was Hamilton's jealousy, combined with his infirmity of purpose and his instinct for keeping a foot in both camps, which, on several occasions, were to make him act in such a manner as to give rise to the suspicion that he was a traitor to his master and friend, the King.

Young Lord Lorn, destined to share with Hamilton the leading rôle in the tragedy upon which the curtain had risen in Scotland, was also a dark and complex character, but of his treachery there could be no shadow of doubt. At his door must be laid the principal share of the blame for the woes of his country during the reign of King Covenant.

He was the heir of a family detested throughout the Highlands, half Gaelic chiefs, half feudal barons. In remote times, the two branches of the Campbells, Clan Diarmaid, had struggled for precedence, a struggle which had resulted in the triumph of the younger branch of MacCalein Mhor when the chief of the elder one, MacArthur, was executed in the reign of James I of Scotland. Having triumphed in this sordid family quarrel, the younger branch went from strength to strength, stretching predatory hands towards the estates of their Highland neighbours, steadily adhering to a system of cunning and perfidy, which gained its usual rewards of temporal power. It was their custom to incite their neighbours to revolt against the Crown; the MacCalein Mhor of the day would then make an offer to the King (who, living in the South of Scotland, knew little of what was passing in the wild Highlands) to reduce the rebels to obedience. When the offer was accepted and the rebels reduced, invariably their lands were given as a reward to MacCalein Mhor, the unwary rebels thus finding themselves dispossessed by the very person who had instigated their rebellion.

By the beginning of the seventeenth century, the Campbells exceeded in numbers and strength every other clan in Gaeldom, and, if the Gordons be excepted, surpassed all the rest put together. Little cared they for the hatred in which their name was held; they could bring five thousand fighting-men into the field; their territory was a compact block of land with an immense sea-coast and rich hill-pastures which supported thousands of black cattle; and it was their boast that their country was so situated that no enemy could invade it. They had annexed Breadalbane and held the head waters of the Tay; south and west lay the sea; eastwards were the Lowlands with which they were ordinarily at peace; to the north was a wall of mountain over which no army could pass. The elder branch of the family had had a favourite brag: "It's a far cry to Lochow."

It was a farther cry to Inveraray, the principal seat of MacCalein Mhor, Earl of Argyll.

The seventh Earl, nicknamed Gilleasbuig Grumach, Archibald the Grim (though the nickname was sometimes, and with more reason, applied to his son), in early manhood had been a typical MacCalein Mhor, annihilating the Clan Gregor, for centuries the Campbells' catspaws but presently becoming more troublesome than useful, and obtaining a grant of their country which included the whole peninsula of Kintyre. But in his maturity he astonished Scotland by acting completely outside the family pattern.

His first wife, Lady Anne Douglas, had died in 1607, and the widower, up in London to claim his rewards for subduing rebels, met and fell in love with the daughter of a Suffolk knight, Anne Cornwallis, a Catholic; not only did Argyll marry her, but he embraced the proscribed religion. This was in 1610. Eight years later, what with his Catholicism and his debts (he had two large families to support), he was obliged to leave Scotland, and in the following February, in the picturesque Scots phrase he was " put to the horn ", that is, outlawed. But in 1627 the new King, Charles I, caused his sentence to be reversed, after he had " offered himself in all dutiful obedience to his Majesty ", and henceforward he lived in retirement in his house in Drury Lane, far from his Highland hills, and plagued by deadly feuds between his two families.

Thus it had come about that when King Charles was crowned in Edinburgh in 1633, the great Clan Diarmaid was represented, not by the seventh Earl of Argyll, but by his heir, the only son of his first marriage, a tall, thin, narrow-chested young man, with red hair and a pronounced squint, Archibald Campbell, Lord Lorn. He was among the earls' sons who squabbled for precedence in the Lang-gait at King Charles's entry; he helped to uphold the canopy as the King rode down for his crowning; he laid his hands between those anointed ones in the Abbey Kirk, and took the solemn oath of homage and allegiance. He was an insignificant and slightly comical figure, with his long nose and his squint, and it is unlikely that the King took much notice of him.

He, like his father, had allied himself with the once all-powerful House of Douglas; in 1626 he had married his second cousin, Margaret Douglas, daughter of William, seventh Earl of Morton. Again like his father he had been brought up by guardians, the principal of whom was Morton, whose daughter he was to marry; and, equally with his father, he was indebted to the King's clemency. For by law the whole of the seventh Earl's estates should have been forfeited to the Crown on his conversion to Catholicism, a forfeiture which, but for Charles's intervention, would have extended to his heirs.

While carrying on the family tradition by annexing the lands of his neighbours, in this case the MacIains, a branch of the great Clan Donald, of Ardnamurchan, until his father's death in 1638 Lord Lorn was principally occupied with family feuds. He hated his father, his step-mother, and most particularly his half-brother James, the only surviving son of the old Earl's second marriage. A portion of the vast family estates, the peninsula of Kintyre, being a recent acquisition and therefore not entailed, could be, and indeed was, left to James, but not before his half-brother had fought for it tooth and nail. The squabble raged for years, Lorn's letters to his principal guardian, the Earl of Morton, growing more and more furious and hysterical. Ultimately James sold Kintyre to his half-brother, went abroad, and died without issue in 1645.

Lorn's relations with his father were almost as bitter. Shortly before his second marriage, Argyll had conveyed the fee-simple of his hereditary estates to his heir, enjoying the income of the property as a life-tenant. But Lorn's behaviour becoming most insolent and unfilial, he resolved to dispose of his fortune in such a way that his heir should enjoy little of it after his death. In 1631, however, King Charles intervened on Lorn's behalf, forcing the old man to renounce even the life-rent on condition that his son provided him with a proper maintenance, and this renunciation was confirmed by Act of Parliament in 1633. The father was forced to submit, though he knew only too well what his son's idea of a proper maintenance would be; but after bidding Lorn remember for ever the King's bounty towards him, he addressed Charles in words which the King would have done well to heed:

"Sir, I must know this young man better than you can do; you have brought me low that you may raise him; which I doubt you will live to repent. For he is a man of craft, subtilty, and falsehood, and can love no man; and if ever he finds it in his power to do you mischief, he will be sure to do it."[44]

King Charles, however, seemed determined to heap favours on the young man. In 1628 he had made him a Privy Councillor; in 1634 he was created an Extraordinary Lord of Session; and shortly afterwards the King gave him the heritable right of the Justiciary of the Isles, with a pension of one thousand pounds sterling a year. But this did not satisfy Lorn's greed; and in

1635 he met with a disappointment which was to turn into a grudge.

The office of Lord Chancellor of Scotland became vacant by the death of the Earl of Kinnoul, and Lorn immediately " dealt " for it. The King, having done so much already for the young man, was displeased by this presumption, and in any case already had determined to bestow the office upon old Archbishop Spottiswoode, for whom, like his father before him, he entertained a great respect. (It was an unwise appointment, for since the Reformation no cleric had held the office, and it was bound to increase the jealousy of the Scots nobles who already looked upon the Bishops with a jaundiced eye, being jealous of their power in Parliament and of their revenues.)

In the following year, Lorn came into collision with Thomas Sydserf, Bishop of Galloway. In his diocesan court the Bishop fined one Alexander Gordon, Laird of Earlstoun, the tutor of Lorn's nephew, five hundred merks for his disgraceful behaviour during the administration of Holy Communion, and banished him for six weeks to Montrose. Lorn paid the fine; and was then enraged by the Bishop's refusal to remit the sentence of banishment. There were high words in the Council, of which both Lorn and the Bishop were members, the latter going so far as to accuse Lorn of lying in his relation of the circumstances. When the storm over the Service Book arose in 1637, therefore, Lorn was already violently and personally anti-Bishops, though officially he was an Episcopalian and a member of the King's Council. In the spring of the following year, when he was in London on a visit to Court, the old man, his father, gave King Charles another warning to beware of him. Argyll advised his Majesty to prevent Lorn's return to Scotland, otherwise the young man would " wind him a pin ", in other words would do him a mischief. But Charles, while thanking Argyll for his counsel, refused to detain Lorn against his will.

What kind of a young man was this who, in the November of 1638, was to make so dramatic an entrance upon the national stage? Like all his race he loved to gain his ends by craft and dissimulation, but unlike them he had a weakness which was to become proverbial: he was the most appalling coward. He was solemn, free from fleshly vice, possessed of immense cunning and few scruples. Under a plain and homely aspect, under the language of piety which he knew so well how to adopt, he was to show himself " the deepest statesman, the most crafty, subtle, and over-reaching politician, that this age can produce ".[45]

His pretence to piety was great. When he was at home at Inveraray or at Roseneath, his two principal seats in the Highlands, he composed both the morning and afternoon sermons for his parish minister. The latter, Alexander Gordon, told Wodrow (that industrious biographer of Covenanting worthies) that Argyll rose at five each morning and continued in private prayer till eight; that besides family worship, he always prayed with his lady morning and evening, his gentleman and her gentlewoman being present; and that he never went abroad, though but for a night, without taking with him his Bible, Newman's *Concordance*, and his "write-book" for the making of notes upon them.[46]

He could be pleasant enough when he saw that it was to his advantage, and according to Clarendon, no man knew better how to play the courtier. His avarice was insatiable, as grew his lust for power when once he had appeared in his true colours in the national quarrel. The worst traits in his character were cruelty and a terrifying vindictiveness. He was cruel in cold blood, says Burnet,[47] a not uncommon vice in a coward; and even his champion, Mr. Willcock, admits his "memory for wrongs received which his enemies came to dread".[48]

Such was the man who shortly was to become dictator of Scotland, and the power behind the throne of King Covenant.

Chapter Six

T HE troubles in Scotland had reached so dangerous a stage with the signing of the National Covenant that the King sent thence a Royal Commissioner, appointing for the post his most trusted Scottish adviser, the Marquis of Hamilton.

Hamilton arrived at Berwick on Sunday, June 3rd, 1638, and an immediate affront was offered to the King whom he represented; a command went forth from the Tables that none should go to meet him. His arrival was made to synchronize with a public fast, authorized by the same body, and rumours had been circulated to the effect that Charles was resolved to resort to force against the malcontents, that there was another Gunpowder Plot designed to blow up the Council who were sitting at Dalkeith, that Edinburgh Castle was being munitioned (which gave the Covenanters an excuse for an informal siege of it), and

that Papists were coming to defend the Bishops. This last fantastic story was the Tables' explanation of the crowds they had
taken care to summon to Edinburgh; they were resolved to show
Hamilton their strength.

The Commissioner rode into Edinburgh on June 5th, and on
Leith Links found the Kirk Militant arrayed to meet him, six
hundred ministers all in their black cloaks. According to Baillie,
Hamilton was moved to tears by this sight, wishing that King
Charles might be there to hear them " so earnestly and humbly
crying for the safety of their liberties and religion ". Be that
as it may, Hamilton refused to listen to the public harangue
these worthies had composed for the occasion; and as he rode
past the grim ranks he was heard to murmur satirically a phrase
in Latin from St. Matthew: " *Vos estis sal terrae.*" A minister
who had not heard distinctly asked one of his brethren what
Hamilton had said, who replied, " Brother, the Commissioner
said it is we who make the kail salt ", alluding to an old Scots
proverb concerning trouble-makers.[49]

Thwarted in their intention of a public harangue, four of the
ministers, describing themselves as " the servants of the Son of
God, and the preachers of the peace that passes understanding ",
went to wait on Hamilton in his lodging. They welcomed him
as " the messenger of the God of Heaven ", and told him they
expected him to " quench this fire of division ", in reward for
which he would " reap the fruit of a sweet remembrance in after
ages, and a wonderful peace and strong consolation when it
comes to the breaking of the eye-strings and giving of the last
gasp ". The effect of this was rather spoiled by a message from
the Tables that if on the Sabbath anyone presumed to read the
Liturgy in the Chapel Royal (the organ of which had been
destroyed by that hot Covenanter, the young Earl of Montrose),
that man should read no more, and that there were a thousand
men provided for the disturbance of it.[50]

That a stronger character than Hamilton could have
" quenched this fire of division " is unlikely; but Hamilton being
what he was it was obvious from the first that, so far as his
master's interests were concerned, his visit was a waste of time.
His letters to the King were almost unintelligible in his panic
and despair, and his desire to keep in with both sides betrayed
him into behaviour which was certainly questionable if not
treacherous. On one occasion, after a Council meeting, he took
Montrose and other Covenanters aside, and said: " My lords
and gentlemen, I spoke to you before those Lords of Council as
the King's Commissioner; now there being none present but

yourselves, I speak to you as a kindly Scotsman. If you go on with courage and resolution you will carry what you please; but if you faint and give ground in the least, you are undone. A word is enough to wise men."[51]

Before returning to London to give the King his contradictory and entirely useless advice, Hamilton attempted to publish the royal proclamation with which he had come armed. In this Charles promised not to press the use of the Service Book, and suggested that all religious differences should be discussed by a General Assembly and a Parliament. But as soon as a day was appointed for the reading of the Proclamation, the Tables summoned their followers to come to Edinburgh and protest against it, "though," admits Baillie naïvely, "what was in the Proclamation we could not learn ".[52] Wariston, who was to read the Protestation, was most upset by a rumour that the Proclamation was "very fair"; and it was not until he had heard it read by the herald that he found it to be "a damnable piece", yet a Protestation had been prepared by him against it, whether it proved "fair" or "damnable". The fact of it was that these Protestations had become automatic; the Tables had not the slightest intention of listening to anything the King had to say; and on this occasion went so far in treason as to declare that if Charles did not indict a General Assembly and a Parliament, they would do it themselves. The thousand Covenanting gentry who, "with their swords loose in their arms", stood round the Mercat Cross while the King's Proclamation was being read by a herald, provided ominous evidence that the Tables, though they lacked authority, had power.

Though the Tables had assured Hamilton that no man was being forced to sign the Covenant, protesting that "they would not admit an unwilling, let be a forced hand ",[53] no sooner had he left for London on July 9th than commissioners, headed by young Montrose, went to extort subscriptions from loyal Aberdeen. At their entry, the Provost offered the customary welcome to visitors of note, sending wine and sweetmeats to their lodgings, but the Commissioners brusquely refused the present, saying they would drink with none till the town had subscribed the Covenant, "whereat the Provost and bailies were somewhat offended ".

In other districts, too, coercion was growing hotter; ministers were deposed for not subscribing, and some suffered violence. "We are grieved," wrote Baillie, "for the stoning of D. Munro, when he came to Edinburgh, where he had much company with the Bishops, and was thought to be a spy to them of the actions and proceedings of the noblemen. The women at Kinghorn, at divers parts of the town, in great multitudes were set for him. Some gentlemen in company defended to their power, and got him on a great horse, whereby he escaped death, but not blood and wounds." It was effective treatment. " D. Munro," Baillie was able to write a little later, " since his strokes, is amongst the foremost at our meetings."

By the time that Hamilton had returned to London from another short visit to Scotland in August, King Charles had considered as well as he could the whole situation, and had resolved upon a policy of conciliation to the limit. He made concessions which ought to have satisfied even the fanatics, since he granted all the demands they had added to that for the abolition of the Service Book. Though the Articles of Perth, the High Commission, and the Book of Canons had been enacted by General Assemblies and made law by Act of Parliament, Charles, at the demand of the Tables, suspended them all, leaving them to be debated by a new General Assembly which he summoned to sit at Glasgow on November 21st, and by a Parliament which was to assemble in Edinburgh on May 15th, 1639.

And since the Covenant professed to be the old Confession of Faith, and the reason for its republication the Scots' fear of Popery, the King himself republished the Confession, and commanded all Scotland to sign it. The latter order he made against his better judgment, persuaded thereto by Hamilton. Charles remembered to have heard his father regret his order for the nation to sign the Confession in 1590 because " it seemed tyrannical over tender consciences to require an oath from all persons, but more especially from women and simple people, who could not judge well, and so were not fit to swear to such nice points ".[54]

As a final concession, the King again pardoned all the illegal acts committed since the beginning of the troubles, the riots, the convening of his lieges, and the maltreatment of his loyal subjects. Thus he had gone as far as any king could go without parting with the ancient prerogatives of the Crown.

When Hamilton brought these extraordinary concessions to Scotland in September, the Council professed profuse and unanimous gratitude. An Act was passed wherein the members expressed themselves as " so fully satisfied therewith, and the same to be so satisfactory for removing all the fears of the subjects anent innovation of religion or laws, that we hold ourselves bound in duty, not only to acquiesce therewith . . . but also to use our best endeavours that all his Majesty's good subjects may likewise rest satisfied therewith; and that they with us, and we with them, may testify our thankfulness for so great a grace and goodness, with all the hearty expressions of dutifulness and loyalty". In a letter of thanks to the King they asserted that "If ever faithful and loyal subjects had reason to acknowledge extraordinary favours shown to a nation . . . then do we of your Majesty's Council of this your ancient Kingdom, unanimously profess, that such acts of clemency vouchsafed us cannot proceed from any prince saving him who is the lively image on earth of the great God ".[55]

Once again, the contents of this Proclamation were disclosed by Hamilton only to the Council before the public reading of it; but on this occasion there can be no doubt whatever that the Tables were made aware of them before that event. For before the date on which the herald was to read the Proclamation at the Mercat Cross, the Covenanting preachers began thundering from their pulpits against what they pleased to term "the King's Covenant", that is to say the old Confession of Faith now to be republished. One prayed to God to "scatter them in Israel, and to divide them in Jacob, who were the authors of this scattering and divisive counsel". Another informed his people from the pulpit that the command to sign the King's Covenant was "an Italian and devilish device, first to make them renounce God, and perjure themselves, and then afterwards there was an intention to destroy their bodies, and so that this subscription imported no less than the destruction both of their bodies and souls ".[56] Rumours were circulated that the King did not intend to keep his word concerning his concessions, and that they were only a trick to lull the people into a false sense of security while he prepared an army against Scotland.

Further to disturb the minds of the people, a "she prophetess" was discovered, a half-witted creature named Michelson. Crowds flocked to hear her when, prostrating herself upon a bed, she foretold the victory of the Covenant and the destruction of its enemies. There was a certain lack of originality in her revelations; "she spoke of Christ, and called him Covenanting Jesus; that the Covenant was approved of Heaven; that the King's Covenant was Satan's invention". But her words were most solemnly taken down, and one minister went so far as to declare that it was Christ Himself speaking through her lips. The Earl of Airth, venturing to cross out the word "gloriously" in a description of her manner of speech, and substitute "goukedly" (crazily), was stoned in the street.[57]

Thus were the people's minds prepared for the reading of the King's Proclamation at Edinburgh Mercat Cross. As soon as the herald had finished reading, Archibald Johnston of Wariston, one of the most fanatical of the Covenanters, stood up on the usual platform prepared for the purpose, and in the usual Protestation (on this occasion a document of sixteen and a half pages) refused the King's Covenant, demanded that no subscriptions to it, whether by the Lords of Council or anyone else, be prejudicial to the National Covenant, and added for good measure that as for the King's pardon they had no need of it, having done nothing unlawful.*

Who were these men who refused such extraordinary concessions, and why did they so refuse? They did not represent the nation at large. Wherever the royal Proclamation arrived before the Protestation, it was cordially received; letters of thanks to the King's Commissioner from magistrates and clergy poured in; twenty-eight thousand people signed the King's Covenant; in many places the Protestation was disowned even by good Covenanters; and one of the four Tables, that of the ministers, showed the utmost repugnance to it.[58]

There were two groups of men who, for different reasons, were determined not to accept the King's concessions, and who were making these strenuous efforts to poison the subjects' minds against their Sovereign. One was composed of the spiritual descendants of those ministers who, all through King James's reign in Scotland, had endeavoured to make the secular power subservient to the spiritual. No concessions would have satisfied these fanatics; they were out for complete theocracy; the King, the Council, the Estates of Parliament, the nation, all were to dance to their tune.

The other group was composed of those nobles and lairds who had been alarmed by Charles's attempted Act of Revocation, who were determined to hold on to all the spoils of the Auld Kirk, and who, many years before, had entered into the Clandestine Band with men of their own ilk in England. "Our Covenanters could not be pleased when their cup was full, conform to the conclusion betwixt them and the malcontents of England, cunningly and obscurely covenanted."[59]

The intention of the second group was to use the fanaticism

---

* "A protestation, however, complete with the most disingenuous reasoning," wrote the Presbyterian historian, Dr. Cook, "and evincing the determination of the leading Covenanters to resist all terms, was read. . . . This conduct of the Presbyterians cannot be justified." (*Hist. of the Church of Scotland*, II, 450-1.)

of the first until the Monarchy was destroyed in everything but name. The intention succeeded. But by a piece of poetic justice, it was that very fanaticism which was to ruin, not only the Monarchy, but the Covenanting potentates and their ally the Kirk.

KING CAMPBELL
1638-1644

Chapter One

WHILE professing no gratitude for the King's concessions, the Covenanters were determined to make every possible use of them for their own ends. They would fill with their own partisans the General Assembly for which the King had given warrant, and in order to do so, they whose cry against "novations" had been so loud, introduced some most startlingly new ones of their own.

More than forty years previously, King James had abolished the Calvinistic practice, disliked by many of the ministers, of sending to the Assembly one lay elder with each two or three clerics. The Tables not only revived this practice but introduced two new ones. They ordered that a lay elder from each parish attend the presbytery to give his vote in the choice of the clerical commissioners to be sent to the Assembly, and since it was not usual for the ministers whose names were in the list of candidates to vote, by this means all the elections fell into the hand of the laity. Secondly, the number of lay elders in the Assembly was now to equal that of the ministers. This was a practice contrary to the Book of Discipline, while the order from the Tables, that lay elders have choice in the election of ministers, was without any precedence whatsoever.

In order to ensure that whatever Acts this packed Assembly passed should be ratified by the parliament of the following year, the Tables directed that the lay elders should be "well affected" noblemen or gentlemen. To make doubly sure, they sent careful directions to every presbytery in Scotland that no commissioner was to be elected who had used the Service Book, who had been a royal chaplain, or a member of the Bishops' Chapters, or a Justice of the Peace, or upon the High Commission. No minister "erroneous in doctrine or scandalous in life" (epithets capable of the widest interpretation) was to be chosen;

and if by some unlucky chance a non-Covenanting minister was elected by a majority, then "all the best affected, both ministers and elders, protest, and come to the Assembly to testify the same ".[1]

Electioneering "stunts" were not neglected. During Hamilton's absence in London before the Assembly sat down, a story was put about that he heartily approved of the Tables' proceedings; this had the effect of bringing in many doubters, and by the time that he had issued a denial it was too late. The "she prophetess" having gone the way of all such novelties, a much more exciting figure was brought upon the stage. This was an apostate Jesuit priest, Thomas Abernethy, who had been unfrocked for seducing a maid-servant, and who now, having taken a wife and got a benefice in Glasgow (making a little fortune on the side by informing against Catholics), solemnly informed the people that the Service Book had been sent by King Charles to Rome before being imposed on Scotland, to be revised by certain Cardinals.[2]

In order to prevent the swarming into Glasgow of unruly mobs during the sitting of this nominally ecclesiastical body, the King had issued a proclamation forbidding any to come thither save those who had business there, and that none should come armed. The Tables retorted that it was lawful for all men to resort to an Assembly at their own expense, "for instructing of their minds in matters of religion"; and "a pretty device" was invented as an excuse for their coming armed. There were Highland robbers abroad, said the Tables, who would be sure to lie in wait for the godly commissioners on their journey to Glasgow, "and that for preventing thereof it was fit that all who were zealous in the Cause should convoy their commissioners thither, and guard them during their sitting, which was done".[3]

One other most important matter the Tables took in hand, and this was to ensure the destruction of the Bishops. Each presbytery was ordered to collect "informations" against the Bishop of its diocese; tales of their drinking, whoring, breaking the Sabbath, playing at cards—all contributions would be thankfully received. "No kind of crime which can be gotten proven of a Bishop will now be concealed", wrote Baillie. He himself was busy dealing with the Presbytery of Glasgow, which was showing a regrettable tendency to insist on a free election of commissioners. Thirty-nine other presbyteries, he pointed out, had chosen their commissioners "as they were desired", and he hoped that Glasgow would not be the first to begin "a dangerous preparative".[4]

Archibald Johnston of Wariston

VERA EFFIGIES REVᵈⁱ
Viri Dᵐⁱ Alex: HENDERSONI
Scoto-Britanni ᵉ

Yow that can find no object where to place
Your wonder. Come behold this gratious face.
Tis He the great Reformer of his dayes
That powrfull Light who spread the brighter rayes
Through Brittain half benighted which did make
Truth to Triumph proud Babells Whoor to quake.

Rev. Alexander Henderson. Moderator of the General Assembly of 1638

From all this it was crystal-clear what the nature of this General Assembly was going to be; and since the Tables had flatly refused to abide by the King's conditions in granting it— that all ministers deposed without authority be restored until legally convicted, that the Bishops have their rents and stipends paid them, and that no layman meddle with the electing of commissioners—Charles had every excuse for refusing to allow it to sit. That he did not so refuse was the measure of his indulgence towards his native kingdom, and a proof that he intended to abide by the concessions he had made.

The date of the Assembly was fixed for Wednesday, November 21st. By order of the Tables the commissioners met at Edinburgh on the 12th, so that they might be directed in the choosing of a Moderator and Clerk, and instructed as to their general behaviour. On the 21st, this blatantly packed body sat down in the High Kirk of Glasgow, and anything less like a General Assembly of the Kirk of Scotland had never before been seen.

"Accordingly we met," Hamilton wrote the King next day, "and truly, Sir, my soul was never sadder than to see such a sight, not one gown amongst the whole company, many swords, but many more daggers, most of them having left the guns and pistols in the lodging." A contemporary described it as resembling a court martial; and there were some commissioners who could neither read nor write and yet were to judge of fine points of theology. Even Baillie was shocked by the disorderly mob which made it difficult for him to get into the kirk; "our rascals without shame," he wrote, "in great numbers, made such a din and clamour in the house of the true God, that if they minted [attempted] to use the like behaviour in my chamber, I could not be content till they were down the stairs."[5]

This first day was spent in a kind of roll-call, but on the morrow the quarrelling began. There was a long wrangle over the legality of some of the commissions, and uproar when Hamilton attempted to read the Bishops' declinator to the accusations against them. On Saturday, the 24th, there was a particularly blatant proof of the way in which the Assembly had been packed.

The Presbytery of Brechin had been one of the few who had insisted on the right of free election, and, by a large majority, had chosen as their lay representative Lord Carnegie of Kinnaird, son of the Earl of Southesk and brother-in-law of that hot Covenanter, the Earl of Montrose. But Carnegie, though he had signed the Covenant, was thought to be but lukewarm in

E

the Cause, and a minority in the presbytery had chosen Erskine
of Dun, a zealot. They had sent Dun's commission to the Tables,
asking for advice; it had been returned with a note on the back,
signed by Montrose and others, with the sublimely simple statement that Carnegie's election was illegal because it was contrary
to the directions of the Tables that only the "well affected" be
chosen.

On this Saturday morning, the Clerk, the fanatical Wariston,
was reading out the commissions, and when he came to that of
Dun he began to read aloud what was written on the back.
Perceiving his *faux pas* he stopped, and was about to pass
hurriedly to the next, when Hamilton demanded a copy of
Dun's commission, both of what was written on the front and
the back. The Moderator at once intervened; what was written
on the back, he said, was something accidental; it was a private
note, and it could not be read in public without permission of
those who had written it.

Hamilton replied with indignation that though he were not
the King's Commissioner but the meanest subject in the land,
he could not, in justice, be denied anything exhibited in a public
court. Not only was he denied it, but even his request that it
should be put to the vote whether or no he should have a copy,
was refused. Since the principal subscriber of that damning
note was the Earl of Montrose, it is possible that the incident
recurred to Hamilton's mind when, some years later, Montrose
changed sides, and that it was not only jealousy which made
him endeavour to prejudice Charles against this erstwhile
Covenanter.[6]

The fight now shifted to the Tables' determination to condemn the Bishops in their absence. It was in vain for Hamilton
to point out that there were legal ways of trying any man, and
that for him to give warrants to a General Assembly to act as a
court of justice would be unlawful and quite without precedent.
But on Tuesday, the 27th, after having been obliged to "moderate the Moderator", he did succeed in having the declinator
read, though the words were almost drowned in laughter and
jeers.

The Bishops refused to acknowledge the authority of the
Assembly, and that for several weighty reasons. First, preparations for it had been begun before the King, who alone had
power to summon it, had published his warrant, and secondly
the majority of the commissioners had neglected to take the
Oath of Allegiance according to many Acts of Parliament.
Further, they had flouted his Majesty's conditions in granting

the Assembly; they had declared, contrary to Acts of Parliament and of five former General Assemblies, that Bishops had no voice in these bodies; they had given lay elders power of election, contrary to the practice of the Kirk, which allowed them disciplinary but not elective powers; and lastly, many of the commissioners had railed against the King's authority, publicly from their pulpits, thereby inciting his subjects to revolt.

There followed a number of protestations from ministers against the constitution of this Assembly, among them one from Dr. Strange, Principal of the University of Glasgow, and from the majority of the ministers of that town. But when the reading of it had begun, Strange asked in considerable agitation that he be allowed to withdraw it. It transpired that, the previous night, Lord Loudoun, the Moderator, and other Covenanters, had visited Strange and had told him that " unless he did withdraw it, he must never look to live quietly in Glasgow or anywhere else in Scotland ", and his tearful wife had repeated to him Lord Lindsay's threat to her, that their family would be utterly ruined if Strange did not withdraw his protestation.[7]

By this time it was clear to Hamilton that no justice whatever could be expected from such an Assembly, and he resolved to dissolve it next day. What he did not realize was that by doing so he was merely playing into the Covenanters' hands. They had done their best to goad the King into withdrawing his warrant for its sitting, so that they could accuse him of breaking his word; now they could say they had been arbitrarily dissolved, which would give them all the excuse they needed for continuing to sit by their own authority, and to do exactly what they pleased.

On Wednesday, the 28th, after a long wrangle as to whether or no the Assembly were the lawful judges of the Bishops, the Moderator was about to put it to the vote when Hamilton, from his chair of estate, curtly interrupted. He could not, he said, allow the Assembly to settle its own competence as judges; he repeated all the King's concessions; and then he produced two papers which caused considerable dismay. They were secret instructions sent by the Tables to one picked lay elder of each presbytery, additional to the instructions sent to the presbytery as a body, and containing this really damning order: " That none be chosen but Covenanters." Their misery, wrote the Tables, would be " inexpressibly great " if a majority in the Assembly was found to be against the Covenant. In other words the Tables knew that a freely elected Assembly would accept the King's concessions.[8]

The Tables did not attempt to disown the papers; the only excuse they made was that they contained private advice sent from one friend to another. To this Hamilton replied drily that since copies of these papers had been sent to him from all parts of the kingdom, and were word for word identical, this seemed strange. Moreover, he said, the elections for the Assembly had been managed precisely on the lines laid down in these instructions. Having made it plain beyond the shadow of a doubt that the Assembly was a packed body, he dissolved it in the King's name.

He was about to leave the kirk, when from one of the seats immediately below him there arose a figure who begged leave to speak. It was the tall, narrow-chested figure of the young man who, by his father's death, had just become the eighth Earl of Argyll.

His voice was low, his speech ambiguous. "We did not well understand him," wrote Baillie. But the Assembly listened with interest, for this was MacCalein Mhor, this was the most powerful noble in Scotland who, as a member of the Council, had signed both the King's Covenant and the fulsome letter of thanks to Charles for his concessions, yet was known to have a personal grudge against the Bishops, and who, during the past tumultuous months, had kept himself very much in the background, no man knowing what went on behind that squinting glance.

He had a command, said Argyll, laid on him by the King, to attend the Assembly as one of the Commissioner's assessors, and he asked all present to bear witness to how fairly he had carried himself in that capacity, but for his part he could never be moved, by private ambition, to flatter the King or persuade him to "run violent courses". He was surprised by this sudden dissolving of the Assembly (and here he lied, for as one of Hamilton's assessors he had been told of the Commissioner's intention), and in his humble opinion the exception against lay elders was not important enough for so drastic a step. He held it fit that the Assembly should consist of laymen as well as clerics, because the two made up one complete body. He exhorted the Assembly to stand fast to the Confession of Faith as it was sworn to in 1581, "and suffer no other expositions to be put upon it". He himself, as a member of the Council, had signed the King's Covenant, "but with that express reservation, that it should be interpreted according to the minds of those who had subscribed it, *anno* 1581".[9]

Certainly an ambiguous speech. He had not explained why,

if it were lawful for laymen to sit in the Assembly, it was unlawful for Bishops to sit in Parliament; nor how it was possible for
anyone present to know what had been in the minds of those
who had drawn up the original Confession of Faith nearly sixty
years previously; nor exactly whose side he was on. The last,
however, he was soon to make plain.

There was uproar as Hamilton left the kirk with his assessors
(including Argyll), the Clerk endeavouring to read a protestation against dissolving, and some of the rabble who packed the
sides of the kirk going so far as to bar Hamilton's way, so that
he was forced to have the door broken open. Having returned
to his lodging, he immediately summoned the Council, and
found that there were two absentees. One was Lord Almond,
who was sick; the other was Argyll. A letter was drawn up to
the King, wherein the Council promised to maintain his
authority with their lives and fortunes, and a proclamation was
issued forbidding the Assembly to sit further.

In the High Kirk, meanwhile, the Moderator was making a
speech. They were at war now, he said, "with the kingdom of
Satan and Antichrist", and though it was late at night he would
put it to the vote, whether or not they should defy the King
and continue to sit. By a large majority it was voted in the
affirmative.

It was war indeed. King Covenant had usurped the authority
of King Charles; and Argyll, as the former's prime minister, was
about to take the stage.

Chapter Two

THOUGH his ambition was insatiable, Argyll's extreme care
for his own safety fitted him more for the rôle of the power
behind the throne than that of open dictatorship. Many dictators had arisen in Scotland when the Monarchy was weak; it was
not yet a lifetime since Regent Morton had substituted the
Bloody Heart, the emblem of the House of Douglas, for the
King's Standard on every fortress in the land. But, a Douglas
himself on his mother's side, Argyll could not but remember the
usual fate of such dictators. Morton, for example, had met a
well-deserved end by the very instrument of decapitation, the
Maiden, which he himself had introduced into Scotland in place

of the sword. Therefore so far as was possible and at least until King Covenant was firmly established, Argyll would walk warily.

But the crisis which arose when the packed Assembly decided to defy King Charles forced Argyll, while endeavouring to leave a door open for retreat in case he had chosen the losing side, to declare himself; it was a choice now between active loyalty and active treason, and for several good reasons he chose the latter. First, he would have behind him the power of what was about to become a Presbyterian Kirk, and he knew well how to talk that language. Next, the Council contained no man brave enough to stand up for the royal authority, and in it were several secret Covenanters. Last and most important, affairs in England were leading up to civil war. The Scots were well aware of this from their agents in England who, according to the terms of the Clandestine Band, were intriguing with the Auld Enemy for that very object. This collusion explains the otherwise mysterious simultaniety with which remonstrances and protestations were presented to the King by the malcontents of both nations; and it explains also why the Scots, poor though they were as a nation, were ready to begin an aggressive war. The King could not raise an effective army against them unless he called a parliament which would vote him the money for it; and a parliament, far from doing this, would attack his Prerogative.

Thus it was that on Thursday, November 29th, Argyll, a member of the King's Council and the recipient of his particular bounty, returned to a General Assembly which was sitting in defiance of the King's order to dissolve.

He had no sort of right to sit here; he was not a lay elder; he had attended previously as one of the assessors of the King's Commissioner. The Moderator, however, earnestly entreated him to remain, "for the common interest he had in the Church", and Argyll graciously consented. "No one thing," wrote Baillie, "did confirm us so much as Argyll's presence; not only the man was the far most powerful subject in our kingdom, but also at that time being in good grace with the King and the Commissioner, we could not conceive but his stay with us was with the allowance of both, permitting him to be amongst us to keep matters into some temper, and hold us from desperate extremes . . . yet afterwards we found, that nothing was more against the stomach both of the Commissioner and King than Argyll's stay."

The first thing the Assembly did was to appoint a committee to consider the King's Covenant, "how far it did exclude or

admit of posterior novations of our Church ", to debate upon
the corruptions in the Articles of Perth, Service Book, and High
Commission (all of which, it will be remembered, the King had
discharged), and above all to examine the accusations against
the Bishops. Another committee solemnly discussed the
iniquities of non-Covenanting ministers. There was a certain
Dr. Panter, for example, Professor of Divinity at St. Andrews,
who had recommended his students to begin their studies with
the Catholic Schoolmen and Fathers and to work their way down
to the Reformers, "a most unhappy and dangerous order",
observed Baillie, though it is difficult to see how they could have
read history backwards.

Moderates like Baillie were being swept along on the car of
revolution, too timid to risk being thrown overboard, too weak
to apply the brake. Thus in the debate as to whether Episcopacy
should be abjured as unlawful in itself, Baillie, who believed
firmly that it was not, who had written that he would never be
swayed by mere numbers, who knew that Episcopacy was to be
found in many of the Reformed Churches abroad, " was as dumb
as a fish ".[10] He was dumb because even he, a sincere Covenanter, had the weapons of deposition and Excommunication hanging over him, ready to fall if he refused concurrence with the
hot-heads who had now seized power.

From November 29th till December 13th the Assembly
listened to long harangues upon the evils of Arminianism,
"though many doubted," remarked James Gordon caustically,
"if all of them understood Arminian tenets or the refutatory
arguments thereof ".* The Service Book was fulminated against
as " heathenish, Popish, Jewish, and Arminian "; petitions were
read from parishes which had some personal grudge against their
ministers and saw the chance of getting them deposed on the
excuse that they were backward in the Good Cause; and yet
another committee was appointed for the inspection and revision
of the multitudinous Acts of the General Assemblies which had
sat since the Reformation. Two days later, Wariston presented
the committee's report on these, " whereat many were surprised
how it had been possible in two days to run over these large
Volumes, which would have been work enough for a whole year
to the most diligent Reviser ".[11]

December 13th was a red-letter day, and crowds fought to get

* The Arminians believed in salvation through works, asserting that Christ
died for all, and that through His death and descent into Hell, even pagans
might be saved. To the Calvinists this was an appalling doctrine, for it
meant that they might encounter in Heaven not only men like Socrates and
Cicero, but even good Papists.

inside the High Kirk to hear the solemn Excommunication of
the Bishops of Scotland who, in their absence, had been found
guilty of all the sins in the calendar and a few newly invented
ones.   Dr. David Lindsay of Edinburgh was "a bower to the
altar, a wearer of the rochet, an elevator of the elements, and an
urger of the Liturgy".   The Bishop of Orkney was "a curler on
the ice on the Sabbath"; Galloway had been heard to swear
when he was angry, and had called his horse "Puritan".   Gentle
and virtuous old Spottiswoode was accused amongst many other
crimes of spending a great portion of his time in inns; which was
scarcely surprising considering that during his period of office
he had made no less than fifty journeys to London.   Only three
of the Bishops escaped condemnation for either adultery, fornication, drunkenness, incest, simony, swearing, or Sabbath-break-
ing; into the lives of those three no enquiry was made, for they
had conformed to Presbyterianism, signed the Covenant, and
were now ministers of parishes.

It was the duty of the Precentor to open this awesome ceremony of Excommunication by reading a portion of Scripture
and a psalm.   On the present occasion his choice of both was
most unfortunate.   He read from St. John's Gospel, Chapter 16:
"These things have I spoken unto you, that ye should not be
offended.   They shall put you out of the synagogue . . ."; and
the psalm he chose was 51:

> "O Lord consider my distress,
>   And now with speed some pity take. . . ."

Having administered a rebuke for such tactlessness, the
Moderator prayed for a blessing on the ensuing ceremony, and
then preached.   "After divisions of his text . . . which I omit
as tedious to be mentioned here, in end he came to tell the
hearers that there was a subordination betwixt God and us, God
the upper end of the line, and we the lower, and the middle tie
Christ, represented there by David our superior; that from God,
by Christ, all graces lineally do descend upon us; that no grace
flows down upon those who are not within that line perpen-
dicular: Then he exhorted all to keep the line, and not to look
to them [the Bishops] who were out of the line.   Some may
think that this application was strained."[12]

At last came the moment which everyone awaited: in a voice
of thunder, the Moderator delivered six of the Bishops into the
hands of the Devil until they should repent.   Those who lay
under this terrible sentence of Excommunication were outlawed

in body and soul. They could hold no kind of office, pursue no trade or profession, claim no debt, bear no witness in a court of law; no man might let them a house, give them lodging at an inn, even bid them good morning. Excommunication made outcasts, pure and simple; and henceforth it was to be the most dreaded weapon in the hands of King Covenant.

Having deposed the rest of the Bishops (save the three who had forsworn themselves and embraced Presbyterianism), depriving them not only of their episcopal jurisdiction but of their seats in Parliament, the Assembly sang another psalm, recited prayers, and were blessed by the Moderator, who wound up the ceremony by warning his hearers of the danger to themselves if they frequented the company of any whom the Assembly had either excommunicated or deposed.

In succeeding sessions the Assembly enacted measures which were calculated to ensure that henceforth the Kirk should be the real ruler of Scotland. All who spoke against the Covenant were to be censured; all who did not ostracize excommunicated persons were to suffer the same dread sentence. Committees were appointed to travel throughout the kingdom and enquire into the soundness of the opinions, and the sanctity of the lives, of ministers, schoolmasters, and regents of universities. "This was the first imposing of committees that ever was heard of in like fashion within this kingdom," wrote Spalding, "and which bred hereafter much sorrow against the King and his loyal subjects."

On Wednesday, December 19th, the day before the Assembly decided to dissolve, that which was to prove the worst evil of all was enacted. A Commission of the General Assembly was appointed to sit permanently and with the full powers of the Assembly; so that never again would Scotland be free from the Kirk's interference in every department of her life. It was a thing without precedent, and its development was admirably described by James Gordon. In the following years, he wrote, "it was licked into a shape, midwifed by politicians, and its power added to it by piecemeal, in a surreptitious way; not all at once, for that would have startled the creators of it in the ministry, who did begin to quarrel with its usurpation too late when by its means they were thrust out by dozens and scores from the ministry, for serving and promoval of the ends of these noblemen and churchmen, whose actions in the end proved the destruction of their illustrious and religious Prince; the laws and liberties of the kingdom; the Church Government and ministry; and, for a conclusion, either did malcontent the chief actors, or made them slaves or beggars or both, and the country a field of blood, rapine, and oppression."[13]

The Commission of the Assembly was to wait upon the Parliament summoned by the King for the following May, and ensure that it ratified all the Assembly's Acts; it is curious that no one seems to have seen the irony of the situation. For one of the Covenanters' chief objections to the Bishops was that by the Constitution they had a voice in Parliament, yet now, instead of those fourteen voices, there was to be the permanent veto of the Kirk in secular matters. The Covenanters had complained bitterly of the High Commission, whose only function had been to discipline unruly ministers and regulate matters pertaining to the Kirk. The Commission of the Assembly was to discipline everyone, from the highest to the lowest, in all matters, both secular and ecclesiastical.

At this penultimate session of the Assembly, Acts were passed declaring that in future the Kirk and not the King had the right to convene Assemblies; making all those censurable who had signed the King's Covenant; and adding a clause to their own Covenant wherein Episcopacy was declared unlawful. And last, but by no means least, the Press was muzzled. On the excuse that several papers had been published against the National Covenant, the Assembly appointed Johnston of Wariston its censor; henceforth nothing was to be printed which in any way concerned religion without that fanatic's *imprimatur*. Thus was revived one of the most pernicious claims of the first Reformers who, in 1553, had arrogated to themselves the censorship of religious books, and in 1574 that of all books whatsoever. King Charles remarked drily on the new censorship, "that it was a pretty Act, that he might print nothing concerning ecclesiastical polity and government, except Johnston should give him leave".

Having enacted all these treasonable and mischievous measures, the Assembly passed a vote of thanks to the King for giving them a free and lawful Assembly, and petitioned him for the ratification of everything they had done, which, they said solemnly, had been aimed only at God's glory, religious reformation, and his Majesty's honour. They had no intention whatsoever, they asserted, of interfering with or encroaching upon other Reformed Churches; and they had written to the Churches of Switzerland and Geneva asking for their approbation. This letter, however, received a most unexpected and unwelcome reply. A Mr. John Diodati was delegated by the rest of the ministers of these Calvinist Churches of Europe to write to the

Kirk that "for their republic and constitution they found presbytery most agreeable and necessary, so behoved to own it; but as for those of Scotland it was fittest for them to close with and retain Episcopacy as most agreeable to monarchial government". But in its sudden taste of power the Kirk could afford to do without the approval of its neighbours, and this and other letters were suppressed.[14]

On December 20th the Assembly at last dissolved itself, confident of the continuance of its reign through its Commission and its innumerable committees throughout Scotland. The Moderator devoutly thanked God, the King, and all present for the success of the proceedings, and then addressed a special speech of thanks to Argyll. The latter replied at great length. He begged his brethren not to misunderstand his delay in declaring himself to be of their party; from the very beginning he had been "set their way", but had postponed declaring himself because, by continuing a member of the Council, he had been enabled to do more for them than otherwise he could have done. "But now of late, matters had come to such a height, that he found it behoved him to join himself openly to their society, except he should prove a knave."[15] The *Large Declaration* of the following year commented drily on this: "What he hath proved himself by this false and close carriage, let the world judge."

Argyll concluded by exhorting them all to remain united; and, addressing himself to the ministers, added something significant. He bade them remember that pride and avarice had brought about the Bishops' downfall, and advised them to shun these two rocks if they themselves would escape shipwreck. It was a warning of strife to come. By the "pride" of the Bishops, Argyll referred to their power and dignity; by "avarice" their having obtained some portion of the benefices of the Auld Kirk. He threw out a strong hint, therefore, to beware of dictating to great men like himself or of seeking emoluments which neither King nor Kirk were going to wring from them.

After Argyll had ended his speech, the hundred and thirty-third Psalm was sung, a prayer was read, and the Assembly broke up, the Moderator declaring that "We have now cast down the walls of Jericho; let him that rebuildeth them beware of the curse of Hiel the Bethelite."[16]

Chapter Three

SAVE for the formality of a declaration, King Covenant had been at war with King Charles from the moment when the General Assembly had refused the royal order to dissolve. And now that war of words was to become one of arms, and preparations for it proceeded apace.

The Auld Enemy was publicly addressed in *A Manifesto to all good Christians within the Kingdom of England*. They had no intention, declared the Covenanters, of invading England; they attested the ever-living God that they had not the least design to wrong any good Protestants among their southern brethren; it was merely that they were alarmed for these brethren, because of the growth of Popery, and because the English Bishops had "set on foot dangerous plots". But unless forced to it, they themselves would employ no other arms but fasting, prayer, and supplications to their gracious Sovereign.

Meantime they continued to blockade their gracious Sovereign's castles, suppressed his proclamations, maltreated his officers who attempted to read them, levied an army against him, and imposed upon his subjects a tax for its maintenance.

For more than a year now they had been buying arms from abroad; now they appointed commanders. They were fortunate in that a large number of Scotsmen, being too poor to maintain themselves at home, had embraced the profession of arms in foreign service, and thus could the Covenanters summon to their aid experienced mercenaries. Chief among these was Alexander Leslie, a veteran who, though he had never managed to get beyond the letter G in the alphabet, had risen to the rank of "Felt Marshal" under Gustavus Adolphus. He was a tubby little man in his middle fifties, with forked beard and military moustachios, canny, avaricious, with a great opinion of himself. Thirty years' soldiering in foreign service had made him "a great rich man"; he had purchased estates all over Scotland, besides two earldoms in Sweden. Sir James Turner, who was to serve with him in Ireland a few years later, wrote of him that he "was of so good a memory, that he was never known to forget himself, nay not in his extreme old age".

Turner himself was typical of many Scots who now came

home to command the Covenant's armies, men who neither knew nor cared about the cause for which they fought, so long as they were paid. "All this while," he wrote in 1641, "I did not take the National Covenant, not because I refused to do it, for I would have made no bones to take, swear, or sign it, and observe it too; for I had then a principle, having not yet studied a better one, that I wronged not my conscience in doing anything I was commanded to do by those whom I served."[17]

The army these officers were to command consisted of twenty-five thousand men, an enormous force to have been raised by so small and poor a country as Scotland. It was well-equipped, the Covenanting ministers having compelled their unfortunate flocks to "shake out their purses" for the purpose; and when, in the late spring of 1639, it lay on the Border, it made a brave enough show, with a colours flying from each captain's tent inscribed with the motto, *For Christ's Crown and Covenant*, in golden letters. Yet it is improbable that had this large host been put to the test it would have conquered in battle. For the Covenant's armies, from the beginning to the end of the forthcoming struggle, suffered from two serious defects.

First, their commanders were hampered by a travelling committee of ministers and laymen who claimed the right to dictate in all military affairs. And secondly, the great majority of the men had been impressed. However willing some of them had been to sign the Covenant, to applaud Protestations, to maltreat Bishops, and to capture unarmed castles, they had no desire whatsoever to fight against their King. They were compelled to fight, just as many had been compelled to sign the Covenant, because they would have suffered in goods and person if they had refused. "Whatever means were used by the nobility or their ministry to persuade the vulgar sort of the justness of their quarrel, yet most part of them, who had been born and bred up under a long peace, could hardly distinguish it from rebellion against the King. This abstracted confidence from the meaner sort, and bred a trepidation in them at the hearing of their own drums, trumpets, and shot."[18] It was these two defects which accounted for the extremely poor part the Covenant's armies were to play in the English Civil War, and the decisive defeats they suffered at home.

On the eve of their invasion of England in what has come to be known as the First Bishops' War, the only active Scottish opposition the Covenanters had to fear was from the personage who ruled the north-east, George Gordon, Marquis of Huntly,

"the Cock o' the North"; and it was now that he began to play,
extremely poorly, a part in the drama which might have been
decisive.

Huntly's father, the first Marquis, had adhered to the Auld
Kirk at the Reformation, and during one of his consequent spells
of imprisonment his heir had been sent to London by special
command of King James, and there had been brought up in
the Church of England. He was in France when his father died
in 1636; shortly afterwards he returned to Scotland to take his
place as Chief of the powerful Gordon clan and as one of the
greatest feudal landowners in Scotland. He found his estates
greatly encumbered by debt, however, and it was this poverty
of his, together with his well-known pride, that the Covenanters
attempted to make use of to get him on their side. They offered
to pay his debts, and to make him their leader, if he would concur with them in their resistance to the King's authority.
Huntly's answer was both gallant and prophetic: "That his
family had risen and stood by the Kings of Scotland; and, for his
part, if the event proved the ruin of the King, he was resolved
to bury his life, honours, and estate under the rubble of the
King his ruins."

It was a resolve he was to keep to the bitter end; but unfortunately he had not the strength of character to display that
active and vigorous loyalty which alone could have prevented
the ruin of his King. He was touchy, obstinate, self-opinionated,
and a slave to his belief in astrology. "He was naturally a
gallant man," wrote Burnet, "but the stars had so subdued him,
that he made a poor figure during the whole course of the wars."
Moreover, though his clansmen obeyed him as their Chief, he
was not loved; even his champion, Patrick Gordon, had to
acknowledge that "service done and not to do, was forgotten,
and old servants for whom there was no use must be brushed
or rubbed off as spots from clothes".[19]

Such was the man who now received from King Charles a commission appointing him Royal Lieutenant of the North, but with
these hampering conditions: Huntly was not to be the aggressor,
and he was to take his orders from the King's Commissioner,
Hamilton, whom Charles was sending to Scotland with nineteen
ships of war and five thousand men. The reason for the first
was the King's extreme reluctance to shed his subjects' blood;
and for the second, Charles's trust in the ability of Hamilton as
a military commander.

On the news that Huntly was raising his Gordons, the Covenant's leaders sent a portion of their army against him, com-

manded by young Montrose with the rank of General; to correct his inexperience in war, old Leslie, in the capacity of adjutant, was to follow with other troops. When Montrose marched into Aberdeen at the beginning of April, he had already, with his keen eye for the picturesque, given King Covenant's army a character and look of its own. Huntly had taken for his badge a ribbon of " a red flesh colour "; Montrose retorted by ordering all his foot soldiers " to take for their colours blue ribbons, which they carried about them scarf-wise, or as some orders of knighthood wear their ribbons. This was Montrose's whimsy." The cavalry carried the spanners for their firelocks slung from ribbons of the same colour, while many of the army pinned blue rosettes into their bonnets. The " whimsy " became the fashion for all Covenanters, who were nicknamed by the English " blue-caps or jockies ".

Huntly now displayed his fatal weakness of character. Hamilton had not yet arrived in Scotland with his ships and men; and Montrose was most decidedly acting the part of the aggressor. It was up to Huntly, therefore, to act on his own initiative, and to offer armed resistance. Instead, he withdrew his army to Inverurie, and there sat still. There followed an incident which, slight though it appeared at the time, was to have enormous and fatal consequences for the royal cause.

Having mercilessly plundered the lands of non-Covenanters, and forced loyal Aberdeen not only to sign the Covenant but to swear to God she did so willingly,[20] Montrose went to deal personally with Huntly. He persuaded the latter to sign a modified version of the Covenant, on the express condition that his Gordons should be asked, not forced, to subscribe, that the Catholics among them should be protected so long as they remained peaceable, and that Huntly himself should be free from molestation.

Montrose returned to Aberdeen, and immediately found himself in trouble with the committee of ministers and laymen who accompanied his army; they were furious that Huntly should have been granted such terms, and they summoned him to Aberdeen under a safe conduct. He came; and was told curtly that he must accompany the Covenanters to Edinburgh, either voluntarily or as a prisoner. To a man like the Cock o' the North it was a simple piece of treachery, and he, who knew nothing of committees, not unnaturally laid it at the door of Montrose. He had the more reason for doing so because Montrose, though his promise to Huntly had been violated by his colleagues, did not throw up his command. It was an insult and an injury which Huntly was never to forgive.

Having forced luckless Aberdeen to pay forty thousand merks as a fine for its resistance to the Good Cause, the Covenant horse left the town on April 28th, taking Huntly with them. Both the Marquis and his heir, Lord Gordon, were promptly imprisoned in Edinburgh Castle, where the Tables appointed five "guardians" to ward them day and night at the prisoners' expense, and where the Marquis and his son were pestered to sign the original version of the Covenant. Huntly wrote a dignified refusal, disposing shortly of the arguments intended to persuade him to yield, "by your hopes of supply from France, and other foreign nations, together with your good intelligence in England", and concluded: "For my own part, I am in your power, and resolveth not to leave that foul title of traitor as an inheritance to my posterity; you may take my head from my shoulders, but not my heart from my Sovereign."[21]

It was at this time, at the beginning of May, that Hamilton arrived with his ships and soldiers in the Firth of Forth. Lying idle in Leith Roads, he occupied himself with writing contradictory advice to his Sovereign, who kept impressing upon him that, being the man on the spot, he must use his own judgment how to act. From his distant headquarters in London, Charles could do no more than advise his Commander-in-Chief "that if you find it not fit to land all your five thousand men upon Lothian-side, then it may be counsellable to send most of your landsmen to the north, to strengthen my party there".

Not only did Hamilton ignore this sensible advice; not only did he refrain from making any warlike move against the enemy; but with that fatal habit of his of wanting to run with the hare and hunt with the hounds, he acted in a way which confirmed the suspicion of many that he was an out and out traitor to his King. He entered into secret communication with the Covenanters on the excuse that it was necessary in the King's interests to confer with their leaders with a view to averting war. According to one contemporary, however, he warned them to settle with the Northern Royalists without loss of time, "or to expect no quarter from the King"; this written advice he enclosed in a pistol, with another note instructing them to draw the charge of the weapon and thus to find its hidden contents.[22]

On May 31st, Huntly's second son, Lord Aboyne, joined Hamilton, bringing a letter from the King which again reminded

Alexander Leslie, afterwards Earl of Leven

George Gordon, 2nd Marquis of Huntly

him how important it was that succour should be sent to the loyal North, which Aboyne was now ready and eager to command. Hamilton greeted the young man with the news that, owing to sickness and lack of victuals, his men were in no condition to fight; if, however, Aboyne himself would go north, he should have a veteran, Colonel Gun, to advise him, and ships and men should be sent after him. No sooner was Aboyne gone than the jealous Hamilton began writing disparagingly of him to the King; and meanwhile Aboyne himself, deceived by the promise of ships and men, and betrayed by Gun, was defeated early in June by Montrose and the Earl Marischal at the Brig o' Dee.

Starved of money to pay his forces, and hampered by the growlings of rebellion at home, King Charles was now forced to open peace negotiations with his Scottish rebels, Argyll being sent for to Berwick to take part in these, " for without him none would mint to treat ". " That man," Baillie wrote of him, " has proven, from the beginning to this day, a notable instrument for the managing of our high and difficult affairs . . . he has laboured what in him lay in his wit for keeping our country in peace, both at home and abroad." His method of keeping his country in peace had been somewhat singular; while Montrose had gone to deal with Aberdeen, Argyll had surprised Hamilton's castle in the Isle of Arran, and had raised his Campbells for the suppression of the King's loyal subjects as far north as Sutherland.

Both conscience and policy inclined Charles to come to terms with the Scots; he had a genuine aversion for war, and he was facing a major crisis in England. Baillie bore testimony to the attitude of the King at this time; he was " very sober, meek, and patient to hear all. . . . His Majesty was ever the longer the better loved of all that heard him, as one of the most just, reasonable, and sweet persons they had ever seen ".

But the utter unreasonableness of the Covenanters made it obvious that this could be but a truce and not a treaty. Every royal Declaration was followed by one of the old Protestations; the King was insulted by Covenanting ministers in their sermons; and, most intolerable of all, the demand was made that " all incendiaries and informers against the kingdom, who have, for their private ends, raised these commotions ", be sent to Edinburgh to receive their just punishment. Since by these were meant anyone who had shown any active loyalty to the King, Charles could scarcely be expected to agree.

At length, however, the negotiations ended in the truce known

F

as the Pacification of Berwick, and the Scottish Commissioners
signed the following note: " In obedience to his Majesty's royal
commands, we shall upon Thursday next, the 20th of this June,
dismiss our forces, and immediately thereafter deliver his
Majesty's castles, and shall ever in all things carry ourselves like
humble, loyal and obedient subjects."[23]   It was a promise they
had not the slightest intention of keeping.

Clarendon summed up the Pacification of Berwick very
succinctly:

"There were not two present who did agree in the same relation of what was said and done, and which was worse, not in the
same interpretation.   An agreement was made in which nobody
meant what others believed he did."

Chapter Four

E VEN before he left Berwick for London in July, Charles was
given evidence that the Covenanters' attitude remained
hostile and insolent. He sent for some of the leaders, hoping,
by a private conference, to arrive at a better understanding.
Among these was Argyll, who had returned to Edinburgh during the peace negotiations. Argyll set out, but went no farther
than the Watergate of that town; there was a rumour, he
declared, that if he accepted the King's invitation he would be
detained prisoner. It was an insult of the first magnitude, and
it decided Charles not to come in person, as he had intended,
to open the Scottish Parliament. "It cannot be thought reasonable," observed the *Large Declaration*, "that We should trust
Our person with those that distrusted Us, after so many arguments and assurances of Our goodness towards them."

In August, Hamilton having refused the honour, Traquair
was sent to Scotland as Royal Commissioner. He found that the
Scots had violated the most important conditions of the Pacification, Leslie still retaining his rank of General of forces which
had not been disbanded, and the fortification of Leith still being
continued. In such impossible conditions Traquair presided over
the new General Assembly, which had been packed as
thoroughly as the previous one.

Having yet once again solemnly abolished the Articles of
Perth, the High Commission, and the Books of Canons and Ser-

vice, having passed Acts which obliged ministers to spend one day each week catechizing their unfortunate parishioners, and to visit houses within their parishes to see that the morning and evening devotions, now made obligatory, were performed, the Assembly vented its wrath upon the *Large Declaration*, newly published, in which was set forth the history of the troubles. Notwithstanding the fact that it was published in the King's name, the Assembly demanded that its author, Dean Balcanquhal of Durham, be sent to Scotland for trial.

For, apart from the fact that it made some pertinent comments upon Argyll's behaviour in continuing to sit on the Council while secretly favouring the Covenanters, the latter had every reason for fearing and hating the *Large Declaration*. It was admirably and concisely written, and it reproduced in full all the proclamations, letters, petitions, and protestations relevant to the events of the past two years. After thoroughly condemning it, the Assembly made a solemn protestation of loyalty to the King, appointed a new Assembly to be held in the July of the following year, and dissolved.

On August 31st, "the last parliament in this kingdom after the ancient form (the royal Prerogative in show being yet entire)", was "ridden", Traquair representing the King, and Argyll carrying the Crown. It was, in fact, the recent Assembly under another name, most of its members having been what were coming to be called, significantly, "ruling elders", a few days previously. It was unique in one respect: the Estate of the Clergy, the Lords Spiritual, for the first time had no place in it. Even in 1560, when all Church jurisdiction in the persons of Bishops had been abolished, and again in 1587, when the temporalities of benefices had been annexed, the clergy had retained their ancient vote in Parliament, and had remained the Third, or more correctly, the First, Estate.

But the Covenanters were now determined to alter the whole framework of the Constitution. The ancient custom was for the King to name eight Bishops, who in their turn nominated eight nobles, who again chose eight barons, who chose eight burgesses. These thirty-two, with eight Officers of the Crown, made up the Lords of the Articles as they were called, whose business it was to receive from the Clerk-Register details of the petitions and the bills which were to be laid before the Estates, and to decide which should be debated and in what order. Such was the peculiar constitution of the Scottish Parliament.

The Covenanters having now abolished one of the Estates in the persons of the Bishops, Traquair demanded that the King

should not be prejudiced in his right by their expulsion, and
that he might have the choice of eight noblemen instead. A
denial of this would have been a denial of the Royal Prerogative,
and since for the moment the Covenanting leaders were not prepared to go so far, they acceded to Traquair's demand. But
only for this once. In future every Estate was to choose its own
representatives. This revolutionary measure, passed by a
majority of only one vote, directly contravened a special Act
made in King James's time, which had declared it to be treason
"to procure the innovation of the power and authority of the
same Three Estates or any one of them". The Covenanters'
retort was that it would be "lese-majesty divine" to observe
Acts of Parliament which had acknowledged Bishops to be one
of the Three Estates.

In October Traquair prorogued this, the "Altercating Parliament", until June of the following year; but the extremists,
headed by Argyll, refused to be prorogued. Their answer to
the moderates who maintained that so long as they had a king
they could not sit without his authority, was an ominous one:
"that to do the less, was more lawful than to do the greater."
In other words it was less unlawful for them to elect Lord Burleigh, one of their number, to preside in the place of the King's
Commissioner, than to declare that Charles was no longer their
King. Meantime they would send commissioners to Court to
air their grievances, and to declare their loyalty to "the descendant of one hundred and eight Kings of Scotland", but if
Charles's answer was unsatisfactory, then they must "take such
courses as may best secure Kirk and Kingdom from the
extremity of misery and confusion".

In actual fact, they were sending commissioners less to lay
their grievances before the King, than to conspire with English
malcontents. One of these was Lord Savile, a bitter enemy of
the man who, in January 1640, was created Earl of Strafford,
and whose drive and personality made him the target of the malcontents' hate. Though again and again the Covenanters had
declared that they had no intention of interfering with other
Reformed Churches, they now wrote Savile suggesting that if
he and his friends would agree to the imposing of Presbyterianism upon England, they would invade with their army, and
thereby force the King to abandon Strafford and give way to all
the demands made upon him by his opponents.

Savile sounded certain of his fellow lords, but found that,
though "they confessed a common cause with the Scots", they
thought the time not yet ripe for them to espouse the Coven-

ant's cause.   Undeterred by this, Savile assured Loudoun and Dunfermline, the principal Scottish Commissioners in London, that if their countrymen would invade, the "honest party" in England would welcome them.   This promise being sent to Argyll in Edinburgh, that cautious personage demanded "ane band"; so a cane was hollowed, a paper, bearing the signatures of Savile and five other peers, was inserted in it, and a man named Frost, afterwards Secretary to the Committee of Both Kingdoms, was sent to Scotland with it, himself disguised as a poor traveller.   His orders were to show the treasonable paper only to Argyll, Rothes, and Wariston, and from them an oath of secrecy was exacted; all they were allowed to make public was that in renewing the war they were confident of "a very great and unexpected assistance".   This indeed proved true, though it was found later that Savile had forged the signatures of the other five noblemen.[24]

An alliance with English rebels was not the only assistance the Covenanters could look for in their determination to renew the war.   From the days of Charlemagne, so tradition had it, France had been Scotland's particular friend; and since the Union of the Crowns in 1603, France had attempted to use the "Auld Alliance" for the purpose of preventing Great Britain from becoming too strong.   For years Cardinal Richelieu and the discontented party in Scotland had had "too straight an intelligence"[25]; and in 1637 that very astute statesman had found a most particular reason for preventing Britain from acting as a Great Power.   For France and the United Provinces were about to make a concerted attack upon the maritime towns of the Spanish Netherlands, and it was necessary to ensure that Britain did not interfere.

Accordingly, Richelieu had sent to England a special envoy, Count D'Estrades, with a promise that if King Charles would observe a strict neutrality, France would lend him aid against his Scottish malcontents.   At the same time one of Richelieu's chaplains, the Abbé Chambres, a man of Scots extraction, was sent to Edinburgh, to promise French aid to those who were soon to become Covenanters, if the King did not accede to French demands.   D'Estrades' mission failed; the King replied bluntly that though he wished for the friendship of his Most Christian Majesty, Louis XIII, there could be no such friendship if the price of it were prejudicial to his honour or injurious to the interests of his people.   If the Spanish ports were attacked by France, the English fleet would be in the Downs with an army of fifteen thousand men for the aid of Spain; and as for the offer of aid against the Scots, "he required no other assistance to punish rebels, than his own regal authority and the laws of England ".[26]

The answer of the Scots was very different. Though they were conducting a bitter persecution of Catholics, and their favourite epithet for all their opponents was "Popish", they eagerly accepted the offer of assistance from a Catholic Power; and they who were busily abolishing Bishops made no bones of treating with a Cardinal. As early as December 1638, they had been buying arms from France; and in April of the following year, when the Covenant's army lay upon the Border, a letter of appeal to King Louis for aid was drawn up and signed by Rothes, Loudoun, Leslie, Montgomery, Mar, and Forrester.

It reminded Louis of the Auld Alliance, and also of "the maxim of policy to assist the weaker, to keep the balance the more even"; and begged him "when matters draw to blood, then really to succour and assist us, either by supply of money and arms at home, or by diverting our invaders [sic] abroad". The subscribers addressed Louis as "au roy", the ritual phrase of subjects addressing their own monarch. Meanwhile, sublimely unconscious of irony, the Covenanters sent into England two thousand copies of a paper in which they warned all Englishmen that if the latter took the King's side in his quarrel with the Scots, the Papists would seize the chance of subduing their land to Popery.[27]

Whether the treasonable letter to the French King was ever sent appears doubtful, though either the original or a copy of it was found long afterwards in the State Paper Office of France. What is certain is that either the letter itself, or a copy, came into the hands of King Charles. According to Guthrie it was the original, and it came into the King's possession in the following manner: "At the subscribing of it there happened to be some great men absent, whom those present wished also might subscribe it. For which end they committed the letter to Mr. Archibald Johnston, appointing him as he found opportunity to get their names to it; but through negligence he lost it out of his pocket, and so it passed from one hand to another, until it fell into Sir Donald Gorram's hand, who delivered it to the Earl of Traquair, and he to the King."[28]

This happened at the time when the Scottish Commissioners were in London, in the autumn of 1639. The King warded three of them in their lodgings, and the fourth and greatest, John Campbell, Lord Loudoun, he sent to the Tower. Loudoun was a known trouble-maker, and for his opposition to the King during the royal visit to Scotland in 1633, he had had his patent of an earldom stopped by special order at the Chancery. "A deft lord he was, who, missing of the Court to civilize his studies, must needs want morality to bring him to manners. And being besides of a cavilling contradictory nature, nothing would seem to him so positive in reason as his own opinion."[29]

When what was to become known as the Short Parliament assembled in April 1640, Charles laid before it this Scottish treason, but the Parliament was too busy hatching treason of its own to take action, and in any case "underhand for the most part wished all prosperity and good luck to the Covenanters". Charles dissolved it on May 5th, and the imprisoned Scots Commissioners were released shortly afterwards.

But long ere this, without waiting for the return of their Commissioners, the Covenanters had been preparing for a renewal of the war. Their chief lack was money, and in order to supply this need, what came to be known as the Blind Band was drawn up, termed euphemistically "A Band for the Relief of the Common Burden", whereby every man's estate was valued and he was taxed accordingly. It was taxation imposed without warrant either from the King or the Parliament, "set forth by subjects upon subjects"; and in addition the ministers were ordered to demand from their pulpits the bringing in of all silver plate to be melted down. Those who brought it willingly were to have a promise of payment at some unspecified date; those who refused were to have it confiscated.

At the same time there was begun a regular besiegement of Edinburgh Castle, held for the King by General Ruthven, and an intensifying of the persecution of non-Covenanters. A royal Proclamation discharging Argyll from his office of Justiciary of the Isles, conferred upon him by the King in 1634, was suppressed, the Covenanters declaring that "they dared not to make any such proclamation against the person of such a prime nobleman", adding with studied insolence that the King had no power to deprive any Scots peer of his offices.[30]

While committing these acts of open defiance, the Covenanters were not unmindful of their obligations under the Clandestine Band, and were busy publishing seditious tracts against the Earl of Strafford and Archbishop Laud, the two chief targets of the English opposition, quaintly terming them "the heads of the Popish faction". They who had just been imploring the aid of the Catholic King of France, and for years had been intriguing with a Catholic Cardinal, gravely begged their English brethren "to look upon the princes in France, who were all busy to bear down the Protestants there", but, mindful of the fact that France, whence they still hoped to get assistance, was the enemy of Spain, added that the latter kingdom was the real instigator of these troubles. Baillie was commissioned to write a book proving that "the faction whereof William Laud is head, is guilty of open Popery"; and to find fresh fuel for such seditious publications, spies were sent to visit the London churches, "to try what crucifixes and new images are at Paul's and the Chapel [Royal]", and to see if they could twist the words of English clergymen to prove them "popishly inclined".[31]

In June, for the first time in the history of Scotland, the Estates assembled without King, Regent, Royal Commissioner, or Honours; the last, the Crown, Sceptre, and Sword, were in the besieged Castle. They chose for their President and figure-head Lord Burleigh, and proceeded to pass laws in the King's name while actively preparing to fight him. It was enacted that the "authors and spreaders" of the Large Declaration be severely punished, that the castles of Scotland be manned and commanded by such as they chose to appoint, that yet another new tax be imposed upon the realm, those who refused to pay it to have their estates confiscated "for the public use", and, following the example of the Kirk, that a huge Committee of Estates be appointed to sit until Parliament met again, one half to attend the Covenant's armies, the other to remain in Edinburgh. Finally a new band was drawn up, to be subscribed by the whole kingdom, acknowledging this entirely illegal parliament to have been a free and lawful one.

Argyll was not a member of the Committee just appointed. Says his biographer, Mr. Willock, "It was in accordance with his policy and temperament to take greater pleasure in exercising power than in having a show of it; so that his abstention from open possession of office is not to be explained so much in his abounding in the virtues of modesty and self-denial, as by a weakness for wire-pulling in secret which seems inseparable from some types of Scotch character."[32] Argyll's contemporary, James Gordon, was less delicate in his summing up of the situation: "But all saw he was major potestas; and though not formally a member, yet all knew that it was his influence that gave being, life, and motion to these new-modelled governors; and not a few thought that this junto was his own invention . . . there was a door left open for him to enter the Committee whenever he pleased, both as an officer of the Army, and upon the call of the Committee."[33]

The fact of the matter was that Argyll had a ploy of his own which he preferred at present to managing in person the Committee of Estates. For the juncture of affairs gave him an opportunity which no Campbell chieftain could resist, the harrying of hereditary foes and the acquisition of their lands.

Chapter Five

O N this eve of the Second Bishops' War the Gordons did not constitute the threat to the Covenanters which they had appeared to be in the previous invasion. Huntly, whose wife, Argyll's sister, had died in the previous July, had been released from his imprisonment as being harmless, and after arranging the marriages of two of his daughters, had gone to Court in November, whither his elder sons, Lords Gordon and Aboyne, had preceded him. The Gordons, therefore, were leaderless; and the only opposition to the Covenant in Scotland was that of the Stewarts of Atholl and the Ogilvies of Airlie.

In this June of 1640, while Leslie marched with the main Covenant army to the Border, Montrose went to deal with the Ogilvies, and Argyll was given a Commission of Fire and Sword against the loyalists of Atholl. From ancient times, nothing had better pleased a Scots noble than one of these commissions, for they legalized the harrying of hereditary foes. Argyll had authority from the Committee of Estates (whose real head he was) to pursue the loyalists " in all hostile manner by fire and sword, ay, and until he should either bring them to their bounden duty, and give assurances of the same by pledges or otherwise, or else to the utter subduing and rooting them out of the country ".

Armed with this formidable warrant, and with four thousand of his Campbells at his back, Argyll marched confidently into Atholl; but when he came to the Ford of Lyon, near Balloch Castle, he found the Earl of Atholl encamped there with twelve hundred of his claymores. A fight, even with such superiority of numbers, was never congenial to Argyll; therefore he made as though he would arrange a truce. He summoned Atholl and eight of his principal gentlemen to come under a safe conduct to confer with him in his tent. Immmediately they came, they were informed by Argyll that they were his prisoners, Atholl was ordered to disband his people, and he and his eight gentlemen were sent captive to Edinburgh. Among these eight was a certain John Stewart of Ladywell, destined to play a major part in the drama of the following year.

Montrose, meanwhile, had had quietly surrendered to him "the Bonnie House of Airlie", the only stronghold of the loyalists of Perthshire and Angus, had placed a garrison in it under a Colonel Sibbald, and had marched away to the Border to join Leslie. Before doing so, however, he had written to Argyll, the Ogilvies' hereditary foe, telling him that Lord Ogilvy, whose father, the old Earl of Airlie, was with the King, had surrendered the house upon terms, and that therefore it would be unnecessary for Argyll to come into those parts.

Argyll ignored the letter. At the beginning of July he appeared with his men before the Bonnie House of Airlie, and curtly ordered Sibbald and his garrison to vacate it. Sibbald naturally demurred, and Argyll was forced, in the discreet words of his biographer, "to exercise a certain amount of pressure". Having turned out Montrose's garrison, he was enraged to find that Lord Ogilvy, whom he had hoped to take prisoner, was not at home, and that, with Montrose's permission, all the valuables of the house had been removed to a place of safety.

But Argyll was not going to be done out of the indulging of his feud. First he proceeded to demolish the house, encouraging his men by "taking a hammer in his hand and knocking down the hewed work of the doors and windows, till he sweat for heat at his work". He then let his Campbells loose upon the lands, burning the crops, plundering the houses of tenants, and driving away the livestock. Everything that could not be carried away was destroyed, and so thorough was Argyll that he did not leave so much as a cock to herald the day to the wretched inhabitants.[34]

Although Airlie had been the only "strength" in the neighbourhood, Argyll next turned his attention to the Ogilvies' other houses, in particular to that of Forthar. He sent one of his sergeants, Dugald Campbell, with a party against it, giving him careful instructions. He was to send the livestock "the nearest way home" (Argyll's home, it is needless to say), and "Albeit ye should be the longer in following me, yet ye shall not fail to stay and demolish the Lord Ogilvy's house of Forthar. See how ye can cast off the iron yetts and windows; and take down the roof; and if ye find it will be longsome, ye shall fire it well, that so it may be destroyed. But you need not to let know that ye have directions from me to fire it: only ye may say that ye have warrant to demolish it, and to make the short work ye may fire it."[35]

When Sergeant Campbell arrived at Forthar, he found there Lady Ogilvy, old Airlie's daughter-in-law, who was awaiting her confinement. Without doing anything to the house, therefore, he returned to his lord and informed him that "it was no strength at all", and contained only a sick gentlewoman and some servants. Argyll turned upon him in fury, told him that it was his part to obey orders, and commanded him to return to Forthar and demolish it. "At the sergeant's parting with him, Argyll was remarked by such as were near to turn away from Sergeant Campbell with some desdain, repeating the Latin political maxim *Abscindantur qui nos perturbant* [Let those be cut off that trouble us]; a maxim which many thought he practised accurately, and which he did upon account of the proverb consequential thereunto, and which is the reason of the former, which Argyll was remarked to have often likewise in his mouth, as a choice aphorism, and well observed by statesmen, *Quod mortui non mordent* [Because dead men do not bite]."[36] Though Lady Ogilvy sent to Argyll, begging him to let her remain at Forthar until her child was born, he not only refused this, but also a request from the lady's grandmother, Dame Marian Douglas, his own kinswoman, to receive the expectant mother into her house of Kelly.

Having settled with the Ogilvies, he turned to the paying off of other old scores; but here he made a nice distinction. Neither the Camerons of Lochaber nor the MacDonalds of Keppoch had signed the Covenant, and Argyll's commission, therefore, gave him the right to harry them. But for the moment Argyll was less a Covenanter than a Campbell. Both the Camerons and the MacDonalds were the feudal vassals of Argyll's brother-in-law, Huntly, and the former clan resented this over-lordship. Himself a Highlander, Argyll knew just the arguments to persuade the Camerons that if they would fight on the Covenant's side they would free themselves from vassalage to a lord who was upon the other. Naturally he did not see fit to mention that if the Covenanters were successful in the coming struggle, he had every intention of seizing his brother-in-law's feudal possessions upon which, for a long time past, he had looked with envy.

The MacDonalds of Keppoch, on the other hand, were friendly to Huntly, and in any case they were MacDonalds, the Campbell's most bitter hereditary foes. So Argyll burned the

Chief's house to the ground, sent some of his principal clansmen to the Edinburgh jail, and allowed the rest to stay at home after paying a substantial "war-tax". Then, his forces much depleted by his leaving two hundred of them to overawe the MacDonalds and by his sending others home with the enormous booty he had acquired during the expedition, Argyll marched by way of Deeside to Edinburgh, where he arrived in the first days of August, and where he had a very particular piece of business to transact.

It had always been the habit of any Scots noble who, when the Sovereign was either absent or a minor, obtained from the Regent a Commission of Fire and Sword, to obtain also, after the execution of that Commission, an "Exoneration". For one never knew what might happen when the Sovereign grew up or returned, or some rival nobleman seized power. Argyll's Exoneration, which he obtained from the Committee of Estates this August, was very thorough indeed.

It ran in the name of the King whose loyal subjects he had been harrying, and it extended to "his colonels, captains, commanders of the army, and to their servants, men, boys, and followers". He and every single person concerned in the late expedition was to be held scatheless "for any violence whatsoever done to the liberty of the subject, or freedom taken with their property, houses, or castles; or for burning of the same, and putting of fire thereinto, or other ways destroying the same howsoever; or by putting whatsoever person or persons to torture or question, or putting of any person or persons to death, at any time betwixt the 18th of June, 1640, and the said second day of August next thereafter".[37]

While Argyll had been committing those acts which had to be covered by so thorough and so ugly an Exoneration, the Committee of Estates had been drawing up a formal declaration of war on the eve of their invasion of England. They were invading, they declared, only in self-defence; but forgetful, it seemed, of their former solemn assurances that they had no intention whatsoever of interfering with other Reformed Churches, they now revealed the fact that God had willed their destruction of the Church of England, "the fountain of Popery", at their hands; when this was accomplished they were hopeful that the Lord would "thrust the Beast and False Prophet back to Rome, if He did not free all the earth from him".

Obscure scriptural allusions followed. They were seeking to remove out of England "the troublers of the kingdom's peace, such as Coraths, Balaams, Doegs, Rabshakahs, Hamans, Tobiases,

Sanballats; and this being done, they declare that they shall be abundantly satisfied". They were not coming to fight, unless forced to it by "the Popish party"; they were coming, the whole twenty-five thousand of them, peacefully to petition the King. Mindful of the average Englishman's intense dislike of their nation, they added a promise that "they will not take so much from England unpaid for as a latchet or a root of garlic".

Though disappointed in the amount of monetary aid sent them by their friends in the south,[38] the vast host under Leslie crossed the Border on August 20th. The Tweed was in spate, and dice were cast among the commanders to decide who should be the first to make the dangerous crossing. The lot fell on Montrose, who plunged cheerfully into the torrent, and, encouraged by his example, the soldiers followed. By the 28th they were encamped five miles from Newcastle, on the north bank of the Tyne, and with the aid of nine pieces of ordnance, cleverly concealed by Leslie, they crossed the ford at Newburn, beating back Lords Conway and Wilmot who had sought to oppose them with some Royalist horse. Thus was the first blood shed.

Their immediate object was to cut off the coal supply from London, and Newcastle being untenable, the King's Governor, Sir Jacob Astley, made them a present of the town and marched towards Durham, "leaving behind," remarked Clarendon bitterly, "the honour and coal of the kingdom". The Covenanters entered Newcastle on the 29th, seized the ships coming in from the Baltic with corn, and got a quantity of arms and ammunition. On the 30th they took Durham, garrisoned all the villages in the neighbourhood and, having committed these acts of war, petitioned the King, as "his Majesty's loyal subjects", that they might come to him without further opposition, their "peaceful" passage at Newburn having been opposed.

They had shown their strength. At home Argyll had forced the surrender of Dumbarton and Edinburgh Castles; and the collusion which for so many years had existed between them and the malcontents of England would do the rest of their business for them. Charles had no money to fight them; and thus it was that the English opposition was able to blackmail him into calling yet another parliament, ostensibly for the supplying of it, actually for the pulling down of their prime enemy, Strafford. "This great policy is unknown to the King," wrote Spalding, "whereby the English Lower House and our confederates were so tied, and each to others obliged." Yet it was plain enough that collusion existed, for among their "supplications" to the

King the Scots included a request for the calling of a parliament in England and the dealing with "incendiaries".

Thus was the Treaty of Ripon born. It was a long birth, beginning in October 1640, and dragging on into the spring of 1641. The reason for the prolonging of the negotiations was that the English malcontents wished to give the Scots Army an excuse for remaining a menace on the Border while they themselves destroyed Strafford and a large portion of the royal Prerogative at the same time. And this despite the expense of maintaining that army. Leslie's men were to have eight hundred and fifty pounds a day, and over and above this they were promised three hundred thousand pounds sterling under the significant name of "Brotherly Assistance"; it was to come out of the pockets of English taxpayers whose country the Scots had invaded.*

In November the Scottish Commissioners for the Treaty arrived in London, avid to assist in the destruction of Strafford and Laud; their bitterness against the former was caused, not only by the fact that he was the staunchest upholder of the prerogative, but because, while he had been the King's Lieutenant in Ireland, he had countered the Covenant by making the many Scots resident there take an oath whereby they abjured it in so far as it was prejudicial to the royal authority. Among these Commissioners was Robert Baillie, and it was remarkable what a change had come over this once kindly and moderate minister. All scruples about treason had vanished, as had former resolves not to interfere with the religious beliefs of other Protestants. He gloated over the thought of giving Laud, "his little Grace", "the last stroke"; he was pleasantly astonished by the open treason being talked in the English Lower House; he wrote happily that "God is making here a new world; no fear yet of raising the Parliament, so long as the lads about Newcastle sits still". His only complaint was that the English, while properly grateful (" their binding word is ever 'Gramercy, good Scot'"), were regrettably slow in paying the Brotherly Assistance.

Throughout Strafford's trial in March, Baillie sent home joyful

---

* Actually the Scots computed the expenses of their invasion at five hundred and fourteen thousand pounds, "a formidable and prodigious sum, more than ever was granted to any king at once." A sordid haggling went on for months, and it was not until the following February that the English Parliament settled for three hundred thousand as "a fit proportion for the friendly assistance and relief formerly thought fit to be given toward the supply of the losses and necessities of their BRETHREN in Scotland, the House taking into its consideration the means of raising the same and the time when it should be paid." (Hamond L'Estrange, 218.)

reports of the insults offered to the King and of the savagery of Strafford's enemies. He described the indecent haste with which the great man was tried, the passionate indignation of his foes when the Upper House gave him eight days to prepare his defence, the Commons' fury that the Lords should give to any-one whom *they* had charged with high treason any benefit of counsel or permission to put his defence into writing. Spite-fully he reported the demeanour of the mobs with which the opposition had taken care to pack Westminster Hall—"much public eating, not only of confections, but of flesh and bread, bottles of beer and wine going thick from mouth to mouth with-out cups, and all this in the King's eye; yea, many but turned their back, and let water go through the forms they sat on". At the same time he had the face to write: "The King is now very sad and pensive; yet no man has the least intention against him; if they had, the Scots, for all their quarrels, would have their hearts' blood: but the farthest is the punishing of false knaves, who has too long abused the King and us all."[39]

Could Baillie have known what the real extent of this opposi-tion to the King was to be; could he have foreseen the scaffold outside Whitehall; could he have imagined that when Episcopacy was rooted out in England something quite other than Presby-terianism would take its place; could he have dreamed that the Covenanters' assistance to their English confederates would result, not in payment and love and thanks, but in the utter destruction, by the Auld Enemy, of Scotland as a sovereign State, he too might have looked "very sad and pensive" at this time.

Chapter Six

THERE was now to take a leading part in the tragedy the romantic figure of James Grahame, Earl of Montrose. He had made his entrance during the tumults which had attended the reading of the Service Book; he had continued to be in the limelight as a prominent Covenanter. Neither he nor anyone else could have foreseen that in the middle of the play he would appear in a completely new guise.

But it was fatally easy for his contemporaries, writing after the curtain had descended, to see him only in that new guise of

Royalist champion, and to delude themselves with the belief
that the other had been but a mask. Thus James Gordon asserts
that Montrose's cheerfulness when he was the first to ford the
swollen Tweed in August, 1640, was only assumed; while Hamond
L'Estrange insists that his appearing active and enthusiastic in
such petty things was only that he might betray his fellow Covenanters to better purpose when he judged the moment ripe. Such
statements do a great injustice to Montrose's character, which
was frank and open to the point of indiscretion, as he was soon
to prove. That a change did come over him, dating from the
summer of 1640, is certain; but the most likely nature of that
change was not that he was becoming a Royalist, but that, while
continuing to hold "left-wing" views, he was becoming jealous
and suspicious of Argyll.

For first of all, Argyll, though inferior to him in military rank,
had demolished the Bonnie House of Airlie after Montrose had
received its surrender upon terms; further than that, Argyll had
turned out the garrison which Montrose had placed in it. Any
young, high-spirited commander would resent such an insult.
Next, Argyll had endeavoured to impeach him; he had
arraigned him on articles drawn up by himself to be tried by a
court martial under the Commander-in-Chief for sparing the
Bonnie House of Airlie. Leslie would have none of so ridiculous
a charge, as indeed Argyll must have known he would not, and
Montrose received from the travelling portion of the Committee
of Estates a formal deed of exoneration.

It had been a hint to Montrose to remember who was the real
master of Scotland and, having administered it, Argyll substituted a bribe. Unknown to the Committee of Estates, he had
drawn up a scheme of "encantoning" Scotland; it was to be
divided into three districts, two south of the Forth, and one
north of it; these three districts were to be ruled by what
amounted to dictators, each with his inevitable committee, and
the dictator who was to rule the country north of the Forth was
to be, of course, Argyll. Through one of his closest friends.
probably Cassilis, he invited Montrose to be on his select committee in this scheme.

The result was to turn Montrose's indignation against the
Campbell into alarm. For he was a Scots noble, and he knew
as well as anyone else in Scotland how many of such men
throughout her history had aimed at, and often obtained,
dictatorship. At about the same time he heard talk which
immensely increased his disquietude. Sir Thomas Stewart of
Grandtully, and John Stewart of Ladywell, two of the gentlemen

View of Edinburgh in the seventeenth century

Lord Lorn, afterwards 9th Earl of Argyll

taken with Atholl by treachery at the Ford of Lyon in June, now told Montrose of the boasts uttered by Argyll on that occasion. He had bragged that he was "the eighth man from Robert the Bruce"; he had talked of deposing the King; his Highland warriors had declared that "they were King Campbell's men, no more King Stewart's"; and some Gaelic verse had been written which Grandtully had seen and which he translated thus: "I gave Argyll the praise, because all men see it is truth; for he will take gear from the Lowland men; and he will cry [be proclaimed] King at Whitsunday."[40]

The effect of all this upon Montrose was to determine him to have "ane band" of his own. Accordingly one was drawn up and signed by himself and some twenty of his friends, including Lord Almond, second-in-command to General Leslie, at Cumbernauld, the house of Montrose's relative, Lord Wigton. The signatories swore to uphold the letter and spirit of the National Covenant "to the hazard of our lives, fortunes, and estates", and protested against "the particular and indirect practising of a few".[41]

Immediately *after* this, Montrose proved his own firm allegiance to the Covenant by being the first to cross the swollen Tweed in the invasion of England. It is true that during the preliminary negotiations of the Treaty of Ripon he wrote to the King, professing his loyalty and ready obedience; but too much importance should not be attached to such professions, seeing that all the Covenanters had continued to make them from the beginning of the troubles. These letters were duly removed from the King's pockets by the traitors in his Bedchamber, copied out, and the copies sent to the leaders of the party. This was in October. Argyll's suspicions may or may not have been aroused by the discovery that Montrose was writing to the King on his own account; but in the following month something happened which proved to the Campbell, not that Montrose was becoming pro-Royalist, but that he was certainly anti-Argyll.

For young Lord Boyd, one of the signatories of the Cumbernauld Band, fell ill, and in his delirium he babbled of the Band and of those who had signed it. His ravings reached the quick ears of Argyll, who hurried to the house of one of the principal signatories, Lord Almond, and dragged the whole story out of him. At Argyll's demand, the Committee of Estates in Edinburgh summoned Montrose to appear before them and answer to the matter; he frankly acknowledged and spiritedly defended the Band as a simple, honest restatement of the original aims of

G

the Covenant. It was an awkward situation for Argyll, particularly so because several high-ranking officers of the Army had signed the Band. All he could do was to burn it and let the matter drop, while keeping a wary eye upon Montrose in the future.

But Montrose on his side was not prepared to forget what he had heard about Argyll's pretensions to dictatorship. He began to talk about them, quite openly, to all his friends, and of his own suggested remedy; he was going to do his utmost to persuade the King to come in person to open the Parliament convened for this summer of 1641, and after Charles had ratified all the illegal Acts of the last Parliament, which had sat without royal warrant, Montrose was going to give him a first-hand account of Argyll's treasonable designs.

By the spring of 1641, therefore, Argyll was out for Montrose's blood. For here was a young man of great personality, of noble birth, extremely popular with the soldiers, and already giving promise of his future brilliance as a military commander, enthusiastic indeed for the Covenant, but neither afraid of the man accepted by everyone else as the natural leader of the movement, nor content to accept King Campbell in place of King Charles. Moreover Montrose possessed a disconcerting knack of discovering his opponents' weak points. Rebuked for " having intelligence with the enemy ", in other words of writing to the King, he asked blandly if they, whose own professions of loyalty had remained so profuse, regarded his Majesty as an enemy. This was particularly infuriating to Argyll who, at his first openly joining himself to the Covenanters in 1638, had impressed upon them their duty of showing themselves good subjects.

But in May Argyll saw a chance of ruining his erstwhile colleague. Certain ministers were called before a select committee of the Committee of Estates, and were examined as to what Montrose had been saying to them. At the end of the month, one of these ministers, John Grahame of Auchterarder, was commanded to repeat his evidence, Montrose being present. It was to the effect that someone had told him that when Argyll was in Atholl the previous summer he had declared that the King might lawfully be deposed, either for leaving his kingdom without a government, for raising an army against his " loyal " subjects, or for destroying their laws and liberties.

The committee immediately demanded of Grahame who had told him this. The minister hesitated, plainly embarrassed, whereupon Montrose cried to him, " Fear not, tell your author."

"Then, my lord," said Grahame, "it is yourself that is my author." The next step was to ask Montrose where *he* had got the story; he replied that this treasonable talk of Argyll had been repeated to him by John Stewart of Ladywell, who had heard it spoken. This, of course, though it was the last thing Montrose had intended, sealed poor Ladywell's fate.

He in his turn was summoned before the committee, and at first he stood stoutly by what he had told Montrose. "My lord," he said to Argyll, "I heard you speak these words in Atholl, in presence of a great many people, whereof you are in good memory." Argyll was righteously indignant. What he had said, he declared, was something quite different; he had found the Stewarts of Atholl antipathetic to the Covenant, and had done his best to persuade them that it was not against the King but only for the upholding of the religion and liberties of the realm, and that if they would not sign it they would imperil all their fellow-countrymen. For it would cause divisions, which would be "a highway to bring in the Englishmen in the land to dethrone the King, and bring the nobles under servitude and slavery. This he remembered to have said, but denied any further ". But Ladywell not only stuck to his story; he signed a paper declaring that every word he had told Montrose was true.

There was a short, sharp way of dealing with such inconveniently honest gentlemen; Ladywell was flung into prison, charged with "lease-making", that is, a sowing of discord between the King and his subjects. Bribes and threats were used to make him forswear himself, and it is extremely probable that torture was employed. For in later examinations he asked permission to give his evidence in writing, "not being able to stand or gang", and it will be remembered that Argyll's Exoneration of the previous summer had expressly mentioned torture. Meanwhile the would-be dictator sought other means for the destruction of Montrose, and he was not long in finding them.

Like all such men he had his spies, and these informed him that Montrose and some of his friends had written to the King, earnestly desiring him to come to Scotland to open the Parliament in August, and that the messenger employed by them was one Captain Walter Stewart, a relation of Traquair. (The choice had been unfortunate, for according to Traquair himself, Captain Stewart was "a timid, half-witted body".) Argyll, therefore, sent some of his men into England to waylay the Captain upon his homeward journey; this they accomplished, and found in the lining of his saddle a packet of letters. These, with the messenger, were hurried before Argyll's own little committee of the Committee of Estates; among the letters was one from the King, which contained nothing more than an expression of thanks for Montrose's protestations of loyalty; but there was also "ane curious piece", a paper full of cryptic terms, the authorship and the meaning of which have proved a mystery to this day, though the general opinion is that Captain Stewart had written it himself.

News that Montrose's messenger had been waylaid reached the King, together with rumours that impinged upon his honour. On June 12th he wrote to Argyll; he had been informed, he wrote, that he had been persuaded to come to Scotland in person in August by certain noblemen who, in return for honours and offices, had promised to divide the Covenanters. "Therefore in the first place, I think fit to tell you, that I intend my journey to Scotland for the settling of the affairs of that Kingdom, according to the Articles of the Treaty [of Ripon], and in such a way as may establish the affections of my people fully to me; and I am so far from intending divisions by my journey, that I mean so far to establish peace in the State and religion in the Church, that there may be a happy harmony amongst my subjects there. Secondly, I never made any particular promise for the disposing of any places in that Kingdom. . . . Thus having cleared my intention to you as my particular servant, I expect, that as occasion may serve, you may help to clear those mistakes of me which upon this occasion may arise."[42]

Argyll proceeded to act as though this letter had never been written. He imprisoned Captain Stewart in the Tolbooth, and Montrose and his friends, Lord Napier, Stirling of Keir, and Stewart of Blackhall, in the Castle; and he sent Lord Sinclair to ransack Montrose's houses to see if he could find, among his private papers, anything which could be twisted into evidence against him. But though Sinclair did his job very thoroughly indeed, breaking open coffers, kists, and trunks (at the same time indulging some personal animosity by "slighting" Montrose's houses of Old Montrose, Kincardine, and Mugdock), all he found for his pains were some youthful love-letters.

There remained Captain Stewart himself, a more promising means of accomplishing Argyll's ends. He was hauled again and again before the latter's committee until his depositions were doctored and concocted into the desired shape. Hearing of this, Montrose and his friends sent to the committee a paper of queries which they demanded be put to Captain Stewart, a demand which, of course, was rejected:

" 1. To interrogate him whether or not he was boasted, threatened, and menaced to depone? 2. If there was not much favour, courtesy, and freedom promised him the time of his deponing, affirming neither his life nor fortune should be in hazard? 3. Whether or not, after deponing, being commanded to swear and subscrive the same, he craved twenty-four hours for advisement before oath, and was refused, but only to hear them read? 4. Whether or not Sir Adam Hepburn [of Humbie, Clerk to the Committee of Estates], having read the deposition, the said Walter desired the same should be changed and altered in some points, and that the Clerk refused the same, without the Committee's advice? 5. Whether or not he was commanded by the Committee to subscrive and swear them as they were, without giving way to change them at all? 6. That he be urged to declare where he wrote those several papers, which falsely are called ours; as that paper called 'The Tablet'; and the other wherein are the Chyrogliphics, of 'Elephant' and 'Dromedary', and the like; and whether we knew anything of the writing, or were accessory thereto."[43]

At the end of June, Balmerino was sent to the Castle to desire Montrose to present himself before the Committee of Estates; the prisoner replied firmly that he would come before a parliament to be tried by his peers, but not before any committee. The Provost was ordered, therefore, to go to the Castle with four hundred men and bring Montrose before the Committee; but it proved a waste of time, for the prisoner simply repeated what he had declared to Balmerino, that he would be tried by his peers, as was his right, and was answerable to none other.

Parliament assembled on July 15th, despite a request from the King that the Estates postpone their assembling until he came down in August. All they would concede was that until August 17th, "they would pass no definitive sentence on any matter of weight, unless necessity constrained them, only they would agitiate and prepare matters".[44] The truth of it was, Argyll was determined to get John Stewart of Ladywell condemned by Parliament and put out of the way before the King came to Scotland.

Bribes had been partially effectual where threats had failed. Durie and Balmerino had visited Ladywell in prison, and had impressed upon him that "Argyll's power was such, that he could not only preserve his life, but also raise him to preferment,

if, for the clearing of him [Argyll], he should convict himself".
So the wretched man had declared that he had invented Argyll's
treasonable talk: "As for those speeches alleged by me to have
been spoken by Argyll at the Ford of Lyon, I confess that, now
having thought better of them, his speech was general, of all
kings; howsoever, by my aforesaid prejudicate opinion of his
lordship's actions, I applied them to the present, wrested them
to my own meaning, and vented them after that kind."

But such a recantation had been far from satisfying Argyll.
Ladywell would not go so far as to deny that Argyll had spoken
of deposing of kings in general, and it was possible that King
Charles's presence in Scotland might give him the courage to
revert to his former story. Therefore did Argyll obtain from
the newly assembled Parliament a warrant to have him tried
for lease-making; and on July 24th he was condemned to death.
Some of his judges were reluctant to impose a capital sentence,
for it was very rare (according to Baillie it had never been known)
for such to be passed on those convicted of this offence. But
Argyll was all-powerful, and he was still very much of the
opinion that "Dead men do not bite".

Too late did poor Ladywell repent his succumbing to bribes.
He confessed to Guthrie, then minister of Stirling, who was with
him for most of the day preceding his execution, and from eight
in the morning until three in the afternoon of the 28th when he
went to the scaffold, that every word he had told Montrose of
Argyll's treasonable talk was true.[45]

He screamed and swooned when he was brought to the
Maiden, the instrument of death set up by the Mercat Cross.
Little did he or anyone else guess that that knife was to drip
with the blood of so many nobler victims of King Covenant; but
it was an ominous prelude to King Charles's second visit to his
native land.

Chapter Seven

TRAGICALLY lacking was this second visit in the joy and splendour of the first.

Argyll had done his utmost to prevent the King from coming at all,[46] but since this proved impossible, he took every means to ensure that things would go his way. The General Assembly was desired to sit down at Edinburgh instead of at St. Andrews as originally intended, so that by their protestations and petitions they might second the demands of the Estates. "Sundry papers were scattered for holding the members of Parliament right"; and in their determination to show Charles their strength, the Covenanters did not scruple to expose their blatant breaking of the terms of the Treaty of Ripon. "Here is to be noted a wonder to all posterity," wrote Spalding: "a monarch, a king, to come to his own subjects to give them a parliament, having their army and regiments lying in his highway, raised against himself, for their own ends; for Leslie was lying at Newcastle, as ye have heard; Major Munro, with his regiment lying in the Merse, about 1400 men; Cochrane, with his regiment of 1000 men, lying in Lothian; and the Lord Sinclair's regiment of 500 lying in Aberdeen."

All noticed how sad Charles looked as, with a very small train, he rode into Edinburgh. He had never recovered, nor would he to the end of his tragic life, from his permitting Strafford's execution in a desperate attempt to preserve his Queen and his Crown. And here in his own native country, as in England, he was surrounded by enemies. "It would pity any man's heart to see how he looks," a correspondent wrote to Ormonde, "for he is never quiet amongst them, and glad he is when he sees any man that he thinks loves him."[47]

Insults were offered him immediately on his arrival. He came to Holyroodhouse on Saturday, August 14th; and on Sunday morning was harangued in the Abbey Kirk, the scene of his splendid crowning, by that stout Covenanter, Alexander Henderson. Tired no doubt from his long journey, the King did not attend the afternoon sermon, an omission for which he was sharply rebuked. But he was determined to do all in his power to please and win over these troublesome subjects of his; he made no complaint for the lack of that Liturgy, in his own Chapel Royal, to which he was so attached, and daily, morning and evening, he listened with patience to Henderson's extempore prayers.

On the 17th the King opened Parliament (a mere formality, since it had sat down a full month before his arrival), and at once a small incident foreshadowed the tone of the proceedings. It was part of the Prerogative for the Sovereign to choose his own Officers, great and small; Charles had not yet appointed an Usher, when a man named Langton "takes a rod and puts himself in possession of the place: The King herewith offended, commands to commit him for his presumption". The Estates were offended in their turn, and calmly enacted that henceforth neither the King nor his successors should commit any official without the Estates' advice.[48]

Charles made a gracious speech, and was thanked by Burleigh, the President. Argyll then rose, and made "a short and pithy harangue, comparing this kingdom to a ship tossed in a tempestuous sea, these years bypast; and seeing his Majesty had, like a skilful pilot, in the times of most danger, steered her through so many rocks and shelves, to safe anchor, he did humbly entreat his Majesty that now he would not leave her (since that for her safety he had given way to cast out some of the naughtiest baggage to lighten her), but be graciously pleased to settle her in her secure station and harbour again".[49]

A few days later, however, Argyll laid aside this high-flown language. The moment had arrived for Charles to exercise the ancient royal right to nominate those he desired to have as members of his Privy Council and as the Officers of Estate. Argyll and his friends objected; "the election of these by the King alone," they declared, "had been the fountain of our evils and was like to be a constant root of corruption, both in Kirk and State, if not seen to". Charles naturally combated this attempt to usurp so essential a part of the Prerogative, and nominated as Chancellor the Earl of Morton. There ensued what Baillie called "a very foul flyting" between Morton and his son-in-law, Argyll.

In his objections to the nomination, Argyll did not mince his words. The office, he affirmed, would shelter Morton from his creditors, and moreover "he is a contemptuous rebel, and often at the horn", "he deserted his country in her greatest need", and he was "decrepid and unable". Good old Morton replied with great moderation; he had never, he said, wronged Argyll, much less his country; as for his debts, he and his friends would see to it that no man suffered by a farthing. He then reminded Argyll that, as the latter's principal guardian in youth, he had been in effect a parent to him for twenty years, and that it was he who had persuaded the King to set aside the harsh law whereby the family of a man turned Papist shared in his material ruin.

He would make no comment, haughtily replied Argyll, on his father-in-law's good offices to him, but had it not been for his own good offices to Morton, the latter "had not been sitting in that place". One of the real objections against Morton (apart from his being a non-Covenanter) was that he had dared to criticize Balmerino, who, Burleigh being old and infirm, had just been elected President of the Estates. In the end Morton humbly entreated the King to nominate someone else for Chancellor, "since he did perceive that his Majesty's naming of him bred such a stir in the House".[50]

Charles thereupon nominated Loudoun, against whom, since he was one of their leading men, the Covenanters could have no objection. But they were determined to show their independence, and made endless delays in consenting to vote upon the nomination, the King continually urging them to do so, adding "that for anything he could perceive, new questions and difficulties did emerge daily, and like mushrooms grew up in one night, to stop the business now in hand". The Estates replied with a deliberate insult; men hesitated to vote freely on the choosing of the Officers, they said, for fear of his Majesty's wrath. With one of his rare flashes of anger, Charles retorted that far from being displeased with any man for voting freely, anyone who did not do so was unfit to sit in the House.

On August 21st, Montrose's petition for a trial was read, but since he refused to sign a submission offered him, "his cause was cast by till the Parliament had dispatched their more weighty affairs". On the 27th, Charles reviewed the Covenant army on the Links of Leith as a prelude to its disbandment; but on the excuse that the King's garrisons in Berwick and Carlisle were not yet removed, Munro's, Sinclair's, and Cochrane's regiments were kept intact.

It was not until October 2nd that at long last the Estates consented to vote on the nomination of Loudoun for the Chancellorship, and after all their delays and objections to voting, it was carried unanimously. Being a Campbell, Loudoun had not failed to point out that the salary pertaining to the office was small, and accordingly he was voted an extra one thousand pounds sterling a year. "Preferment," he said, in a pretty little speech of thanks for the office, "comes neither from the east nor the west, but from God alone; and I acknowledge I have this from your Sacred Majesty, as from God's Viceregent on earth, the fountain of all earthly honour here."

There followed new "stirs" over the offices of Treasurer and Clerk-Register. For the first Charles nominated Lord Almond who, as second-in-command to Leslie in the recent invasion, should surely have been acceptable. But not, it seemed, to Argyll. He had always been a dear friend of Almond's, said Argyll, but the public weal must come before personal friendship. (In other words, Almond had been one of the signatories of the Cumbernauld Band.) The Estates, who had been quite ready to concur in the nomination, at once put upon it that power of veto which they had just wrested from the King, and for the granting of which they had all risen to their feet "and bowed themselves to the ground".[51] Under all these insults and irritations, Charles retained an extraordinary patience. "His Majesty takes infinite pains," Sir Harry Vane, the English Secretary of State who had accompanied the King to Scotland, wrote to Nicholas in London, "is in business from morning until night, and will certainly part fair with these people."[52]

The Estates were still wrangling over the nominations when, in the second week of October, they were interrupted by the sensational and extremely obscure affair which became known as "The Incident".

On Monday, October 11th, the King, in obvious distress, laid before Parliament what he described as "a very strange story". On the previous evening, Hamilton had come to him when he was walking in the gardens of Holyroodhouse, and "in a philosophical and parabolical way, as he sometimes had used", had babbled that his life was in danger, that his enemies had calumniated him to his Majesty, and that he begged leave to retire from Court. That very night he, with his younger brother William, who had been created Earl of Lanerick and Secretary of State for Scotland on the death of Lord Stirling in the previous year, and Argyll, had fled to Hamilton's feudal keep of Kinneil, twelve miles from Edinburgh.

The reason for Hamilton's flight, declared Charles, must be either fear, "which he thought could not be inherent in many Scots, much less in him", or else distrust of his royal master. It was this latter possibility which caused the King so much distress, and with good reason. For not only had Charles regarded the man as one of his closest personal friends, but some years previously, when the Marquis had been accused of a plot against his life, he had shown the measure of his own trust by ordering Hamilton to sleep in the royal Bedchamber. As for Lanerick, he was, said Charles, a very good young man and he knew nothing against him, and for Argyll, "he wondered what should move him to go away; he knew not what to say of him".

The news of the flight of the three noblemen was received with horror, and a most ridiculous panic ensued. Edinburgh citizens set a guard about their dwellings; representatives of the English House of Commons, who had been attending the Scottish Parliament for the purpose of "keeping a good correspondence", sent expresses home to have the Trained Bands called out to protect London and Westminster from mythical and anonymous plotters. Sir Thomas Hope, Lord Advocate, begged Charles to remove from about his person "all common incendiaries of the kingdom"; and ministers roundly declared from their pulpits that there had been a plot to assassinate the three noblemen, described by them as "chief patriots and pillars of the Kirk of God".

The details of the conspiracy were variously given, but the favourite version was that Hamilton, Argyll, and Lanerick were to have been roused from their beds at dead of night, brought to the King's Bedchamber, arrested as traitors, delivered to the Earl of Crawford who, with armed men, was to be waiting at the foot of the back-stair, hustled into a coach, carried to the shore, and put on board one of the King's ships which, said rumour, had been riding in Leith Roads for weeks for this very purpose. Thence they were to have been carried to London to answer a charge of high treason, and if they resisted, Crawford had orders to stab them. The three "chief patriots" being thus removed, the sinister programme was to have been completed by the violent dissolution of the Estates by an armed force composed of Highland barbarians, Border ruffians, and Irish cutthroats; Colonel Cochrane, seduced from his allegiance to the Covenant, had sworn to bring his regiment to overawe Edinburgh; and the Castle was to be delivered to Montrose.

In the midst of the panic and the uproar, Charles demanded one thing and one thing only: a public examination of all who had spread these fantastic tales. The Estates immediately and emphatically refused; the examination, they said, must be made by one of their committees, at which, of course, the King would not be present. The wrangle continued for days, the Estates adding fuel to the fire by bringing in a report that the Earl of Carnwath had said to one, William Dick, "that now we had three kings in Scotland, and by God two of them behoved to want the head ". William Dick was called, and declared that indeed Carnwath had spoken these words to him, "with great execrations of Hamilton and Argyll".

On October 21st, despairing of persuading Parliament to consent to a public examination, and feeling keenly that his honour was at stake, Charles consented that a committee of four nobles, four barons, and four burgesses should sit in secret that afternoon. On the 28th they made their report—if it deserves that name: the three lords had had good reason for their flight, since their going away was only "to avoid tumults". The Estates ordered an official letter to be written, begging the fugitives to return, since his Majesty's business suffered by their absence.[53]

The most probable explanation is that The Incident was a ruse of Argyll's, the object of which was twofold. During the time the King had been in Scotland, Montrose had written three letters to Charles; in the first two he had begged for an audience with his Majesty; in the third he had put his cards on the table and offered to prove that both Hamilton and Argyll were traitors. Undoubtedly these letters were copied by the traitors in the Bedchamber, and the last of them put Argyll into an awkward predicament; for it was possible that the King would consent to see Montrose in private and give credit to what he said. Accordingly, though Montrose could not be accused of being in the plot to slay the three noblemen, since he was closely confined in the Castle, it was inserted into the story that that stronghold was to have been delivered to him when the dastardly deed was done, thus implicating him in the conspiracy.

The Incident accomplished another object which was of equal importance to Argyll. There were a few, a very few, Scots nobles who remained actively loyal to the King; among these were the Earls of Carnwath and Crawford. Robert Dalyell, second Earl of Carnwath, had taken the King's side from the beginning of the troubles, and therefore was styled by Baillie "a monster of profanity". Ludovic Lindsay, sixteenth Earl of Crawford, was also a staunch Royalist, and was to fight gallantly for the King during the Civil War. These two, therefore, together with Colonel Cochrane, whose allegiance to the Covenant was considered doubtful, had the leading parts assigned them in the ridiculous plot; while the lesser men who had refused to bow the knee to "King Campbell" were to be dismissed from the King's service under the conveniently vague epithet of "common incendiaries and stirrers-up of tumults".

Early in November, Argyll and Hamilton returned to their

seats in Parliament, and were received as heroes who had narrowly escaped martyrdom. Baillie, an ardent admirer of Argyll, admits that the latter's "late danger" had enormously increased his power. A few days previously, the King had communicated to the Estates the news that rebellion had broken out in Ireland, which necessitated his return to London as soon as possible, and he begged them to hasten the rest of their business. The Estates were not unduly perturbed, since only two pieces of business remained: the filching of the temporalities of the dispossessed Bishops, and a jostling for the remaining offices. Argyll did very well for himself out of the former; he got the temporalities of Argyll and the Isles, in addition to the benefices of eight parish kirks formerly belonging to the Priory of Ardchattan.

For the remaining offices, Wariston passionately wanted the Clerk-Registership, but despite his well-known zeal for the Covenant it was given to Sir Alexander Gibson of Durie, who had bribed Will Murray of the Bedchamber, one of Argyll's secret agents, with "a velvet cassock, lined with fine furrings, and a thousand double pieces therein".[54] Many wondered, wrote Baillie, at this snub administered by Argyll to his old crony Wariston, who had to be content with knighthood and a place on the Session, which gave him the forensic title of Lord Wariston.

The most lucrative of all the offices, that of Treasurer, Argyll had earmarked for himself, but here, and here only, Charles remained firm. He insisted that the Treasury be put into commission, after the English fashion, and Argyll found himself obliged to share it with the Chancellor, the very young Earl of Glencairn who was Hamilton's friend, Hamilton's brother-in-law, Lord Lindsay of the Byres, and the Treasurer-Depute. For Huntly and seven other lords nominated by the King as members of his own Council, zealous Covenanters were substituted; and the lists of all officials, great and small, given in by Charles were subjected to the most jealous scrutiny, and the names of those not deemed forward enough in the Good Cause remorselessly struck out.[55]

A commission was then appointed to attend the English Parliament, "not so much for the perfecting of our Treaty," admitted Baillie, "as to keep correspondence in so needful a time"; the Earl of Crawford and others connected with The Incident, having served their turn, were released from their imprisonment; and all that remained was the bestowing of honours. Alexander Leslie was created Earl of Leven, and an order was given for the payment to him of one hundred thousand merks out of the Brotherly Assistance, when it could be wrested from English pockets. The "little old crooked soldier" was so delighted that he swore that "when his Majesty would require his service, he should have it, without ever asking what was the cause".

A patent creating him Marquis of Argyll was then delivered to "King Campbell" by King Charles. The squint-eyed gentleman received it on his knees, rendering his Majesty humble and hearty thanks for so great a grace and favour which, he said solemnly, was far beyond his own merit and expectation. According to a contemporary, Argyll had a particular desire for this honour, because of an "old cuss" which had prophesied that the red-haired, squint-eyed Earl of Argyll would be the last to bear that title.[56] Apparently the dictator was indifferent to the second part of the "cuss"—that whenever MacCalein Mhor should take up arms against his lawful Sovereign, the family would be extinguished.

The honours Charles bestowed on what was to prove his last visit to his native land, were, observed Clarendon caustically, "in proportion to the capacity and ability they had for doing him a mischief"; the sole result of the visit, added the historian, was the making of "a perfect deed of gift of that kingdom" to the King's most bitter enemies. Indeed Charles had conceded to the limit, and beyond; and when, on November 18th, he rode south to a troubled England, he may have taken at their face value the farewell words of the Estates, that he was parting "a contented prince from a contented people".[57]

But he left behind him another monarch, "King Campbell", who now was supreme indeed. Rothes, the father of the Covenant, had died in London nearly three months previously, England having proved so congenial to him that he had turned courtier and negotiated for the hand of an English heiress. Wariston, a useful tool, had just been put in his place by the dictator, Balmerino and the others were to be kept firmly in theirs, and Loudoun, a Campbell connection, was Chancellor. Hamilton, who seems to have been genuinely scared by the faked plot called The Incident, was now so friendly with Argyll that he was soon to suggest a marriage between his eldest daughter and Argyll's heir, Lord Lorn, when they should come of age.

As for Montrose, he and his friends were released on probation, having lain seven months in jail without trial. For lack of this they would be unable to clear their names from the vague accusations made against them, and Argyll took care to make it clear to them that they owed their escape from execution solely to his clemency. That Montrose had learned his lesson seemed evident from the fact that after his release he went to live in semi-retirement with his wife and sons at Kincardine.

But like many a tyrant before and since, King Covenant and King Campbell were not content with the supreme power at home; they must extend it over their neighbours. And in this lay the seed not only of their own ruin but of Scotland's likewise.

Chapter Eight

ON August 22nd, 1642, the Royal Standard was raised at Nottingham, and the long "cold war" between King Charles and his English opponents gave place to the thunder of cannon and the clash of steel.

The General Assembly had sat down at St. Andrews in July, and to them as well as to his Scottish Council, the King had sent an account of the intolerable demands made by the House of Commons, "that finding how much We are injured by them in Our just and legal Prerogative, Our Council might, in name of Our Kingdom, declare their sense of these wrongs to the Parliament, by what Commissioners they please". But the Assembly had received other letters which they deemed more important.

To that from the English Parliament, which had desired them to remember their Covenant (rather strangely, since it had nothing to do with England), they penned "a pleasant answer". To the appeal from twenty-five London ministers for the blessings of Presbyterianism, and to another from the Estates' Commissioners in London desiring the same, the Assembly sent a paper containing the tenets and discipline of the Kirk, drawn up by Alexander Henderson. Lastly they deigned to reply to their King, soliciting him to make the Church of England conform to the Scottish Kirk.[58]

They who had been so indignant at having the Service Book imposed upon them, they who had declared *ad nauseum* that they had not the least intention or desire to interfere with other Reformed Churches, were now resolved to impose upon England an alien creed. They knew as well as anyone else that the vast majority of Englishmen were either averse or indifferent to Presbyterianism, but proselyting zeal was strong upon them, and the respectful tone in which the English rebels addressed them had gone to their heads.

The leading-light of this Assembly, as elsewhere in Scotland now, was the Marquis of Argyll. He sat there as a lay-elder from the Presbytery of Inveraray, as an assessor to the King's Commissioner, the Earl of Dunfermline (whose wife, a Douglas, was Argyll's kinswoman), and as a Commissioner of the Estates. "I admired," wrote Baillie, "the industry of Argyll. All the diets of our Synod he kept, and did give most and best advice in every purpose . . . our privy committee, both before and after the Assembly, he never missed; the committee for visiting the Universities he punctually attended, and yet never complained of weariness." Southesk, Montrose's father-in-law, "sat at his footstool, and oft whispered his not very savoury advice".

But Argyll had no need of advice, "savoury" or otherwise, for his dictatorship was open now, and both friends and foes must do his bidding. To the appeal of the King who had just created him a marquis, to live up to "your large expressions at my last being in Scotland", Argyll replied with advice to his Majesty to come to terms with his English rebels—which would be their terms, as he very well knew. In sending commissioners both to the King and Parliament, Argyll appointed those he chose, whether they were willing or not. "Sundry would fain have been employed, and lest they should have gotten themselves named, Argyll in his cunning way got them on the committee of nominators." Of the five ministers appointed, both Henderson and Baillie begged in vain to be excused, and of the three ruling elders "Cassilis was much averse and made great opposition. Every man said something, but no man was gotten excused".[59]

As soon as open hostilities had broken out between the King and the Parliament, it was clear that Scottish aid to one side or the other might well prove decisive and could command a high price. During the early stages of the war, however, Argyll deemed it safer to watch the progress of the struggle from a ringside seat, while taking care to keep down Scottish loyalists, and to cultivate the friendship of Hamilton, whose standing and man-power would have made him formidable had he shown any active loyalty. "The Marquises of Hamilton and Argyll's intimate friendship," observed Baillie with satisfaction, "kept down

the malcontents from any stirring." It was true that Hamilton
could never resist having a foot in both camps, but his present
idea of serving his King was so fantastic that Argyll could well
afford to treat it with contempt. It was a proposal that the
Queen should come to Scotland to negotiate a settlement between
the King and his English rebels; and it is interesting to speculate
whether the Catholic Henrietta would have been required to
sign the Covenant.

But by the late spring of the following year, 1643, the tide of
war was flowing so strongly in the King's favour that Argyll
became alarmed. He had gone too far in treason to withdraw;
he had ignored the appeal from the master who had loaded him
with honours; and in a debate in the previous December it had
been he who had got a decision against publishing a royal
Proclamation. On being informed by Lanerick, who had
brought it, that its publication was demanded by the King,
Argyll had replied that " they sat there to good purpose if every
message to them was a command ".[60] If King Charles's cause
triumphed, therefore, King Campbell's reign, perhaps even his
head, was doomed.

On May 11th, on the excuse that the Royalist Northern Army
was a menace to Scotland's security, Argyll, solely on his own
authority, summoned a parliament. Even so stout a Covenanter
as Sir Thomas Hope was a trifle shocked by this; but that cunning old lawyer, while admitting that by the laws of the land
no parliament could be convened without the King's authority,
soon suggested a way out of the difficulty. A Convention
could be called, he said, "and gave them a precedent thereof, which happened in the time of King James V. Those
that had insight into Scots history, knew well enough that
this instance was no way applicable to the case now under
debate."[61]

Two solemn fasts, and many protestations that they were the
King's "faithful and humble subjects and servants", preceded
the opening of this Convention, in which Argyll made sure that
no one who sympathized with the King should sit. From the
first, admirable amity prevailed between it and the Commission
of the General Assembly, papers passing backwards and forwards between the two bodies, and ministers kindly advising on
the manifold dangers of the kingdom, though "in this we carefully abstain from the mentioning of arms, that the envy of
this conclusion should not justly be put on us ".[62]

The first care of the Convention was to intimidate certain
important personages who otherwise might have proved trouble-

H

some. For saying that "Scotland was not content with their own
rebellion to have troubled the King, but also would yet again
join with the rebels in England, for to ruin the King and his
children", Lord Carnwath was fined ten thousand pounds Scots.
Traquair, "thought to be a great stickler in our State affairs",
was summoned to appear before the Convention, but wisely kept
out of the way. Morton, Lanerick, the second Earl of Kinnoul,
and others, who, on their way home from visiting the King at
Oxford, had written to the Queen who was at York to beg for
three or four thousand men to be sent to the aid of loyal Lord
Derby, were forced to sign a written apology. Hamilton, who
in April had been created a duke, dared to vote that the constitution of the Convention was limited and not absolute; as a
result he was so threatened that he did not venture to appear
in the Parliament House again, and a few months later went
to England.

Meanwhile the Convention, which had been shocked beyond
measure by the "intermeddling with England" by Morton and
his friends, were impatiently awaiting the arrival of commissioners from the English Parliament. They had to wait some
time, and that for a regrettably sordid reason; the English rebels
were hoping against hope that the vast expense of Scots aid in
the war might be avoided. Argyll beguiled the time with what
might appear to have been a curious occupation; he attempted
to win over the man he so recently had endeavoured to ruin,
the Earl of Montrose.

But Argyll was fixed in his belief that every man had his price;
and according to this theory, no time could be more auspicious
than the present for buying the services of one who had proved
himself the most popular and brilliant young soldier the Covenant possessed. For earlier in the year, Montrose, whose retirement had given him the opportunity for some serious thinking,
had gone to see the Queen, newly returned from a visit to Holland where she had been pawning her jewels to buy arms for
her husband's soldiers, and had endeavoured to impress upon
her the danger that Scotland, dominated by Argyll, might come
to rebel England's aid. Hearing of this, Argyll had sent that
mercurial creature, Hamilton, to counteract Montrose's influence; and since Montrose was known to the Queen only as a
prominent Covenanter (and, in justice it must be said, to Hamilton also in the same light), this had not been difficult to perform.
Montrose, politely snubbed by her Majesty, had returned home,
and Argyll hoped to catch him on the rebound.

He desired a conference with him by proxy; and on a day in

June, Alexander Henderson and Sir James Rollo, the latter being the brother-in-law of both Argyll and Montrose, met the latter, accompanied by Lords Ogilvy and Napier, on the banks of the Forth. Tempting offers, including the Lieutenant-Generalship of the Army, and "whatever else he could desire and they bestow", were made by Henderson and Rollo. If, as Wishart affirms, Montrose had consented to the interview for the purpose of discovering Argyll's real intentions, he was not disappointed. Henderson told him that the Covenanters and the English rebels "had unanimously resolved either to die or to bring the King to their terms".[63] Montrose made no direct answer, excusing himself on the grounds that neither Henderson nor Rollo could produce authority from the Convention for the large offers they had made him.

Late in July a Mr. Cobbett arrived from England, and on August 7th one member of the House of Lords, two of the Commons, and some ministers, landed at Leith. They attributed their delay in coming to the fact that they had been busy "discovering plots", and they brought a woeful tale of the Parliament's defeat everywhere in the field, culminating in the recent storming of Bristol by Prince Rupert. "They would never," remarked Baillie, "in earnest call for our help, till they were irrecoverable; now when all is desperate, they cry aloud for our help; and how willing we are to redeem them with our lives, you shall hear."

The Assembly had made careful preparations for the reception of the Commissioners, appointing the inevitable committee to confer with them, arranging "a place commodious above us in a loft" for their attendance as private spectators, and composing a speech of welcome. "Some did run so far back as to remember how Queen Elizabeth helped the Lords of the Congregation in the Scottish Reformation in opposition to the Queen Regent; and therefore it was but justice that they should now repay them with the like assistance." Perhaps they remembered also Elizabeth's generosity to those who had rebelled against Mary Stuart and her mother.

The Commissioners presented to the Assembly "a long-tailed supplication". They begged to be allowed to ease their overburdened hearts in reverend Scottish bosoms. "Surely," they cried, "if ever a poor nation were upon the edge of a most desperate precipice, if ever a poor kirk were ready to be swallowed up by Satan and his instruments, we are that nation, we are that kirk. . . . Our God, who in his former judgments was a moth and rottenness (and yet had of late begun to send us health and cure) is now turned a lion to us, and threatens to rend the very calf of our hearts." If their own blood could ransom the rest of the saints from the rage of "the bloody Popish faction", they would shed it gladly, but alas, that rage was insatiable.

Since God seemed angry with English saints, albeit they had lain in the dust before Him, they implored the brotherly prayers and assistance of the Elect of Scotland, who might be more acceptable to an offended Jehovah. Naturally they omitted to mention the fact that those who had sent them had just invited English Catholics to fight for them, promising a suspension of the Penal Laws if they would do so.[64]

All this was leading up to the drafting and signing of "ane band", and this time it would not be a clandestine one. But in regard to the terms of it, there was a significant difference of opinion. The Kirk wanted another religious covenant; so also did Argyll, not only because it was absolutely necessary to humour the Kirk, his principal ally, but because the King's victories everywhere made a civil league highly dangerous. The English Commissioners, on the other hand, while professing to desire nothing so much as the blessings of Presbyterianism for their nation, wanted Scots military aid, without which their defeat was certain, and for which they were prepared to pay through the nose. The Solemn League and Covenant, now drafted, was a compromise between the two; what the Kirk failed to realize was that in one important clause it was deliberately misled.

This was in the first Article, and the very clever way in which it was worded was due to the cunning of one of the English Commissioners, Sir Harry Vane the younger. He knew, as the Scots did not, that a very large proportion of the English rebels disliked Presbyterianism almost as much as they abhorred Episcopacy, and that they were, in fact, "Sectaries" or Independents. These had to be humoured, and a way of humouring them, without on the other hand offending the Kirk, was opened to him by the Kirk's overweening pride. He worded Article I so that both sides swore to endeavour "the reformation of religion in the kingdoms of England and Ireland, in doctrine, worship, discipline, and government, according to the Word of God, and the example of the best Reformed Churches". To the Covenanters there was only one best Reformed Church, and that was their own.

Thursday, August 17th, "was our joyful day of passing the English Covenant," wrote poor Baillie, little knowing how he and his brethren were being tricked. To them it was a charter for imposing their creed upon England, which they appeared to regard as a land of heathen darkness. They acted, remarked Sir Philip Warwick indignantly, "as if they were to convert an unsanctified heathen nation; and Timothy and Titus are upon all occasions proved not to have been bishops as a distinct order from presbyters, and the rites of the Church [of England] of no better appellation than superstitions, and the bowing at the name of Jesus hath a book written against it with no less title than *Jesus Worship Confuted*; so as if a Mahometan had heard it cried in the streets to be sold, as it was (as I heard a gentleman say passing by) surely he might justly have thought this nation at that time was denying their Saviour".[65]

The parties to the Solemn League and Covenant (which hence-forth was to be *the* Covenant, the National one being quite outmoded), besides pledging themselves to endeavour the extirpa-tion of "Popery, Prelacy, superstition, heresy, schism, profane-ness", swore to preserve the rights of Parliament, to defend the King's person and authority in the preservation and defence of the true religion and liberties of the kingdoms, "that the world may bear witness with our consciences of our loyalty, and that we have no thoughts nor intentions to diminish his Majesty's just power and greatness"; to bring to justice "all incendiaries, malignants, and evil instruments"; to keep "a blessed peace" between the two kingdoms; and "to assist and defend each other, and never to suffer ourselves to be divided, whether to make defection to the contrary part, or to give ourselves to a detestable indifference or neutrality in this cause . . . and what we are not able ourselves to suppress or overcome, we shall reveal and make known, that it may be timely prevented or removed".[66]

There was nothing in this Covenant, be it noted, about the sordid question of payment for Scots aid. That was settled privately. One hundred thousand pounds sterling was to be paid in advance for the maintenance of a Scottish army, twelve thou-sand for the levying of it, twelve thousand merks "for the wants and necessities of the Scottish army in Ireland" (Scotland had sent a considerable force into that country, ostensibly to assist in quelling the late rebellion there against the King), and a further hundred thousand merks for the collectors of these taxes. Without this money, Covenant or no Covenant, Argyll would not budge.

On August 18th a Commission of eight was appointed to go to London to witness the signing of the Covenant by the English Parliament, and a proclamation was issued in the King's name, containing the heads of the agreement, and ordering all fencible men between the ages of sixteen and sixty to be in readiness, with full arms and forty days' provisions, to march to the rendezvous the Convention would appoint.

All through the rest of August, and throughout September, nothing was heard in the land but " touking of drums and proclamation from cross to cross". The ministers drew up lists of the fencible men in their parishes, informed the people that they were to fight "the English Papists", threatened the reluctant with Excommunication, and saw to it that all heritors gave in lists of their rentals for making up a war-tax. Leslie, created by the King Earl of Leven but two years previously, accepted the chief command. "It is true," confessed Baillie, " he passed many promises to the King, that he would no more fight in his contrary; but, as he declares, it was with the express and necessary condition that Religion's and Country's rights were not in hazard; as all indifferent men thinks now they are in a very evident one." David Leslie, son of Sir Patrick Leslie of Pitcairly, a soldier who had learnt his trade in Swedish service, came over to take up the post of Major-General; and the army these men were to command would, it was hoped, reach the enormous proportions of thirty-two thousand foot and four thousand horse.

On September 1st the Covenant was signed by the Assembly of Divines in London, a Presbyterian body; on the 2nd by the House of Commons; and on the third by the Lords. In the latter its passing was facilitated by the absence of those lords who had formed a peace party. The cry for peace was rising everywhere in England, and the Covenanters, who had used " the holy sisters" of Edinburgh to such good effect during the Service Book riots, were shocked by the reports of women besieging the doors of Westminster, clamouring for peace on any terms. "This tumult could not be suppressed but by violence, and killing some three or four women, and hurting more of them, and imprisoning many."[67]

The Covenant was brought down to Scotland again in October, and on the 11th an ordinance was passed for a national subscription to it. Printed copies, containing blank sheets for signatures, were sent to every presbytery; it was to be read by the ministers one Sunday, and signed the next " by all his Majesty's subjects of this kingdom, and that, under the pain, to such as shall postpone or refuse, to be esteemed and punished as enemies to religion, his Majesty's honour, and peace of these kingdoms, and to have their goods and rents confiscated, and that they shall not enjoy any benefit, place, nor office within this king-dom".[68] The old mischievous epithet of "Popish" was used to persuade the people to sign; ministers instilled into their flocks that it was not against the King, but only against "the malignant prelates and papists of England", that they were being called upon to fight. Nevertheless, as Baillie admits, a great many signatures were obtained only because the frightful penalties for refusing were read out before the Covenant.

This document, which committed Scotland to a major war, had been rushed through by the Parliaments of both kingdoms, and by the Assembly. "It was thought strange," Burnet commented sarcastically, "to see all their consciences of such a size, so exactly to agree as the several wheels of a clock; which made all apprehend there was some first mover that directed all their motions: this by the one party was imputed to God's extraordinary providence, but by others to the power and policy of the leaders, and the simplicity and fear of the rest."

The power and policy of the leaders, who really amounted to Argyll, were seen at first-hand at this time by a Frenchman, M. de Boisivon. It will be remembered that the Covenanters had tried their utmost to get French aid in their earlier struggles with the King, reminding Louis of the Auld Alliance, and of how it was good policy to help the weaker side. The signing of the Solemn League and Covenant inevitably meant that the King would be the weaker side, and Boisivon was sent to Scotland to prevent, if he could, this alliance between rebels.

He found, however, that a change had come over the Covenanters since the days when they had sought French aid. They spoke insolently of their own King, and with little respect of France, and in their present power-drunk mood, not even the threat of a rupture of the Auld Alliance had any effect. "They feel certain they could, if united," Boisivon wrote to Brienne, French Secretary of State, "conquer all the princes in Christendom—their plans are so vast, and their presumption so great, that there is no hope of obtaining anything of them. . . . The Marquis of Argyll is absolute here: he is in the highest degree intelligent in all that relates to Scotland, but knows nothing of anything beyond his own country."

As for old Leven, he was seeing himself as a second Gustavus Adolphus who, with a smaller army, had overrun all Germany. Boisivon was present when Leven, in a large gathering of nobles, exclaimed to Lord Home: "Consider, my lord, what glory it would be before God and man if we were to drive the Catholics out of England and follow them to France, and, in imitation of the late King of Sweden, rally around us all those of the [Protestant] religion in France, and plant, either with consent or by force, our religion in Paris, and thence to Rome, drive out Antichrist, and burn the town."[69]

The enormous host of the Covenant was now ready to invade. The very herdsmen had been taxed, and the lairds mulcted in the extent of a third of their estates, in order to equip it. Each foot soldier had cost unfortunate Scotland one hundred merks, and each cavalryman, with his horse, nine-score pounds. But before crossing the Rubicon, in this case the Tweed, Argyll, who had the odd title of President of the Army, had an important piece of business to transact. Though Huntly had been put to the horn in the previous August, which meant that anyone who sided with him would partake in his outlawry, the Gordons remained a potential danger, especially when the Covenant's army was over the Border. Argyll, therefore, "dealt" with his nephew, Lord Gordon, Huntly's heir, who had returned to Scotland.

Some three years previously, Argyll had persuaded his nephew to sign the National Covenant in order to protect himself and his clan; he now pointed out to the young man that in this new crisis the only two ways in which he could save his estates was either to "wink" at the Covenanters' doings, or else to side with them. He reminded Lord Gordon that it had always been the custom in times of trouble for Scottish nobles to espouse one side and their sons, with their permission, the other, a convenient arrangement by which, whatever the issue, the family escaped ruin and shared in the rewards.[70] Gordon having agreed at least to "wink" on this occasion, Uncle Argyll went confidently over the frozen Tweed, no doubt agreeing with Baillie that "all things are expected from God and the Scots".

The vast army came marching up to Newcastle on February 3rd, 1644, but seeing that it would require a long siege, Leven decided to push on to Sunderland, which was entered without opposition on March 4th. Argyll had been enjoying himself in the ordinarily uncongenial rôle of military man, capturing a small fort on Coquet Island, and turning it into a Covenant stronghold. But at Sunderland he was very much annoyed to hear that, despite all his precautions for the keeping of Scotland quiet, Huntly was "up" in the north.

Huntly had risen, as it happened, more to protect his own estates from the consequences of his outlawry than for the King's cause, and apart from his own weakness of character which ensured that the rising would be abortive, his clan was hopelessly divided. His heir was with Argyll; his second son, Aboyne, was with the King's armies; with his third, young Lord Lewis, he was on the worst possible terms. For in 1641, when the family were in London, Lord Lewis had made off with a cabinet containing the whole of his father's jewels, and now, in the March of 1644, he came to Edinburgh to see what he could get in the way of favours from Argyll, just arrived there with a commission to raise five thousand soldiers against Lord Lewis's father. Naturally Uncle Argyll welcomed this hopeful lad, and enlisted him on the side of the Covenant.

By the beginning of April, Huntly had got as far as having banners made, with a red lion rampant and the motto *For God, the King, and against all Traitors*; also a quantity of black taffeta scarves for himself and his officers, "which was a sign to fight to the death, but it proved otherwise". From then until the end of the month he simply marked time, while the Kirk solemnly excommunicated him (contrary to its own discipline, since the General Assembly was not sitting), and Argyll combed the Lowlands for soldiers. On the 26th, King Campbell was at Dunnotar, awaiting the arrival of the Earl of Lothian's men, eight hundred recruits from Perthshire, and the Forbeses, who hitherto had sat upon the fence, a very favourite occupation of that clan. On May 1st Huntly went hastily to Strathbogie, his principal seat, and though over fifteen thousand of his friends and clansmen met him there, he refused to think of fighting, and fled into the wilds of Caithness, leaving his army to take care of itself.

His abortive rising was over; there remained Argyll's vengeance on those who had given him a fright. While unfortunate Aberdeen once more was being occupied by a Covenanting army under Lords Burleigh and Elcho, Argyll marched with four hundred Irish soldiers of Lothian's regiment to the Place of Drum, an ancient house in the neighbourhood belonging to Sir Alexander Irving, whose son had risen under Huntly. Both the old laird and his son were absent, and the house was occupied by Lady Irving and her daughter-in-law, Lady Mary Gordon, Argyll's own niece. Argyll immediately turned them out, not even allowing them to take a change of clothing, and then proceeded to plunder the house and estate. He got a rich haul. Besides livestock, meal, malt, and inside plenishings, he found a trunk containing jewels and silver plate valued at over twenty thousand pounds.[71]

Leaving fifty musketeers and some pieces of ordnance at the Place of Drum, he marched thence to the Place of Kelly, the

home of Gordon of Haddo. With Argyll was his nephew, Lord
Gordon, to whom Haddo offered to surrender if he might live
secure. Argyll intervened with a curt refusal, sent Haddo and
his friends off to prison, and put a garrison in the house. Having graced the Provincial Assemblies at Aberdeen and Elgin
with his presence (where he commanded the ministers to inform
against any of their brethren whom they suspected of being
backward in the Good Cause), Argyll returned to the former
town on May 28th where, with Elcho and Burleigh, he was made
a burgess, and "gat the wine freely". Next day the wretched
Aberdonians were informed that, Dundee having advanced a
thousand pounds towards the expenses of the expedition, it was
expected that Aberdeen would not be outdone in generosity, and
the inhabitants, freeman and serf alike, were taxed to provide
the like sum.

Leaving a party of his Campbells to plunder Covenanters and
anti-Covenanters indiscriminately,[72] Argyll returned to Edinburgh where, on June 4th, the Estates of Parliament (not a
Convention this time) had sat down without the King's authority.
As on a former occasion, Argyll took care to get himself
"exoned" for his conduct in the North, and the Estates, having
done this, gave him "hearty thanks for that he has acquit himself like a good and faithful patriot".[73]

All seemed right with King Campbell's world. A letter arrived
from the English Parliament, declaring that the brotherly aid
of the Scots would never be forgotten by them or their posterity;
and, what was more to the point, another from the Scottish
Commissioners in London with the information that twenty
thousand pounds sterling was being sent to the Covenant's army
at York that week. There was good news, too, from the North;
Irving the younger of Drum, his wife, his brother, and some
friends, who had been attempting to join Huntly in his retreat,
had all been captured. The capture had been effected by Lord
Sinclair, son of the Earl of Caithness and a relation of Lady
Drum's; and the Estates, being "marvellous blythe for getting
such a rich prey", appointed Sinclair twenty-three thousand
merks as a reward, and ordered that all men speak well of him
for capturing his own kinswoman.

Argyll was sitting happily down in one of his beloved committees, which he had appointed to try these and other prisoners
from Huntly's abortive rising, when he received some bad
news.

It was nothing very alarming—a small invasion from Ireland,
led by a personal foe of Argyll, one Alastair MacDonald, who,

with a following of ragged Scoto-Irish, had landed on the west
coast. It was irritating and tiresome; but it could not have
warned Argyll that it was the prelude to disgrace and defeat,
that he would not feel so pleased with himself for a long while
to come, and that a greater than poor Alastair MacDonald was
about to challenge the power of King Campbell.

THE CHALLENGE OF MONTROSE
1644-1645

Chapter One

ALASTAIR MACDONALD was a picturesque ruffian, an Islesman of enormous strength, lion-like in courage, a born fighter. He was commonly called by his father's nickname of Colkitto or Coll, which meant "Coll who can fight with either hand". His entrance on the stage was suitably melodramatic, for it was heralded by a generous display of signs and omens. The sun had appeared "like a large pound of blood"; celestial music of organs had been heard in churches, to the scandal of the godly who had abolished earthly organs; and "a heaven mounted piece of ordnance" had sounded in the ears of every man, woman, and child in Scotland at one and the self-same moment.

He had been sent over from Ireland by his kinsman, the Earl of Antrim, with sixteen hundred recruits, to strike a blow at King Covenant; but Coll had more personal scores to settle. His father and his two brothers had been imprisoned by Argyll many years previously, and Coll himself had been forced to flee to Ireland; landing now in Ardnamurchan, an ancient territory of his kinsfolk, he proceeded to drive out the Campbell settlers and to ravage the country with fire and sword.

This news reached Argyll on July 9th in a letter from the Captain of Dunstaffnage Castle; he sent against the invader two warships which he had borrowed from the English Parliament, and himself remained in Edinburgh until the Estates should rise. On the 12th arrived the tidings of the utter defeat of the King's Northern Army at Marston Moor, but the Covenanters' joy was somewhat damped by the fact that the English rebel army was taking the whole credit for the victory. Cromwell had written roundly to Colonel Valentine Walton: "Our own horse, save for a few Scots in our rear, beat all the Prince's horse"; and much was made of the fact that during the early part of the fight, when Rupert's Cavaliers looked like being victorious, old Leven had been the first to flee. It was the first ominous hint of discord between the Covenanters and their southern allies.

On July 19th two of the prisoners captured after Huntly's abortive rising, Sir John Gordon of Haddo and John Logie, were executed in Edinburgh. Logie was a kinsman of the Earl Marischal, and the fruitlessness of the Earl's attempts to persuade Argyll to save the victim's life made Marischal somewhat cold in the Good Cause. Both men died very bravely, despite the unnerving and horrible innovation of the degrading of the Arms of Haddo upon the very scaffold. On the 29th, Chancellor Loudoun closed this session of Parliament with a speech in which he entreated the Estates to stand fast for the honour of their King, two of whose loyal subjects they had just executed.

"He wished everyone to fetch water to extinguish the fury of this flame, and not oil to nourish it; and lastly besought the great Creator of heaven and earth, who according to the good pleasure of his will did govern the actions of men, to preserve from danger the King's person, to establish peace and truth in all his dominions, and to remove the crying sins of the land, which was the cause of so heavy an indignation upon it."[1]

Argyll was now free to lead an army against the trifling forces of Colkitto, who, a most indifferent general, had been getting himself into serious difficulties. The ships which had brought him over had been burnt by the two English men-of-war borrowed by Argyll; Coll's name was not sufficient to raise the clans to his aid; the Gordons had made their peace with the Covenant, and indeed were now being recruited for it by Lord Gordon, who had been given the title of Lieutenant-General of the North.

Cut off by sea, his appeals for help from the clans falling on deaf ears, and menaced by the armies Argyll was gathering against him, Coll seemed in a fair way to be exterminated. As a last and desperate resort he sent a messenger to find the one man he thought might be able to help him, James Grahame, recently created Marquis of Montrose.

II

In order to understand how Colkitto, who had invaded Scotland in the King's name, came to appeal to a man who had been one of the King's most prominent opponents, it is necessary to glance at Montrose's career since that interview with Henderson and Rollo on the banks of the Forth in June, 1643.

He was young, active, and devoted to the profession of arms, and it was impossible for such a man, who was also genuinely patriotic, to be content for long with retirement from public affairs, especially in so major a crisis. His old whole-hearted allegiance to the Covenant had gone; his distrust and hatred of Argyll had intensified with the latter's open dictatorship. In the autumn of 1643, therefore, he had taken the only way left open to him; in company with Lords Ogilvy, Kinnoul, Niths-dale, Crawford, and Aboyne, he had gone to the royal head-quarters at Oxford, and there he remained for six months.

It was the turning-point in his career. At the end of that time, he who had partaken in so many acts of defiance, and of downright treason, against his King, was not only a convinced Royalist, but Charles's most devoted follower. It was more than admiration and loyalty; it was a deep personal love of Charles Stuart; and it was to colour and to sweeten the tragic lives of them both.

For Charles on his side, surrounded by squabbling courtiers and secret traitors, responded warmly to the devotion of this vigorous young Scotsman, and presently gave him the place in his heart which Hamilton had at last vacated. Charles was no fool, and for a long while he had suspected (with how much pain!) that this childood friend was a broken reed if not a traitor. The King's continuing to employ Hamilton had had its cause in the haunting memory of how he had failed Strafford. "The failing of one friend," he had written to Hamilton in December 1642, when that personage was reported as being inti-mate with Argyll, "hath indeed gone very near me; whereof I am resolved that no consideration whatsoever shall ever make me do the like."[2]

But when Hamilton and his brother Lanerick had arrived in Oxford a year later, Montrose, who himself had been so deep in the counsels of the Covenanters, had been able to convince Charles of the Duke's double-dealing, in which Lanerick had concurred; and both brothers were arrested. Since a trial by their peers was impossible in the present situation, Hamilton was sent prisoner to Pendennis Castle, while Lanerick was warded in his lodging. The younger brother contrived to escape, went to London, and thence to Scotland, where he appeared openly on the side of the Covenanters.

Meanwhile the military situation had been entirely changed

by the Scots' invasion in January 1644. It was not so much the impossibility of defeating even so vast a host in pitched battle; that, indeed, might well have been accomplished, as Montrose was to prove on a smaller scale, since the majority of the rank and file were pressed men who had drawn the sword only because a refusal to do so would have meant outlawry. It was the menace of the presence of the Scots up there in the North of England which crippled the King, and which was, in fact, to defeat him. For by it, Charles's excellent strategy was thrown out of gear. His aim from the beginning of the war had been to draw his Northern and his Western Armies gradually together like pincers, until they met in the neighbourhood of London; by isolating London, the treasure-house of the kingdom, the seat of the rebel government, and by cutting off her supplies, the King might well have won the war.

This strategy was made impossible by the invasion of the Scots. All Leven had to do was to sit up there in the North, paralysing the forces of Lord Newcastle, until such time as English rebel forces approached to engage that earl in battle, as eventually they were to do at Marston Moor. There was only one way in which to remove this menace: to create a diversion in Scotland which would force Leven to withdraw from England with his army to defend King Covenant at home.

It was precisely this that Montrose proposed to do, and though it seemed a hopeless venture, since the King could spare him but a very few troops, he now displayed that spirit which was to make his name immortal. "I will not," he said, "distrust God's assistance in a righteous cause, and if it shall please your Majesty to lay your commands upon me for this purpose, your affairs will at any rate be in no worse case than they are at present, even if I should not succeed."

All he asked was a commission as Lieutenant-General of Scotland (wisely refusing that of Viceroy lest it create new jealousies), a small body of horse from Newcastle's army to enable him to cut his way through to the Lowlands; and, if possible, a few troops from Ireland to land in the west of Scotland and keep Argyll busy defending his own territories. Thus, in March 1644, the newly created Marquis of Montrose set out from Oxford, a slim young man with searching yet candid grey eyes, an air of resolution and hope, and a heart on fire with that love for his master and friend which was to be henceforth the main-spring of his life.

The difficulties before him were obvious; he was to overcome

The Marquis of Montrose

The Marquis of Argyll

all but one, his own past. This was the crucial fact, and it is seldom given its true weight in Montrose's story. It was the fact which made what might have been a decisive campaign against King Covenant a mere interlude in that tyrant's reign.

For Montrose had not been a Covenanter for the sake of expediency, nor only because he believed in the religious side of that cause. He had not stopped short when, in the early troubles, it had become plain that his colleagues, under cover of religion, were out to change the whole Constitution and to rebel against the King. He had been a whole-hearted, hot-blooded, utterly convinced Covenanter, making himself conspicuous during the reading of Protestations, punishing loyal Aberdeen, breaking up the organs and turning out the chaplains at the Chapel Royal in Edinburgh, signing the treasonable letter to the French King, the Blind Band, and that awkward note on the back of the commission which had caused such a furore in the General Assembly of November 1638. Last but by no means least, he had been the first to cross the swollen Tweed in the Covenant's invasion of 1641.

To the great majority of the Royalists, therefore, no less than to the Covenanters, Montrose was a renegade and a turncoat; and to the former at least there seemed no reason why he should not turn his coat again. It was this, and not just jealousy, which prevented other Scottish nobles (with the exception of old Airlie and his Ogilvies) from joining with him after his first brilliant victories.

Worst of all was the mortal offence he had given, in his Covenanting days, to the one personage in Scotland from whom he could get cavalry, the Cock o' the North. To Huntly, Montrose was, and remained, the man who had betrayed him in the April of 1639. That such betrayal had been unintentional, that Montrose had been overruled by his travelling committee, meant nothing to this proud Highland Chief. A man, a fellow noble, a Scotsman, had betrayed him; and George, Marquis of Huntly, lacked that greatness of character which counts a personal betrayal less than a common cause.

III

Montrose's first appearance as a Royalist commander was not promising. In April 1644, he attempted to rally the Lowlands for the King, but immediately it became apparent that, either because of jealousy or genuine mistrust, Royalists such as Niths-

dale, Traquair, Hartfell, and Morton, would have none of him.
Of the Irish levies which the Earl of Antrim had promised to
send over there was no sign; and presently all Montrose could
do was to march southwards again in response to a summons
from Prince Rupert, who was marching rapidly through Lanca-
shire to relieve beleaguered York.

Montrose was not in time to share in Rupert's defeat at Marston Moor, but with that defeat the whole of the North of
England was lost to the King, and there seemed nothing for
the young man to do except return to Oxford and surrender his
new commission. But the spirit of the hero, the lone champion,
was strong within him, and he resolved, as he expressed it in
his verse, to put his fate to the touch, "and win or lose it all".
Disguised as a servant, and with but two companions, he turned
northwards again, his purpose being to break through the Covenant's cordons, win to his own country of Angus, and raise his
kinsfolk there. The journey of nearly a hundred miles was
made in four days; and on an evening in August Montrose was
knocking at the door of a kinsman, Patrick Grahame of Inchbrakie, of Tullibelton between Perth and Dunkeld. His disguise
had not been penetrated; neither friend nor foe knew that
Montrose was back in Scotland. It was by the luckiest chance
that Colkitto's messenger, with his frantic appeal for help, called
at Tullibelton to ask directions to Carlisle, where Coll supposed
Montrose to be.

A few days later occurred that scene which has been depicted
so often: the ragged levies of Colkitto hemmed in among the
braes of Atholl, threatened not only by the forces of the Covenant which were hot-foot on his trail, but by the Atholl-men who,
while they detested the Covenant, were determined that no
"Irishes" were going to live upon their lands. And then the
situation saved by a hair's-breadth, the sudden appearance of a
slim young man in Highland dress, walking briskly across the
moor with one companion, the shouts of greeting from the
Atholl-men, the astonished delight of Colkitto, the production
by Montrose of his commission to command King Charles's as
yet non-existent Scottish army, and the unfurling next day of
the Royal Standard on a knoll above the Tilt, so near the spot
where, forty-five years later, another Grahame was to conquer
and die in the Battle of Killiecrankie.

One of Montrose's first acts, the overture to his campaign, was
to write to his former colleague, the Marquis of Argyll. He
besought the dictator to return to his allegiance, "and submit
yourself, and what belongs to you, as to the grace and protec-

tion of your good King, who, as he hath hitherto condescended unto all things asked, though to the exceeding great prejudice of his prerogative, so still you may find him like an indulgent father, ready to embrace his penitent children in his arms, although he hath been provoked with unspeakable injuries. But if you shall still continue obstinate, I call God to witness that, through your own stubbornness, I shall be compelled to endeavour to reduce you by force. So I rest, your friend, if you please, Montrose."[3]

To such an appeal Argyll was deaf; at such a threat he could afford to laugh. Benorth the Grampians was one Covenanting army; Elcho was at Perth with another recruited from Fife and the Perthshire Lowlands; Burleigh with a large host was at Aberdeen. All these had been raised to exterminate Colkitto and his Scoto-Irish; and behind Colkitto, at a respectful distance, Argyll was pursuing with his formidable clan. "Argyll, after he had learnt the way whither the miscreants had run, followed as armed men might; which was, four or five days' journey behind them," wrote Baillie, not intending sarcasm.

Montrose knew nothing of such cautious methods. He had gathered a few recruits, and it was his business to fight at once before the armies of the Covenant converged. He chose the one nearest to him, and at the end of August marched boldly on Perth.

Gladly did Elcho accept the challenge. He had between six and eight thousand foot, seven hundred horse, and nine pieces of artillery; also the solemn promise of the Kirk that his should be the glory of wiping out this insignificant but impudent threat to King Covenant's reign. "If ever God spake truth out of my mouth," the Rev. Frederick Carmichael proclaimed from his pulpit on Sunday, September 1st, "I promise you, in His name, assured victory this day." So the Covenant's army marched confidently out of Perth, accompanied by a large number of townsfolk as spectators, to eat up the little army of Montrose—three thousand foot at most, no cavalry, and so little ammunition that many of the soldiers had only sticks and stones. Elcho encountered this pitiful force at Tippermuir; and half an hour later he and his men were fleeing for their lives to the safety of Perth, which, as soon as Montrose came hammering on the gates, surrendered without a parley.

Up in London the Assembly of Divines, composed of English and Scottish ministers, were enjoying themselves in day-long debates upon minute points of doctrine, when the shattering news arrived. After the first shock had passed, they settled down to "the most free and strong parley that ever I heard", as Baillie, one of their members, described it, as to what could have provoked Jehovah thus to forsake His Covenant, whether it was the sins of the Parliament, the sins of the Army, the sins of the Assembly, or the sins of the people.

The important question was still being thrashed out when, eleven days after the battle, Argyll tiptoed cautiously into Perth which the active Montrose had vacated a week previously to pursue the campaign thus happily inaugurated.

IV

Argyll had scarcely reached Perth when he received a further shock: Montrose had captured Aberdeen. It was clear that the time had come for the dictator really to bestir himself; accordingly he moved majestically northwards, sending urgent messages to the Covenanting nobles and gentry of the neighbourhood to join him, somewhat heartened by the news that Montrose had left Aberdeen and was marching up the Don valley in an attempt to raise the Gordons. For Argyll was confident that this would prove a hopeless task; only one of Huntly's sons, Aboyne, was on the Royalist side, and he was safely in beleaguered Carlisle; the other two were in the Covenant's army under Burleigh (just defeated by Montrose), Huntly was still lurking in the wilds of Strathnaver, and the clan, though individual members of it joined the King's Lieutenant-General, was too hopelessly divided to rise for him in strength.

On September 17th Argyll arrived at the Place of Drum, the owners of which were in the Edinburgh Tolbooth, and next day sent to Aberdeen a proclamation declaring Montrose and his followers traitors, and offering twenty thousand pounds reward for the capture of his former colleague, dead or alive. This proclamation was made in the King's name against the man the King had just created his Lieutenant-General. About the same time Argyll welcomed into his camp a man who, already guilty of two murders, had just perpetrated a third, James Stewart of Ardvoirlich, a member of Montrose's forces. Shortly after Tippermuir, he had stabbed to death his friend and patron, young Lord Kilpont; fleeing to Argyll, he was welcomed gladly, and given "considerable commands".[4]

It was not until the 21st that Argyll "comes quietly upon the night to Aberdeen", and by that time no less than five regiments of foot and one of horse were there to protect him, all

living at free quarter. Yet, though Montrose was now but half
a day's march away at Inverurie, Argyll made no attempt to
attack him, waiting until his foe had begun to move off towards
Strathbogie before beginning a cautious pursuit, and beguiling
the time with a fresh ravishing of Huntly's lands, which Lords
Gordon and Lewis, who were now with their uncle, were forced
to witness.

A report that Montrose was dead of a serious illness heartened
Argyll at the end of the month, and the Almighty was sincerely
thanked from pulpits, some ministers being rash enough to
assure their flocks that the Lord had slain him with His own
hand. But by October 4th there was definite news of his
recovery, and that he was getting his little army into Atholl.
There now began what Baillie described as " a strange coursing ",
Montrose leading a rapid dance and Argyll lumbering some
seven or eight days in his rear, from Spey to Tay, from Tay to
Don, from Don to Dee. On the 24th, Argyll was back in Aberdeen once more, collecting reinforcements; on the 26th, learning
that his enemy was again at Strathbogie on the heart-breaking
business of trying to persuade the Gordons to rise, he marched
to Inverurie, where he was joined by Lothian's regiment. For
once Montrose very nearly had been caught unawares by a force
at least four times larger than his own; he withdrew his little
army to Fyvie Castle, a seat of the Earl of Dunfermline on the
Ythan.

The situation was a very grave one for Montrose. For not
only was he compelled to face a vastly superior army, but his
own was seriously depleted by the absence of Colkitto and the
majority of the Scoto-Irish, hitherto the backbone of the army,
who had gone off some time before to recruit among Clan
Donald. Montrose was without bullets and almost without
powder; and worst of all, a small party of Gordon horse who
had been induced to join, deserted, in full view of their com-
rades, at the very first skirmishing.

But such a crisis called forth Montrose's genius. For bullets
he melted down all the pewter vessels in Fyvie; and when the
Covenanters delivered a general attack, he called upon the few
Irish remaining with him to charge with broadsword and pike.
The gallant warriors attacked to such good effect that not only
did they drive back the foe but were able to get the powder
they so sorely needed from the discarded pouches of the Covenanters. The Royalist musketeers immediately opened fire, using
for ball the pewter melted down from the domestic utensils at
Fyvie. "I have certainly broke one traitor's face with a chamber-

pot!" merrily called out one of them as he fired. On October 30th Argyll withdrew his men across the Ythan, and under cover of darkness Montrose marched quietly away in the direction of Strathbogie.

Following more cautiously than ever, Argyll busied himself with work which was always more congenial to him than fighting. The winter was drawing on, and Lowlandmen would be reluctant to continue the campaign in that wild country. So from the shelter of Dunkeld, Argyll began tempting away Montrose's officers with free passes and an indemnity for any who wished to go home; a number succumbed to this temptation, among them Colonel Sibbald, who had been one of Montrose's two companions on that long ride north from Carlisle. Argyll was thus happily employed when the incredible news reached him that his enemy, whom he had believed to be somewhere in Badenoch, was marching over the snowbound roads into Atholl. Argyll did not await him; he bade his men shift for themselves, fled to Perth, and thence to Edinburgh, where he laid down his commission.

By this time it had become horribly clear that Montrose, however small his army, was not a foe to be despised, and there was no competition for the office Argyll had vacated. Neither Lothian nor Almond, now Earl of Callander, would accept it, and it was decided that a professional soldier must have the job forced on him, "else it must have lain". The choice fell upon William Baillie who, after the surrender of Newcastle to the Covenant on October 9th, had received an express from the Estates requiring his return to Scotland. He was the illegitimate son of Sir William Baillie of Lamington, a good soldier, but a somewhat embittered man. His father's attempt to legitimize him by marrying his mother had proved vain, as had his own endeavour, over many years, to prove himself "the righteous air" to Lamington.

Baillie's experience in the Covenant's army in England had shown him the mischievous effects of civilians interfering in military affairs, and now, having the command of the army in Scotland forced upon him, he was resolved to have no such interference. But he had reckoned without Argyll. "Because I would not consent to receive orders from the Marquis of Argyll," he wrote in his *Vindication* of the following year, "(if casually we should have met together), after I had received the commission to command in chief over all the forces within the Kingdom, my lord seemed to be displeased, and expressed himself so unto some, that if he lived, he should remember it; wherein his lordship indeed hath superabundantly been as good as his word."[5]

But for the moment Argyll was content to take what he considered a well-earned rest. After a stay in Edinburgh, where he was cheered by the sight of a rich haul of prisoners from the capture of Newcastle, including the Earl of Crawford, he retired in the middle of December to his principal seat of Inveraray. Little did he dream how soon he would be forced to play the military man again.

V

Exactly what Montrose was doing at this time Argyll did not know and can scarcely have cared, for of one thing he was certain: at Inveraray he himself was safe from any foe. There was only one route by which an enemy could come upon him, the old raiding-road out of Lorn, and to this tortuous track Argyll believed himself to have the only key. Often had he been heard to say that he would give all he had rather than that a foe should discover it.

But even in that eventuality, it seemed impossible that an army could traverse such a track, particularly at this season of the year. There is a vivid contemporary description of the country through which it ran:

" Argyll is the wildest country of all, and there is a proverbial saying, that it is far enough to follow plunderers to Loch Tay, for that is the first obstacle encountered, and seems to have *Ne plus ultra* written upon it. And even before it is reached, a short distance takes many days to traverse, with no regular road, with continually alternating ascents and descents, and long detours, and numberless streams to be crossed, equally difficult for ferry or ford. There are very few trees to conceal or adorn the landscape. There is no track the traveller can follow, except along the shore, and this is frowned upon by rocks, and interrupted by pools of water alternately spreading and subsiding, and the whole region seems to devour the wayfarer rather than carry him with it. The soil is full of caves and holes, and barren spots, or covered with mosses, with innumerable bog-holes of black and brackish water."[6]

It was through such country, shrouded now in snow, that Montrose swooped suddenly upon Argyll, secure, as he thought himself, in the heart of it.

To Montrose the expedition was a waste of precious time; for his main object was to get into the Lowlands and thus to force Leven and his host to withdraw from England lest he attacked them in the rear. But his own little force was composed mainly of Highlanders, and he was obliged to humour them and their feuds. They begged him to take into consideration "MacCalein Mhor his grandeur, and how much it did importune the King's service to have his wings clipped, for thereon did depend their future good success, since on him alone the Covenant relied; and on his private ambition, joined to his present greatness, had more advanced the present rebellion, and keeped down the King's just interest, than the whole body of the Covenant besides ".[7]

In the middle of December, therefore, now rejoined by Colkitto, who was among the most enthusiastic for this punishing of an hereditary foe, Montrose took that very raiding-road to which Argyll supposed himself to have the only key. It was a MacDonald of Glencoe who acted as guide upon that dreadful and exhausting journey; the little Royalist force had ploughed its way over the snowbound track to within two miles of Inveraray before wild-eyed herdsmen came running to Argyll with the incredible news. Argyll acted promptly. He got into the nearest fishing-boat at the loch-side and bade the oarsmen pull for their lives down Loch Fyne to the shelter of his castle of Roseneath.

Left leaderless and unprepared, the unfortunate Campbells could make no resistance to their hereditary foes, who exacted a terrible vengeance for old wrongs. Here the victors lived for some weeks on the fat of the land, while Argyll lay trembling with rage and fear at Roseneath, excusing his flight by a fall he had had some weeks previously, which had hurt his face and arm, so that he was disabled from using either sword or pistol. He had been "forced", therefore, by his friends, to flee from Inveraray.

VI

At the end of this eventful year of 1644, Montrose marched out of Argyllshire towards the north, where Seaforth had an army of five thousand men in the neighbourhood of Inverness; this the King's Lieutenant-General proposed to attack before it could join with the army under Baillie, which lay at Perth. But when Montrose had marched as far as Kilcumin, the celebrated MacDonald bard, Iain Lom, brought him grave news:

Argyll was behind him with three thousand men, eleven hundred of whom he had taken from the unfortunate Baillie, and was burning Glen Spean and the Lochaber braes.

Argyll had no intention, as it happened, of attacking Montrose in the rear. His design was to follow at his usual respectful distance until Seaforth had engaged the foe, and then to come up in time to take credit for the victory. The panic terror which had seized on him a month previously had given place to a burning itch for revenge. At Inverlochy he paused to indulge his Campbells with the burning of homesteads, little dreaming that Montrose had got news of his pursuit and had resolved to deal with him instead of with Seaforth.

It was the kind of decision typical of Montrose's genius. "He thought it would prove a matter of far greater importance, and at the same time of less danger, if he could attack Argyll, and show that he could be defeated in the Highlands, where he was revered, by the ignorant country people, like a god; and if he succeeded, he was convinced that Seaforth's army, terrified with the report of a victory obtained over Argyll, would easily be reduced and brought to order."[8]

Argyll was sitting quietly at Inverlochy when news was brought of armed men approaching. He was not unduly alarmed, for he imagined it to be some hereditary foe bent upon a foray. It was the bitter cold evening of February 1st, and he was entertaining guests to supper, a minister, Mr. Mungo Law, a bailie of Edinburgh, and Sir James Rollo.

All through that icy night, famished and exhausted after a march over passes blocked with snowdrifts, Montrose and his men lay waiting for their rearguard to come up. It was bright moonlight, and soon Argyll was made uneasy by the reports of his scouts that the enemy, whoever he was, had the appearance of waiting for daylight to give battle. The injuries to Argyll's arm and face were healed,[9] but most conveniently began to trouble him again; accompanied by his friends, whom he had invited to witness his forwardness in the Good Cause, he got into his galley, the *Dubhlinnseach*, or black-sailed, leaving the command of his army to Sir Donald Campbell of Auchinbreck, the best warrior of Clan Diarmaid. From this safe refuge he watched the virtual extermination of his fighting-men.

It was dawn on St. Bride's Day when Montrose attacked. The Campbells fought gallantly, but they were no match for the Royalists, famished, exhausted, and outnumbered though these were. At least fifteen hundred of the Campbells, including Auchinbreck, fell in the battle and the pursuit, and the fighting power of Clan Diarmaid was broken for ever. As for Argyll, he crammed on sail and fled from the scene of disaster, appearing ten days later in the Parliament House at Edinburgh, with his left arm tied up in a scarf, "as though he had been at bones breaking".

The Chief whose crest most appropriately was a galley had utterly disgraced himself; yet so complete was his dominance over the Estates that they begged their President to "render him hearty thanks for his great pains and travails taken for the public, and withal entreated him to continue in so laudable a course of doing, for the weal and peace of the country".[10]

VII

The brilliant victories which Montrose had achieved in a few months did not enable him to overcome the fatal handicaps under which he had laboured from the beginning. He could get no support from those great men who secretly hated the Covenant; and although Lord Gordon now joined him, the Gordons as a clan remained hopelessly divided. It was impossible, therefore, to put into action the scheme which the King suggested: that Montrose should march into the Lowlands, and that Charles, with such forces as still remained to him, should join him there.

But the mere thought of such a possibility (disclosed to them in an intercepted letter, the bearer of which they promptly hanged) alarmed the Covenanters, who sent expresses to Leven for yet more reinforcements. What they needed even more was money, for the "General Commissar" of their armies had just presented his accounts, which amounted to 1,991,576 pounds Scots. No more cash could be squeezed from the Scottish taxpayer, but there remained "delinquents and malignants" who could be fined. The Estates busied themselves in the dividing of these into classes, and deciding on the amount of the fines to be imposed on each.

Early in May came a further blow: Montrose gained a decisive victory over Sir John Hurry at Auldearn, a village between the valleys of the Nairn and the Findhorn, the Covenanters losing some two-thirds of the men they had brought into the field. All that now remained to the Covenant was Baillie's small army which blocked the way to the Lowlands, and a newly raised force the command of which had been given to Lord Lindsay of the Byres at his own request. He had trenchantly criticized Argyll as a commander, and he was determined to show King Campbell how to fight. The Estates bestowed on him the title of Earl of Crawford, the rightful possessor of which was still lying a prisoner in the Tolbooth,* where he was joined at this time by seventy-year-old Lord Napier, the latter's son-in-law, daughter-in-law, and two young daughters, and Montrose's second son, now his heir, Lord Grahame, a boy of nine.

The plague was raging in Edinburgh, and it was at Stirling that the Estates assembled in July. By that time Montrose had given Crawford-Lindsay such a fright that he had scuttled away into Angus without waiting to meet the foe, and the Royalist commander had beaten Baillie soundly at Alford on the Don, Baillie narrowly escaping with his life. The defeat had not been his fault, for here as elsewhere he had been overruled in everything by his travelling committee, and on his arrival at Stirling he vindicated his conduct in a long document. The Estates, having no other soldier fit or willing for the chief command, compelled him to continue in it, though without a commission, until September 8th, taking care, however, to appoint an even larger committee to accompany the wretched Baillie to the remains of his army which lay at Perth. Six nobles, including Argyll, six barons, and six burgesses, together with representatives of the Kirk, were to "advise" the Commander-in-Chief henceforth. Having passed an Act for the levying of a new army of ten thousand foot and five hundred horse, the Estates adjourned to Perth (the plague having followed them to Stirling), where they met again on July 24th.

Though he was still unable to persuade any important man to join him, Montrose's two recent victories had enabled him to recruit a larger army than he had ever possessed, and he was more hopeful of the Gordons. Huntly's heir had been killed at Alford, but his brother, Lord Aboyne, had escaped from beleaguered Carlisle on the eve of Auldearn, and was now endeavouring to raise some cavalry among his clan. While awaiting his return, Montrose decided to give the Covenanting government a fright.

He mounted some of his foot on baggage-nags, and paraded them before the horrified eyes of the Estates who watched from the safety of Perth. For several days, from their camp at Methven, the Royalists kept up this bluff; then, having no wish

* In order to avoid confusing the reader, Lindsay is referred to in future as Crawford-Lindsay to distinguish him from the rightful owner of the first-named title.

to engage in battle at least until Aboyne rejoined him, Montrose
retired to Little Dunkeld. The Covenanters' method of aveng-
ing themselves for the trick which had been played them was
to butcher the camp-followers, including women, who were
straggling behind.[11] For this they had just received a good
precedent, for after their recent victory at Naseby their English
brethren had engaged in the like atrocities.

Montrose, meanwhile, rejoined by Aboyne, and commanding
four thousand four hundred foot and five hundred horse, was
ready to put into action his plan of marching to the Border.
But before he could achieve this, one more battle must be fought,
on the issue of which might well depend the future of the royal
cause in Scotland. The Covenanting army recently recruited
was more numerous than his own; Lanerick had raised the
Hamilton tenantry in Clydesdale and was about to march
towards Baillie, who was expecting also new levies from Fife.
If all these forces were allowed to join, Montrose, though by
his lightning movements he might gain the Border, would have
in his rear a most formidable foe. He resolved, therefore, to
fling himself between Lanerick and Baillie; as for the Fifeshire
men, though hot for the Covenant they were farmers and shop-
keepers, and the farther they were drawn from their homes, the
more reluctant they would be to fight. If he could beat the
main Covenant army under Baillie, Montrose judged rightly
that he would have little to fear from Lanerick.

The Covenanters remained unaware of his purpose. When
they heard that he had crossed the Forth, they fondly imagined
that he was making "a running march before them", in other
words was fleeing. In actual fact, by August 14th he had got
between Baillie and Lanerick, and was encamped in an upland
meadow about a mile north-east of the town of Kilsyth. One
thing, however, was clear to Baillie: at all costs Montrose must
be prevented from gaining the Border, and if the Covenant's
army marched hastily along the north side of the Ochils it could
cut him off.

Once again Baillie had reckoned without Argyll. Precious
time must be wasted while that potentate paid off old scores on
the way, burning Lord Stirling's castle of Menstrie and the
house of Grahame of Airth. It was not until the evening of
August 14th that the Covenanters encamped at Hollinbush on
the road from Stirling, a little over two miles from where
Montrose lay. Here Baillie made a last attempt to exert his
authority. He told his committee of civilians that they must
wait to give battle until Lanerick, then only twelve miles from

them, came up with his reinforcements; he begged them to realize the serious consequences should they be defeated yet again; he pointed out that they had now no other army in Scotland. But the nobles on the committee, each having been beaten by Montrose (except Crawford-Lindsay who had been merely frightened), were itching to revenge themselves upon him in a body, and fight they would next day whether Lanerick had joined them or not. "I found myself so slighted," wrote poor Baillie afterwards, "in everything belonging to a commander-in-chief, that for the short time I was to stay with them, I would absolutely submit to their direction and follow it."

At dawn on the 15th, the Covenant's army scrambled through cornfields and up the steep slopes of the Campsie Hills until they had gained a position on high ground below which, across a burn, lay Montrose. The obvious and sensible course was to embattle here and await the imminent arrival of Lanerick and his Clydesdale levies, but even in this Baillie was not allowed to have his way. His committee, convinced that Montrose was doomed to defeat, and terrified lest he might escape, decided that he must be outflanked immediately, a course that would take their army straight across Montrose's front. When Baillie's efforts to convince them of the madness of this manœuvre proved of no avail, he insisted that the votes of the committee be taken upon it; it was done, and decided in the affirmative, the only dissentient being Balcarres.

The result of the ensuing battle was to make Montrose master of Scotland, and this despite the fact that not one man of note fell on the Covenanting side. No sooner had the Royalist trumpets sounded a general advance, than the foe " did fly all of a sudden, their horse riding over their foot, and among the horse the nobles the first of any ". Leaving the common men to their fate, and trusting to the fleetness of their blood-horses, the lords, the gentry, and the ministers galloped off in all directions, anxious only to find a safe refuge. Glencairn and Cassilis fled to Ireland, Lanerick (who had been too late for the fight) to Berwick, Loudoun and Crawford-Lindsay to England, Baillie and Balcarres to Stirling.

It need scarcely be said that Argyll was among these fugitives. He had made his will before the battle, so that "many concluded that he meant to show a firm front, and cast his life upon the hazard of victory". Even before the engagement, however, he had decided once again that discretion was the better part of valour, and had given the command of his regiment to his major, Hume. At the sound of Montrose's trumpets, he was the first to turn tail. He never looked over his shoulder until he had galloped twenty miles to South Queensferry, where for the third time he sought safety in a boat. Even then he did not feel secure until it had weighed anchor and he was well out to sea.[12]

When news of the catastrophe reached Edinburgh, there was panic. The Royalist prisoners were hastily released, and two of them, the Earl of Crawford and Lord Ogilvy, were implored by the townsfolk to accompany a deputation to Montrose and intercede on their behalf. They had, in fact, no need for such intercession, for Montrose's demands were most temperate. All he asked was that Edinburgh Castle be surrendered to the King's officers, that the townsfolk renounce all correspondence with rebels and return to their allegiance, and that all the Royalist prisoners be sent to him at Glasgow. The deputation eagerly agreed to these terms, but the only article they carried out was that concerning the prisoners.

Early in September, the Covenant leaders in their several refuges received a ray of hope. The honours of Kilsyth belonged to gallant old Airlie and his Ogilvies, and Argyll, in his letters to his nephew Aboyne, had made the most of this, rightly counting on Gordon jealousy. A letter from Lord Ogilvy, warning Aboyne that Argyll, "notwithstanding of any promises or oaths that he may have seemed to make to you, does intend nothing but your dishonour, the utter extirpating of all memory of your old family, and if it could lie on *your* hands, the ruinating and betraying of the King's service", proved of no avail, and Aboyne deserted Montrose, taking the Gordon cavalry with him.

Nor was this all. It was the invariable habit of the Highland clans to return home after a battle, partly to attend to their agriculture and their hunting without which their families could not live, partly to carry home the booty. It was a tribute to Montrose's genius that he had prevailed upon these mountaineers to fight so far from their glens; but not even his genius could keep them at his side in the Lowlands when there was no fighting on hand. They had every excuse for melting away, as now they did; the same could not be said for Colkitto. After Kilsyth, Montrose had received from the King a patent creating him Viceroy of Scotland, and the new Viceroy's first act was to honour his old comrade-in-arms by knighting him. But Sir Alastair MacDonald remained Colkitto, whose thirst for revenge upon hereditary foes had not been quenched by Inveraray and Inverlochy. Taking the seasoned Irish warriors with him, save for five hundred who refused to leave Montrose, he marched off with the intention of rooting out Clan Diarmaid for ever.

Such was the situation when, in this September of 1645, Montrose began his march to the Border, and thence, as he hoped, to redress the balance of the English Civil War.

VIII

The decisive victory of Kilsyth appeared to have removed the handicaps under which Montrose had laboured hitherto. At long last the non-Covenanting nobles seemed eager and ready to fight under his banner, and to provide an army which would more than compensate for the desertions of Aboyne and Colkitto and the absence of the Highland clans. The Border lords, the Earls of Traquair, Home, Hartfell, Annandale, and Roxburgh, and the Marquis of Douglas, all were profuse in their promises to raise their tenantry; only Lanerick refused to leave the Covenanting side he had lately espoused. To Montrose's appeals he answered bluntly, " that he was resolved to have no correspondence with that side of the question, and would not therefore encourage them with vain hopes ". Well had it been for the Viceroy, and his master, if Lanerick's fellow nobles had been as frank.

For among all these Border lords, only Douglas, Annandale, and Hartfell were sincere in their promises of help. Moreover the help that these could give had been greatly exaggerated. The days were long past when a Douglas could bring thirty thousand fighting-men into the field, and it was only some twelve hundred, which included the faithful Ogilvies, that Montrose found awaiting him at the rendezvous at Torwoodlee on September 7th. He was still optimistic, however; there were Traquair's levies to come in, and at Kelso he was to meet Home and Roxburgh. The first duly arrived—one troop of horse under Traquair's son, Lord Linton; but when he reached Kelso, Montrose found, not Home and Roxburgh, but ominous news of them. They were the prisoners of David Leslie.

After the disaster of Kilsyth the Covenant's leaders had sent expresses to their army in England, demanding that a strong force be sent home to their relief. The appeal reached Leven when he was beiseging Hereford, and David Leslie, who had proved himself the best commander King Covenant possessed, was dispatched northwards with four thousand men. Collecting reinforcements from the garrisons of Newcastle and Berwick

on the way, Leslie crossed the Border on September 6th. His
original plan had been to take up a position between Forth and
Clyde and cut off Montrose's retreat into the Highlands, but
news reached him which caused him to discard this plan for
one of immediate attack.

It was news of the pitiful weakness of the Royalist army, and
it came from Traquair, Roxburgh, and Home. The first-named
sent it to Argyll, who was now with Leslie's army, at the same
time sending orders to his son, Lord Linton, to withdraw himself and his troop from Montrose's camp. Home and Roxburgh
had entered into a secret correspondence with Leslie when the
latter had reached Berwick, and had invited him to apprehend
them, that they might save their face by pretending that they
had been made prisoners against their will. By this revelation
of the weakness of his foe, Leslie's course was plain. He marched
straight up Gala Water, forded Tweed, and late on the night
of September 12th he was within three miles of Montrose's
camp on the flat ground of Philiphaugh near Selkirk, ready for
a surprise attack.

Montrose was utterly unexpectant of battle, and for the first
time in his campaign he had laid aside, during that fatal night,
his usual custom of personally setting the watch. He sat up
through the dark hours writing a long dispatch to the King,
leaving to his officers the posting of pickets and the sending out
of scouts. Either these latter were criminally careless or else
there was fresh treachery; at all events at daybreak they positively assured Montrose that there was no enemy within a ten-
mile radius. Thus it was that the Royalists were leisurely cook-
ing their breakfast when, from out of the thick mist of that
September morning, there rushed upon them six thousand
veterans.

Douglas's moss-troopers fled at the first shot; all that remained
were a hundred faithful horse commanded by old Airlie, and
the five hundred Irish who had stayed with Montrose when
Colkitto had deserted him. Harried by a murderous musket-
fire on both flanks, the gallant Irish stood sturdily, while
Montrose and his handful of cavalry charged Leslie's solid ranks.
But there could be no doubt of the issue; his cavalry reduced
to some thirty troopers, Montrose was persuaded to flee at last,
since in him alone lay the hope of fighting another day. The
Viceroy galloped across the moors into Tweeddale, and passing
Traquair's house paused to ask for aid. But Traquair sent a
deliberately insulting message that neither he nor his son was
at home. He was very much at home when the victors of

i 6   a Solenn   4 3

LEAGVE AND COVENANT,

for Reformation, and defence of
Religion, the Honour and happinesse
of the King, and the Peace and safety of the
three kingdoms of

ENGLAND, SCOTLAND, and IRELAND.

WE Noblemen, Barons, Knights, Gentlemen, Citizens, Burgesses, Ministers of the Gospel, and Commons of all sorts in the Kingdoms of England, Scotland, and Ireland, by the Providence of God living under one King, and being of one reformed Religion, having before our eyes the Glory of God, and the advancement of the Kingdome of our Lord and Saviour Iesus Christ, the Honour and happinesse of the Kings Majesty and his Posterity, and the true publique Liberty, Safety, and Peace of the Kingdoms, wherein every ones private Condition is included, and calling to minde the treacherous and bloody Plots, Conspiracies, Attempts, and Practices of the Enemies of God against the true Religion, and professors thereof in all places, especially in these three kingdoms ever since the Reformation of Religion, and how much their rage, power and presumption, are of late, and at this time increased and exercised, whereof the deplorable state of the Church, and Kingdom of Ireland, the distressed estate of the Church and Kingdom of England, and the dangerous estate of the Church and Kingdom of Scotland, are present and publique Testimonies; We have now at last, after other means of Supplication, Remonstrance, Protestations, and Sufferings, for the preservation of our selves and our Religion, from utter Ruine and Destruction, according to the commendable practice of these Kingdomes in former times, and the Example of Gods people in other Nations; After mature deliberation, resolved and determined to enter into a mutuall and solemn Legue and Covenant; Wherein we all subscribe, and each one of us for himself, with our hands lifted up to the most high God, do sweare;

The first part of the Solenn League and Covenant as it was published in England

Rev. James Guthrie. One of the most fanatical of the Covenanting ministers

Philiphaugh called upon him some hours later, and he tendered fulsome congratulations on their success which had been due so largely to his own treachery.*

Meantime the Covenanters were celebrating their first victory in a manner which accorded with their pitiless creed. The hundred Irish who remained alive after the battle surrendered on quarter; having laid down their arms, they came to deliver themselves up to Leslie, led by their officer, Stuart, Montrose's Adjutant. Immediately a howl of fury arose from the ministers on the travelling committee; it would be an act of impiety, they cried, to spare such wretches. Argyll, who was with the army, concurred. Thus was Leslie prevailed upon to pretend that he had promised quarter only to Stuart the Adjutant, and the army was let loose upon the defenceless, unarmed Irish, who were butchered, every man of them, in cold blood.[13]

There remained the fugitives from the battle, and the camp-followers. Among the latter were three hundred "married wives of the Irishes"; some were pregnant, others had infants in their arms; these, together with the cooks and boys, were slaughtered in a manner too horrible to record. An exhaustive search was made for the fugitives; those found wandering over the moors were stabbed or shot; eighty women and children were thrown, in one day, over the bridge at Linlithgow, the few who tried to clamber up the banks to save themselves were thrust down again by the butt-end of muskets. Six more were drowned at Elgin.[14]

These were the humbler victims of King Covenant. As soon as it was known that Montrose had failed in a fresh attempt to induce Huntly to bring out his Gordons in force, the executions began upon the more important prisoners. Neither Parliament nor the General Assembly was sitting, but the permanent Committees of these twin powers cared nothing for the law which required that a man must be judged only by his peers and by a lawfully convened court of justice. The bloody play began with the execution at Glasgow of Sir William Rollo,

* It is satisfactory to be able to record that Traquair, who had been raised by King Charles from private gentleman to earl, gained little by his betrayal. Hated by his own tenants for his oppressions, and distrusted by the Covenanters for his well-known craftiness, in his latter years he was reduced to such a degree of poverty that he was forced to beg, and died in the fields of his own estate, it was believed of hunger. This was in 1659. "And at his burial he had no mort-cloth, but a black apron; nor towels, but dogs' leashes belonging to some gentlemen that were present; and the grave being two foot shorter than his body, the assistants behoved to stay till the same was enlarged, and be buried." (*Staggering State*, 45. N. Wishart, 199. N. Burnet. *Hist. of My Own Times*, 35.)

K

brother of Sir James who had married Argyll's sister Mary as his
second wife; of Sir Philip Nisbet, who had fought for the King
in England; and of a lad of eighteen, Alexander Ogilvy of
Innerquharity, whose death was a mere sacrifice to the bitter
enemy of his race, Argyll. As the Rev. David Dickson stood by
the scaffold, watching the dripping knife fall a second and third
time, he rubbed his hands and was heard to exclaim:

"The wark gangs bonnily on!"[15]

Two Irish officers, Colonel O'Kean and Major Lachlan, were
hanged at Edinburgh, and then there was a pause. For news
had come that Montrose had gathered fifteen hundred men and
was threatening Glasgow from Lochlomondside. But as soon as
Leslie had driven off these raw levies, the Maiden was put upon
a cart and trundled up to St. Andrews, where the Estates, because
the worst epidemic of the plague ever known in Scotland was
still raging in most of the other towns, were about to assemble.
The remaining Royalist prisoners of note were brought to the
Castle there, to await their execution without the formality of
a trial.

Wariston opened the session with a long harangue, urging
that justice be done upon all Malignants, and declaring that
their former remissness in this duty had brought upon his
brethren God's favourite punishments of sword and pestilence.
That which he quaintly described as "the massacre" of the
godly at Kilsyth must never be forgotten; and he required that
the Estates be purged, since Parliament "was become like to
Noah's Ark, which had in it both foul and clean creatures".
Meanwhile the Commission of the Kirk was sending remonstrance after remonstrance against the dilatoriness of Parliament
in executing the remaining prisoners, reminding the Estates
"how displeasing unto the Supreme Judge of the world, how
dangerous unto yourselves, how grievous unto the hearts of the
Lord's people, and how advantageous to the enemy, your former
delays have been". Pulpits thundered to the same tune. "Thine
eye shall not pity, and thou shalt not spare" was the favourite
text; and the Rev. Robert Blair preached a sermon before the
Estates on the words: "I will early destroy all the wicked of the
land, that I may cut off all the wicked doers from the city of
the Lord."

The Estates' reply to the Kirk's remonstrances was most
gracious. They thanked their reverend brethren for "their
modest and seasonable petitions", and bade them be confident
that "with all alacrity and diligence they would go about and
proceed in answering the expectation of their reasonable

desires ", begging the Kirk to implore God's blessing to assist them in this good work.[16]

Accordingly, early in the year 1646, Nathaniel Gordon, who had been Montrose's faithful companion-in-arms ever since the first victory at Tippermuir, met the sharp embrace of the Maiden. He was followed by Sir Robert Spottiswoode, son of the old Archbishop, who had never been in arms against the Covenant, but was condemned for accepting from the King the office of Secretary in place of the faithless Lanerick, and for bringing Montrose his patent of Viceroy. Spottiswoode was denied the immemorial right of addressing the people from the scaffold, and even his private devotions were interrupted by a minister who bawled forth the most indecent execrations against both himself and his dead father.[17]

Andrew Guthrie, son of the Bishop of Moray, was the next victim; and two days later the knife fell on the neck of William Murray, aged nineteen, whose elder and only brother, the Earl of Tullibardine, though his influence with the Covenanters was great, made no effort whatsoever to save his life. Three other potential victims eluded the vengeance of King Covenant.

One was Stuart the Adjutant. He had been condemned despite the decision after Philiphaugh that he personally, and not the Irish he had commanded, had been promised quarter; history is silent as to the details of his escape from jail. The second was the object of Argyll's particular animosity, Lord Ogilvy, old Airlie's heir. Confined in the Castle of St. Andrews and awaiting death, Ogilvy obtained, through the influence of Lanerick, whose kinsman he was, a visit from his mother, his wife, and his sister. A little later the guards escorted to the gate three weeping ladies; and it was not until next morning that the warders discovered that one of these "ladies" was in fact the prisoner dressed in his sister's clothes; by that time Ogilvy had found a safe retreat. Baulked of his vengeance on a mortal enemy, Argyll himself spared the third victim, Hartfell, by way of tit-for-tat, since Hartfell was an hereditary foe of the Hamiltons.

The Estates wound up their work of vengeance by ordering that "the Irish prisoners taken at or after Philiphaugh, in all the prisons of the Kingdom, especially in the prisons of Selkirk, Jedburgh, Glasgow, Dumbarton, and Perth, be execute without an assize or process, conform to the treaty betwixt both kingdoms" (that is, the Solemn league and Covenant). All those who had been "active" for Montrose, a word admitting of the widest interpretation, but were not condemned to death, were

to be fined from three to six years' rent, and "notwithstanding
of these fines, the Parliament and its committees, as they shall
think expedient, should banish, confine, or imprison all such
within the class as they should think to demerit a higher
censure than their fines, and might prove dangerous instruments
to the peace of the country".[18]

Montrose also had prisoners from his several victories, confined in Blair Castle. His answer to those who urged him to
retaliate by executing these, lights this black aftermath of his
defeat. "Let them set a price upon our heads," he cried; "let
them employ assassins to murder us; let them break their faith
and practise the utmost pitch of wickedness; yet shall that never
induce us to forsake the glorious paths of virtue and goodness,
or strive to outdo them in the practice of villainy and
barbarity."[19] It was the same spirit in which his royal master,
immediately after the great victory of Kilsyth, had offered a free
pardon without exception to all who would return to their
allegiance.

Montrose's gallant challenge had been made, and had failed.
It had proved, though an epic, but an interlude, the flash of a
meteor which made the night but darker when it vanished.
King Covenant was settled more firmly than ever upon the back
of Scotland, and for a long while yet she must bow to his pitiless
rule.

PART THREE

THE SELLING OF THE KING
1645-1647

Chapter One

HISTORIANS who admire the Covenant have drawn a veil over the state of the ordinary people of Scotland during this fantastic period of her history. And not without reason. For never had those people suffered a greater oppression or an interference which extended to every department of their lives.

The Kirk, whose arrogance King James VI from policy, and his son from principle, had tried to curb, was now supreme. Its General Assembly, permanent now through the Commission of that body, wielded a power far exceeding that of the Pope. The crazy fanaticism of John Knox was back again, and that sombre ghost, with its mad eyes and patriarchal beard, must have gloated over a Scotland become at last the Calvinist's Sion. A man or woman could be censured for "an uncomely gesture", for wearing a new fashion, for dancing at a wedding, for eating at his or her own table food which the Kirk considered too luxurious for their status. The Monday markets were forbidden again, because they entailed travelling on the Sabbath; trading with Spain and Portugal was banned because of the possibility of "religious contagion"; carriers and travellers were compelled to produce testimonials from the place where they spent the ritualistic Sabbath rest; money-lending was prohibited; merchants must either close their booths for the fasts, which sometimes lasted for a whole week, or find themselves sitting on the Stool of Repentance.*

The Kirk claimed the right to appoint regents at the Universities. In the disputation for a regent's place in St. Leonard's College at St. Andrews in 1649, three ministers had decisive votes

---

* Yet Argyll's impudence was such that he was solemnly to inform the English Parliament that "It is a maxim of the Church of Scotland that ministers shall not meddle in civil affairs." (Burton, IV, 330.)

in the election; "these were the first ministers that ever had voice in the election of a master to any of the Colleges there; the custom formerly and of old was, that every college had liberty to choose their own masters".[1] The civil penalties which the first Reformers had attached to Excommunication, and which had been abolished by James VI, were revived. On the other hand the pre-Reformation Sunday, which even those zealots had viewed with an indulgent eye, or at least had winked at (Knox had visited Calvin on a Sunday evening and found him playing bowls), was now done away with.

Two members of the kirk-session, accompanied by a bailie, passed through the town every Sabbath, searching houses and reporting to the presbytery all who were absent from the kirk, and these were severely punished. A man was censured for visiting his sick mother on the Sabbath; nor was it only on Sundays that such Sabbatarianism was compulsory. There were afternoon lectures on week-days, there were Days of Thanksgiving and Days of Humiliation. On these no merchant durst open his booth, nor a farmer attend to his harvesting. "But here it is to be marked," wrote Spalding in September 1641, "that this day of thanksgiving was straitly kept, the weather being wonderful fair, the poor people rather wishing to have been at home winning their corns in such fair weather, nor so often to be brought in with the crafts and commons, both of burgh and land, sometimes for giving of thanks, and sometimes for fasting, upon work days . . . whereas some poor people, living from hand to mouth, fasted the day of thanksgiving because they durst not labour for their food." On this occasion insult was added to injury when, in October, the people were compelled to fast in order to implore God's removal of the rain which was ruining the harvest they had had to neglect for a thanksgiving day in September.

The same writer gives details of a typical fast-day. "Upon the seventh of July, we had a fast, entering the church by nine hours, and continued praying and preaching till two hours. After sermon the people sat still hearing reading till afternoon's sermon began and ended, which continued till half hour after six. Then the bell rang to the evening prayers, and continued till seven." This was in 1644, and the King and his family were prayed for, as well as the armies which were fighting against him.[2]

The original opposition to King Charles had been due, ostensibly at least, to his "novations" in the matter of the Service Book. King Covenant multiplied "novations". In 1641

fishing was forbidden from midnight on Saturday until midnight on Sunday; for the first offence the culprit was punished,
rather strangely, as a fornicator, for the second as a "double
fornicator", and for the third as an adulterer. Not only was
there no religious observance of Christmas and Easter but for
several days before these festivals the fleshers were forbidden
to sell any meat, so that the people should be prevented from
having their immemorial good cheer.[3]

Since the Reformation, the old prayers such as the Lord's
Prayer, the Creed or "Belief", and the *Gloria* or "Conclusion",
had been in constant use. These were now abolished as superstitions, and on one occasion the abolition gave rise to a bizarre
incident. The people of a parish in Angus had not heard of the
new decree, and at the end of a psalm were beginning as usual
"Glory be to the Father", when their minister furiously interrupted them by bawling, "*No* glory to the Father, *no* glory to
the Son!" It was only on rare occasions that the unfortunate
people were able to get back at their tormentors who had
imposed these innovations. Thus a Covenanting soldier, being
found in "uncivil conversation" with a woman in the College
Church of Aberdeen, reminded the kirk-session which was about
to censure him that, according to the new teaching, a kirk was
no more holy than any other place.[4]

It was only to be expected that since the most innocent recreation could not be indulged in without the risk of punishment,
and spies infested the ale-houses to catch a man out in some
homely oath, serious moral crime should be treated with the
utmost severity. Fornicators were made to sit on the Stool of
Repentance for twenty-six successive Sundays, garbed in sackcloth which, in some parishes, they had to provide at their own
expense. The adulterer must stand at the kirk-door, barefoot
and bare-legged, while the congregation entered and again when
they dispersed, and during sermon he was placed before the
pulpit with a paper round his head inscribed with the details of
his crime. For repeated immorality, the kirk-session of Dunfermline ordered a woman to be scourged, branded, carted
through the streets, and banished from the town.

This bitter code had its inevitable result, not only in an
increase of the immorality it affected to cure, but in a terrible
outbreak of unnatural vice, which was said to have been
unknown in Scotland before the Reformation. By the time that
King Covenant had reigned for several years, it had reached the
most alarming proportions. The diarists of the period, Nicoll
and Lamont, give innumerable instances of "bestiality", for

which both the man and the animal were burnt alive, the human culprits being often "young boys". In the August of 1657, an old man and his daughter were drowned together at Glasgow for incest. The penalties for adultery were the most common cause of infanticide, and as the Duke of York, afterwards James VII and II, was to remark many years later, "rather made scandals than buried them".

The only remedy the Kirk could offer was still harsher punishment, a still greater interference with the daily lives of the people. Nicoll records *daily* hangings, scourgings, nailing of ears to the gallows, and boring of tongues.[5] In 1650 he noted that "for eschewing and downbearing of sin and filthiness in Edinburgh, it was enacted, that no woman should vent or run wine or ale in the taverns of Edinburgh, but only men-servants and boys". Needless to say, such measures proved wholly ineffective. In 1650 one of Cromwell's soldiers wrote of the Scots: "For the sins of adultery and fornication they are as common amongst them as if there was no Commandment against either (they call those only broken women that have had but six bastards)"; and in the same year Cromwell himself wrote that "the people generally are so given to the most impudent lying and frequent swearing as is incredible to be believed".[6]

It must not be imagined that the entire ministry of Scotland concurred in this tyranny; but the minority that did not come into line were as persecuted as the laity. In 1649 eighteen ministers were deposed and five suspended by a Visitation of one of the Assembly's committees. In the following year the Rev. Gavin Stewart of Dalmellington, and a goldsmith named James Macaulay, were punished for not yet having signed the Solemn League and Covenant, the first being deposed, and the second, who died without signing, denied burial in the kirkyard.[7]

But even ministers who had subscribed to both Covenants were not free from the tyranny of the Kirk. If a travelling committee disapproved of a preacher's sermon, he was not only prohibited from preaching, but compelled to maintain a substitute at his own expense. Those who had been censured but were penitent, must preach a penitential sermon; if this, when put into writing and submitted to the Moderator of the Provincial Assembly, was not deemed satisfactory, the penitent must compose another, and he must continue in this way until he had given satisfaction.

One of the worst oppressions was that of "transportation". General Assemblies or their Committees removed ministers from one parish to another, whether they themselves or their parishioners or even their presbyteries were willing or not. Even so enthusiastic a Covenanter as Robert Baillie had become, strongly disapproved of the practice. Transportation, he wrote in July 1648, "I love worse and worse; the most are evidently packed businesses, little for the credit either of the transporters or the transported". In 1642 he himself had been uprooted from his well-loved charge of Kilwinning, Ayrshire, after he had been there ten years, and transported to Glasgow, to his great grief and despite the protests of his parishioners. One wonders what admirers of the Covenant would have said if Charles I had acted in like manner.

Perhaps the most terrible of all the cruelties of King Covenant was the witch-hunt. Witchcraft had not been a capital offence until the Reformation, and for many years after that upheaval the moderates merely concurred in the superstitious spirit of the age. The Covenanters on the other hand deliberately provoked it. Ministers were directed to invite from their pulpits any of their flock who suspected a neighbour of "witchery" to make a public accusation, thereby appealing not only to the superstition of their parishioners, but to private grudges.[8]

The General Assembly of 1640 ordered ministers "carefully to take notice of Witches, Charmers, and all such abusers of the people", and the frequency and solemnity with which Assemblies debated on the crime encouraged the ignorant to believe in it, and exhibitionists to accuse themselves. In Fife, a Covenant stronghold, thirty witches were burnt in the space of a few weeks in 1643; at Torryburn near Dunfermline, one out of every three old women is said to have been persecuted as a witch; and in one afternoon in July 1649, Sir James Balfour saw "commissioners severally directed by the Parliament for trying and burning of 27 witches, women, and 3 men and boys".[9]

It is difficult to bring oneself to read the details of the tortures inflicted in order to persuade these hapless creatures to "confess". Suicides became frequent, the victims being unable to endure the thought of the trial they must undergo, and which they could not evade by flight, since they were hunted from place to place. One of the favourite forms of discovering a witch was by "pricking". The victim was blindfolded, men supposed to be experts in discerning certain "devil's marks" upon the body were called in, and a long pin was thrust into these blemishes. If no blood was drawn and no pain felt, it was an infallible sign of witchcraft in the victim. Scotland was the nursery of this art; warrants and substantial fees were given to the prickers, and in 1649 one of them was invited to Newcastle, the magistrates of that town promising him twenty shillings sterling for each conviction.[10]   Perhaps the most hideous custom of all was that of ministers offering accused witches their lives if they would make "a general discovery" of others.

An English journalist, writing in 1652, recorded the accusing before the English Commissioners of a multitude of the victims of King Covenant.   No less than sixty were accused of moral crimes, some of which had been committed twenty years before; others had been brought before the Kirk for witchcraft and had confessed.   "The Court demanding how they came to be proved witches, they declared that they were forced to it by the exceeding torture they were put to, which was by tying their thumbs behind them, and then hanging them up by them; two Highlanders whipt them, after which they set lighted candles to the soles of their feet, and between their toes, then in their mouths, and burning them in the head; there were six of them accused in all, four whereof died of the torture."[11]   Others had their nails torn off by pincers, or their mouths lacerated by the prongs of an iron hoop knows as a witch's bridle, or had haircloths dipped in vinegar wrapped round their naked bodies to fetch off the skin.   Such atrocities were not only approved of, but often superintended by, the ministers.

There was one small section of the community which had suffered since the Reformation a bitter and unceasing persecution, and which under the Covenant was almost wiped out. These were the Catholics.   In 1643, Boisivon, the French agent who visited Edinburgh that year, affirmed that there were not more than five hundred of them in Scotland, and that their plight was more wretched than those who lived under infidels. On the signing of the National Covenant in 1638, one Jesuit rather naïvely had hoped that since the Covenanters professed to be demanding liberty of conscience, "this consideration may induce them to desist from persecuting the Catholics".   Instead, not only were the latter persecuted for adhering to the faith of their fathers, but for not signing the Covenant.

The Annual Letters of the Jesuit Fathers reported in 1642 that "for the last four years and more, the Catholics have borne the fury of the storm of persecution, and during this time the greater number of them have been ejected from their houses and sent to prison, and their property dispersed or lost".   One aged Catholic knight, who had returned from the exile consequent upon his adherence to his religion, to serve his King, died in prison aged eighty-six, and at his funeral his coffin was pelted with stones and filth.   In 1641 Fr. James Macbreck wrote the

Father General that since his coming to the Scottish Mission of the Society in 1615, "neither I nor any other Catholic have since the first overthrow of the Catholic faith in this country, ever before experienced a trial so universal and terrible as this".[12] It was greatly to the credit of these Scots Catholics that, notwithstanding the persecution they had suffered under James VI and Charles I, they remained loyal to the latter during the Civil War, thus subjecting themselves to a double persecution as Catholics and "Malignants".

Oppressed and tyrannized over in every department of their daily lives by the Kirk, the unfortunate people of Scotland were brought by the civil powers to a degree of poverty which even so poor a nation had never experienced since the Wars of Independence. For there was continual taxation which, though it had no legal authority whatsoever, must be paid in order to avoid imprisonment or worse. In the autumn of 1640 the people were forced "under the pain of plundering" to make twenty thousand pairs of shoes, twenty thousand suits of clothes, and twenty thousand shirts for the Covenant's army, the material to be paid for, but the work to be done free.

Taxation of all kinds, fines, and "voluntary contributions to the Good Cause", enormous though the sums were, could not meet the cost of the rebellion. Many towns had their plate seized and melted down; in 1644 "The Committee begins now to discuss the wealthy widows in Aberdeen, and to borrow money from them upon band as well as from the men"; and in 1648 a new device was invented. This was to summon before a committee those suspected of being secret Royalists, and to order them to "lend" money to the Government to the extent of some hundreds of pounds sterling, whether they had it or not. Those who refused had the amount doubled; those who protested that they lacked the money, were offered it by the committee upon bond for a certain unspecified time. If the debt and the interest were not then paid, the unfortunate had his goods seized and his person flung into prison. So excellent a device was this considered that the Committee of Estates quarrelled with the Commission of the Kirk as to which had had the honour of inventing it.[13]

No picture of Scotland under the reign of King Covenant would be complete without a glimpse of the extraordinary fanaticism which was the hall-mark of the genuine Covenanter as distinct from those who, like Argyll, used religion as a cloak for their own lust for power. The diaries of Alexander Brodie, Robert Blair, Sir Thomas Hope, Johnson of Wariston, and to a lesser degree the Letters and Journals of Robert Baillie, give a vivid insight into the mixture of superstition, emotionalism, private judgment gone mad, and the appalling lack of charity and humour which made up the true Covenanting spirit.

The Lord was sought in every detail of daily life, and was expected to answer "articulate". It was Wariston's habit, especially before undertaking anything which entailed personal risk, to "cast the lot", and in practically every case it fell, as he himself admitted in his more honest moments, according to his own inclinations. Revelations were vouchsafed almost daily, either by the Lord's voice speaking in the zealot's ear, or in dreams; and no matter how often they proved incorrect, absolute belief in them persisted. Wariston was hugely delighted by such a revelation given to him in July 1650, on the news of Cromwell's arrival at Berwick, "that, as God brought Duke Hamilton in London to public justice, and Ja. Grahame [Montrose] in Edinburgh, so would He bring Cromwell, Commander-in-Chief of the invading army, to public justice in Edinburgh ere long".

The learned Sir Thomas Hope, Lord Advocate, solemnly noted down his dreams which, he believed, were full of supernatural warnings. Two specimens may be regarded as typical: "24th June, 1643. This night I thought that a tooth, which was loose, fell out of my gums, and that I took it in my hand and kept it, thinking to have it set in again. These repeated dreams portend some calamity to me or mine. . . . June 25th. Sunday at night I dreamt that while I was pulling on my left boot, both the tags of it broke. The Lord prepare me."

The true Covenanter regarded as wicked the most innocent of pastimes if they gave pleasure, for all joy derived from the things of the world was sinful. "This day I intended to plant and graft trees," wrote Brodie on one occasion, "and was a little employed therein. I desired to have my sinful affection pardoned in going about these natural things." Converted at the age of seven, the Rev. Robert Blair "durst never play upon the Lord's Day; yea, though when the schoolmaster, after catechizing his scholars upon that day, would have dismissed us with express orders not to go into the town, but to the fields to play, I obeyed him in going to the fields, yet I refused to play with my companions, as against the commandment of God".

Wariston made the lives of his wife, his thirteen children, and his friends a misery by his addiction to a holy gloom. Asked to say grace at a bridal feast, he turned it into a prayer for God's pardon for the sins of the bride, the groom, their respective families, and their guests, and later rebuked his wife for dancing at the festivities—"a gross fault". At family prayers it was his habit to enumerate the sins of his wife, children, and servants, and when necessary to appoint a household fast. On occasions he would make his wife kneel beside him while he prayed aloud for forgiveness for their "excess of carnal affection". On the other hand he felt no need for forgiveness for helping himself to money entrusted to him by kinsfolk and clients, considering that the Lord had "cast it into my lap".[14]

A dreadful lack of charity and common pity distinguished such men. Wariston gloated over the story of how some lass had danced at her brother's wedding, and "the next day took an apoplexy and is dying of it without ever recovering any of her senses, language, or motion". He rejoiced over the death of poor little Princess Elizabeth in her lonely prison room at Carisbrooke in September 1650, and even the burning of Holyroodhouse in the same year was a matter for congratulation, because it was a certain sign of God's wrath against the Royal Family. When his own wife fell sick, he informed her that it was a judgment on her for attending to mundane matters when she ought to have been attending sermons, a particularly cruel charge seeing that he left the management of all his material affairs to her. Even Baillie, by nature a kindly man, could write of a supporter of "Erastian" tenets: "God has stricken Coleman with death; he fell in an ague, and after four or five days expired. It's not good to stand in Christ's way."

To the Covenanter, "Christ's way" was exclusively that which accorded with his own judgment. It was heresy not to believe that the Pope was Antichrist, that Papists and Malignants were automatically damned, that the Elect were predestined to eternal bliss. On the other hand the Kirk could change its views upon such vital matters, and punish those who did not accept the change. Cornet Baynes, an English soldier, wrote during the English Occupation: "Three of the enemy's ministers are come under our protection; one of them saith he is excommunicated for not answering whether Cromwell is Antichrist or not".[15]

Such was the savage and pitiless creed which, during its long tyranny, ruined Scotland's material life, dishonoured her name, and left her a legacy of gloom and bigotry which she was never wholly to eradicate.

Chapter Two

FOR a while after the signing of the Solemn League and Covenant, the two parties to the bargain had remained harmonious. The Scots Army was worth its enormous price (very little of which had yet been paid) by the mere menace of its presence up there in the North of England, and the Committee of Estates dealt firmly with the hundreds of deserters from Leven's camp who tried to get back to their homes and their trades. Strict orders were given to magistrates to "decimate" the fugitives, hanging every tenth man, and sending the rest back to the front with "a mark of infamy". Any person found sheltering such deserters had half his movable goods confiscated, and the other half given to the informer.[16]

Up in London the Assembly of Divines harmoniously debated such interesting matters as the scriptural authority for ruling elders, the Scots wisely avoiding the thorny subject of Independency "till it please God to advance our army, which we expect will much assist our argument". Fasts occupied a great deal of the Assembly's time, and Baillie gives details of a typical fast-day kept on the news of Huntly's abortive rising in May 1644:

"After Dr. Twisse had begun with a brief prayer, Mr. Marshall prayed large two hours, most divinely, confessing the sins of the members of the Assembly in a wonderfully pathetic and prudent way. After, Mr. Arrowsmith preached one hour, then a psalm; thereafter Mr. Vines prayed near two hours, and Mr. Palmer preached one hour, and Mr. Seaman prayed near two hours, then a psalm. After, Mr. Henderson brought them to a short sweet conference of the heart of the sins confessed in the Assembly, and other seen faults, to be remedied, and the convenience to preach to all sects, especially Anabaptists and Antinomians. Dr. Twisse closed with a short prayer and blessing."

There were minor unpleasantnesses. In December 1643, the Scottish members of the Assembly refused to attend Pym's funeral sermon, "for funeral sermons we must have away with the rest"; and they were affronted by the desire of some of their English colleagues to adjourn for Christmas. The English ministers got their way, "yet we prevailed with our friends in the Lower House to carry it so in Parliament that both Houses did profane that holy day, by sitting on it, to our joy, and some of the Assembly's shame". When the Scots Army actually crossed the Border in January 1644, the English ministers became more amenable; "the relics of the Service Book, which till then were every day used in both Houses, are at last vanished," rejoiced Baillie. "Paul's and Westminster are purged of their images and organs, and all which gave offence. My Lord Manchester made two fair bonfires of such trinkets at Cambridge."

The first really jarring note sounded in the December of 1644, the year which had witnessed the turn of the tide in the favour of the English rebels. In the House of Commons, Cromwell, who, since Marston Moor, had been the rising man, accused Lord Manchester of neglecting to fight the King at Newbury, and in his reply Manchester described Cromwell as one who "has spoken contumeliously of the Scots' intention in coming to England to establish their Church government, in which Cromwell said he would draw the sword against them; also against the Assembly of Divines; and has threatened to make a party of Sectaries, to extort by force, both from King and Parliament, what condition they thought meet. This fire was long under the embers; now it's broken out, we trust in good time. It's like, for the interest of our nation, we must crave reason of that darling of the Sectaries, and in obtaining his removal from the Army . . . break the power of that potent faction. This is our present difficult exercise," added Baillie; "we had need of your prayers." They had indeed.

With the raising of the great New Model Army in 1645, Baillie's alarm and indignation increased. For, like Cromwell who was its moving spirit, many of the officers and men were Independents, and these were now added to Montrose and Malignants on Baillie's list of "prime enemies". Because it was the New Model which won the great victory at Naseby, no rejoicing was made by Baillie and his fellow Scots.

Nor was Independency the only bone of contention between the two allies. In May 1645, the Rev. George Gillespie wrote Baillie that in the North of England "the counties cry out they are exhausted and undone for ever, the Scottish army having taken so much money off them by assessments; and now the Parliament having forbidden those assessments, our army cries out they will be starved, whereupon the Parliament hath given them leave to take free quarter and billet, upon tickets given for whatsoever is so taken, but do not permit them to sesse [levy taxes]. This pleaseth the common soldiers, but not the officers, who say still they must have monies. . . . I might enlarge myself on this sad subject, which has made some of our countrymen, from more passion than deliberation, both say and write, that they fear it will turn to a national quarrel."

Bad feeling continued to grow. "We are hated and despised daily by many here," wrote Baillie from London in July; and in October: "Our doing nothing since the taking of Newcastle; our lying still in the north so long; and when we moved, our running back to Carlisle; when we were drawn up to Hereford, our lying there for no purpose; and when we returned, our plundering all the way, are much exaggerated." While admitting the plundering, he excused it because "their withdrawing of all the promised pay the seven last months, not giving one month's pay, has forced us to take by violence for our subsistence, and disabled us to do any service, of purpose to make us odious".

This, had he but realized it, was the key to the mystery of the sudden change of attitude in his southern brethren. The Scots had served their turn; and the aim of the Independents in the Parliament and the Army was to get rid of them without having to pay them the vast sums promised for their aid in 1643. To the English people at large they had always been an object of contempt and hatred; and by withholding their pay it was hoped that the northern counties, exasperated by their living at free quarter, would rise up against them and drive them out.

In January 1646, Baillie heard a report that the King, beaten in the field, and in danger of capture, was considering the placing of his person for protection in the hands of the Scots. Baillie was shocked and dismayed; it would prove, he wrote, "a fountain of most dangerous and horrible evils . . . for if we should in so base and treacherous a way join with him, we would be able to do him no real help at all; but I hope there is nothing of the report true". He was not in the confidence of the Covenant's leaders, and therefore he did not know that in their growing rift with their former allies the possession of the King's person was regarded by them as a trump card; and that, far from joining with him, they had a purpose far more base and treacherous.

*   *   *

In the August of 1645 there had come to England a man who

was destined to play an important part in the events of the following year. His name was Jean de Montereul. He was in his early thirties, a brilliant young member of the Paris Bar, cultured, of enormous industry and great intelligence, described by Cardinal de Retz as one of the handsomest men in Europe. On this his second visit to England his ostensible business was to find recruits for French service, and to spend his spare time hunting for rare manuscripts and tapestries for his patron, the power behind the French Throne, Cardinal Mazarin.

But his real mission was one of diplomacy. It was still to the interest of France to prevent Great Britain from becoming sufficiently united as to constitute a menace to her power; and in his first letter to Mazarin after his arrival in London, he summed up the situation thus: "I shall simply indicate to your Eminence that it appears to me that France has a two-fold interest in preventing the King of Great Britain from coming to terms with the Independents; first, because it would be the complete ruin of the Scots, whom France ought to maintain, as a power she will one day be able to oppose to England; and again, it is preferable that the agreement be effected by France, rather than by the Spaniards, whose services the Independents will be found to have had in coming to terms at present."[17]

But beneath the cynical realism of the diplomat, Montereul had a large heart and a keen sense of personal honour. Like many another man, close acquaintance with King Charles was to bring him a very real regard for the Stuart. On the other hand, as a Catholic he had an amused contempt for the internal squabbles of the Protestants; he regarded both Anglicans and Presbyterians as heretics; and he could never understand why the King was so consistently to refuse to sign the Covenant, since he himself saw little difference between the two creeds.

This man of the world, after his first talk with the Scots Commissioners in London, perceived one thing clearly: that underneath their religious cant their real anxiety was for the money promised them by the English in return for their invasion of 1644. It was on this score that they were anxious for peace, "since while the war lasts," he wrote, "they cannot obtain payment for what is owing to them by the English, and it is probable they will have still greater difficulty in obtaining it if the Parliament remains victorious, since it is true that benefits conferred by states are easily forgotten and very often repaid by insults; thus everything tends to induce the Scots to come to terms with the King".

By the end of 1645 the Civil War was as good as over, and the

L

defeat of the King had revealed three distinct parties among the victors: the New Model Army which had won the war and which was the stronghold of Independency; the Parliament, which had created the New Model, and which was largely Presbyterian; and the Scots. Each of these three parties was now endeavouring to negotiate a treaty with the King on terms which would be advantageous to their respective interests. Since the New Model represented the strongest party, and it was still France's policy to assist the weaker, Montereul set himself on the one hand to frighten the Scots Commissioners by pointing out to them the serious consequences to themselves if the King came to terms with the Independent Army; and on the other to make them see in the light of common sense their fixed intention of forcing Presbyterianism upon England.

"I could not well understand," he wrote to Mazarin, "how they wished to establish in the Church of England a form of government that their King did not wish, which the English rejected, and which even those who were most attached to their interests did not even desire in the manner they proposed to introduce it; and I could not but express my great surprise at the strong stand they took on a matter which did not concern them, but their neighbours." The Scots, after talking piously of their duty to seek the salvation of their fellowmen, blurted out that they could not feel secure from the Auld Enemy unless she embraced their religion. Montereul replied with his usual realism that "I failed to see how they could have greater security against the English by the introduction of Presbyterianism into their country, since uniformity of religion did not prevent nations from going to war, when other considerations excited them to it".

In January, 1646, he went to see the King at Oxford, and gave him his considered advice. Since England, he said, would never consent to have Presbyterianism forced upon her, especially by a foreign nation as was Scotland, his Majesty could use the Scots by consenting to their demands to establish their creed, and then trust to a parliament to disestablish it as soon as he had regained his throne. He was speaking, so he believed, as one statesman to another, and Charles's reply astounded him: "he at once told me his conscience would not allow him to consent to the ruin of the religion he had sworn to maintain, and that he would rather lose his crown than his soul".

It was the stand Charles was to maintain, despite every argument of men of the world, every accusation of obstinacy, every bribe and every threat offered him by his fellow-countrymen, every entreaty of his beloved wife, until that January morning three years later when, rather than violate his conscience and his Coronation Oath, he sacrificed not only his crown but his life.

Yet there were several considerations, Charles told Montereul, which inclined him at this juncture to seek refuge with the Scots. He believed them sincerely anxious for peace; he could not believe that they would wish him to force Presbyterianism upon an unwilling England; and he was desperately anxious for the safety of Montrose. The French envoy, who had summed up the Scots with cynical shrewdness, was dismayed by Charles's illusions concerning them as displayed in the first two considerations; but he was touched by the nature of the King's concern, not merely for a loyal subject who deserved his protection, but for Montrose the friend. "He went so far as to say," wrote Montereul, "he would in future consider him as one of his children, and that he wished to live with him henceforward as a friend rather than as a king."

His own growing admiration for Charles impelled the Frenchman to intensify his efforts to induce his Majesty to come to terms with the Scots as the only means of saving his throne, perhaps even his life. For the King's situation was becoming ever more desperate. He had no longer an army of any consequence either in England or Scotland; the Prince of Wales was in imminent danger of capture by Fairfax; his younger children were prisoners; and there was an ominous rumour that in case he consented to come to London to negotiate personally with the Parliament, the principal apartment in the Tower had been furnished for his reception.[18]

Throughout February the scene continued to darken. Dartmouth, the last seaport in Royalist hands, had been taken by storm on January 18th; on February 3rd Chester surrendered, and on the 16th Hopton was defeated at Torrington. Soon the New Model would be able to concentrate its strength against Oxford, the royal headquarters, and, if he remained there, to capture the person of the King. The Independents were talking openly of their intention to depose him, to declare the Prince of Wales (whom they had failed to catch) an enemy of the State, and to crown the King's youngest son, the little Duke of Gloucester, making the Earl of Northumberland Protector. Meanwhile, to counter the possibility of the King's going to the Scots, Fairfax advanced a portion of his cavalry between Oxford and the Scottish camp at Newark.

One hope only remained to Charles; it lay in the growing

friction between the allies which had defeated him, and particularly in the coldness, developing into downright hostility, of the English towards the Scots. "The divisions between the two nations are so great," observed Montereul, who had returned to London, "that the resolution to oblige the Scots to send back two thousand horse was carried in both Houses of Parliament, so that both nations are merely awaiting the signal, so to speak, to begin to quarrel." Such was the situation when the Scots Commissioners in London gave to Montereul that promise the violation of which was to brand them with eternal infamy:

"That the King of Great Britain would not only be in safety in their army, but that he would be received there with every respect and all obedience due to him."[19]

Cynical though he was, Montereul did not question the keeping of so solemn and definite a promise made by eminent men, the representatives of their government; but, very naturally, he desired to have it in writing. This the Scots Commissioners absolutely refused, giving as their reason that the English would reproach them with the violation of that Article in the Solemn League and Covenant in which both parties had sworn never to suffer themselves to be divided. For the same reason the Commissioners were desirous that the King, when he came to them, should leave behind him "any of those against whom the English Parliament has shown the greatest irritation, in order that it may not be said they received into their army those whom they knew to be the enemies of this Parliament". While regarding with contempt such quibbling, Montereul was deceived into believing that "what they promise will be performed", and he had no hesitation in assuring Mazarin that the King would be in safety in the Scottish camp.

He had misjudged not only the Scots but the King. Charles's keen anxiety for his friends, and particularly for Montrose, had led Montereul to believe that if he could induce the Scots to promise them protection, Charles on his side would make the concession of signing the Covenant. Accordingly the Frenchman paid particular court to Chancellor Loudoun, the least fanatical of the Commissioners, and managed to wring from him the promise that the King should not be required to abandon any of his friends, and that if Montrose would consent to leave Scotland for a short period, his estates and all his offices would be restored to him. Further than this, Montereul persuaded Loudoun to concede that in regard to the Covenant all the King would be asked to do was to express, in a letter to both Houses, his approval of it. This, argued the casuistic Montereul, would not oblige him to keep it, since he had not actually signed it.

But Charles was not casuistic; and he could not express approval of a covenant the intention of which was to force Presbyterianism upon England, the head of whose Church he was. In his letters to his wife, who was urging him to take the Covenant in order to save his crown and possibly his life, he tried again and again to make his position clear. "For I assure thee," he wrote, "I put little or no difference in setting up the Presbyterian government or submitting to the Church of Rome. Therefore make the case thine own. With what patience wouldst thou give an ear to him who would persuade thee, for worldly respects, to leave the community of the Roman Church for any other? Indeed, sweetheart, this is my case; for suppose my concession in this should prove but temporary, it may palliate tho' not excuse my sin." "And consider," he wrote touchingly in another letter to his beloved wife, "that if I should quit my conscience, how unworthy I make myself of thy love."[20]

Convinced at last that this was the rock on which all his negotiations must founder, Montereul, by his eloquence and diplomacy, wrung from the Scots Commissioners a final and most vital concession. While still refusing to put anything in writing, they gave him their solemn promise "that the King of Great Britain will neither be obliged to sign nor to approve the Covenant". If he would place himself in the hands of the Scots, he would be safe "both in person, honour, and conscience". It was *this* concession which induced Charles to the fatal decision of entrusting himself into the hands of his fellow-countrymen.[21]

At the end of March, his ears ringing with the appeals of each member of the Scots Commission to persuade the King to go to their army, Montereul left London for Oxford. Having arranged with Charles that the latter should follow him to the Scottish army, and with the Scots that they should send a detachment of their horse to protect him on his journey, the French envoy arrived on April 7th at the Covenant's camp before Newark, which town they were besieging. He discovered immediately two things.

First that the Scots had not the slightest intention of abiding by the promises made to him by their Commissioners; and secondly that he was deprived of all means of communicating with Charles, and thus was unable to warn him against putting himself in the hands of these traitors.

Chapter Three

O<small>N</small> April 6th Charles wrote to the Queen, enclosing a particular account by Secretary Nicholas of the conditions on which he was going to the Scots. "I shall be received into the Scotch army," he wrote, "as their natural Sovereign, with freedom of my conscience and honour, and all my servants and followers are to be there safely and honourably protected."[22]

There followed a painful period during which he heard nothing from Montereul; it was not until the 16th that the latter found means of communicating with Secretary Nicholas and warning him of the Covenanters' perfidy. In regard to church government, they desired his Majesty to grant the imposing of Presbyterianism upon England as quickly as possible; and as for his friends, they would receive only his nephews, the Princes Rupert and Maurice, and one of his gentlemen, Mr. Ashburnham. Even these must be surrendered by them to the Parliament if it should choose to demand them.

"This is all the account that has been taken here," wrote Montereul indignantly, "of the assurances given in the name of the King my master [Louis of France], and of the promises I had from them in London, and the best I was able to obtain from them after a long discussion, for what they proposed at first was still more rude." He was at his wits' end to give advice, but while considering that if Charles could make other arrangements it would be best for him to do so, "I am still bold enough to assure him that though he will not find all the satisfaction he may wish, he will at least find every possible safety" if he went to the Scots.

Montereul's news roused in Charles a rare anger. "In short," he wrote to the Queen, "the Scots are abominable relapsed rogues, and Montereul himself is ashamed of them, they having retracted almost all which they made him promise me."

A moment had now arrived when the King must act and act quickly, for in a few days Oxford would be closely invested by the New Model. Determined to avoid capture by the soldiery, he prepared to escape from the city, commanding his nephews, Rupert and Maurice, to accept a pass from the Parliament to go overseas, and permitting to accompany him only Ashburnham and a Dr. Michael Hudson. On April 22nd he wrote the Queen, telling her of his intention to escape he knew not whither, and concluding: "In the meantime I conjure thee, by thy constant love to me, that if I should miscarry (whether by being taken by the rebels or otherwise), to continue the same active endeavours for Prince Charles as thou hast done for me, and not whine for my misfortunes in a retired way, but, like thy father's daughter, vigorously assist Prince Charles to regain his own."[23]

At three o'clock in the morning of the 26th, the little party rode over Magdalen Bridge; and for days they wandered aimlessly and in great peril, protected only by a pass which Hudson had obtained from a captain who was going to London on the business of compounding for his estates. On one occasion a trooper of the New Model actually rode a stage in their company, not recognizing the King, whose hair and beard had been shorn by way of disguise.

From Baldock Charles sent Hudson to Montereul who was at Southwell, to see if by any chance the Frenchman had succeeded in bringing the Scots into a better frame of mind. It appeared that he had. If the King would come to their camp, not only would they send out a party to escort him safely thither, but they would "condescend to all the demands which the King and Montereul had agreed to make to them, before Montereul came from Oxford". What both Charles and the French envoy failed to see was the reason for this sudden *volte face*. News had leaked out that the King had left Oxford, no man knew whither, and the Scots were in a panic lest he should either have gone to London to negotiate with the Parliament, or have come to terms with the Independents. The former was still supposed to be their friend; but it had made it brutally clear to them that it was going to manage its own affairs without regard to the Solemn League and Covenant.[24]

The Covenanters still refused to put anything in writing, but Hudson, backed up by Montereul, prevailed so far as to obtain permission for himself to set down on paper, "to avoid mistakes", the conditions under which they were now willing to receive their Sovereign:

" 1. That they should secure the King in his person and honour. 2. That they should press the King to do nothing contrary to his conscience. 3. That Mr. Ashburnham and I should be protected. 4. That if the Parliament refused, upon a message from the King, to restore the King to his rights and prerogatives, they should declare for the King, and take all the King's friends into their protection. And if the Parliament did condescend to restore the King, then the Scots should be a means that not above four of them [the Royalists] should suffer banishment; and none at all, death. This done, the French agent sent me word, that the Scots seriously protested the performance of all these [promises]; and writ a little note to the King to accept them and such security as was given to him on the King's behalf."[25]

Armed with these solemn promises, which were better even than those given to Montereul by the Scots Commissioners in London, Hudson returned to the King, who, because of these promises the sincerity of which he could not doubt, finally decided to take refuge with his fellow-countrymen. He could not know that they were willing to promise anything so long as they could entice him into their hands. He could not know that their purpose in doing so was either to force him to impose their religion on England and Ireland, or else to use him as a supreme asset in their bargaining with their former ally for their pay. He could not know that they had every intention of forswearing themselves as soon as he was in their power.

In actual fact they began to forswear themselves even before he arrived in their camp. They refused to send out the promised party of horse to meet and escort him, and for some days Montereul was in a fever of anxiety lest he had been captured or killed *en route*. But the weary King and his two companions arrived safely in the Scottish camp at six o'clock in the morning of May 5th; his reception is described by Sir James Turner, who was still serving in the Covenant's army as sergeant-major in Lord Sinclair's regiment:

"There did Earl Lothian, as president of the Committee, to his eternal reproach, imperiously require his Majesty (before he had either drunk, refreshed, or reposed himself), to command my Lord Bellasis to deliver up Newark to the Parliament's forces, to sign the Covenant, to order the establishment of presbyterian government in England and Ireland, and to command James Grahame (for so he called great Montrose) to lay down arms; all which the King stoutly refused, telling him that he who had made him an earl, had made James Grahame a marquis. Barbarously used he was, strong guards put upon him, and sentinels at all his windows, that he should cast over no letters."

Having seen for himself the uselessness of further resistance by stout Lord Bellasis, the Royalist Governor of Newark, Charles sent him orders to surrender the town on terms. As soon as this was done, the Scots struck camp and, taking the King with them, began a rapid march towards the Border, where they proposed to sit down and bargain with their former allies, secure in the knowledge that they could retreat into their own country if need arose. But they had no intention of leaving England without their money.

At Newcastle, where they encamped, their treatment of the King became harsher. Already he had been pestered to sign the Covenant, "so ungraciously that they could not have done differently," wrote Montereul, "had they wished to give him an aversion for the establishment of their Presbyterianism". All their promises had gone with the wind. Ashburnham was forced to flee in order to escape arrest by them; the mayors of Durham and Newcastle, who came to pay their respects to the King, were forbidden to do so; and Charles was treated openly as a prisoner.

Worst of all, perhaps, was the Covenanters' refusal to believe that his resistance to the attempts made to force him to sign the Covenant was grounded in conscience. The "sweet Prince" and "our own native-born Sovereign" of Baillie's early letters, had now become "that obstinate man", who, if he refused to surrender his friends and betray the Episcopacy he was pledged by his Coronation Oath to maintain, was mad. Charles's protests against the assaults upon his conscience, "I never," wrote Baillie, "took to be conscientious, but merely politic, and a pretence to gain time", while as for the Coronation Oath, "No oaths did ever persuade me that Episcopacy was adhered to on any conscience".[26] A conscience was, apparently, the exclusive possession of the Covenanters.

The only excuse the Scots had for denying the King's sincerity was his consistent willingness to listen to their theological arguments, and the courtesy with which he repaid their insolence. He supported their rude treatment "with an equanimity that I cannot enough admire," wrote Montereul, "having a kindly demeanour towards those who show him no respect, and who treat him with very little civility." The temper of his jailers was not improved by the fact that in theological argument Charles was infinitely the superior of their ministers. The papers which passed backwards and forwards between the King and Alexander Henderson on the subject were printed, and, as Burnet put it, "had his Majesty's arms been as strong as his reason was, he had been every way unconquerable, since none have the disingenuity to deny the great advantages his Majesty had in all these writings. And this was when the help of his chaplains could not be suspected, they being so far from him."[27]

But though well able to fight single-handed in such wordy battles, the deeply religious King felt most acutely the lack of the ministrations of his chaplains and the comfort of the Anglican worship to which he was so devoted. His loneliness at this period is awful to contemplate. In his letters to his wife he touchingly referred to the infrequency of hers, the majority of which were intercepted. "Indeed I have need of some comfort, for I never knew what it was to be barbarously baited before, and these five or six days last have much surpassed in rude pressure against my conscience all the rest since I came to the Scotch army." And again: "I cannot but remember thee that there was never man so alone as I . . . all the comfort I have is thy love and a clear conscience. I know the first will not fail me, nor (by the grace of God) the other."[28]

His jailers now took from him the other companion of his journey to them, Dr. Michael Hudson, thus violating one more of their solemn promises, and increasing the King's anxiety for the rest of his friends, and especially for Montrose. Disillusioned now about the worth of Scottish promises, Charles could think of no way to protect his champion except to arrange through Montereul that Montrose and the remainder of his forces should be allowed to go to France as recruits in the French armies. When, at the end of May, Montereul himself left for France in order to inform the Queen and Mazarin of the state of Charles's affairs, he had hopes of saving Montrose by this means, "but," he wrote from the depths of his own disillusionment, "I am in a country where people's promises and their performance of them are somewhat different". While he himself was both baffled and irritated by Charles's consistent refusal to violate his conscience in order to save his throne, he was shrewd and honest enough to admit that "perhaps were he to grant it them, they might do nothing for him of what he wishes".

On the eve of Montereul's leaving Newcastle there arrived there Chancellor Loudoun, who was followed shortly afterwards by "King Campbell" himself. The delay in the coming of the dictator was due to the fact that he had been experiencing a tiresome and humiliating time at home.

Some fifteen hundred of his Campbells, forced out of Argyllshire by Colkitto (who was still busy settling old scores) had been making themselves a nuisance to the country by their burning and stealing. In February they had been overtaken at Callander by seven hundred Atholl-men who were determined to protect their homes from the marauders. The Campbells, ordinarily brave enough, appear to have been infected with the same spirit which had caused their lord to flee from three separate battlefields, and though more than double the number of their assailants, had turned tail and fled.

Argyll was at Stirling on his way to Ireland to fetch over from thence the Scottish regiments ("that being strengthened with that accession, their power might be so formidable to the English as to make them, to eschew a national quarrel, deal more thankfully with the Covenanters"), when he encountered his Campbells with their tails between their legs. Though for the present he had no use for them, he was obliged to arrange for their maintenance; but his first attempt to do so was a dismal failure. He tried to plant them on the shire of Renfrew, which was hot for the Covenant; it was not, however, amenable to having Campbells quartered upon it. The Renfrew people went so far as to threaten to drive the Campbells out by force if they were not removed, so Argyll sent them into the Lennox, to live on the lands of Lord Napier and other Royalists there.[29]

Having solved this little problem, Argyll hastened to Newcastle, where he stayed for a fortnight and then departed to London, "with great professions of doing me service there," Charles wrote to the Queen; "his errand (as is pretended) is only to hasten down and moderate the demands which are coming to me from thence". In another letter he wrote wearily, and with a most uncharacteristic cynicism: "Argyll is very civil and cunning, but his journey to London will show whether he be altered or not (if he be, it must be for the better)."

The demands to which Charles referred were in the form of nineteen propositions drawn up by the Parliament; by these Charles was to sign the Covenant himself and impose it on England and Ireland (a sop to the Scots, who might be useful in persuading him to sign), and give the control of the Militia and of the Navy to the Parliament for twenty years, at the end of which time Parliament would decide upon their future management, with or without the King's assent. Thus Charles was to give away the ancient rights of the Crown not only for himself but for his posterity.

A copy of the Nineteen Propositions was delivered to the Scots Commissioners in London; and on June 25th Argyll made a speech to Committees of both Houses in the Painted Chamber. His biographer, Mr. Willcock, observes of him on this occasion: "His romantic personality as a Highland chieftain of princely rather than patrician rank, the commanding position he was known to have attained in Scotland, his stalwart and successful resistance to the royal policy, and his recent misfortunes in warfare, must have all contributed to the interest of seeing and hearing him on that day."[30] If there were any of the military Members present, his "misfortunes in warfare" can scarcely have impressed them.

Like most of his speeches, this one was ambiguous. "We are to look that we persecute not Piety and peaceable Men," he declared, "who cannot through scruple of Conscience come up in all things to the common rule; but that they may have such a Forbearance as may be best according to the Word of God, may consist with the Covenant, and not be destructive to the Rule itself."[31] His method of honouring his promises to do the King service and moderate these Propositions which would have destroyed the Monarchy in everything except name, was to announce that he and his countrymen thoroughly approved of them, and that his own hope was for an actual union between the two nations. Thus in Richard Cromwell's Parliament in 1659 he was to be able to remind the House that "I was here in '46, in your service".

On July 7th his commission from the General Assembly to sit in the Assembly of Divines was approved by both Houses, and accordingly he was escorted with great ceremony to the Jerusalem Chamber and greeted by the Moderator in a flowery speech. "In the midst of all difficulties we have ever found encouragement from that famous, religious, and pure Church implanted in that Kingdom. . . . And to crown all the rest it is the joy of our hearts to find a person of so great honour and renown, in which the greatest safety of the Kingdom of Scotland is reposed. . . . We look upon your Lordship as the greatest instrument under God", and so on.

While Argyll was thus enjoying himself in London, there had arrived at Newcastle an erstwhile friend of the King's, the Duke of Hamilton, released by the New Model from his Cornish prison. He who once upon a time had expressed such abhorrence of the National Covenant, now straightway urged Charles to sign its far more intolerable successor: "God," he assured his Majesty, "would never lay it to his charge, since his inducements to it were so strong and unavoidable." Needless to say, Hamilton's arguments had no more weight with the King than the rest, and in August the Duke left for Scotland. He returned in September with Cassilis and Crawford-Lindsay on a commission from the Committee of Estates to press Charles to sign the Nineteen Propositions; according to Burnet, Hamilton came unwillingly upon this errand, "but there was no avoiding it"— why, it is difficult to imagine. Shortly afterwards he left for

Scotland once more, never to see again the master he had served so ill, except for one moment when the King was on his way to execution.

It was now clear to everyone (and the King cannot be excepted) that the alternative to accepting these Propositions was deposition or something much more sinister. Tracts were being circulated in London to prepare the people's minds for the former; and some while before, Baillie had written the ominous sentence: "I abhor to think of it, what they speak of execution." The only hope remained in the Scots. Loudoun had declared to the English Parliament that his countrymen "would not do so base an act, as to render up their prince's person, who was come to them for safety in so great a danger; and that this act could not consist with their duty and allegiance, or Covenant, or with the honour of their army, it being contrary to law and common practice of all nations, in case even of private men".[32]

While Montereul, who had arrived in London from France in July, tried every means to induce the Scots Commissioners to honour such solemn statements, M. Bellièvre, President of the French Law Courts, and newly appointed Ambassador to England, went to Newcastle, where he arrived on July 30th. Here he joined his voice to the chorus which urged Charles to save himself on any terms, neglecting, as he wrote to the French Secretary of State, "neither prayers nor threats". On the other hand he did everything he could think of to induce the Scots "to oppose the ruin of their King and take upon themselves the glory of his re-establishment. To accomplish this I try to awaken in them all that concerns their honour, with some mention of money, of which I have offered very considerable sums to private individuals, and I believe I should not be disavowed [by France] if they had done what I had reason to calculate on from people really avaricious, but poor, without credit and very selfish."[33]

But whatever sense of honour the Covenanters possessed had long been stifled; and as for money, they were out for far greater sums than any Bellièvre could offer. They were out for what England owed them for their "brotherly assistance" in defeating the King in the field; and in return for that they were prepared to deliver Charles, their "own native-born Sovereign" whom they had sworn to protect, into the hands of those who were talking openly of his deposition, secretly of his death.

Chapter Four

O<small>N</small> August 18th, in the midst of a description of the trial of the godliness of certain elders, Baillie wrote a line or two on the squalid question of money. The Parliament at last was prepared to put its hand into the pockets of English taxpayers as the only means for getting rid of the Scots on the one hand, and of getting hold of the person of the King on the other. One hundred thousand pounds sterling was their offer; but the Scots were "peremptor" for more than double that sum down, besides future settlement of the debt to the last farthing. There ensued a haggling which went on for months.

When President Bellièvre had gone to Newcastle, he had left behind him in London his younger brother; and on September 6th Bellièvre junior sent a report on this sordid wrangle. The Parliament had now offered two hundred thousand pounds, half of it down, and half as soon as the Scots had left the kingdom. "But the Scots, having always stated and offered to show that they owe in England the two hundred thousand pounds that they demand, which they wish to pay before leaving the kingdom, there is reason to believe that they will not be satisfied with this, in which case some of the members of the Lower House have decided no longer to offer a lump sum, but to demand to have a reckoning with the Scots, hoping to show that they have received more contributions which they have levied, than they claim on their account."

The Scots, however, continued to hold out for their two hundred thousand cash down, and as a gentle hint to the Parliament that they were prepared to give value for money, they inserted into a paper on the subject the question, "What was to be done regarding the person of the King of England?" It proved effective; in the middle of September the Parliament gave in. The Scots were to have the two hundred thousand before leaving the kingdom, fifty thousand in three months' time, a similar sum in six months, and one hundred thousand within the space of two years.

Next arose the delicate question, where was this enormous sum to be obtained? The obvious place was the City, but when the Mayor and Common Council suggested taxing the merchant corporation, the latter did not seem inclined to give their money willingly. The City was strongly Presbyterian, and therefore, as Baillie declared, "our loving friends; but," he added, "before they will part with more money, they will press hard the disbanding of their own army as well as ours". There was nothing the Parliament would have liked better, but the New Model had not the slightest intention of being disbanded, and was too formidable to offend. At last an English Presbyterian divine suggested a way out, which was to assign the principal and interest of the loan upon the sale of the Bishops' lands, thus making sure that the City would oppose the King tooth and nail if he persisted in standing by the Bishops.

Having achieved the real purpose for which he had come to London, the bargaining for the "brotherly assistance", Argyll prepared to return to Newcastle. At the end of September, Baillie wrote to David Dickson: "It's like you may see the Marquis of Argyll shortly. The Lord help him out of his troubles; his enemies are many, and friends for any purpose but few; yet God is not dead." Possibly Baillie was unaware how extremely well Argyll had done for himself out of the public transaction.

He was to receive thirty thousand pounds for himself, ten thousand of which was to be cash down, and another fifteen thousand for his friends, while his Campbells were to be maintained by a "voluntary" contribution from all the parishes in Scotland. In the debates on the subject in Parliament, on the eve of Argyll's leaving for Newcastle on his way home, "Sir Henry Mildmay made a long speech in praise of Argyll, saying, That he and his party, and the Scottish clergy, were the only men that upheld the English interest in Scotland, and were better friends to us than all Scotland besides; wherefore he moved, that Argyll might be paid his 10,000 l, and the rest continued at interest at 8 l per cent". Hamilton likewise received thirty thousand, Wariston a modest three thousand, "and several of the Kirk's ministers were enriched".[34]

All that remained was the collection of the money and the giving up of the King's person. At the beginning of October, when Montereul had returned to Newcastle, he found Argyll's party there suspiciously anxious to induce Charles to go voluntarily to London, on the excuse that he would be better able to negotiate with Parliament in person. The truth was, of course, as Bellièvre junior had written to Brienne, that "the Scots are much at a loss, fearing, on the one hand, the disgrace they cannot escape in delivering him up, and on the other, the danger that threatens them if they refuse". For both the Independents and the common people were violently hostile to them, and Baillie was "in great fears the country shall break out in violence against our army" if it did not remove itself.

Throughout October and November the enormous price of betrayal was being collected, though the threatening advance of the New Model towards the Scottish camp indicated that the Independents still hoped to force the Scots to withdraw without their pay. While in Newcastle Argyll was saying that the promises his countrymen had made to the King would be honoured so long as Charles, even though a prisoner of the Parliament, was served on the knee, in London Baillie was rejoicing in the fact that at last the money had come in. "This night," he wrote, on December 8th, "I count us as good as agreed for the sending down of our money, and the return of our army; I think on Monday, if not sooner, it will go. We receive, at Northallerton, one hundred thousand pounds, and the other beyond the Tyne, when Newcastle is delivered; before a month, all is like to be ended."

Four days later Sir Robert Moray wrote to Hamilton: "The King hath heard of the particular appointment of the payment of the 200,000 *l.* and the march of our army with his wonted unmovedness." It is said that the only comment Charles made was, "I am ashamed that my price is so much higher than my Master's".

There followed, however, weeks of further haggling before the bargain was completed. The Scots desired hostages to ensure that the second hundred thousand would be paid them half a mile outside Newcastle when they had crossed the Tyne; the English demanded the like until Carlisle and Berwick were delivered to them. There were unseemly squabbles over the nature of the securities to be given to the Scots for the remainder of their money; there were frantic endeavours on the Scottish side to persuade the English to give them troops for use in Scotland; and there were internal quarrels in the Parliament about the disposal of the King once it had got him into its hands. Many were extremely averse from his being brought to London, "having no doubt," Bellièvre junior wrote to Brienne, "but that the people would deliver him in order to restore him to the throne, so great is the desire they say people have to do it".

On Christmas Day, carts laden with specie left London, escorted by three thousand horse and two thousand foot under the command of old Skippon who had been appointed Governor of Newcastle. At the same time the Scots Commissioners took their leave of Parliament, and received a public snub. It being moved in the House that they should be thanked for their civilities and good offices, it was carried by twenty-four votes that they should be thanked for the former only. "And so all those noble characters they were wont to give of the Scottish Commissioners, upon every occasion, concluded now in this, that they were well-bred gentlemen."[35]

The Commissioners of both Houses appointed to receive the person of the King left London on January 23rd, 1647, and arrived at Newcastle on February 4th. President Bellièvre had already left the Scottish camp, telling the Covenanters roundly, in taking leave of them, that they had lured their King into their midst under false pretences; but Montereul had returned thither after a brief visit to Edinburgh, and made one last attempt to induce the Scots to see themselves as others saw them.

It was in vain. The Committee of Estates, they said, had sent them positive orders to deliver up the King; and not even the astonishing constancy with which Charles supported their betrayal, nor his failure to speak one word of reproach, awakened in their breasts a feeling of shame. On Saturday, February 11th, the Scots, "as if vain of their infamy," wrote Montereul, "paraded all their cavalry through the centre of this town, and before the King's residence, and left it to the English garrison that arrived about two o'clock, and delivering up their King at the same time to the English Commissioners, no one being allowed to be present when they took leave of him, perhaps in the fear that, whatever precautions they might take, they might be reproached with their treachery in presence of the English".

Thus the two partners in the Solemn League and Covenant bade farewell to one another with no love lost on either side. As for the common people, they showed their opinion of the Scots in no uncertain manner. As the carts laden with the reward of betrayal rumbled over the cobbles, closely guarded by Leven's troopers, shouts of "Jews!" arose above the sound of the wheels, and it was only by dint of blows and threats that the English prevented the townsfolk from stoning the Scottish soldiers.[36] In London, meanwhile, a pasquinade was being sold in the streets:

> "The Scots must have two hundred thousand pound
> To sell their King and quit our English ground;
> And, Judas-like, I hope 'twill be their lots
> To hang themselves—so farewell lousie Scots!"[37]

"They entered the Kingdom contrary to all Faith and Grati-

M

tude, as well as Loyalty and Obedience, and at last quitted it
with Ignominy and Dishonour: Never were people more com-
plimented at their Arrival, more oblig'd while they were wanted,
and more contemn'd at their Departure. They departed with
a Reward, but likewise with a Curse, as many observe; for from
that time they never flourish'd, or prosper'd in any one undertaking."[38]

PART FOUR

THE STRUGGLE FOR POWER: ARGYLL *versus* HAMILTON 1647-1648

Chapter One

IT was now the spring of 1647, and everywhere former allies were busy falling out among themselves. In England the breach between the New Model and the Parliament which had created it was growing ever wider; in Scotland dissensions began among the Covenanting leaders. One of the first clashes was on the subject of money.

Not content with the vast sums he had obtained from England, Argyll clamoured for the arrears of the pension bestowed upon him in his youth by the King he had just betrayed. Montereul, who was in Scotland on his business of collecting recruits for French service, described the scene which ensued. Argyll represented to the Estates "the services he had rendered to the Kingdom, and exaggerated in servile terms the losses he had sustained, representing the misery to which he was reduced, stating, as I am assured, that he had no bread for his wife and children, and demanding that his pension be paid out of the first sums at the disposal of the Treasurer".

Lanerick rose at once and said he found it strange that Argyll should ask for something which was clean contrary to the rules of Parliament, which laid it down that the Officers of Estate should receive their pensions first and those who had private pensions from the King afterwards. To this Argyll's kinsman, Chancellor Loudoun, retorted that Argyll's demand was so well founded that he himself was content to receive his pension after him, and he had no doubt that other Officers of Estate would be so likewise. He was at once contradicted by Lanerick, who said acidly that, not being named Campbell, but Hamilton, the Chancellor must excuse him if he did not decide to follow his example. Argyll lost his temper, and "forgot himself so far as to say that this treatment, which he had so little expected, would cause him to decide on asking a passport to leave the kingdom". The result of such a threat from King Campbell was to cause the Board of Exchequer to order that the pensions of Argyll and Loudoun be paid before those of anyone else.[1]

Thus there began to appear the beginnings of two distinct parties in Covenanting Scotland, the Hamilton clique and that of Argyll. "It is to be remarked," Montereul wrote Mazarin, "that the more the King's affairs are depressed, the more the division, which was thought to be more pretended than real, between the Duke of Hamilton and the Marquis of Argyll increases, so that they are of opposite opinions in everything but what concerns the ruin of their King; and that although they speak to each other and dine together very often, it is seen that they look upon themselves as the only persons who can mutually destroy each other, and that while the Marquis will not brook having a master, the Duke does not want a companion."

In his determination to remain dictator, Argyll was perfectly willing to continue fawning upon the Auld Enemy, and to throw away the national heritage. He told Montereul that "England and Scotland would unite so closely as to form but one kingdom, as they were one island, and that their peoples had no longer but one religion"; the second statement was as manifestly false as the first was unpatriotic. The long history of Scotland's struggle to retain her independence was known to no one better than Argyll; and apart from the Church of England, to which the vast majority in that nation were warmly attached, both Parliament and Army were riddled with a multiplicity of sects which detested the Presbyterians as heartily as the Presbyterians detested them.

The Estates rose towards the end of April, having transmitted their authority to the usual Committee; and Argyll left Edinburgh to go to the army which, under David Leslie, had been mopping up the remains of revolt at home.

Despite an attempted trick to capture him, Montrose had succeeded in leaving Scotland in the previous September, but Huntly remained in arms in the North, and Colkitto was somewhere in Kintyre. When the Covenant's army reached home after selling the King, five thousand foot and twelve hundred horse had been kept under arms, and with these Leslie had marched off to capture Huntly's strongholds, and, if possible, Huntly himself. Before accepting this commission, Leslie had asked permission to come to terms with the Cock o' the North if the latter surrendered, but this the Estates, under the influence of Argyll, absolutely refused, and Huntly, his son, Aboyne, and

Colkitto, were all exempted from pardon. Argyll had waited a long time to get his talons upon his brother-in-law's estates, and he was growing a little impatient.

Having captured Huntly's strongholds, Leslie left Sir John Middleton to pursue the Gordon Chief who, as usual, had taken refuge in the wilds of the Highlands, and marched to deal with Coll. On May 16th he was joined by Argyll at Dunblane; on the 21st they were at Inveraray, and reached Kintyre on the 24th. Lacking the leadership of Montrose, Colkitto allowed them to pass unmolested through the narrow passes of that peninsula, where a successful attack might well have been delivered; and putting three hundred of his soldiers into a small fortified house called Dunavertie, where they had "not a drop of water but what fell from the clouds", went himself to Islay, and, leaving his old father there, retired to Ireland.

The horrible story of Dunavertie may best be told in the unemotional words of Sir James Turner, who was serving as Adjutant under Lieutenant-General Leslie:

"We besieged Dunavertie, which keeped [held] out well enough, till we stormed a trench they had at the foot of the hill, whereby they commanded two strips of water. This we did take in the assault. Forty of them were put to the sword. We lost five or six, with Argyll's major. After this, inexorable thirst made them desire a parley. I was ordered to speak with them; neither could the Lieutenant-General be moved to grant any other conditions, than that they should yield on discretion or mercy; and it seemed strange to me to hear the Lieutenant-General's nice distinction, that they should yield themselves to the kingdom's mercy, and not to his. At length they did so; and after they were come out of the Castle, they were put to the sword, every mother's son, except one young man, Mackonnel, whose life I begged, to be sent to France with a hundred country fellows whom we had smoked out of a cave, as they do foxes, who were given to Captain Campbell, the Chancellor's brother."[2]

It would appear that Leslie himself was reluctant to permit such butchery, but, as at Philiphaugh, it was Argyll and the Kirk who had the final say. Leslie's chaplain, John Nevoy, threatened him with the curse which befell Saul for sparing the Amalekites; and Argyll and Nevoy between them so worked on Leslie that "the army was let loose upon them and killed them all without mercy. Whereat David Leslie seemed to have some inward check: For while the Marquis and he, with Mr. Nevoy, were walking over the ankles in blood, he turned about and said, *Now, Mr. John, have you once gotten your fill of blood?*

This was reported by many that heard it."[3]   The commander of Dunavertie, a MacDonald, was strung up on the spot but, the gibbet being found to be so short that his feet touched the ground, he was subsequently shot.

Thence the Covenanters marched into Islay, and invested Dunneveg, the fort in which Colkitto's father was sheltering. The old man, accepting Leslie's safe conduct to come and speak with a friend of his, the Governor of Dunstaffnage Castle, was promptly made prisoner, tried by a jury of Campbells, his hereditary foes, and hanged. Leslie and Argyll were marching on to Jura and Mull, when an express arrived with the news of the abduction of the King from Holmby House by the New Model Army, and the Marquis returned post haste to Edinburgh.

Here he found Montereul, who requested that he might have all the prisoners captured during the recent campaign as recruits for French service, offering five hundred jacobuses for them. Torn between his greed and his reluctance to allow any enemy to escape from his clutches, Argyll's cunning hit upon a way out of the dilemma. He suggested that, instead of the prisoners, Montereul should have some of the Gordons, under the command of Huntly's third son, Lord Lewis, who, he said, he thought he could persuade to enter the service of France " if good terms were offered him ". In other words, he wanted France to provide for his nephew, while he annexed that nephew's patrimony. On hearing a rumour that Colkitto was trying to negotiate an agreement with the Estates whereby he should captain some recruits for Spanish service, Argyll flew into a rage, and told Montereul that the only agreement the Estates would ever make with Coll " would be whether they would make him shorter or longer than he was, that is to say, by consulting whether it were better to behead him or to have him hung ".[4]

The news of the abduction of the King, and still more of the march of the abductors upon London, alarmed not only the English but the Scottish Parliament, while the discreet withdrawal from the former of the leading Presbyterians, made " the Scots look upon the ruin of their religion as inevitable, attended also by that of their fortunes, which," added the cynical Montereul, " they consider much more important than their religion ". " The imprudence and cowardice of the greater part of the City and Parliament," Baillie wrote furiously to his cousin Spang, " which was triple or sextuple the greater, has permitted a company of silly rascals,* which calls themselves as yet no

* The great New Model! The Presbyterians, both English and Scots, had always underestimated the power of the Army.

more than fourteen thousand, horse and foot, to make themselves master of the King, and Parliament, and City, and by
them of all England. . . . Parliament and City, as their masters
command, are ready to declare against us if we should offer to
arm: But if the King would call, I doubt not of the raising of
the best army ever we had, for the crushing of these serpents,
enemies of God and man."

The real fear was, of course, that the King might come to
terms with the Army, terms which, harsh though they would
be, at least would leave him the liberty of conscience denied him
by the Covenanters and their friends in the English Parliament.

Montereul had now come round again to his former opinion
that the rivalry between the Hamilton and Argyll cliques was
more apparent than real; he was misled by the fact that both
urged him to petition the Queen to send the Prince of Wales to
Scotland. What he did not realize was that, in the crisis which
was now coming to a head in England, the possession of the
Prince's person would be an enormous asset to both parties in
Scotland. To the Hamilton clique he would be a rallying-point
for the Royalists, as whose champion Hamilton, who had never
lost the King's affection, might appear; while Argyll and his
ally the Kirk could either force Prince Charles to sign the Covenant or else sell him as they had sold his father.

The first real clash between the rival potentates came in a
debate on the disbanding of David Leslie's forces. Hamilton
pressed for disbandment on the grounds that the army was not
only useless but burdensome to the kingdom; Argyll retorted
that never had there been so great a need for keeping up the
army, seeing that the King's person, which, he somewhat
belatedly remembered, they were pledged to defend by the terms
of the Covenant, had been seized by the Independents. Both
Hamilton and Argyll were well aware that they might need an
army, but whereas the first desired to disband the present one so
that he might raise new forces of his own, the second was
resolved to keep David Leslie's in being, because it was strongly
Covenant. Argyll's ally the Kirk drew up Remonstrance after
Remonstrance against disbandment, declaring Kirk and Kingdom to be in mortal danger; but the Hamilton faction, now
growing stronger, prevented these from being published. Hamilton himself decided to "wait upon events", and retired for a
while to his country seat, hoping that the elections for the new
parliament would give him the majority he required to triumph
over his rival.

Meanwhile renewed panic was caused by the news that

London had abandoned her line of forts to the New Model and had submitted to its will. Their Presbyterian allies thus lost to them, and the King in the hands of the " Sectaries ", the Committee of Estates resolved to send commissioners to "comfort and encourage" both the King and the Parliament, and to prevent the former from coming to terms with the Army. The English Parliament on their side sent letters to Argyll, expressing the hope that the rumour of the raising of a new army in Scotland was false, and declaring their confidence that Argyll would be an instrument to prevent it, and to maintain a good understanding between the two kingdoms.

The battle over the disbanding of David Leslie's forces continued throughout September. By Argyll's influence the matter was referred to a committee whose members the Marquis summoned from the remotest parts of the kingdom, and who, being his nominees, voted that, until it was seen how events went in England, the army should not disband. For the easing of taxation they obliged many of the officers to forgo "voluntarily" a third part of their pay, "for which simplicity the Kirk cried them up as good patriots; and this was enough to put these simpletons in the full possession of a fool's paradise".[5]

But in October the battle between Hamilton and Argyll turned in favour of the former, for the elections for the Parliament which was to meet in March gave the Duke an overwhelming majority. It was a genuine Royalist reaction, and it was very significant of the mood of the country; for more than half the burgesses and nearly half the gentry, hitherto the backbone of the Covenant's cause, had seceded from the camp of Argyll. There can be no doubt whatever that it sprang from a national disgust at the selling of the King, an act for which Argyll and the Kirk had been responsible.

Chapter Two

T HE end of the year 1647 was also the end of the resistance (such as it had been) of the Gordons. Two of Huntly's principal followers, Gordon of Newton and young Patrick Leith, Laird of Harthill, were executed in November; the former had received a special act of pardon from the King, which pardon Balmerino suggested should be attached to the severed head of the victim after execution.[6] In December Huntly himself was betrayed by one of his own people, brought prisoner to Edinburgh, and flung into the common jail. It was known that Argyll thirsted for his blood, but his friends pinned their hopes on Hamilton's ascendancy, hopes which appeared to be justified when, in the Committee of Estates, Huntly's condemnation to death was delayed, by one vote, till the meeting of Parliament.

Hamilton was now in active communication with the King. A threat of assassination had induced Charles to escape from Hampton Court and take refuge in the Isle of Wight, where he believed that Robert Hammond, Governor of Carisbrooke Castle, would give him protection (a belief which proved unjustified); and in December the Scottish Commissioners who had been in London since October, visited him there. They were Hamilton's brother Lanerick, the Earl of Lauderdale, who was one of the leading men in Hamilton's party, and, rather surprisingly, Chancellor Loudoun, who was supposed to be attached to Argyll. Between these Commissioners and the King, Lord Traquair had been going backwards and forwards, negotiating a secret treaty; when the Commissioners came to Carisbrooke, ostensibly to protest against proposals made to Charles by the English Parliament, this treaty, which became known as the Engagement, was signed.

Charles on his side promised to establish Presbyterianism in England for three years, at the end of which time the settlement of religion was to be decided by Parliament after consultation with the Assembly of Divines, who were to be reinforced by twenty members nominated by the King. The Covenant was not to be imposed, however, on any who conscientiously objected to it, and in the Royal Household the Anglican worship was to remain undisturbed. Charles impressed upon the Commissioners, and took them as his witnesses, that he did not bind himself in any way to forward the Presbyterian cause in England.

The Engagers on their side promised that if the two Houses of Parliament would not agree to a general disbandment of the New Model and a personal treaty with the King which should preserve his just rights, the Scots would invade England on his behalf.

The terms of the Engagement were to be kept secret for the present, but Charles, most unwisely, ordered that they should be disclosed to Argyll. It was partly the King's ineradicable belief in the good faith of those who had shown themselves most hostile to him, partly because the concurrence of Argyll in the

Engagement would have meant a united Scotland behind it. Moreover Charles honestly believed that the concessions he had made would satisfy even so strict a Covenanter as Argyll was supposed to be. The King wrote him, therefore, the following letter:

"Argyll, howsoever, heretofore, you and I have differed in judgment, I believe now that the present state of affairs are such, as will make you heartily embrace my cause, it being grounded upon those particularly that were given in question between you and me: and for those things wherein you and I yet may be of several opinions, I have given such satisfaction to the Scots Commissioners, that with confidence I desire your concurrence in what hath been agreed between them and me, knowing your zeal to your country, and your many professions to me: as this bearer will more at large tell you, to whom referring you I rest, Your most assured real constant friend, Charles R. I desire you to believe whatsoever Traquair will tell you in my name."[7]

Shortly before this letter arrived, Argyll, alarmed by the growing ascendancy of the Hamiltons, had been thinking seriously of his own safety. He had approached Montereul with the suggestion that he might be given the command of Sir Robert Moray's regiment in the service of France; imagine, said he, how good this would be for recruiting. "It has occurred to me," wrote Montereul blandly, "that the bad condition of Presbyterianism and the Covenant in England at present, through which the Marquis has subsisted until now, leads him to augur badly for himself for the end of these troubles, and causes him to believe that he may one day require a protection as powerful as that of his Majesty [of France] and perhaps also a safe retreat."

It can scarcely be doubted that it was Argyll who disclosed to his old ally the Kirk the terms of the Engagement. At all events, by the middle of January 1648, the Kirk, which had been in a most militant mood, clamouring for its army to invade England and take revenge on the erstwhile ally who had broken the Covenant, now suddenly changed its tune. God was powerful enough, it said, to punish the Independents without the help of man. "Here," wrote Sir James Turner with his usual tartness, "you see an army necessary and not necessary, for one and the same cause. You will think this strange, but I will unriddle you. Necessary for the King's defence, and to withstand the power of the Independents, so long as old Leven and David Leslie commanded it; not necessary for these or any other causes, if Duke Hamilton and Earl Callander had the conduct of it."

Rumours of the treaty between the King and the Hamilton party had reached also the English Parliament, which, early in February, sent commissioners to Edinburgh to protest against it. They were a Colonel Birch, who had succeeded the Scots in the command of Hereford, Mr. Stephen Marshall, an Independent, described by Montereul as "Preacher Marshall, a man of small knowledge and scanty eloquence", and Mr. Ashurst, "an honest cutler". It was not a tactful selection to have sent to Presbyterian Scotland, and the Kirk can scarcely be blamed for straightway administering a gratuitous snub. It passed an ordinance whereby no English minister should be permitted to preach in the Edinburgh churches, though no request of this nature had been made.

The only personage who made the English welcome was Argyll, a fact which caused great surprise, since he professed to be so strict a Presbyterian, and so recently had been clamouring for the Covenant's army to fight the Independents. He went so far as to propose to furnish a place of residence for the Commissioners at the expense of the Crown, a proposal promptly turned down by the Committee of Estates, Glencairn telling him sharply that they were no friends to the English. This rebuke, however, had some personal animosity in it. At the end of January there had been a great law-suit between Glencairn and Eglinton over precedency; the Lords of Session had given a verdict in favour of Glencairn, though Argyll had brought all his influence to bear on the side of Eglinton.[8]

On February 25th the terms of the Engagement were made public by the Chancellor and Lauderdale, who had returned to Scotland almost simultaneously with the arrival of the English Commissioners. The Kirk at once sent a demand that nothing be agreed upon without its consent, to which the Hamilton party retorted that "they would soon have reason to regret the Bishops, that they had driven away because they wished to have too large a part in civil matters". Pulpits began to thunder against this sinful Engagement, George Gillespie, Moderator of the General Assembly, filling his prayers with "sundry implications against his prince", and one minister informing Hamilton from the pulpit that the curse of God would fall on him and all his posterity if he leagued with Royalists. In the next breath he "flew into a passion against the English Commissioners who were present at his preaching, and reproached them as traitors and perjurers, without employing any circumlocution".[9]

Since the English Commissioners were here for the very purpose of protesting against the Engagement, this seemed a little unfair; but the truth of it was that the Kirk itself was in a confusion which soon was to lead to a major rift; meanwhile it could not make up its mind which it hated most, Engagers or Independents. The English Commissioners were not unduly disturbed by its hostility, for they trusted to Argyll to keep it in order, and Argyll they had taken care to buy. Hamilton remarked to Montereul that the large sums of money the Commissioners had brought with them to expend in bribes were scarcely necessary, since Argyll kept an agent in London solely for the purpose of receiving English gold.[10]

The full triumph of the Hamiltons was seen when the new Parliament assembled in Edinburgh on March 18th. Of fifty noblemen, only eight or nine were of the Argyll faction, while, as Baillie admits, not only had the Hamiltons a huge majority in the other Estates, but also the best speakers. The Kirk did its best; it published a Declaration against the sinful Engagement and ordered it to be read from every pulpit; but in his alarm at the turn of events, Argyll desired a stronger ally than the Kirk. Unbeknown to his reverend friends, he sent the Earl of Lothian to England to negotiate a secret treaty with the Independents. Unfortunately for him the head of the Independents was Cromwell who, saying that " he would make more out of the Scots by threatening them than by giving them anything", advanced troops towards the Border.[11] The time for an alliance between Cromwell and King Campbell was not yet ripe.

All these reverses had made Argyll's temper smoulder, and three days after the opening of Parliament, it flared. The Treasurer, Crawford-Lindsay, had long been a rival of King Campbell for the leadership of the Covenant, and on this Friday afternoon in the Parliament House, Argyll suddenly accused Crawford-Lindsay of having said he was the better man. What the Treasurer replied to this childish challenge we are not told, but whatever it was, Argyll stalked out of the House, sent for a Major Innes who had been present when the alleged words were spoken, and finding that Innes prudently refused to say whether he had heard them, sent him to Crawford-Lindsay to demand a positive statement on the matter. The Treasurer replied haughtily that he would not be accountable to Argyll for anything he had said, but was ready to make it good with his sword.

To the amazement of his friends, Argyll accepted the challenge, desired Crawford-Lindsay to name the time and place, and so far forgot his Covenanting piety as to agree to fight on the Sabbath which was also a public fast-day. The two lords, with their seconds, duly arrived at Musselburgh Links at seven in the morning of the day appointed; but the childish quarrel had the most ridiculous ending. It was a cold morning, and Argyll demurred at taking off his doublet and boots; it would appear that his opponent's temper likewise was cooled by the rawness of the weather. At all events when, an hour later, their friends who had got word of the affair came rushing out to part them, they found challenged and challenger quietly setting down on paper the cause of their quarrel.

They were formally reconciled by the Council that same evening, but Argyll found himself in the humiliating position of being ordered to do penance by his ally the Kirk. He acknowledged that his act had been "a scriptural desertion", was publicly rebuked for it by the Commission of the General Assembly, which accepted his penitence while admonishing him to "take heed that he fall not into such a sin and scandal in time coming".[12]

Argyll's public difficulties were growing every day more serious. Hitherto he had always been able to rely on the backing of the Kirk, but its present attitude was so fantastically absurd that it was like to alienate all moderates. For it presented to the Estates a new oath which it demanded should be imposed on the kingdom; Scotland was to swear to do nothing for the King until he had signed the Covenant, to put down all sects in both kingdoms, and to make no alliance with anyone who had ever fought on the Royalist side. The Kirk followed this up by a demand that these Articles be added to the Coronation Oath.

All Argyll could do was, by fair means or foul, to prevent Hamilton from raising an effective army in accordance with the terms of the Engagement. With this end, he engineered a petition from the principal officers of Leven's old army to "secure the Kingdom of Christ" before any new forces were raised to secure the kingdom of King Charles; the attempt misfired, however, for, since Major-General Middleton and other high-ranking officers refused to sign the petition, it would merely have disclosed the divisions in the army, and was not presented. Argyll's utter insincerity as a Covenanter was proved once and for all when, on April 11th, he, Cassilis, Wariston, and a very few more, voted against a motion that the King be brought to London in honour, freedom, and safety, that the English be required to disband their army of Independents, *and that religion be established in England according to the Solemn*

League and Covenant.[13]   The fact of the matter was, of course, that King Campbell was still hoping for an alliance with him who was soon to become "King Cromwell".

At the end of April the Articles of the Engagement were passed by the Estates, Argyll scarcely allowing a word to pass without proposing an amendment.   A proclamation calling Scotland to arms was published early in May, and at the same time a formal demand was sent to the English Parliament for the redress of Scottish grievances.   Of the army now to be raised, Hamilton was elected General with only seven dissentients, of whom Argyll was the chief; Callander, hitherto violently jealous of Hamilton, accepted the post of Lieutenant-General; David Leslie was offered the command of the cavalry, and on his refusal it was given to Middleton; William Baillie got command of the foot, and many general officers of the old army obtained their former ranks in the new one.   Old Leven was thanked for his past services and was appointed to the nominal command of any forces which might be raised for the defence of the kingdom when the Engagers marched into England.

Before adjourning, the Estates passed an order that anyone who opposed, by any means whatever, the raising of men for the army of the Engagement, be declared a traitor to the realm. This was clearly aimed at Argyll and his friends, Cassilis and Eglinton, who were among those appointed to raise levies. Argyll not only disregarded the order, but in his determination to regain dictatorship, did his utmost to embroil Scotland in another civil war, and betrayed his country by inviting its most deadly enemy to invade it.

He sent a Major Strachan to Cromwell. Strachan's errand was kept secret for the time, "but shortly afterwards it broke out how it was to desire Cromwell to send a party to Scotland, with which the opposers of the Engagement might join for making a division".[14] As soon as he had dispatched Strachan on this detestable mission, Argyll himself started to prepare the way in Scotland. He went to Fife, thence to Stirling, and thence to Dumbarton, to persuade the people in these places to rise against the Engagement whenever the call should be given; and then, having given an account of these doings to his friends at the Earl of Eglinton's house, he went home to Inveraray. He was armed with a colonel's commission to raise his people for the Engagement; he intended to use that commission to levy troops against it.

Chapter Three

N o t since the tide had turned against the King in the middle of the Civil War had there seemed a better chance of his regaining his throne than in this early summer of 1648.

In England, and in Wales, old Cavaliers and ex-Roundheads were uniting to rise in strength; Byron had seized Warrington; Sir Marmaduke Langdale had between six and seven thousand men in arms near Carlisle; even in East Anglia, which had been steadily Roundhead throughout the Civil War, men were mustering for their King. Petitions from men of all parties poured into the Parliament for a personal treaty with Charles, that from Essex bearing twenty-four thousand signatures. A part of the fleet had mutinied and had sailed away to offer their services to the young Prince of Wales; the New Model was riddled with Levellers who detested Cromwell, and was mutinous for lack of pay; the City was so hostile that he was forced to withdraw his troops from the liberties.

But it is scarcely an exaggeration to say that all depended on Hamilton. The enormous New Model Army was perfectly well able to deal with scattered and sporadic risings in England, and could always be relied upon to forget its arrears of pay when there was fighting to be done. But if Hamilton, who had the sinews of war the English Royalists lacked, who had raised an army whose numerical strength was equal to that of the New Model, had marched at once, or even had repeated the strategy of the Covenanters in their invasion of 1644 and remained a menace on the Border, the issue of the Second Civil War could scarcely have been in doubt. Hamilton's delay in marching, and, when at last he did so, his criminal stupidity in leaving Argyll free to stab him in the back, ruined the chances of the King's restoration.

His conduct in regard to Argyll made many continue to think that the hostility between them was a sham. A more likely explanation may be found in his own weakness of character which prevented him from acting boldly and coming down firmly on one side or the other. What he ought to have done was to imprison Argyll; he had every excuse for doing so, since the secret of Strachan's errand to Cromwell had leaked out, and thus there was proof that Argyll was a traitor not only to his King but to his country. It was pressed by several in the Estates that the Campbell should be proceeded against on the charge of flouting the Parliament's decree that none oppose the raising of the Engagement's army under pain of treason; but Hamilton "slighted" the motion, and actually sent Argyll a courteous invitation to come and take his place as a colonel in the army.

Hamilton's only excuse for such weakness and folly was that Argyll seemed likely to have lost his old and essential ally the Kirk, for he had been "trafficking" with its bitter enemies, the Independents. But Argyll had his own methods for keeping the Kirk on his side. Just as in 1638 the Covenanters had spread the malicious rumour that the King did not intend to abide by his concessions, so now Argyll assured his reverend friends that Hamilton did not intend to honour the Article in the Engagement whereby Presbyterianism was to be established in England for three years.[15]. It was an Article which in any case was unsatisfactory to the Kirk; and moreover even Independents were less obnoxious than "Malignants". The fanatical ministers preached harder than ever against this sinful Engagement, so that Lanerick suggested to his brother the expediency of imprisoning these trumpets of sedition; but here again Hamilton had not the strength of character to put dangerous enemies under lock and key.

All through May the English Royalists sent express after express to the Engagers, urging the necessity of an immediate march, and warning Hamilton of the menace of Argyll. "I think Argyll's designs were never so dangerous as at present," Byron wrote to Lanerick; other correspondents declared that the Campbell was so "industrious and malicious" with his frequent letters to the Independents that it was essential he be secured, and that "there are expectations here that Argyll will declare against the other party, having assurance that the trumpets of Sion will sound a hot charge for him". But apart from the menace of Argyll, there were fatal dissensions in the Engagers' camp, and it was, wrote a correspondent of the Hamiltons, "by such disputes, scruples, and procrastinating distempers that your best and most cordial friends suspect your power, the King's party your affection, and your enemies to condemn all you say and do".[16]

The Estates rose on June 10th, and it astounded everyone that Hamilton nominated Argyll and his small following as members of the usual Committee which, during the interim, was to have the full powers of Parliament, "notwithstanding they had openly deserted the Parliament, and were actually employed in stirring up disobedience thereto". So anxious was Hamilton not to offend Argyll, that instead of releasing Huntly, he left him to the mercy of his mortal foe, merely ordering his transference from the common jail to the comparative comfort of the Castle. Two days after the rising of Parliament, Hamilton had a last warning of what the results of his weakness were going to be.

Argyll had not been very successful in his attempts to persuade the people of Fife to rise in opposition to the Engagement; hot though they were for the Covenant, they were difficult to raise except in defence of their homes, and all they would promise now was that they would appear in arms only if others did so first. In the dour and fanatical south-west, Argyll had found those others; certain Ayrshire gentry had organized resistance, and, aided by the fiery ministers, had assembled some two thousand foot and five hundred horse. Argyll then drew up the regiment he had raised by virtue of his commission from the Engaging Parliament, mustered it in the neighbourhood of Stirling, and sent word to Cromwell's capable young commander, George Lambert, who was lying near the Border, to join forces with the Ayrshire men.

The latter assembled on Mauchline-moor on June 12th, and were about to choose officers when Middleton, with a few troops of the Engagement, came suddenly upon them. The gentry immediately decided to lay down their arms, but the poor peasants, urged and threatened by the ministers who dominated them, refused to disband, and a bloody struggle ensued, in which Middleton was wounded and saved from defeat only by the timely appearance of Callander and his cavalry. Some hundreds of the insurgents were killed, many made prisoner, and the rest fled. Once more the blood of the slain lay upon the heads of the ministers. "There is indeed," admitted Baillie, "in our people a great animosity put in them, both by our preaching and discourse." Too late was he beginning to realize that "it were for the good of the world, that churchmen did meddle with ecclesiastical affairs only".[17]

Though the insurgents had been defeated, their rising was a bad augury for the success of the Engagement, and other circumstances did nothing to improve it. Pulpits continued to ring with invectives and threats, the same mobs of women who had flung stools and tried to lynch bishops during the beginning of the Troubles were "crowing" after Hamilton and flinging stones

N

at him as he passed down the street. The levies fell far short of expectation, thanks partly to Argyll and the Kirk, and partly to the depressed state of the kingdom, for the plague was still raging in the large towns, and intemperate rain was ruining the harvest. Men were too confused by rival ministers, too poor and miserable, to answer the call of the drums.

The army levied was rent with feuds. Hamilton and Callander, the latter a professional soldier who "understood well the Dutch discipline of war, which he observed with a strictness which seemed not free of affectation", were at loggerheads again, and the inferior officers were divided into the General's faction and that of the Lieutenant-General. Chancellor Loudoun, who had been compelled by the Kirk to do penance for his sinful compliance with "these unlawful courses" (his agreeing to the terms of the Engagement), loaded one of his horses with a trunk containing his valuables, and went home to his country seat and to his old occupation of sitting-on-the-fence. The few Covenanting nobles were also in their rural retreats, quietly allowed by Hamilton the opportunity of raising their people as soon as the army of the Engagement should be over the Border. "Enemies," wrote Montereul, with his usual dry humour, "were never seen to treat each other with so great moderation."

Another enemy, however, the erstwhile ally which had called in the Scots to its aid in 1643, was behaving in a manner far from moderate. Furious denunciations and rude pasquinades against the Scots came echoing from the south, while booted feet tramped ominously nearer to the Border. "But one letter written by an English refugee in this kingdom," wrote Montereul, who was still in Edinburgh, "has offended this Committee more than all the others; he after having written all he could to the disadvantage of this country, and after having quoted what the poet [Cleveland] says, that if Cain had been Scot he would have received for punishment of the murder of his brother not to leave his country, rather than to wander through all the world, he adds that when the Devil offered all the kingdoms of the world to Jesus Christ, he would have rendered the temptation more powerful if he had put his thumb on Scotland, in order to hide so wretched a country."

The army of the Engagement marched at long last on July 18th. Though far smaller than it should have been, it numbered ten thousand foot and four thousand horse, a vastly superior force to any with which Montrose had won his victories. But not only was it disunited, and commanded by a man who, brave enough personally, was utterly without the gift of leadership, it marched too late. The New Model had dealt with the English risings; and Cromwell, having quelled revolt in Wales, was marching rapidly to join Lambert at Carlisle.

Immediately the Engagers were over the Border, the General Assembly sat down at Edinburgh to make trouble. They framed a Declaration against the unlawfulness and sinfulness of the Engagement, termed its opponents "the Israel of God", appointed Visitations to depose any ministers who had not preached against it, drew up a list of "the chief insolencies committed by the soldiers", and ordered this Declaration to be published throughout Scotland. Montereul's brother, left behind in Edinburgh when his elder had gone to London, wrote that the Assembly was now debating whether the Engagers should be accused of being Erastians, "which I hope you will not find it strange that I have not yet heard of, since I am told the Parliament of England, that knows, tolerates, and professes even many different heresies, has declared in the last reply that it has made to the Scots, that it had not yet heard of this one".

Argyll did not grace the Assembly in person, but his absence was not a serious handicap, since his closest friends were among the ruling elders, and "it was carefully provided that in all presbyteries they should be chosen who were most zealous for the Covenant".[18] Before it rose on August 18th, the Assembly had decided that the Communion should not be administered until the kingdom had expiated its crime in allowing an army to be raised for an uncovenanted King. Until it was seen what success that army met with in England, the Covenant's leaders stayed in their homes, and the ministers worked off some of their malice by "calling names and flinging about excommunications"; but, prophesied Montereul's brother, "if anything happened to the army it is to be feared they would do something more disagreeable".

Something did happen to the army. Early in September news reached Scotland of its utter defeat at Preston; Hamilton had surrendered himself to the victors on the condition that his own and his followers' lives be spared.[19] The wretchedly managed Engagement was over; and all that remained for Argyll was to crush its adherents at home and become "King Campbell" again.

Chapter Four

As soon as the news of Hamilton's defeat reached Scotland, the Argyll clique acted.

The zealots of the south-west, to the number of six thousand, and commanded by Eglinton, Loudoun (now a Covenanter once more), David Dickson, and other ministers, marched on Edinburgh, whence Dickson's reverend colleagues went out to meet the insurgents, opened the gates, and received them with joy. And now, for the first time, occurs the term "Whig". The south-west of Scotland, the greatest stronghold of the Covenant, was a sour, infertile land which could not support itself. It was the custom, therefore, of its inhabitants to drive their pack-horses during the summer months to Leith to buy corn. The common expression used in urging on the horses was *whiggam*, and the drivers were nicknamed whiggamores. Thus this march on Edinburgh became know as the Whiggamore Raid, and the term Whiggamore, usually shortened to Whig, was used henceforth to denote the adherents of King Covenant.*

The Committee of Estates did not remain to face the insurgents; its members fled, leaving Lanerick to name himself General of those few troops which his brother had left behind him on his march south. With these he succeeded in joining Sir George Munro who, having fetched over a regiment from Ireland, had been absent from the defeat at Preston, and upon news of it had retreated towards the Border. Together, Lanerick's and Munro's forces amounted to five thousand horse and six thousand foot, mostly veterans.

Argyll, meanwhile, collecting the remnants of the fighting-men of his clan, marched to Stirling, where he was joined by some four hundred levied by his friends in Dunbartonshire. Here, having set his Campbells to guard the gates of the town, he went to the Tolbooth with his officers, held a committee, ordered the magistrates to provide food and drink for his men, and invited himself to dinner with the Earl of Mar. The meat was just being set upon the table when news arrived that stole Argyll's appetite.

* The term was not used in English politics, however, until long after the Restoration.

Despite the large army under his command, Lanerick had refrained from marching on Edinburgh, which he very easily could have taken, and had come northwards at a leisurely pace, refusing to allow Munro to turn and attack the raw levies of the Covenant under David Leslie who were following in a very cautious manner. Indeed, the only man on either side keen on fighting was Munro. He, hearing that Argyll was "keeping a committee" at Stirling, galloped ahead with the advance-guard of Lanerick's army, intent on capturing the town, the castle of which was being held for the Engagers. As he approached, a courier came galloping from Stirling with the information that the Barras-port was manned by Argyll's troops, and that he must pass through the park in order to gain the bridge and prevent Argyll's flight. The Governor of the Castle, meanwhile, displayed the King's colours over the walls, and caused his cannon to play upon the bridge, hoping thus to bottle up Argyll within the town.

But never yet had anyone been able to prevent Argyll from saving his own skin. The difficulties Munro experienced in breaking open the park gates and a part of the wall to admit his cavalry, gave King Campbell his chance. Mounting a swift horse which he kept by him for just such emergencies, he fled, never drawing rein until he reached North Queensferry where, for the fourth time in his military career, he sought safety in a boat.

His unfortunate men, thus left leaderless, instead of attacking Munro's troopers as they entered singly into the deer-park, milled around in hopeless confusion, and, attempting to retreat after their lord, were overtaken by Munro's men, who killed a number of them, took many prisoners, and pursued the rest, who flung themselves over the bridge into the Forth where, attempting to swim to safety, most of them were drowned.[20]

It would have appeared, therefore, that at least in Scotland, the Engagers had got the better of the Covenanters. But Lanerick's conduct, like that of his brother on former occasions, turned victory into defeat. His neglect either to march on Edinburgh or attack David Leslie seems capable of no other explanation than the one given by Wishart, that "he had long before this time determined to accommodate matters with Argyll and his faction at any rate, and had taken the field rather to show his power, and thereby more effectually to conciliate their favour, than out of any design to act offensively against them; for it is now notoriously well known, that he had some time ago sent messengers privately to Argyll to treat concerning an accommodation, without showing any concern for his soldiers, and those whom he had engaged to take up arms ".[21]

On September 15th, both sides in the late petty struggle sat down at Stirling to debate a treaty, Argyll, who had recovered from his fright and returned thither, offering the most intolerable terms. Lanerick and his friends were demurring at these, when Argyll produced his trump card. He had sent commissioners to Cromwell, he said, to invite him to come to the Covenanters' aid, and Cromwell had accepted.

There was nothing for it then but for Lanerick to give in. By the terms of the treaty both sides were to disband their forces by October 5th, and Munro's Scoto-Irish troops were to leave the kingdom within eight days, without any safe-conduct or provision being made for them on their way to the coast, on pain of being treated as enemies of the kingdom. The poor soldiers were mercilessly used by the Westland Whigs on their journey. As for Lanerick and other principal Engagers, Argyll would endeavour to secure their lives and estates, but as for what the Kirk might decide on this matter, "we cannot meddle without breach of Covenant". A few days later a proclamation commanded all persons who had been "in the late unlawful Engagement" to depart twelve miles from Edinburgh.

Argyll was now energetically recovering his position as dictator. Disregarding the fact that their nominations as members of the Committee of Estates had been made conditional on their carrying out the Acts of the late Engaging Parliament, he and his friends used these nominations to make themselves the governors of the kingdom. They sent a message to the English Parliament, excusing the long silence of their party by the fact that they had had an army of Malignants (Engagers) to settle with; the two Houses were begged to keep some forces on the Border in case these Malignants made further trouble, and to retain, "as pledges of the peace of the kingdoms", all noblemen and officers captured during Hamilton's invasion. "You shall endeavour," the messenger was instructed, "that honest men who have suffered for opposing the Engagement be not prejudiced, but furthered in payment of the sums assigned unto them before the Engagement, out of the two hundred thousand pounds sterling, and brotherly assistance for public debts or losses."[22]

Having sent this broad hint to the English Parliament to pay up the vast sums assigned him when he was in London in 1646, Argyll prepared to welcome to Scotland the man who was the leader of the Independents, and who was soon to become dictator of England. Cromwell had accepted the cordial invitation sent him by those whom he termed "the Good Men of Scotland". He crossed the Tweed on September 20th, and a day or two later was met at Mordington by Argyll, Elcho, and Sir John Scott. Six miles outside Edinburgh the party was greeted by Major-General Holbourn, and Cromwell was escorted in great state to the capital.

Here he was entertained with the honours usually reserved for the Sovereign. Argyll feasted him in the Castle, the guns of which fired salutes; he was then conducted to Moray House in the Canongait, the finest in the city, which had been prepared as his residence.[23] As their honoured guest was he received by Argyll's Committee of Estates, and he presented to them "a writing", in which he demanded that which they were only too ready to grant, that none of those concerned in the late Engagement, even those who had approved of it, should have any public employment in Scotland.

Thus between Cromwell and the Covenant's leaders all was harmony; but between the former's soldiers and the ordinary people of Scotland, it was otherwise. Every day there were complaints of the insolent carriage of the English, which resulted in brawls which sometimes ended fatally. The old quarrel between Independency and Presbyterianism flared up; one of Cromwell's officers was so affronted to hear a preacher pray for the success of the Covenant that the minister was threatened "most beastlie", and informed that "they had in England trodden his Covenant under their feet, and they hoped before long to consume it in Scotland with fire, and with disgrace to extinguish the memory thereof". Thick though he was with the Covenant's leaders, Cromwell abstained from attending the services of their Kirk, but preached sermons in his own lodgings, "whenever the spirit came upon him; which took him like the fits of an ague, sometimes twice, sometimes thrice a day".[24]

But Argyll and his more intimate friends continued to "haunt" Cromwell, paying daily visits to Moray House. A few months later a strong rumour was circulated to the effect that during these visits Cromwell had disclosed to Argyll his intention to put the King to death by virtue of a mock trial.[25] What passed between the dictator of Scotland and the future dictator of England will never be known, for the interviews took place in the strictest privacy; but on the whole it seems unlikely that this was so.

For the killing of the King would have very different consequences for Argyll than they would for Cromwell. It would mean, inevitably, a violent Royalist reaction throughout both kingdoms, and while the New Model Army remained strong enough to deal with this in England, Argyll had no comparable force to curb it in Scotland. The perpetual imprisonment of the King was what would have suited Argyll, and possibly Cromwell led him to believe that this was what was intended, and that he would be allowed a free hand in Scotland so long as he kept the Kirk from meddling with English affairs. It is unlikely that either potentate was completely honest with the other. Years before, a correspondent had written to Ormonde that Argyll "is so subtle that he can hugely dissemble"; and in reply to a fellow minister who had been edified by Cromwell's pious tears and his zeal for religion, Robert Blair had exclaimed, "And do you believe him? If you knew him as well as I do, you would not believe one word he says. He is an egregious dissembler and a great liar."[26]

News that a treaty was on foot between the King and the English Parliament made Cromwell prepare to hasten to London, speeded by the compliments and good wishes of Argyll, who sent the Rev. Robert Blair and Sir John Chiesley to assist him in crushing these negotiations with the King. Cromwell on his side promised to leave some troops under Lambert in Scotland until Argyll had consolidated his power; and, in its joy at the crushing of the Engagers, the Kirk went so far as to term Cromwell their Deliverer. He replied to this in the usual scriptural terms, "laying his hand upon his breast, and demurely looking on their grave countenances".[27]

Thus ended the year 1648. To all outward appearances, in the words of King Charles at Carisbrooke, "Herod and Pontius Pilate were agreed."

PART FIVE

ALLY TURNS ENEMY
1649-1651

Chapter One

SIXTEEN hundred and forty-nine opened for Argyll with deceptive brightness. On January 4th the Estates assembled, whose chief business was to take vengeance on the remains of the Engaging party, and to prevent future effective resistance from anyone qualified for the conveniently vague term "Malignant". Chancellor Loudoun opened the proceedings with what Baillie described as "a long tedious speech of an hour and a half's length", speaking as hotly against the Engagement as though he had never taken its side, much less had been one of those who had negotiated it.

Next day the House listened to an equally long harangue by Argyll. This he divided into five heads, which, being in a playful mood, he called the breaking of the Malignants' teeth, promising that the next speaker, Wariston, would break their jaws. Under the first head came those Engagers who had been entrusted with high office; under the second those who had sat in the former Committee of Estates, and "who by their tyranny had oppressed the subjects"; under the third were Malignants formerly fined by the Estates and now again relapsed into their sinful ways; under the fourth those who had been "eager promoters" of the Engagement; and under the last all who had petitioned for the advance of its army. These five heads Argyll termed his "classes"; and in a speech lasting two hours, Wariston explained how each class was to be punished according to its deserts.

Next day the debate on the Act of Classes (as it came to be called) was interrupted by an express from the Scots Commissioners in London. The military under Cromwell, they wrote, had purged the English Parliament of all those in favour of continued negotiation with the King, and Charles was to be "tried" by a High Court of Justice set up by the Army.

It was a delicate situation for Argyll, since, by the terms of both Covenants, he was pledged to defend the King's person. Sitting on Sunday, January 7th, the Estates under his guidance drew up cautious instructions to their Commissioners in London. The Commissioners were not in any way to justify the King's actions or the Engagement, and they were to take care to say nothing which could give offence to their English brethren or which might sow the seeds of a new war. All they were to do was to endeavour to delay their said brethren's "meddling with the King's person", and if the brethren persisted, then to enter a protest, "that this kingdom may be free of all the desolation, misery and bloodshed that inevitably will follow thereupon, without offering in your reason that princes are exempt from trial of justice".[1] In other words, Pontius Pilate washed his hands.

Whilst the Estates, assisted by six ministers, were drawing up these futile instructions, a dispute arose on Wariston's moving that a fast be kept. Those in whose breasts remained a spark of loyalty or a residue of care for their Sovereign's life, argued that the delay of three or four fast-days might prove fatal, since during that time the express could not be sent to the Commissioners in London; though what the express was expected to achieve it is difficult to imagine. It was put to the vote; those who voted to fast first and send the express afterwards were Argyll, Wariston, David Dickson, and Sir Thomas Ruthven. Finding so large a majority against him, and no doubt realizing that his recent intimacy with Cromwell might have bred a suspicion that he had agreed to the latter's present conduct towards the King, Argyll made "a fair apology", and submitted to the vote of the majority that the messenger be dispatched without delay.[2]

The fast was kept on the 10th, and next day was passed the Act of Classes, perhaps the most iniquitous of all the ordinances of King Covenant, and the source of endless trouble and dissension. No time was lost in putting it into operation. Eight Lords of Session were dismissed "as being tainted with the crime of loyalty", as Guthrie sarcastically put it; Crawford-Lindsay, Argyll's old rival, was turned out of the Treasurership, and Argyll, Cassilis, Eglinton, and Burleigh were made joint commissioners of that office. The Privy Seal was taken from Roxburgh; and in place of Lanerick, who had lain under some measure of restraint since the treaty at Stirling, Sutherland, Cassilis and Lothian shared the Secretary's place between them. Wariston got his long-coveted post of Clerk-Register in place of Sir Alexander Gibson of Durie; and Cassilis was given yet a third office, when there was bestowed upon him Crawford-Lindsay's seat among the Lords of Session.

The Act of Classes established the complete domination of Argyll. Not only did it rid him of old rivals and lukewarm friends among his peers, but it put all, from the highest to the lowest in the land, at his mercy and that of his ally the Kirk. The fourth head in it was especially designed as a sop to the Kirk, many ministers being uneasy over the alliance with the Independent Cromwell; into this fourth class came all those guilty of "uncleanness, swearing, drunkenness, neglect of family worship", and so on, the Kirk, of course, to be the sole judge. Anyone who had shown sympathy with the cause of the Engagement came into the third class, and was disqualified from holding any office, even that of the deacon of a craft, for five years. No man included in any of the classes could be re-admitted to office after the punitive period was ended, unless he had given satisfaction both to the General Assembly or its Commission and to the Committee of Both Kingdoms.

It was Argyll's most dizzy moment of power. He was more secure in his dictatorship now than when he had been "King Campbell" on the eve of the First Civil War. For Montrose was defeated and in exile; Hamilton was defeated and in an English prison; the King was defeated and in the hands of Argyll's ally, Cromwell; Huntly was defeated and was about to be dealt with by Argyll himself; and now, by the Act of Classes, all other rivals and enemies, great and small, could be kept in permanent subjection.

But early in February news arrived which was to alter the whole situation: the King had been put to death.

There followed that which Argyll must have known was inevitable, a wave of horror sweeping through Scotland; and a demand for the proclaiming of the boy of nineteen who was now King Charles II. It will be remembered that, all through the struggle for power between Hamilton and Argyll, each had clamoured for the sending of the Prince of Wales to Scotland. But in this changed situation, Argyll desired nothing less than his coming, or indeed his proclaiming, which inevitably would offend the new ally, Cromwell. Yet the old ally, the Kirk, was adding its voice to the chorus which demanded the proclaiming of the new King and an invitation to him to come to Scotland, subject, of course, to his signing the Covenant; and all Argyll could do was to offer such intolerable terms to the young man that, of his own accord, he would refuse to come.

Charles was proclaimed in Edinburgh on February 5th, and

two days later the Estates drew up a letter to the new King. It directed his Majesty to shun the company of Malignants and the counsels of the ungodly, "And that your Majesty would avoid all the temptations and snares that accompany youth, and humble yourself under the mighty hand of God, and seek him early, and labour to have your senses exercised in his Word, and that your Majesty would establish Presbyterial government, and allow and enjoin the Solemn League and Covenant, and employ your royal power for promoving and advancing the work of uniformity of religion, in all your Majesty's dominions". This letter, together with one of similar insolence from the General Assembly, was carried over to Charles in Holland by Sir Joseph Douglas.

Commissioners from the Estates and the Assembly went over in March; the former were the Earls of Cassilis and Lothian, Sir John Chiesley, William Glendinning, and Alexander Jaffray, Provost of Aberdeen. The bunch of preachers sent by the Assembly were directed to make a thorough prying into the King's private life, "what form of worship he uses in his family; what ministers he hath with him; whether he seeks God in private or not". Also to "represent unto him the sins of his House. . . . You shall show him that we look upon the idolatry of his Mother [with whom the Covenanters had been in active correspondence during the period when they were trying to induce the late King to outrage his conscience] as a main cause of the evils, both of sin and punishment, that have afflicted these kingdoms. And thereupon seriously to represent unto him the evil and danger of Popish marriage, and labour to dissuade him from marrying any that is not of the Reformed Religion."[3] Since by the Reformed Religion was meant Scottish Presbyterianism, the King's choice of a wife was somewhat limited.

The first thing the Commissioners did on their arrival at the exiled Court was to demand the removal from it of "the most bloody murtherer of our nation", Montrose. To this Charles refused to make any answer, and to the further demand that he impose, on his own authority, Presbyterianism on England and Ireland, he gave a decided negative. The Commissioners came back with what they termed "A Plain Reply", which was very plain indeed. They were shocked beyond measure that no notice had been taken of their demand for Montrose's removal, and deeply hurt by his Majesty's refusal to impose their creed on other people. "We do not conceive what in this Covenant can stumble your Majesty," they wailed. If Presbyterianism was the one true religion, as the Lord had revealed to them that it was, it was Charles's bounden duty to impose it on his other kingdoms.

"Your Majesty and all the world may see," they continued darkly, "to the very great grief of our souls, the wrath of the Lord burning like a flame; no better mean know we to quench it than for your Majesty to be humbled under his mighty hand, to seek and rely on his favour, to be zealous for advancing his affairs, to establish the Solemn League and Covenant, to provoke him no more by holding up in his House, against the hearts of all the orthodox abroad, and of the godly at home, human inventions borrowed from Rome, most unhappy to Britain." Either their intelligence or their sincerity must be questioned in their additional remark that "all Scotland, the most of England, the best part of Ireland, do judge the abolition of Episcopacy, of Prelacy, of Liturgy, and joining in a Covenant for that end, a necessary duty", since they themselves lamented the considerable body of Malignants still in Scotland, and England, their late ally, was ruled by the Independents.

The King's reply to these intolerable demands was temperate. Scotland should have her Presbyterianism, but he would not, and indeed could not, impose it upon England and Ireland without the advice of the Parliaments of those kingdoms. As for the Malignants, a term used now to cover both Montrose and his bitter enemies the Engagers, the King suggested an indemnity for all persons excepting only those who "upon sufficient and due evidence in a lawful trial", should be found guilty of participation or acquiescence in the late King's murder. It was a suggestion in accordance with the young King's present aim, which was to unite all parties in Scotland against the common enemy, the military clique which was becoming supreme in England. Finding, however, that the Scots would not budge an inch from their exclusive attitude, Charles concurred with the majority in his Council who, headed by Sir Edward Hyde, advised him to endeavour to go to Ireland, where loyal Lord Ormonde still held out for him.

That the Scots' demands were indeed intolerable was admitted even by those whom the Covenanters had referred to as "the orthodox abroad". Baillie's cousin, Spang, a staunch Presbyterian, pleaded hard with the Kirk to remit its rigour. He demurred at the Act of Classes: "passion," he wrote, "has been too great in that Act; for it is judged a greater sin not to protest against the late Engagement than to be an ordinary drunkard, since it is declared punishable by a more severe punishment". He earnestly entreated his cousin to represent to his fellow ministers "how much the fame of rigidity, used by them against the last year's Engagers, is like to endanger the reputation of our Kirk abroad, and like also to make presbyterial government hateful".

He warned the Covenanters that they might be made "through their own experience, to feel what it is which now, without pity, is executed upon others. Generally the great power which the Commission of the Kirk exerciseth displeaseth all: It is but an extraordinary general meeting, and yet it sits constantly and more ordinarily than any synod; yes, and without the knowledge of provincial synods and presbyteries, deposes ministers, enjoins, *pro authoritate*, what writs they please to be read, inflicts censures on those who will not read them. If the Kirk of Scotland look not to this in time," concluded this true prophet, "we will lament it when we cannot mend it."[4]

The Kirk, however, was deaf to such warnings, and so also was the once moderate Baillie, now one of the Kirk's Commissioners to the King. He and his colleagues were certain of getting their way with Charles, deceived by his mild manner towards them, his youth, and his easy graciousness. Having bestowed upon him "the National Covenant, the Solemn League and Covenant, the Directory, the Confession of Faith, the Catechism, the Propositions of Government, bound together in a book so handsome as we could get them", the Commissioners were delighted by the grace with which Charles received this charming present. "His Majesty is of a very sweet disposition," Baillie wrote home; "it were all the pities in the world but he were in good company. . . . He is one of the most gentle, innocent, well-inclined Princes, so far as yet appears, that lives in the world: a trim person, and of a manly carriage; understands pretty well, speaks not much; would God he were amongst us."

While in Holland Baillie was writing this patronizing description of his Sovereign, in England and in Scotland two of the King's father's principal adherents were being put to death by powers which had no existence in law.

The Duke of Hamilton had been brought to Windsor in the previous December, and here, for a few moments and for the last time, he had met the master to whom he had proved such a broken reed, the royal master who himself was on his way to a mock trial and a violent death. Though, according to Clement Walker, Hamilton stooped very low in his efforts to escape a like fate, offering to join interests with Argyll and to concur with the English Independents,[5] he consistently refused to involve others in his own ruin.

Cromwell visited him several times in prison, and made strenuous efforts to wring from him the names of all those Englishmen who had participated in the Engagement, promising him his life if he would disclose them. To his honour, Hamilton refused. Fearing that his brother Lanerick might be a prisoner in Scotland (though in fact he had escaped to the Court of the young King), Hamilton wrote him in lemon-juice, the favourite invisible ink of the day, a touching little note: " I under the power of the sword and merciless men, no favour to be expected, oft examined, but nothing discovered, being ignorant: perhaps you will abide the same trial; beware, if you do."[6]

Yet it was in fact the fatal irresolution of Hamilton himself which in the end destroyed him. A faithful servant contrived a plan for his escape, warning him, however, that on no account must he attempt to enter London by night because of the troops which patrolled the streets. The plan was successful in so far as Hamilton escaped from Windsor, but disregarding the warning, he was recaptured in Southwark. Even then he might have got away, for his captors had not recognized him, and had taken him up only for being upon the streets at four in the morning; but with incredible stupidity, while he was detained in the guardhouse he lighted his pipe with "several great papers". The suspicions of his captors were aroused, and searching him they found other papers which disclosed his identity. With characteristic fatalism he exclaimed: " It was God's will it should be thus."

He was closely warded at St. James's, in company with the Earl of Norwich and Lord Capel, two of the Royalist leaders in the Second Civil War, while the English military potentates sent to their ally, Argyll, to know his pleasure concerning the noble captive with whom he had once been so friendly. Argyll was only too eager to have this dangerous rival put out of the way, and remained deaf to the entreaties of Hamilton's daughter and other kinsfolk that he should intervene. With his usual hypocrisy he gave as his reason for refusing, that since those who now had the power in England had murdered their Sovereign despite the protests of the Scots Commissioners, it was unfit that Scotland should make any more addresses to such men.

Hamilton's trial before the so-called High Court of Justice dragged on until March 6th, when he, with Norwich, Capel, and Sir John Owen, were condemned to death. In Hamilton's case it was a particularly flagrant outrage of justice, since he was a prisoner of war who had surrendered on promise of his life, and as a Scotsman he could not lawfully be tried in England. An hour before his execution, Cromwell sent some of his officers to him in a last attempt to make him disclose the names of his English confederates in the Engagement; but Hamilton replied that "if he had as many lives as hairs in his head, he would lay them all down rather than redeem them by such base means".[7]

The better side of his strange character enabled him to make a good end. On his way to execution he called for pen and paper, and wrote a hasty note to his brother, commending to his care the poor servant, Cole, who had contrived his abortive escape from Windsor. In his speech on the scaffold he admitted all he owed to the late King's favour, and how much reason he had had to love him, both as master and friend; and being desired to change his position because the sun shone full in his face, he answered pleasantly, "No, it would not burn it, and he hoped to see a brighter sun than that very speedily."

Hamilton suffered on March 9th, and a fortnight later a similar scene took place in Edinburgh. His long incarceration in the common jail before being transferred to the Castle, together with his grief for the King he had served so poorly, had made old Huntly so sick that his death was daily expected. His sister, therefore, the Marchioness of Douglas, together with his three daughters, the Ladies Haddington, Seton, and Drummond, Argyll's nieces, went to that potentate and on their knees begged for a few days' respite from the sentence of death which had been passed on Huntly, "that his life might expire by a natural infirmity, and not by violence".[8]

The Estates, indeed, had intended to do no more than sentence Huntly to life imprisonment; for, apart from the fact that the old man could not possibly constitute any further menace to the reign of King Covenant, they were aware that to kill a man only for executing the King's commission was making a dangerous precedent. But Argyll was still firmly of the opinion that dead men do not bite, and in a meeting of the Estates from which all nobles except the Chancellor had absented themselves, sentence of death was passed. On March 22nd the sick old Gordon, dressed in the mourning he had worn ever since the murder of his royal master, walked cheerful and unmoved to the scaffold, remaining to the end the spirited Cock o' the North. A minister asking him if, for the peace of his conscience, he did not wish to be released from the sentence of Excommunication passed upon him years before by the Kirk, he replied, "That he was not us'd to hear false prophets, such as he was, and desir'd him to be gone."[9]

With Huntly's death Argyll obtained two things he had long.

desired. The first was the feudal jurisdiction which had been exercised by his victim over a large portion of the Highlands; the second was the ruin of the House of Gordon. The eldest son had fallen during Montrose's campaigns; the second, Lord Aboyne, was dying broken-hearted in exile; the third, who now became Marquis of Huntly, was that wild Lord Lewis who once had stolen his father's jewels, and who was content, at least for the moment, to be guided in all things by Uncle Argyll.

Chapter Two

IT is possible that, by insisting on Huntly's death, Argyll had hoped to achieve a third aim, and for the moment it seemed that he had. The execution of one who had borne his father's commission, and had suffered only on that account, was scarcely the kind of thing to incline Charles II to accept the Scots' invitation to come over to them; and during this summer Argyll had a very special reason for hoping that Charles would not come. For there were ominous reports that before dealing with loyal Ireland, Cromwell intended to bring an army down on Scotland for daring to proclaim King Charles II. The last thing Argyll can have desired was to have the ally to whom he had betrayed his country on the eve of the Engagement, whom he had entertained in Edinburgh but a few months before, and from whom he had parted on such amicable terms, turn into an enemy.

The Scots Commissioners in Holland, on the other hand, were dismayed by the young King's refusal to accept their terms and come over. Severally and collectively they continued to importune him, enlisting in their cause his brother-in-law, the Prince of Orange, and, strangely enough, his mother, whose idolatry they had declared to be one of the chief causes of God's wrath. While strongly against Charles's surrender to the demand that he impose Presbyterianism on England and Ireland, the Queen saw Scotland as her son's only hope; but the boy was not to be moved, and in July, "in discomfort and grief" at the failure of their mission, the Commissioners left Holland.*

Argyll's secret relief at the King's refusal to come to Scotland

---

* Emotions which must have been increased had they but known that in the same ship with them was a disguised Jesuit priest, Fr. George Leslie, David Leslie's cousin. (Blairs' Papers, 18.)

was short-lived, for the Kirk he had ridden so long and so success-
fully had now got the bit in its teeth. It had put up with the
necessity of accepting Cromwell's aid against the Engagers, but
now that the Engagers were beaten, it remembered its old
quarrel with the Independents, and assumed its most militant
aspect.

It should have been obvious to the meanest intelligence that,
lacking not only the enormous asset for bargaining which the
possession of the King's person would have been, but likewise an
army, defiance of Cromwell was simple madness. Yet the Kirk's
answer to the suggestion of a treaty with England was that it
would treat only if its former allies there returned to their duty
according to the Solemn League and Covenant, which, it
declared, they had broken by their failure to impose Presbyterianism upon England and Ireland. The English retorted that the
Scots also had broken the Covenant by invading under the
Engagement, "an advantage," wrote the indignant Baillie,
"which they would openly make that use of, as to have it a
breach of all their obligations to us. To this we made no reply;
for what need paper-disputes at such a time?"

The situation was saved for the moment by Cromwell's
decision to settle with Ireland first; but for Argyll at least it was
complicated by the young King's resolve to go thither likewise
and try what Ormonde and the Irish Royalists could do for him.
A restoration by such means was the last thing Argyll wanted;
and he attempted, therefore, to come to a secret understanding
with Charles, without the knowledge of the Kirk.

While Wariston, the Kirk's mouthpiece, was absent from the
Parliament House, Argyll moved "off-hand" to send Lothian
alone to the King, who was now in Jersey, with a new address;
the Estates, packed with Argyll's adherents, agreed to the suggestion without presuming to enquire into the contents of this
address. "But incontinent thoughts began to arise about the
matter; some began to be jealous of Argyll, that he was inclined
to a new trinketing with the King by himself"; suspicion was
increased by the fact that Lothian, who was to go upon this
errand, was Argyll's most particular friend. The affair reached
the ears of the Kirk, which, thoroughly alarmed, used its power
to get that "unripe motion" quashed and Lothian's employment
revoked; and in the last sitting of the Parliament an address to
the King, inspired by the Kirk, was voted to be carried to Charles
by Winram of Libberton, an advocate who, in 1638, had undertaken to carry to Court the "Supplication" of the General
Assembly justifying its abolition of Episcopacy.[10]

By the time that Libberton was ready to set out, Ormonde
had been defeated at Rathmines, Cromwell had landed in Ireland, and all hopes which the King had placed in that country
were scattered. The Kirk seized eagerly on this advantage to
send with Libberton an invitation to Scotland on even harsher
conditions than before. In this nadir of his fortunes, the unfortunate Charles was ready to treat with anyone who could get
him back his birthright, and he agreed to negotiate with another
Scots Commission at Breda in the spring, writing to Argyll to
entreat him " to the moderating of their instructions as much as
reasonably you may". Libberton wrote in the same strain to
the Kirk; "I persuade myself," he wrote, "it will be the wisdom
and piety of the Commission to send such as may gain the King
by the spirit of meekness, and not such as say there is no help
for him in God."[11] But the King and Libberton might have
spared themselves the pains of writing; Argyll would do his best
to see that the terms offered were so intolerable that Charles
could not accept them.

Libberton returned to Scotland from Jersey at the beginning
of February, 1650, and on March 9th the Commissioners who
were to treat with the King at Breda took shipping at Leith.
Their orders were to treat for the space of thirty days and no
longer; if the penniless exile surrendered to their demands, they
had a warrant under the Great Seal to bestow upon him three
hundred thousand pounds. In the middle of the month, the
Marquis of Montrose sailed to the Orkneys for what was to prove
his last campaign.

When, early in the previous year, Montrose in his exile had
heard of the execution of the royal master he had come to love
so well and had served so faithfully, he had fallen down in a
dead swoon. On recovering from the shock, his life had narrowed
into one purpose: to overthrow the government of Argyll which
had made that murder possible. With the wave of loyalty which
had swept through Scotland, a Royalist rising under the leadership of the man who had defeated the Covenanters so many
times during the Civil War seemed to have every prospect of
success. For months, therefore, previous to this March of 1650,
Montrose had been furiously active, negotiating for supplies of
arms and money and mercenary soldiers throughout Europe.
In place of the Gordons, who had proved such broken reeds, he
had the promise of aid from the weathercock Seaforth, Chief of
the great northern clan of Mackenzie, and he could count with
certainty upon his old friends the MacDonalds.

The young King who was now his master was a very different

man from the idealistic Charles whose head had fallen on the scaffold outside his own royal palace of Whitehall. Young Charles's childhood had ended abruptly when, at the age of twelve, he had been present at the raising of the Royal Standard at the beginning of the Civil War; from his sixteenth year he had known nothing but exile; he had grown up amid the intrigues and perpetual quarrelling of councillors and courtiers who were penniless like himself; he had been snubbed by his fine French relations, dogged by spies, frustrated at every turn in his efforts to aid his distressed father. His formative years had been passed without that father's influence, and the conditions of his life had forced him into a premature maturity, giving him a dependence on his own considerable shrewdness, a profound knowledge of men, and an absence of illusion. He had none of the idealism of either his father or Montrose; life was a battle of wits, and he believed in fighting intriguers with their own weapons.

Now when the chance of regaining his throne by way of Ireland failed, and Scotland remained his only hope, Charles's most formidable problem lay in the fact that there were three distinct parties, each desiring his presence there, each detesting the other. Lauderdale, for instance, a prime Engager and a member of Charles's wandering Court, swore in a passion that though he wished nothing more in this world than to see the King restored, he would rather he never should be than that Montrose should have a hand in it.[12] The Covenanters, of course, hated Montrose and the Engagers almost equally; and since the Covenanters held the power in Scotland, the King's immediate problem was how to get there on any tolerable terms.

The solution he arrived at, while it can scarcely be defended from a moral standpoint, was a neat piece of statecraft which might well have succeeded. Montrose should have his way and lead a Royalist expedition into the north; if he defeated the Covenanters in battle once more, as there seemed every chance of his doing, they would be frightened out of their stubborn exclusiveness, and Charles would be able to treat on terms which, he hoped, would satisfy all parties.

Montrose knew all about this design of the King's. Charles had written him several times, enclosing the addresses the Covenanters were making to him in Jersey. In January 1650, the King had sent him a "public" letter and a private one; in the first he wrote that "as We conceive that your preparations have been one effectual motive that hath induced them to make the said address to Us, so your vigorous proceeding will be a good means to bring them to such moderation in the said treaty, as probably may produce an agreement, and a present union of that whole nation to Our service". In the private letter he assured Montrose that "I will never fail in the effects of that friendship I have promised . . . and that nothing can happen to me shall make me consent to anything to your prejudice".[13]

But the weeks went by and there was no news of Montrose, no glad tidings of a Royalist victory; and the Scots Commissioners, the period of thirty days which the Estates had laid down being expired, were threatening to return to their own country and abandon all further negotiations. On May 1st Charles gave in, and signed the Treaty of Breda. (Like most seventeenth-century treaties, it was not a treaty in the modern sense of that term, not a binding understanding but an agreement accepted *ad referendum*.) On the same day, unaware that Montrose, whom the Mackenzies had failed as completely as the Gordons had failed him in the old days, had been defeated at Carbisdale, Charles wrote to him to lay down his arms (a letter which never reached the Royalist General), and on the 8th he wrote to the Committee of Estates requiring that Montrose's forces be allowed to leave the country unmolested.

By the 12th, rumours of the disaster at Carbisdale had reached the exiled Court, and Charles ordered Sir William Fleming, who had not yet left for Scotland with the letter to the Estates, not to deliver it unless Montrose was still unbeaten and at the head of a reasonably strong army; if he had been defeated, the letter was not to be delivered, and this for a particular reason.

For Charles already had come to a private agreement with the Scots Commissioners at Breda for Montrose's safety, and he preferred to trust to this rather than to an appeal to the Estates which would have meant, in fact, to Argyll, Montrose's bitter personal foe. The proof that there was this private agreement lies in the notes upon it made at the time by Charles's secretary, Robert Long: "Order to Montrose to lay down arms, and leave cannon, arms, ammunition brought from Gottenburgh to Orkney, or deliver 'em to Sheriff of County. 1000 rix dollars paid to his use in Sir Patrick Drummond's hands, indemnity for Mon. E. Seaforth, Kinnoul, Lords Napier and Rhea, Sir James Macdonnel, etc. This upon K's agreement with Scots Commissioners. Sir W. Fleming sent with the orders, all his [Montrose's] officers and soldiers indemnify'd. M to stay in safety for a competent time, and ship to lie provided for transporting where he pleased."[14] "It is impossible," remarks Dr. Gardiner, "after reading this note, to doubt that Charles did the best he could—

short of breaking with the Covenanters—to bring Montrose off in safety."[15]

It is impossible also to believe that Charles either wished or tried to disavow the authority he had given Montrose to invade Scotland. The King could not have done so even if he had been base enough to desire to, for it was known both in Scotland and abroad that Montrose had the King's commission. When, later in the month, Montrose was brought to the Parliament House to hear his sentence, Loudoun informed him that it was he and his like who were "a great snare to Princes, and drew them to give such bloody commissions"; Montrose himself, in his speech on this occasion and again upon the scaffold, asserted that he had come to Scotland at his Majesty's command; and at the end of May, not knowing he had been executed, the French Government sent to the Estates an appeal for his life, in which he was spoken of as being captured "while fulfilling the commission of our very dear and well-beloved brother and cousin, the King of Great Britain".[16]

But it was still the purpose of Argyll to prevent the King from coming to Scotland, and with the defeat and capture of Montrose he saw a chance of alienating the Royalists from their master. He caused to be read in the Parliament House a letter, supposed to be from the King, wherein Charles disclaimed all responsibility for Montrose's invasion. The letter was never allowed to be shown to the House, and presumably was destroyed, for no trace of it has ever been found. It is generally believed to have been a fabrication of Will Murray, Argyll's tool. "It is impossible to believe," wrote Buchan, a severe critic of Charles, "that the King, who was no fool, and had the rest of the correspondence in his memory, could have been guilty of so futile and purposeless a piece of treachery, by which no one could be deceived."[17] Unfortunately both for Charles's moral reputation and for Argyll's hopes, the King, despite this aspersion on his honour, held to his resolve to come to Scotland.

Montrose, who had been surprised at Carbisdale in Caithness by David Leslie's advance-guard under that same Colonel Strachan who had been Argyll's messenger to Cromwell in 1648, was captured a few days later. His wounds neglected, his body racked with fever, he was brought on a slow progress to Edinburgh, exhibited everywhere like a wild beast, with a herald proclaiming before him: "Here comes James Grahame, a traitor to his country." He arrived at Leith in the afternoon of Saturday, May 18th, and thence, mounted on a cart-horse, was brought to Edinburgh, where Argyll and the Kirk had made every preparation for his speedy dispatch before the King had time to intervene on his behalf.[18]

As soon as the welcome news of Carbisdale had arrived, the Estates had sat to consider the fate of Montrose if their troops succeeded in capturing him. He had been outlawed in 1644, and no time, therefore, need be wasted in trying him. Left to themselves, there can be little doubt that the Estates would have ordained his beheading, the customary method of executing prisoners of noble rank; but Argyll was determined to taste to the full the sweets of revenge against this man who had made him scuttle away from three battlefields. The sentence, therefore, was that Montrose should be hanged, and that after death his head and limbs be struck off and affixed to the pinnacles of the chief towns in Scotland, the highest prick of the Edinburgh Tolbooth being reserved for his head.

Even Sir James Stewart of Coltness, the Covenanting Provost of Edinburgh, remonstrated with Argyll for so barbaric a sentence. "'What need,' said Sir James, 'of so great butchery and dismembering? Has not heading, and public affixing of the head, been thought sufficient for the most atrocious State crimes hitherto? We are embroiled, and have taken sides; but to insult too much over the misled is unmanly.' Yet there was no remedy. Argyll pushed the vengeance of Church and State against Montrose."[19]

The streets were packed with people, who had been incited by the ministers to jeer at him and pelt him, when Montrose, bound to a chair on the hangman's cart, his arms tied so that he could not defend his face from the mob, was brought from the Watergate to the Tolbooth. But contrary to godly expectations, no jeers were heard, no filth was flung. The people looked with sympathy upon that drawn yet serene face and upon the body wasted with fever. Only one insult was offered, and that came, not from Edinburgh's " holy sisters ", the termagants who long ago had tried to lynch the Bishops, but from a lady of rank.

Upon the balcony of Moray House in the Canongait, that fine house where Cromwell had been lodged in 1648, there sat Argyll's heir, Lord Lorn who, a few days previously, had married the Earl of Moray's daughter, Lady Mary Stewart. With the bride and groom was Argyll's niece, Huntly's daughter, the Countess of Haddington; inside the room, peeping between the shutters, could be seen the faces of Argyll and Wariston. As the tragic figure on the hangman's cart passed beneath the balcony, Lady Haddington's voice broke the silence with a jeering laugh. Immediately a gentleman in the street below called

up to her that it would have become her better to have sat in
that cart as a punishment for her notorious adulteries.[20]

Apparently by orders which he had received beforehand, the
hangman halted the cart when it came beneath this balcony, so
that Argyll might gloat upon his fallen foe. Lorn mocked and
laughed, but as the grey eyes of Montrose, bright with fever,
encountered the squinting glance of Lorn's father, Argyll was
observed to draw back into the room and close the shutters. "It
is no wonder," cried an Englishman in the crowd, "you start
aside at his looks, for you durst not look him in the face these
seven years bygone."[21]

On Monday, May 20th, Montrose was taken to the Parliament
House to hear his dreadful sentence; and at two in the afternoon
of the following day he was brought from the Tolbooth to the
gigantic gallows, thirty feet high, which had been erected
between the prison and the Tron Kirk. Perhaps he remembered
that prophecy which Rothes had made in jest when, an ardent
young Covenanter, Montrose had climbed on a barrel in his
enthusiasm during the reading of a Protestation. But years of
active loyalty had more than redeemed that youthful folly; in
his last letter to the King, written from Kirkwall in the Orkneys
on March 26th, he had declared a passionate resolve to "abandon
still my life to search my death for the interests of your Majesty's
honour and service"; and he was dressed like a bridegroom as
he came to abandon his life on this May afternoon. "He stept
along the street with so great state," recorded an eye-witness,
James Fraser, "and there appeared in his countenance so much
beauty, majesty, and gravity as amazed the beholders."

The vast concourse which had gathered to see him die was
reverently silent; only the ministers plagued him with their
exhortations and denunciations, and Lord Lorn jeered, staying
afterwards to witness the butchery on the dead body, and
triumphing in every stroke.[22] Montrose's last words before the
weeping hangman turned him off the ladder, were, "God have
mercy on this afflicted land". When the butchery had been
carried out, the trunk was buried in the felons' pit on the
Boroughmuir, the limbs sent to Aberdeen and other towns, and
the head set upon the highest prick of the Tolbooth, a new cross-
piece of iron being made to secure it, lest the victim's friends
might attempt to take it down.

Contrary to all decency and custom, the bloody scaffold was
left standing, for Argyll still had a use for it. Eight days after
Montrose had paid the price of loyalty, two of his friends were
executed by the Maiden, Sir John Spottiswoode, grandson of the

dead Archbishop, and Major-General Hurry. The latter had turned his coat so many times that the Estates would have been content to banish him; he was a good soldier, and their clemency might have persuaded him to fight on the Covenant side again. But the Commission of the Kirk insisted on a capital sentence, and sharply rebuked the Estates for trying to save the life of one "whom the Lord had appointed to die for being a man of blood".

On June 4th there were two more victims, Sir Francis Hay of Dalgetty and Colonel Sibbald; and on June 22nd, the very eve of the King's arrival in Scotland, the grisly scaffold was bespattered with the blood of Captain Alexander Charteris. This scaffold was nicknamed by the people "the Altar of Argyll and the ministers", and with grim humour some wag remarked that the Kirk "delighted not in unbloody sacrifices".[23]

Chapter Three

MUCH has been made of the fact that Charles II signed the Covenant, the price of Scottish aid, without the slightest intention of keeping it; and while on moral grounds his action must be condemned, yet the circumstances provided a certain excuse for it. The Scots had leagued with English rebels to defeat his father; they had sold his father after promising him protection; they had harried and butchered his loyal subjects; and they had invited him over to suit their own ends. He would do, therefore, precisely that which so many vainly had entreated his father to do in order to save his crown : sign the Covenant and trust to an English parliament to resist the imposing of it.

But very little has been made of the fact that the Covenanters were perfectly aware that Charles had surrendered to their terms because it was an ultimatum. He had signed from *force majeure*, and he had made it crystal-clear to them that there was no question of his being converted to their creed. Throughout the negotiations at Breda, and until his actual landing in Scotland, he continued to attend the Anglican service, and received Holy Communion on his knees under the very noses of the Commissioners. One of these afterwards had the honesty to admit that the moral blame for the Treaty of Breda lay heavier upon themselves than on Charles.

"We did sinfully both entangle and engage the nation and ourselves," wrote Alexander Jaffray, "and that poor young prince to whom we were sent; making him sign and swear a Covenant which we knew, from clear and demonstrable reasons, that he hated in his heart. Yet finding that upon these terms only he could be admitted to rule over us (all other means having failed him), he sinfully complied with what we most sinfully pressed upon him; where, I must confess, to my apprehension, our sin was worse than his."[24]

After a very stormy voyage, the ship carrying Charles and his small retinue anchored in the mouth of the Spey at the end of June; here he signed both Covenants, "and had notable sermons and exhortations made unto him by the ministers," wrote Sir Edward Walker, Garter King at Arms, who accompanied him, "to persevere therein". The news of his arrival was brought by Arthur Erskine of Scotscraig two days later to the Estates, who immediately settled down to delete from the list of friends and servants the King had brought with him, those they deemed obnoxious. While they were thus employed, the common people were enthusiastically celebrating his arrival. "All signs of joy were manifested through the whole kingdom; namely, in a special manner in Edinburgh, by setting forth of bale-fires, ringing of bells, sounding of trumpets, dancing almost all that night through the streets. The poor kail-wives at the Tron sacrificed their maunds and creels, and the very stools they sat upon, to the fire."[25]

On July 1st, Libberton and Brodie arrived with a full report of the negotiations at Breda, and copies of the Covenants signed by the King; on the 4th an Act was passed, ratifying the Treaty, together with an invitation to Charles to be present at the next session of Parliament, "and there to receive his royal crown". After a proclamation of his entry into the government of the kingdom had been read at the Mercat Cross, a few yards from the spot where Montrose and his fellow Royalists had met their death so recently, the Estates adjourned, appointing the usual Committee to reign in the interim.

The nobles then rode northwards to meet their King who, on his first landing, had gone to Huntly's seat, the Bog of Gight, and to conduct him to Falkland Palace. There was immediate unpleasantness over the fact that Charles had brought with him certain of the Engagers. Though he protested that it was a breach of the Treaty of Breda, Lanerick, now Duke of Hamilton, and others were commanded to withdraw themselves, while some were allowed to remain only after they had done public penance for their part in the Engagement. Engaging nobles who came to kiss the King's hand were forbidden to do so; among these was old Carnwath who, at first insisting on his right to greet his King, was prevailed upon to withdraw by Sir James Balfour, who had an order from Wariston and Sir John Chiesley to hang him unless he complied.[26]

The remaining lords and gentlemen in the King's train were then divided into sheep and goats, the latter being dismissed as insufficiently godly. Among the former were nine English nobles, surprisingly headed by that notorious profligate, the Duke of Buckingham. But Buckingham, a skilful actor, could ape a pious manner when it suited him, and Argyll, who had a keen nose for a possible traitor, may well have seen the weakness in that handsome face.

While the rest of the Covenanting potentates went their several ways until Parliament reassembled, Argyll, his son Lorn, and Lothian, brought the King southward to Falkland. There is a tradition that during this progress, on which Argyll rode at the King's left hand and Buckingham at his right, a woman who was believed to be a seer called out to Charles to beware of the man who rode on his left, who had taken off his father's head and who, if he did not take care, would have his own next.[27]

On this his first journey through his father's native kingdom, Charles was given a foretaste of what was in store for him. The common people who flocked to see and cheer him, were driven off; towns which offered him gifts of money were rebuked for it; and at Aberdeen he was lodged in a house opposite the Tolbooth on which he could not avoid seeing one of the decomposing hands of the dead Montrose. On his arrival at Falkland, Lord Lorn was appointed the captain of his bodyguard, for the purpose, it was believed, of spying on the King and reporting all his words and acts to his squint-eyed father; while Argyll himself set about maturing a plan which, when it had become certain that not all his harsh conditions were going to prevent the King from coming to Scotland, he had begun while Charles was still at Breda.

It was nothing less than a proposal that Charles should marry Argyll's eldest daughter, Lady Anne Campbell, " a gentlewoman of rare parts and education "; this, said Argyll, would unite all interests in Scotland, " and make them all of a piece ".[28] Now, when the King had arrived in Scotland, the scheme was made into a sort of ultimatum. Argyll told his Sovereign that he could not serve him " unless he gave some undeniable proof of a fixed

resolution to support the Presbyterian party, which he thought
would be best done by marrying into some family of quality
that was known to be entirely devoted to that interest; this he
thought would in a great measure take off the prejudice both
kingdoms had to him on his mother's account, who was
extremely odious to all good Protestants; and he thought his own
daughter would be the properest match for him: not without
some threats if he did not accept the offer, as the King told
Colonel Legge, who was the only person about him that he could
trust with the secret ".[29]

Legge's opinion was that Argyll would never have dared propose such a thing unless he had been very sure of his power in
Scotland, and that therefore it was necessary to play for time by
telling the dictator that, in common decency, his Majesty could
come to no conclusion without consulting his mother. "But
this answer was far from satisfying the Marquis, who suspected
Colonel Legge had been the adviser; and he committed him next
day to the Castle of Edinburgh."[30] Nevertheless it was an answer
with which Argyll was forced to be satisfied, for Charles insisted
on consulting his mother by letter, privately telling the messenger that he need not hasten his return.

In other matters the King was now paying the price of out-
raging his honour and his conscience by coming to Scotland on
the Covenanters' terms. His condition while at Falkland is
pithily described by Clarendon:

"He was not present in their councils, nor were the results
thereof communicated to him; nor was he, in the least degree,
communicated with in any part of the government: yet they
made great show of outward reverence to him, and even the
chaplains, when they used rudeness and barbarity in their repre-
hensions and reproaches, approached him still with bended
knees, and in the humblest postures. There was never a better
courtier than Argyll, who made all possible addresses to make
himself gracious to the King, entertained him with very pleasant discourses, with such insinuations, that the King did not
only very well like his conversation, but often believed that he
had a mind to please and gratify him: but then, when his
Majesty made any attempt to get some of his servants about
him, or to reconcile the two factions, that the kingdom might be
united, he gathered up his countenance and retired from him,
without ever yielding to any one proposition that was made to
him by his Majesty."[31]

The utter stupidity of Argyll and the Kirk in not coming to
terms with the Engagers was soon to become apparent. For

Cromwell, having crushed Royalist Ireland, was marching to subdue Presbyterian Scotland.

By the end of July, with a large force of veterans, he had crossed the Border and lay at Musselburgh, where he turned the kirks into stables for his horses, used the seats and pews for firewood, and burnt the surrounding cornlands in order to deprive Edinburgh of food.[32]   In Edinburgh itself there were preparations for a resolute defence against the invader.   Barricades were erected across the streets, the walls were manned and colours planted in defiance, the houses outside the Flodden Wall were demolished to prevent their providing shelter for the enemy, a trench was dug at the foot of the Canongait, and even the four pinnacles of the Netherbow, " which was a very great ornament hitherto", were sacrificed, that cannon might be planted on top of the gate.   From the highest prick of the Tolbooth the mouldering head of Montrose looked down upon these warlike activities.

On the 29th, as a very great concession, the King was allowed to review the Covenant's army assembled at Leith.   He was received by the common soldiers with enormous enthusiasm; they chalked the royal initials on their arms, and one of them wrote in white chalk on the back of his coat " I am for King Charles".   (This unfortunate man was caught by the English in a skirmish, had his eyes put out, was stripped naked, and sent back to the Scottish leaguer.)[33]   Nothing could be plainer than that in the coming struggle, which was one for Scotland's survival as a sovereign State, the presence of the young King with his army was vital to that army's morale.

But Charles's popularity alarmed the Covenanters.   " The army's exclamations and carnal carriage in his presence," wrote Wariston, "more than the Lord's, was ominous in my thought that, at the best, we get a mixed dispensation . . . Lord, reckon with us at any other time, in any other way, but deliver us this time from this enemy."   He spoke his mind freely to Charles, assuring him that God would be jealous of such enthusiasm shown for a creature, and very probably was "changing the quarrel to undo us".   The King must go away at once, said the ministers; and so on August 2nd, "sore against his mind", he retired to Dunfermline.

But Covenanting stupidity did not stop at removing the army's rallying-point, the popular person of the King.   The Engagers and other Malignants had offered to raise a separate force, and in case that of the Covenant were defeated in battle, to continue the fight against the invader, in the interim offering their wives

and children as hostages, and promising to lay down their arms
if the Covenanters were victorious. The offer was brusquely
refused, the ministers affirming that it was better to fight with
a handful of the Elect than with a mighty host tainted with
Malignancy, which, they added, was the sin against the Holy
Ghost.[34]

They then set about a thorough purging of their own army,
appointing a special committee to enquire into the godliness of
every officer and man. Disregarding the imminence of battle,
the Committee for Purging sat daily, while the ministers filled
their sermons with arguments for the necessity of this work. God
had shown many times in the past, they cried, that He "laid
aside many and made use of few"; He would by a little army of
the Elect soon "muddle away" the vast host of Cromwell.
While Wariston gloated over tales of the wickedness of the Independents, and of how Cromwell, "that proud piece of clay", had
said that he was as assured of victory as of his own salvation,
the Committee for Purging dismissed from the Covenant's army
eighty veteran commanders and three thousand common men,
substituting "ministers' sons, clerks, and other sanctified
creatures, who hardly ever saw or heard of any sword but that
of the spirit".[35]

The purging mood being strong upon them, the Committee
turned their attention to the King's Household, and although
Argyll had been through it with a tooth-comb several times
already, they dismissed three of Charles's gentlemen, and recommended four nominees of their own as Grooms of the Bedchamber. But even this was not enough to placate Jehovah.
Nothing good could be expected from Him until Charles had
signed a Declaration which had been delivered to him on August
9th, and in which he must attribute all the past woes of Scotland
to his father's opposition to the work of reformation and his
mother's idolatry.

He had been made to re-sign the Covenant twice since his landing, and had put his name to endless confessions of personal
sinfulness, but this was too much, and he refused to sign so
detestable a document. The usual committee, consisting of
Wariston, Robert Barclay, Argyll's old pedagogue, and three
ministers, arrived at Dunfermline to bring him to reason. "We
told him," recorded Wariston, "his standing or falling depended
on this, and it would be counted the great prognostic of the
success of the battle, which we knew not how soon it might be";
if the Covenant's army was beaten, the blame must lie at
Charles's door. "We all spake very freely, and the Marquis [of

Argyll] with us ". but Charles still refused to vilify his father's memory. He was a cynical young realist, but his love for his father had been the strongest emotion of his youth; he fasted every Tuesday, the day of his father's murder, " that he might not forget a day so fatal to him and all Great Britain ".[36] Even when Argyll told him privately that it was necessary " to please these madmen ", the ministers, Charles was not to be moved.

The Covenanters' retort was to meet in the West Kirk of Edinburgh and draw up a Declaration of their own. In order, they said, to clear themselves from any misunderstanding with the English, they declared that they disowned the King's quarrel until " he disclaims his and his father's opposition to the work of God, and to the Covenant, and likewise all the enemies thereof ". It was a threat, and not an idle one. There were many extremists who would have liked nothing better than an excuse to sell the young King as they had sold his father.

On August 16th, Charles gave in. Having obtained the trifling concession that the Declaration be re-written, with some of the ruder epithets against his parents deleted, he signed the detestable document. That same evening he was removed to Perth, where, as a reward for his capitulation, the Crown and Sceptre were fetched from Stirling, though nothing was said about his Coronation. Meanwhile, while the opposing armies exchanged broadsides, the Kirk drew up an exhaustive list of the sins of the Royal Family, for which they appointed a special fast. The most important items in it were James VI and I's " defection from the National Covenant " (the Confession of Faith of 1580), Charles I's " obtruding upon the Kirk of Scotland the Service Book ", his Popish marriage and the idolatry of his wife, Charles II's treaty with the Irish, and his being " involved in the opposition to the work of God, and giving commissions to Malignants ", in other words to Montrose.

While Charles, hugging an empty stomach on fast-days and dozing through endless sermons, was being thus humiliated, the canny Argyll was making provision for the future if the Covenant's army should prove successful against Cromwell. " M. of Argyll," Secretary Nicholas wrote to Hyde, " (who underhand doubtless doth set on the ministers to make these mad and unconscionable demands) hath pressed the K. to give security, that the Scots shall have satisfaction in case they shall beat Cromwell. And I believe one part of that security will be, that they may have the D. of York in their power; which if they shall compass . . . then they may be sure to have a good price from the rebels of England for the K. and his brother together, and then there will be an end, if not of Monarchy in England, yet I doubt not of that Family."[37]

Such was the prelude to the Battle of Dunbar. Only four days previous to it, the Committee for Purging dismissed from the Scots Army that hitherto impeccable Covenanter, the Earl of Eglinton, and issued an order forbidding any to drink or converse with those whom it had cashiered.

Chapter Four

DESPITE the purging of the Covenant's army, and the replacing of so many experienced officers and men by saints who scarcely knew one end of a pike from the other, there remained a chance, which the fanatics little deserved, of their beating Cromwell.

For the latter, always a poor strategist, had got himself into very grave difficulties. When he had crossed the Border in July, he had had seventeen thousand veterans under his command, a force which very easily could have defeated the Covenanters in pitched battle, even though they were numerically superior. But there were two things he had neglected to do. One was to make provision for the possible necessity of retreat; he had left no lines of communication behind him, and no detached bodies to hold essential points. The other was his failure to take into account the excellence of David Leslie as a commander, and consequently Leslie's present strategy of playing for time.

There was one other circumstance in the Scots' favour which was no fault of Cromwell's: the weather. It was proving the worst summer within living memory; day after day came pouring rain, and the English had no tents. The result was an increasing number of sick men, and an inevitable lowering of morale, intensified by lack of proper food, for the country through which they marched had been eaten bare; they themselves had destroyed the cornlands, and there was no means of getting supplies from England.

By the end of August the situation had grown so bad that Cromwell accepted the necessity of withdrawing from Scotland. There were two possible ways of effecting this. One was to get as many as possible of his troops on board a few English ships which lay off Dunbar, and leave the rest to their fate; the other

King Charles II in 1650

Contemporary English
satire on Charles II and
the Scots

was to march down the only road which led along the East Coast to Berwick. He chose the former. On Saturday, August 31st, he burnt his huts in his camp at Musselburgh, and began his march to Dunbar.

Leslie, however, with something between twenty and twenty-two thousand men under his command, had no intention of letting the invader escape. He hurried after the retreating English, harassing their rear, and the next day, September 1st, prepared to deliver a general attack. Though many of his men were raw levies, there can be little doubt that the sheer weight of numbers would have made that attack successful. But he had reckoned without the plague of all the Covenant's armies, the committee of ministers who travelled about with them. It was the Sabbath, they reminded Leslie, and men must not profane it by fighting. It was exactly the kind of interference the King had foreseen when, as early as July 19th, he had written Argyll from Falkland, entreating him to impress upon the committee to leave such decisions to the military commander.[38]

Leslie acquiesced, partly because he was himself a sincere Covenanter, partly because the alternative was to lose his command. But he remained an excellent soldier, and on Monday, the 2nd, he executed two tactics which together ensured that his enemy should not escape him. He drew up his main army on some rising ground above Dunbar, so that he stood above Cromwell's retreating forces, menacing them with his cannon; and he sent a strong detachment to hold the defile called Cockburn's Path through which the English must pass if they attempted to withdraw into England by land. It was the best possible strategy in the circumstances, and it deserved success.

Thus matters stood until the evening of that day, when the representatives of the Kirk committed their crowning piece of folly. As with Baillie at Kilsyth, so with Leslie at Dunbar, the committee of ministers decided upon tactics of their own, or, as they would have said, on those revealed to them by the Lord of Hosts. They insisted that Leslie withdraw his main army from its excellent position on the heights and come down into the level ground where, next morning, it must make that general attack which they had prevented on the Sabbath. Leslie had no choice but to concur.

All that night, under the rain and the gale, the Scots stood to their arms; but towards morning, Major-General Holbourn (later strongly suspected of being a collaborator of the English) gave order to the Covenanting infantry to extinguish the matches with which the powder in the muskets was fired, and

P

to seek some rest among the stooks of mouldering corn. Some of the horse, meanwhile, was sent out to forage; the rest unsaddled their beasts and lay down to sleep. The fantastic folly of the ministers, and the treachery or stupidity of Holbourn, gave Cromwell a chance he was not slow to take. Advised by his scouts of this singular behaviour of the enemy, he gave orders for a stealthy advance to be made, screened by the gale, before it grew light. Somewhere around half past four, therefore, with the first glimmerings of day, the Scots beheld their erstwhile trapped enemy marching down upon them in order of battle.

Even then the numerical superiority of the Covenanters might have told, for, with so many of his men sick, Cromwell cannot have had much more than half the strength of the Scottish host. But the Covenanters were taken by surprise; a number of them were raw levies; the musketeers' match could not be rekindled in a moment under that pouring rain; many of the horses were unsaddled, and others were not yet returned from their foraging. Worst of all, the men were almost immediately left leaderless, the committee of civilians being the first to flee, and the officers following their example.[39] It was less a battle than a rout; the casualties on the Covenant's side were only between eight and nine hundred, mostly of the infantry, the horse having saved themselves by flight.

The tale of the disaster reached Perth late that night, Argyll himself breaking the news to the King. Just before the tidings arrived, the Rev. Robert Durham, whose rigidity and moroseness had made him the Kirk's choice for the office of principal chaplain to the King, had informed Charles " that now God had put a glorious victory into his hands, which he must not ascribe to any other cause, but that he was entered into the Covenant of God ". He would have done well to have remembered the unfortunate result of the Rev. Carmichael's like presumption, when he had promised Lord Elcho a glorious victory at Tippermuir.

The ministers immediately set about finding scapegoats. First they upbraided the Almighty for permitting His Elect to be defeated by Sectaries; then they raged against " the carnal confidence that was in so many of the army, into the despising of the enemy and promising victory to themselves " (which was precisely what they had impressed upon the saintly soldiers they must do), and lastly they rounded on the King. It was the presence of " this thing that troubleth our Israel " which had caused God to forsake His Chosen; it was impossible for Scottish arms to triumph while this son of a man of sin and a woman of idolatry, himself a hypocrite, polluted their New Jerusalem.

While Cromwell was entering Edinburgh in triumph, the Commission of the Kirk at Stirling was issuing "A Short Declaration and Warning to all the Congregations of the Kirk of Scotland ", showing the mind of Jehovah in this crisis. The godly were not to believe the calumnies which were "blazing abroad " anent the conduct of their army, though on the other hand that conduct could not be entirely justified. God's people must "eye the Lord, and look up to the hand that smites them "; it was the King's part to mourn for all the grievous provocations of his father's House and for his own sinfulness, which between them had been a main cause of this disaster. "It concerns our Nobles and Judges to consider whether their carriage in public matters be straight and equal, or rather savouring of seeking themselves and the things of this world; and how they walk in their families, and in their private conversations." The officers of the army and even some of the ministers, must weigh well what the Lord had against them, for "doubtless even among these is much negligence ".[40]

Of the real cause of the defeat, the dismissal of experienced officers and men on the eve of battle, and the criminal pride and folly of the travelling committee in interfering with military affairs, there was not one word.

Many ministers refused to read this Declaration from their pulpits until pressure was brought to bear upon them. For the split which was to wreck the Kirk, which in a short time was to put an end to the reign of King Covenant, was beginning. By its own tyranny and presumption the all-powerful Kirk was tottering at last; and there may well be truth in the story that King Charles, on hearing that Cromwell had smashed the Kirk's army, fell down on his knees and thanked God.

Chapter Five

T HE defeat of the Kirk's army at Dunbar gave Charles a chance of which he had almost despaired. The blow had caused many, even among the ministry, to realize that it was no longer a question of fighting for the Covenant, but a struggle for Scotland's very existence. It was clear that a new army must be raised, and to anyone of average intelligence it was clear also that such an army must be made up of men of all shades of opinion in religion and politics who had a common love for their country, and would combine rather than see her occupied by the Auld Enemy. And the only man to raise and command such an army was the energetic and popular young King.

From the first it had been Charles's aim to use Scotland as a recruiting-ground, and with Scots arms to fight his way to England and his throne. But before he could march, it was essential to ensure his leaving behind him a united Scotland. It was Hamilton's failure in this which had ruined the Engagement. First of all, therefore, the King attempted to satisfy the greed of Argyll. The latter's reputation for cowardice had caused him to be regarded as a Jonah by the soldiers and therefore he would be better left behind on the march to England; when, in 1644, he had returned to Scotland to carry thither the news of the Covenant's success at Newburn, the soldiers had rejoiced at his going, because they had "an apprehension that his company was unfortunate in war, and that they would prosper the better to be rid of him".[41]

On September 24th, the King wrote Argyll a letter which he hoped would keep the Campbell out of mischief. In consideration for his "faithful services", Argyll should be made a duke, a Knight of the Garter, and a Gentleman of the Bedchamber, as soon as it pleased God to restore the King to his throne. In addition there should be paid him the sum of forty thousand pounds sterling which he claimed was owing to him out of the public money.[42]

It is possible that the hope of such lavish rewards might have kept Argyll quiet until he saw the result of the King's march into England. But there were those in Scotland more difficult to deal with even than King Campbell. The Western Army of the Covenant had not been present at Dunbar, and remained intact; until new forces could be raised, it was Scotland's only defence against the invader, apart from the remains of Leslie's army. This western host was composed of the extreme Covenanters, those very Whigs who had risen during the Engagement. The defeat of Leslie enabled them to clamour for his dismissal, but while the Estates refused the petition, they weakly gave an independent command to the most michievous of the military Whigs, Colonel Strachan.

It was the height of folly, for Strachan had actually fought in Cromwell's army against Hamilton, had remained with him until the execution of Charles I, and was suspected, correctly as it proved, of being as ready as ever to betray his country if not given his own way. Before sending Strachan and his friend Sir John Chiesley to take command of the Western Army, the Estates suggested that they should include in it such of the former Engagers who had done penance; whereat "Sir John Chiesley rose up laying his hand upon his sword, and protesting that he would rather join with Cromwell than with them, and so went away to take up his own charge".[43]

Strachan and his colleagues proceeded to make plainer yet their intention to divide Scotland. In the Provincial Synod of Glasgow they drew up a document which amounted to a disowning of every authority except their own. It became known as the Western Remonstrance, but might well have been called the Third Covenant; it was condemned by the Estates as "ane band of a high and dangerous consequence", and indeed it was. In it, the extremists censured the Estates and the Kirk for inviting Charles to come to Scotland, entirely disowned the King's cause, and asserted that the Solemn League and Covenant forbade an offensive war against England.[44]

This attitude of the main fighting force of the kingdom, an attitude which revealed to Charles his very real personal danger, induced him to embark upon that pathetic little adventure known as The Start. A mixed party of northern Royalists and former Engagers had invited him to escape from his virtual imprisonment at Perth, and put himself at their head. Early in October, taking advantage of the fact that Argyll was absent in his own domains, Charles attempted to put this plan into action. It is doubtful whether, in any case, it would have succeeded, for, except for gallant old Airlie, the northern leaders were of poor stuff; its certain failure was due to the treachery of the Duke of Buckingham.

Buckingham, who had grown up with Charles, as Hamilton had grown up with his father, was utterly untrustworthy, and the young King's confidence in him was an example of the fatal weakness of the Stuarts in trusting those they loved. As soon as Charles had ridden out of Perth on the afternoon of October 4th, with five gentlemen and no baggage, and on the excuse that they were going hawking, Buckingham marched straight to the Covenanting authorities and disclosed the whole plan. Two days later the weary and dispirited King was brought back to Perth by the armed forces of the Covenant commanded by Colonel Robert Montgomery.

The failure of The Start encouraged the western fanatics to draw up a second and even more insolent Remonstrance, which revealed the extent of the rift which was taking place in the

Covenant's camp. They demanded the resignations of Argyll, the Chancellor, Lothian, and others whom they blamed for the King's attempt to escape; that the Treaty of Breda be declared unlawful; and that Charles's governing power (which in any case he had not been allowed to exercise) be suspended until he had given evidence of a genuine change of heart, "whereof," observed Baillie sarcastically, "they were to be the judges, who were never like to be satisfied". There was, moreover, a strong hint that the King should be imprisoned, and the chief Malignants executed. Even this did not satisfy Strachan, who now openly expressed his desire for a treaty with the invader.

The moderates in the Kirk (if such a term may be used to describe men like Baillie) were shocked by this attitude of their extremist brethren. "I sent to my Lord Argyll and you the two Remonstrances," Baillie wrote to David Dickson on November 18th, "in my judgment very insolent and scandalous pieces. If you connive with them, and permit two or three bold men to carry the Commission of the Church to allow any such write, I think you consent to put upon the Church the foulest blot that ever yet it got. . . . If my Lord Argyll at this strait should desert the King, and verify the too common surmises of many, which I trust shall be found most false and shortly shall be refuted by his deeds, I think, and many more with me of the best I speak with, that it would be a fearful sin in him, which God will revenge."[45]

The fact of the matter was, the official government both in Kirk and State was now between the devil and the deep sea; on the one hand were the extremists, now known as the Remonstrants, who would admit of no authority except their own; on the other were the old Engagers and the various shades of Royalists who had engineered The Start. The Government's only asset lay in the possession of the King's person, and from now onwards, for the first time since his coming to Scotland, pains were taken to placate him, and he was allowed to be present at the meetings of the Committee of Estates. Not that the Covenant's leaders had experienced a change of heart towards him; "Argyll," wrote Nicholas to Lord Hatton, "will sooner trust Cromwell (who I believe is not much more guilty of the death of the late K. of blessed memory than his lordship) than the K. our master"; but he was an invaluable pawn in their game; and not only did they accede to his demand for a complete indemnity for those who had contrived The Start, but at long last they appointed a committee to debate upon the order of his Coronation.

But on the other hand they had not the courage vigorously to defy the western fanatics. As Baillie had hinted, there were rumours that Argyll was intriguing with the latter, and that there was some real fear of this is evident from the fact that the members of the Committee of Estates were called upon individually to swear that they had had no hand in drawing up the Western Remonstrance. An Act condemning it was then framed, yet so fearful were the Estates of giving offence to the revolutionaries that every other word was scrutinized to see that it was not too harsh. The description of "scandalous" must have "conceived" inserted before it; for "destructive" to his Majesty's government, was substituted "prejudicial". When the Act was finally drawn up, Argyll was sent with it to get the approval of the Commission of the Kirk who, while finding that there were "many sad truths" in the Western Remonstrance, expressed themselves as "dissatisfied" with that document. The Kirk could scarcely do less, seeing that the Remonstrants had dared to censure the Commission of the General Assembly.

Having passed this futile Act, Kirk and State applied themselves to the winning over of their dear but erring brethren. Four whole days were spent discussing the question in Argyll's private apartments, so that things might be carried "in a smooth way". The fact that Cromwell was rampaging throughout the south of Scotland was far less important to the rulers of that country than was the endless drawing up of counter-remonstrances to the party of hot-heads who had flouted their authority.

"Though it was visible," wrote Baillie, "that every day the kingdom languishes under these debates, which impeded that action, there was no remedy : by no persuasion the Remonstrance could be taken up [withdrawn]; yea, the gentlemen gave in a petition to the Estates at Perth, in the presence of the King, urging the answer thereof, from which petition they would not pass; yea, when they were most earnestly dealt with to conjoin their forces, all that could be obtained, both by public and diverse private entreaties, both of their best friends, Argyll and others, there was a willingness to join on two conditions: The first was, an express laying aside the King's quarrel . . . the other, to keep none in the Army at Stirling but according to the qualification in the Act [of Classes]. When in these two all the gentlemen and officers were found peremptor, the conference on the Friday, the fourth day of it, was broken off as fruitless: though, for their satisfaction, the Parliament had been shifted from the Wednesday to the Friday, and from the Friday till the Tuesday again, for all the issue of blood, and starving, that was every day over the kingdom."

The spinelessness displayed by the Estates in their dealings with the Remonstrants argues strongly that the former contained secret sympathizers. When, being ordered by the Estates to lay down his commission, Strachan flatly refused, a motion to arrest him was defeated on the grounds that this would only irritate his colleagues. Again, though a majority found the Remonstrance to be high treason, "the respect most of them had to the persons found guilty" prevented the imposing of any penalties.

Only the same explanation can account for the extraordinary behaviour of the Kirk. Never yet, since its grasping of the supreme power, had it been so flouted and insulted as it was by the Remonstrants. They had even set up what they termed "The Presbytery of the Western Army" in competition with the Commission of the General Assembly. One of the ministers accused the latter to its face of approving nothing that was right, declared that a hypocrite like Charles II should not be permitted to reign over Scotland, and advocated a treaty with Cromwell. These zealots, the followers of a God who delighted in revenge and in persecution to the limit, rebuked the Kirk for "not using the Gospel-way allowed by God for gaining others, however carried away with errors", and, most astonishing of all, reproved it for "pitching on our form of presbyterial government, as the uttermost attainable perfection of reformation".[46]

Yet the Kirk, which for years had excommunicated right and left, which had deposed and censured and punished for every imaginable and unimaginable kind of sin, refrained from punishing these rebels who were advocating a treaty with the invader of Scotland and the head of the Sectaries, and who were daring to imply that Presbyterianism was not the only true religion. It was not until Strachan had actually gone over to Cromwell, and his colleague, Colonel Ker, had been defeated by Lambert and was therefore harmless, that the Kirk passed a sentence of Excommunication upon these two ringleaders.

Strachan and Ker, refusing to lay down their commissions, had been allowed to return to their troops; but the Estates ordered Colonel Robert Montgomery to go after them and take the chief command. Though Montgomery not unnaturally "showed great aversion from any such junction", he obeyed, sending word to Ker that he was coming. Rather than be subordinate to any commander appointed by the Estates, Ker attacked Lambert at Hamilton at four o'clock in the morning of December 1st, found the enemy all too ready to receive him, and "the fearful consequence of that pride of stomach" was the complete rout of the Western Army, Ker's men fleeing singly, and the English pursuing as far as Kilmarnock and Paisley. Ker, who was wounded, was among the prisoners. According to Baillie he "might have 'scaped if he would", but evidently, now that he was defeated, Ker felt that Cromwell would prove a less remorseless captor than the Kirk.

The next day, two or three hundred men who had rallied at Kyle were disbanded by Strachan, who, with Sir John Swinton, at last declared himself by going over to Cromwell's side. The first thing they did was to persuade young Dundas, Governor of Edinburgh Castle, which until now had held out against the invader, to hand over this, the principal fortress of the kingdom, to the English. Cromwell was now master of the whole of the south of Scotland; his forces over-ran the countryside without opposition, destroying cattle and crops, and putting Glasgow and other towns under "grievous contributions".

Chapter Six

T H E defeat of the Western Army did not enable Scotland to unite in the struggle for her existence. In this hour of her greatest peril she had never been more rent with rival factions, the main parties dividing into small ones, so that besides the Royalists, the Engagers, the Remonstrants, and the Covenanters, there were Anti-Covenanters, Cross-Covenanters, Old-horns, New-horns, Cross-Petitioners, and half a dozen more.[47]

Such was the unpromising material out of which King Charles must create the force with which he was determined to invade England, if, by strategy and good fortune, he could evade the victorious army which had smashed Leslie at Dunbar and Ker at Hamilton. Once he was over the Border he was convinced that the English Royalists would rally to his side; he did not realize how much he had offended them by signing the Covenant and thus pledging himself to impose Presbyterianism upon England, nor how deep was the hatred of the common people of that nation for the Scots who had lived on the northern counties during the Civil War.

Meanwhile the defeats of Leslie and Ker had given Charles one advantage; they provided an unanswerable case for repealing the Act of Classes. Whatever their differences, all men must take up arms and unite against the invader, unless they would see Scotland made a province of the Auld Enemy. First, however, Charles held the Estates to that promise which they had made him when first he had come over from Holland, and had never yet fulfilled: that he should be crowned.

Grudgingly the Estates and the Kirk assented, the latter comforting its wounded pride by preparing to make the ceremony as humiliating as possible for the King. On Christmas Day, while Cromwell's army was holding a solemn thanksgiving for the treachery which had given them Edinburgh Castle, the King's Scottish subjects were being made to fast for his sins. The Kirk then settled down to a fierce internal squabble on the question of which sins to choose for further fasts, a question complicated by the fact that Remonstrants and Anti-Remonstrants could not agree on what constituted a sin and what did not. Day in, day out, they argued, while Cromwell was expected at any moment to march on Stirling "to mar the Coronation"; untroubled by this, the Kirk ordered the Coronation to be postponed until January 1st, in order that a Day of Public Humiliation might precede it, on which Scotland must fast for the sins of the Royal Family as far back as King James V. King Charles II, who somehow had managed to retain his sense of humour, remarked that it might be proper to add a lamentation for the fact that he had ever been born.

There must have been some present in the old Abbey of Scone, on New Year's Day of 1651, who remembered the Coronation of the King's father in the Abbey of Holyrood eighteen years before, the pageantry and the colour, the singing of the choir, the firing of salutes, the nobility in their crimson robes, the distributing of gold and silver pieces. How dramatic, and how melancholy, was the contrast between the two occasions. On this bleak January morning, the nobles of Scotland were not so much crowning King Charles as endeavouring to prolong the reign of his rival, King Covenant. Once again, for at least the third time since he had come to Scotland, Charles was obliged to swear to both Covenants; the sermon preached by the Rev. Robert Douglas was merely a lengthy exhortation to defend them. Many plagues, prophesied Douglas, would fall upon the King's head if he failed in this, and he added a defence of subjects who resisted the royal authority. The only cause for rejoicing was that "by the blessing of God, Popery and Prelacy are removed; the Bishops, as limbs of Anti-christ, are put to the door; let the anointing of kings with oil go to the door with them, and let them never come in again". When Argyll placed the Crown upon the King's head, the Moderator prayed that the Lord would purge it from all the transgressions of its previous wearers.

It is interesting to speculate upon the thoughts of Argyll while he was thus engaged in crowning his Sovereign. Charles had evaded all his attempts to make his daughter Queen Consort; and the possibility of a restoration by means of a Scottish army, which inevitably now would be largely composed of Royalists and Engagers, cannot have been pleasant to the dictator who had given mortal offence to both these parties. "I confess I cannot bring myself to believe," Nicholas wrote to Hatton, "that Argyll will ever endure the K. to have an army at his devotion, while Hamilton is powerful with his Majesty, but that being conscious of what mischief he hath done his Majesty, and to the family of Hamilton, he will either betray the K., or himself rather trust Cromwell than his Majesty."

When the Court returned to Stirling after the Coronation, Argyll made a last attempt to wean Charles from his favouring of Malignants and Engagers. One night after supper he followed the King into his closet, and there "dealt freely" with him. Charles was "seemingly sensible, and they came that length to pray and mourn together till two or three in the morning; and when at length he [Argyll] came home to his lady, she was surprised, and told him she had never known him so untimous. He said, he had never such a sweet night in the world, and told her all; what liberty they had in prayer, and how much concerned the King was. She said plainly they were 'crocodile tears', and that that night would cost him his head."[48]

But the fooling of Argyll was only for Charles's few moments of leisure; all his youthful energy was concentrated upon creating that army by means of which he hoped to regain his throne. Though the common people were enthusiastic for him, now that he was allowed to recruit in person, he was obstructed perpetually by the great ones both in Kirk and State who were either definitely hostile or but lukewarm in his cause.

Among these was Chancellor Loudoun, who did his utmost to obstruct the processes against two of the most fanatical Remonstrants, James Guthrie and David Bennet, who, for their seditious writings and preaching, were summoned to appear before the Estates; neither the King nor the Estates, declared Loudoun, were the proper judges of sedition. Sir Alexander Hope advised the King to come to terms with Cromwell, and treat "for the one half of his cloak before he lost the whole"; Wariston, who for weeks had been in Edinburgh on the pretext of persuading the

English to let him have the Registers of the Council stored in the Castle, was having frequent meetings with Cromwell; and Holbourn, the Governor of Stirling Castle, already suspected of treachery at Dunbar, was thought by many to be in secret communication with the invader. It is little wonder, therefore, that the distracted young King told a friend that he did not know whom to trust; and well might Baillie exclaim: "Alas, that so good a King should come among us to be destroyed by our own hands, most by traitors, and divided!"

Argyll's chief occupation was the nominating of his friends for the inevitable committee of civilians who would accompany the army into England. On March 26th, the Estates wrangled for four hours on the matter, Argyll objecting to every name suggested by the King, while Loudoun and Lothian upbraided Charles with what they pleased to call his "inconstancy" in preferring the Hamilton party to those who had invited him to Scotland. Nevertheless, the King got his way; he had the country behind him; and it was a small triumph for him when, on March 31st, the barons and burgesses earnestly solicited him to take the sole command of the army upon himself. He answered "that he was confident there was none there that would distrust him, since he had as much at stake as any other whatsoever had".

Parliament rose on this last day of March, a new one being appointed to meet on May 21st, at the same time as the sitting down of the General Assembly. In the interim the Remonstrants did their utmost to prevent Scotland from uniting in the national cause, and to bully their more moderate brethren to come into their camp. They went, wrote Baillie disgustedly, "in a way of confusion, and will not state a question; never tells positively and clearly what they call a Malignant, and what a Malignant party, and what places of trust, and what convincing signs of repentance. It seems to me their way is indirectly for destroying this Church and Kingdom . . . I suppose that they will, by force of arms, with the bloodshed of all who stand in their way, when they see it time, suppress the present Army, Parliament, and Commission of the Church, and frame both Church and Kingdom according to their own model."

What Baillie failed to realize was that this was the inevitable sequel to the troubles of the thirties. The Kirk had defied the supreme civil authority, the King; by preparing a Protestation against every royal Proclamation before the contents of the latter were known, it had shown that, despite all its professions of loyalty and its pious talk, it was out to usurp the power of the

Crown. Now its own authority was being challenged by a party of extremists, and it was as unable to curb them as the King had been to curb the rebels of 1638. The constitution of the Kirk was that of a highly organized bureaucracy, and it was just as simple to pack kirk-sessions and presbyteries and synods as it had been to pack the General Assembly which had declared war on Charles I.

Nevertheless, when Parliament reassembled in May, the Act of Classes was rescinded despite the Remonstrants' efforts to keep this iniquitous Act upon the Statute Book. Those who had taken part in the Engagement could now be included in the army which was soon to march into England, after they had done penance in their parish kirks. They were required by the Estates to sign a declaration, swearing "that we shall never, directly, nor indirectly, seek to revenge ourselves any way upon any man, for opposing us in the matter of the sinful Engagement, or for opposing us in, or censuring us for, any malignant course whatsoever".[49]

When, in July, King Charles set out at the head of a mixed army of Royalists, Engagers, and Covenanters, to give Cromwell the slip and march into England, the situation appeared very similar to that of Hamilton's invasion in 1648. For there remained in Scotland the two potentates who had made trouble as soon as Hamilton's back was turned: Argyll and the Kirk.

King Campbell had ruled for so long that his attitude at this critical moment appeared vital and evident to friend and foe alike. Wariston affirmed that for the King there was "no getting England without Scotland, nor Scotland without Argyll, nor him without his daughter"; Baillie reiterated over and over again that by every means possible the King must keep Argyll on his side. Argyll's enemies, on the other hand, pressed Charles to imprison the dictator before the army marched, but the King refused to do so, giving as his reason that Argyll "would not attempt anything while the army was entire: if it prevailed, he neither would nor could do any harm; and if it were defeated, it would be no great matter what he did".[50]

It was an extremely shrewd judgment. Charles, and Charles alone, seems to have realized that the situation in this summer of 1651 was vitally different from that of the summer of 1648. The rule of King Campbell was over; he was hated by the Royalists, by the Engagers, and most of all by the common people upon whom his iron hand had lain so heavy. He was blamed by the Remonstrants for allowing the King to come to Scotland; his old ally Cromwell had turned enemy. In this same month of July, an English news-sheet reported: "Argyll is gone down the wind; nobody takes any notice of him; as he rides along, private troopers jostle him almost off his horse."

And that other potentate, that other older ally of Argyll, the Kirk which had borne him to power on the wave of its own fanaticism in 1638, that too had gone down the wind. Though few realized it as yet, its power had been smashed for good and all at Dunbar, when the tyranny and pride of its ministers had turned victory into defeat. Dunbar, far more than the Union of 1707, was "the end of an old song", the song of Scotland's proud sovereignty and independence. For the first time since the days of Bruce, she was to become a conquered and occupied country; and the shame and the humiliation she was now to undergo she would owe, not to a foreign invader, but to a home-bred tyrant, King Covenant.

PART SIX

THE BITTER HARVEST OF
THE COVENANT
1651–1660

Chapter One

WHEN, having captured Perth on August 3rd, Cromwell began his pursuit of King Charles and his army, he left to complete the conquest of Scotland a ruthless, experienced mercenary, George Monck, Lieutenant-General of the Ordnance. Monck had under his command ten thousand men, the greater part of the train of artillery, and the English garrisons in Edinburgh, Leith, Perth, and several smaller towns; but with even a fraction of that strength his task would have been easy, for the weakness or treachery which had infected the Scots commanders who had been left behind to defend their native soil, made resistance impossible. Already, in July, there had been a disgraceful exhibition at Inverkeithing, when Lieutenant-General Holbourn, encountering Lambert, had behaved so badly that "the whole army exclaimed against him".

On August 6th, Monck summoned Stirling, which immediately capitulated; the castle, unable to withstand a cannonade, surrendered on the 14th. On the 28th, he captured the Government itself. The Committee of Estates was sitting at Alyth, protected by an armed guard under old Leven; they were surprised by five hundred English horse, who routed the guard and seized the members of the Committee, amounting to thirty-eight persons, stripped them of their valuables, and sent them off by sea to London, where most of them remained in prison until the Restoration. Argyll was not among the captives; he had sat snugly at home in his Highland fastness since the King had left Scotland.[1]

By this time rumours had come filtering north of some great action fought by the Scots army in England; at first it was believed that the King had defeated Cromwell, and Glasgow and the other towns remaining in Scottish hands lit bonfires for a victory. But the truth was known all too soon; Cromwell had utterly defeated the King at Worcester on September 3rd, the anniversary of Dunbar; the Covenant horse under Leslie had not struck a blow. For their ministers had been at them; the King had attended the Anglican service in Worcester Cathedral two days previously, and no good Covenanter must fight for such a renegade. Among those who had fought gallantly that day was the second Duke of Hamilton; he was wounded in the leg and died a few days later. He was more fortunate than many of his compatriots. "The gentlemen prisoners," wrote a Catholic priest, "are used as ill and basely as the most simple soldier, going barefoot and bare-headed, used like very slaves, getting nothing but brown black bread sparingly, and water; the English call them hogs, pigs, and dogs. Many of them die of misery and are buried ere they be fully dead without compassion. The cursed Covenant is the cause of this barbarous cruelty."[2]

In Scotland the invaders appointed October 24th as a day of thanksgiving to be kept throughout the land for the defeat of Scottish arms, celebrating it with feasting and the shooting off of cannon. The conquered people, who so often had had their trade interrupted by the fasts and thanksgiving-days of the Kirk, now experienced the like tyranny under their conquerors: "Some poor people who were spinning that day, lost their wheels and were broken."[3]

Early in September, Aberdeen and Montrose had surrendered to the English, and on the first of the month Monck had stormed one of the few towns to offer resistance, Dundee. It was full of wealthy merchants who had fled from Edinburgh, thinking to find security here, and the booty from these alone was estimated at two hundred thousand pounds sterling. Monck gave a warning on this occasion of what other towns must expect if they dared resist him. The Governor, Robert Lumsden, was killed after quarter had been granted him, two of the town's three ministers were sent prisoner to England, despite the fact that they had clamoured for the surrender of Dundee before its storming, and for forty-eight hours Monck's soldiers were let loose upon the wretched inhabitants. Between eight hundred and a thousand of them were slaughtered, together with two hundred women and children.[4]

Throughout the winter and spring of 1651-2 the tale of conquest continued. Huntly (Lord Lewis Gordon) signed articles of capitulation on November 21st, and Balcarres on December 3rd. Inverness was occupied at the end of November; Dumbarton

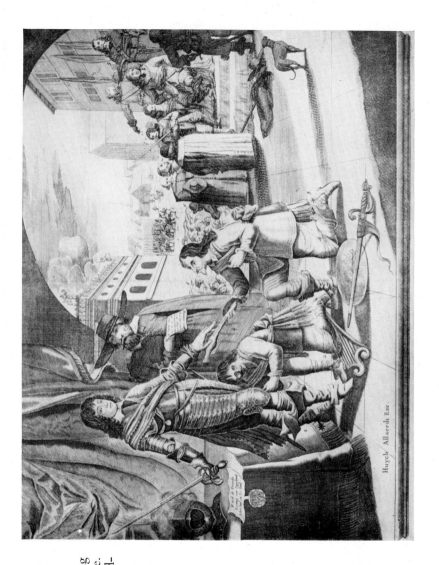

The crowning of King
Charles II at Scone.
From a Dutch broad-
sheet

Huych Allaerdt Exc.

General George Monck

yielded in January; and Dunottar, the last of the Scottish "strengths" to fly the Royal Standard, fell at the end of May. By this time Monck had left Scotland in order to try the waters of Bath for a serious illness, and Major-General Richard Deane was left to mop up the pockets of resistance.

All this while the ex-dictator Argyll had remained quietly in his once-impregnable Highland fastness. He and Chancellor Loudoun were almost the only important personages left at liberty; with so many prisoners of rank captured at Worcester and at Alyth, "all the nobility of Scotland that are at liberty may sit about a joint-stool", as *Mercurius Politicus*, the English official news-sheet, unkindly put it. For weeks the Chancellor had been trying to lure Argyll out of his fastness, to co-operate with him in forming some sort of a government, and eventually Argyll agreed to meet him, with a remnant of the gentry, at Rothesay. The meeting took place, and it was decided to hold that parliament for which the King had given his warrant before leaving Scotland, in the middle of November at Finlairg, near the west end of Loch Tay, a place which could be guarded against a surprise attack. Since all the principal towns were occupied by the enemy, the proclamation was made at Killin; but before this pitiful parliament could meet, Argyll was making overtures to the invaders.

He opened proceedings with a most characteristic letter to Monck, who at this time was still in Scotland:

"Sir, I know the truth of Solomon's saying, that in the multitude of words there wants not sin, therefore in that I will not transgress; but as I believe all good Christians in every business do propose a good end (or at least ought to do), so should they resolve upon just and righteous ways to obtain it. I judge no man, yet I desire to know from you, as one having chief trust in this kingdom, if it were not fit that some men who have deserved trust in both kingdoms may not meet to good purpose in some convenient place, as a means to stop the shedding of more Christian blood? which hath a loud cry in the Lord's ears against the unjust authors and contrivers of it. I shall say no more until I hear from you, but that I am, sir, your most humble servant, Argyll. 15 of Oct. 1651."[5]

Monck replying curtly that he could not treat without the authority of the Parliament of England, Argyll tried again. He proposed a visit and a personal talk with Monck and his officers. A pass was sent him for this purpose to come to Perth with not more than thirty of his servants, there to meet a Colonel Brayne and a Major Pierson on November 19th, but he was required not

Q

only to discountenance the forthcoming Scottish Parliament which he and his compatriots had proclaimed at Killin, but to use his best endeavours to hinder it from meeting. Since this would have meant a definite declaring of himself upon the side of the invaders before he knew what terms they might offer him, Argyll immediately developed a convenient sickness which prevented him either from keeping the appointment with Monck's officers or attending the Parliament at Finlairg. The latter duly met; it consisted of three gentlemen, who sympathized with Loudoun and went home again.

There was now sitting at Dalkeith a Commission of English officers, whose main business was the imposing upon Scotland of the Oath of Allegiance to the Commonwealth of England. Besides this they were authorized to " settle " the finances of the conquered country by taxing her for the maintenance of the invading army, and to administer a rough and ready justice, both civil and military. To these Commissioners Argyll sent his steward, Mr. Campbell, in February 1652, after Monck's departure for Bath, excusing himself for not having done so before on the grounds that he had been ignorant of the Commission's existence.

He was confident, he wrote, " when other information and particulars concerning him are rightly weighed, they shall be found light in the balance of righteous judgment, as in relation to men, with whom he says he hath ever studied to walk uprightly, as the Lord was pleased to furnish him with light and direction, which he hopes for the time to come, by His grace and strengthening him, never to be found otherways ". This ambiguous message was interpreted brutally and briefly by an English soldier: " Argyll is willing to come in."[6]

It was a correct interpretation; but Argyll was going to fight very hard to come in on his own terms. He was not going to have English soldiers quartered on him if he could help it, as they were quartered on most of his compatriots, and he was going to use all his cunning to persuade the conquerors to pay him the enormous sums which, he claimed, were owing to him from the public money. These matters being settled to his satisfaction, he was perfectly willing to betray both his country and the King whom he had crowned the previous year.

Throughout the spring and summer, Argyll continued to write fawning, rambling letters to the Commissioners, stressing the fact that he had always walked by the rules of conscience and duty, that " it is still my desire to shun all occasions which may lead me beyond my own station and calling ", and that all he desired was the peace and union of the two nations. The English news-sheets commented contemptuously on his "trafficking" with the conquerors of his country. "There hath been lately some further overtures from Argyll," one of them reported on April 24th, "but what they signify or the Commissioners have done therein is not publicly known, yet we hope he will get nothing by his jugglings and dissembling devices, which are so generally known." And a little later: "Argyll is now again seeking to come in, the pitcher goes often to the conduit, but at last is dashed in pieces. He solicits hard, and sends letter after letter, and one messenger after another, using all the means he can through his best policy to obtain some singular act of favour. But I cannot understand that he will much advantage himself by his policy, for we are, I hope, sufficiently satisfied with his put-offs and over-reaching intentions, which will be a snare probably to himself."

By July Argyll had exhausted the Commissioners' patience, and had been forced to agree to terms which, while better than he deserved, fell far short of those for which he had negotiated. Troops under Colonels Reid, Overton, and Blackmore were sent into Argyllshire to obtain his submission, and an English soldier waxed alliterative over the wildness of the country through which, long ago, Montrose had led his little army—"such Mountains and Mosses, such Places and Passes, such Lakes and Loughs did never poor people wander". However they received a most effusive welcome. They were met at Tarbert by Argyll's steward, "with a compliment", and at Inveraray the officers were entertained with much state, while the common soldiers were given the best hospitality of the clansmen.

Articles of Agreement were signed on August 19th, Argyll on his side undertaking to do nothing directly or indirectly to the prejudice of the English Commonwealth or the authority exercised by it in Scotland. But with his usual cunning he managed to qualify this promise by inserting the phrase that it was not to be understood as "hindering his good endeavours for the establishing religion according to his conscience". His conscience had always been an elastic thing, and it did not now prevent him from swearing to inform against any of his compatriots who attempted to throw off the yoke of a foreign conqueror.

Deane, as the representative of the Commonwealth, promised in return to respect Argyll's person, rank, and property, and to abstain from placing garrisons in either of his principal seats. Five garrisons, however, were to be planted in his territory: at Dunstaffnage, Dunolly, Lough, Kincairn, and Tarbert. Since

Argyll remained the principal potentate in Scotland, and also because he was known as a very slippery customer, the gist of his submission was published: "My duty to Religion, according to my oath in the Covenant always reserved, I do agree (for the Civil part) of Scotland being made a Commonwealth with England, that there shall be the same Government without King or House of Lords derived [extended] to the people of Scotland, and that in the meantime, until this can be practicable, I shall live quietly under the Parliament of the Commonwealth of England and their authority."[7]

But Argyll was still resolved to get better terms for himself, and in order to do so he staged a show of his strength as a Highland chief. He sent between a thousand and fifteen hundred of his Campbells to lie in wait for the English soldiers as the latter marched through a narrow defile on the borders of his country; they were not to attack the English, but they were to show them how easy an attack would be by lightly armed mountaineers in such a wild country against troops who were strangers to it. The English arrived safely at Dumbarton, whither Major-General Deane had come from Inveraray by sea; he brought the news that three of the five garrisons he had just planted in Argyllshire, Lough, Kincairn, and Tarbert, had been surprised by the Campbells. "I doubt whether we will or no," wrote one of the English soldiers indignantly, "these things are in order to war with these base and beggarly wild beasts, which we would willingly have avoided for many weighty reasons, especially their poverty and unaccessibility of every pass and place, where every hill, whereof the country totally consists, is no less than an invincible garrison."

Argyll, of course, disclaimed any knowledge of these doings; but apart from the fact that his clansmen would never have defied the invaders without his permission, there is the testimony of a certain English officer, Adjutant-General Smythe, which proves Argyll's determination to make a show of strength, and thereby to get better terms.

After the Articles of Agreement had been signed on August 19th, Smythe was left in charge of some vessels laden with provisions, and a man-of-war, the *Elias*, at Inveraray; the provisions were for the garrisons just planted in Argyllshire. On August 22nd, the day after Deane and his troops left, a certain Scotsman came aboard the *Elias* and informed Smythe that Argyll's people were in arms, that some of the English soldiers had been slain by them and others taken prisoner, and that two of the garrisons had been seized by the Campbells.

"Whereupon," declared Smythe, "I went to the Earl [sic] of Argyll to know the truth (being within half a mile of his house when the ship was riding in the river). And when I was within twelvescore yards of his house, I see many men in arms drawn up within a hundred yards of his house. As soon as I came near them they did throw a dirk either at me or at the coxswain of the boat who was with me. I did perceive they intended to stab one of us. At my entering into the said Earl of Argyll's house, for my endeavouring to save the coxswain (which I did apprehend they would have murdered) they broke my head.

"Immediately I went to my Lord Argyll, and did acquaint him that I had intelligence that many of the soldiers belonging to the Commonwealth of England were slain and taken prisoners, and our garrisons surprised within his bounds, contrary to his agreement with Major-General Deane. My Lord Argyll answered me that he knew nothing of it. I told him there were many men in arms about his house, near the number of two hundred: he denied that he knew of any. I told his lordship that I had been abused by them: he told me he would not stand to talk any more with me. Then I desired to know of him whether he would keep me, and give order for my safe return: he would give me no answer, but shut the door and went away from me, and would not speak to me any more. . . . In my return from the said Lord Argyll's house I was necessitated to give moneys to two of his servants (unknown to my Lord Argyll) to go along with me to the boat; if I had not done so I suppose they would have stabbed me; for several of the seamen which set me on shore, and stayed with the boat till my return to them, were sore wounded, and one slain."[8]

Argyll's ruse was successful. It had revealed to the invaders, who knew Argyll well by reputation, that this slippery customer was capable of causing a great deal of inconvenience if he chose, while always disclaiming responsibility for the acts of the clansmen he ruled so absolutely. Scotland was a conquered kingdom now, but the army of invasion was made up of men who were ignorant of the wild Highlands, the most difficult kind of country to police; only once had Argyll's fastness been stormed, and that had been by fellow Highlanders under Montrose. On the other hand, Argyll's past made it plain that he could be extremely useful to anyone who made it worth his while.

Thus it was that in October he secured for himself very much better terms than those which he had obtained in August. No compensation of any kind was demanded for his clansmen's acts of hostility; in future there were to be no English garrisons in his territory; and the number of soldiers quartered in Argyllshire was reduced to one hundred and twenty foot and twelve horse. Only upon some urgent occasion were additional forces to be allowed to march through the Campbell's domain, "for the peace of the Island, or reducing those that might be refractory". Argyll considering this latter phrase to be ambiguous, he wrote to Deane to have it clarified. On November 6th, shortly before he was recalled to London, leaving Colonel Robert Lilburne as acting Commander-in-Chief, Deane replied in a most cordial and respectful letter, explaining that certain of Argyll's feudal vassals might be "deficient" in paying the tax imposed upon the nation, and that in that case force would have to be employed.

In return for all these privileges, Argyll was required to do only one thing: he must surrender eighteen brass cannon and five hundred muskets which he had in his possession. It is unlikely that he felt the loss very keenly. For he was paid one shilling and fourpence for each English pound weight of brass, and eight shillings sterling for each musket. Truly did an English news-writer observe: "The Marquis is no stranger to the art of Politicks."

Chapter Two

SCOTLAND was now suffering that most bitter of all fates which can befall a proud people, occupation by an alien race. She who had struggled so long and so fiercely against the aggression of the Plantagenets and the Tudors, she whose most precious possession was her sovereign independence, was to become a mere province of England, and now there was no Wallace or Bruce to set her free.

Until the May of 1652, the Commission of English officers formed the government of the conquered country; on May 18th of that year, their place was taken by seven Commissioners, four of these being Englishmen and the rest those collaborators whom the English contemptuously referred to as "assured Scots". This Commission appointed new sheriffs and judges, admitting only those willing to take the Oath of Allegiance to the English Commonwealth, and saw to it that the people paid the taxes imposed upon them for the maintenance of the army of occupation. Ten thousand pounds sterling a month was the sum imposed, but

both Deane and his successor Lilburne found it impossible
to squeeze more than eight thousand five hundred out of this
always poor and now ruined people.

Though the rule of the English was less tyrannous than that
of Argyll and the Kirk had been, it remained an alien rule, and
it was hated by the people at large. A news-letter from Leith,
describing the proclamation at Edinburgh Mercat Cross of an
order for the sending of twenty-one deputies to the English
Parliament, mentioned with pained surprise its reception by the
townsfolk: "After the reading whereof the soldiers gave several
shouts, as complying with the Parliament in their free conferring
of liberty upon a conquered people, but so senseless are this
generation of their own good that scarce a man of them shew'd
any sign of rejoicing." The average Scotsman concurred with
the sentiment expressed by the Rev. Robert Blair: "As for the
embodying of Scotland with England, it will be as when the poor
bird is embodied into the hawk that hath eaten her up."

Apart from the intolerable burden of taxation, many Scotsmen
found themselves in the humiliating position of tenants to
English landlords. For, needless to say, the great ones of the
invading army had done very well for themselves. Colonel
Ingoldsby had got the manor and park of Hamilton, Colonel
Whalley those of Liddington; Major-General Lambert had been
rewarded with lands worth one thousand pounds a year, Monck
had got Hamilton's feudal keep of Kenneil, and he, with four
other commanders, were enriched in addition to other rewards
by estates which brought in five hundred pounds annually.

The native rulers of Scotland, the nobles, were either in cap-
tivity or else had submitted to the invaders; every town of
importance was occupied; and the people, left leaderless, could
offer no resistance. There remained to be dealt with the once
all-powerful Kirk. It had defied two Kings; it had bullied
innumerable Parliaments; it was not going to submit without a
violent struggle to the ally who had enlisted its aid in 1643. In
the September of 1651, when the military conquest of Scotland
had become a certainty, Monck had received instructions as to
how he was to deal with the Kirk: "Their ministers you may
suffer to preach, so long as they keep within the bounds of their
proper function in preaching the Gospel of Christ; but if they
meddle with matters of State, or the power of their jurisdiction,
command them out of all places within your power, and if t' ey
do not obey, secure them." Well had it been for Scotland if, ong
ago, King Charles I had been as ruthless.

Before the horrified eyes of the Elect, English soldiers usurped pulpits, preaching with their swords laid on the pulpit-cushion, or hanging by their sides. A dozen different sects proclaimed by their existence that liberty of conscience which the Kirk hated above all things. Why, wailed the ministers, if freedom to worship as they pleased was given to "Antitrinitarians, Arrians, Socinians, Pholimians, Familists, Seekers, Antimonians, Polagians", and so on, was it not extended to Papists and Prelatists? "A door is opened and an inlet made," cried the Kirk, "unto the worst of those who bear the name of Christians, yea, unto Jews and Mahometans, and heathens, to converse and dwell and profess their religion in this land."[9]

Worse even than this, the conquerors interfered with the beloved discipline of the Kirk, and even indulged in a mild form of persecution. The English appointed fast-days and days of thanksgiving without reference to the Commission of the Assembly, and their military minions interrupted services and despoiled churches. In several kirks the Stool of Repentance was pulled down; in others the soldiers sat on it as a sign of contempt during sermon; the sackcloth was taken away; and, as a crowning insult, some ministers were fined forty shillings each for riding to a General Assembly on the Sabbath.[10]

The moderate party in the Kirk, termed the Resolutioners, were beginning to realize that the woes which had befallen Scotland had been due to the tyranny of the Kirk in the past; and one of these ministers, the Rev. Robert Ramsay, actually admitted as much in a sermon preached at Glasgow. He spoke of "our too much meddling in civil affairs, which was not the example of our Master . . . I will not speak, he says, of our sitting, voting, and ruling of committees and other public meetings; which is much too frequent. Whereas we should have been peace-makers, we have been fomenters of divisions, and dividers of the people of God. Our preaching of the ministry has been rather for our own maintenance than for edification. That in our ecclesiastical censures, we have too rigidly dealt with some on the one hand, and too favourably with others, rather seeking out their shame than their sin, their punishment rather than their amendment. So we have domineered with cruelty."[11]

There were not many so honest as Ramsay; but it was plain to the Resolutioners that if the Kirk were to regain its hold over the people, the two parties into which it had split must unite again, and they were beginning to desire peace with their brethren on any tolerable terms. But the extremists, called indifferently Remonstrants and Protesters, were so bitter against the moderates that they were ready to traffic with the English conquerers, the hated Independents, rather than compose their differences with the Resolutioners. They refused to acknowledge the authority of the recent General Assembly, because it had agreed to the rescinding of the Act of Classes, and such refusal struck at the very root of the Kirk's authority. So bitter grew the strife that in the summer of 1652, Baillie, a Resolutioner, spoke of "the preparing of cudgels by too many of that side, to have fallen upon us in our very pulpits for no cause at all".

Though the Kirk was too obsessed with its internal squabbles to give a lead, and the ex-dictator Argyll, on a visit to Edinburgh, was hooted after by the townsfolk, who yelled at him, "Traitor! thou has killed one King and banished another!", it was unthinkable that the conquest of this fiercely independent people should go unchallenged. Leaderless and betrayed though they were, the common folk regarded their conquerors with a hatred which burnt more fiercely as time went on. Lilburne, the honest plodding soldier who was now acting Commander-in-Chief, deplored this attitude in almost every dispatch he sent to London. "Even in all these people," he wrote, "there is a secret antipathy against us, do what we can to oblige them"; and one of his officers wrote in a similar strain, "The country people show themselves our enemies on all occasions".

This attitude of the people, together with the outbreak of war between the Commonwealth and the Dutch in the summer of 1652, made possible a rising which, had there been a Montrose to lead it, might well have proved successful. The Highland clans had formed themselves into an Association in the previous year, and in October 1652, one of the Chiefs, Glengarry, wrote to Charles II (who, having escaped from England after Worcester, was living in exile once more), asking for "letters of encouragement", and for Sir John Middleton to be sent as General, with money and arms which it was hoped the Dutch would supply.

Middleton, wrote Hyde, "is the soberest man I have met with and very worthy of any trust, having the greatest sense of the errors he hath formerly committed [he had been a Covenanting commander] and the best excuses for them that I have found for any". But unfortunately he was not the man to make a rising successful. As a Lowlander he did not understand the Highland way of fighting, and was unacceptable to many of the Chiefs; his past history as a Covenanter made him suspect among the genuine Royalists; and the part he had taken in the Engagement had put him under the ban of the Kirk. For the moment he was unable, on account of sickness, to go over to Scotland; and at the end of December, 1652, the King sent a commission to the Chiefs, constituting them a Council of War, and authorizing them to choose a temporary commander.

Early in 1653, Argyll began to fulfil that part of his engagement with the invaders whereby he had promised to inform against his own countrymen if the latter showed themselves hostile to the Commonwealth. He sent Lilburne a letter, "signifying the great and frequent meetings of Glengarry and the other Highlanders and Islanders; but what the intent of their meeting may be, he saith he knows not". Lilburne at first refused to credit the information; but on February 18th he wrote Argyll that "I am apt to believe something is intended by Glengarry and his accomplices". He had heard that some of Argyll's own people were involved in the business, and while warning the Campbell Chief of this, added that he was not much concerned about a possible rising "by such a rabble". To this Argyll replied solemnly that so far as he knew none of his own people were involved.

In actual fact, his own heir, Lord Lorn, was one of the leaders of the rising; and here arises an interesting question. It may be remembered that during Huntly's abortive rising for Charles I during the Civil War, Argyll had given his nephew, Lord Gordon, the advice to act in accordance with an old Scottish custom, that is, to appear on the opposite side from the one espoused by his father, in order that, whatever the issue, the family estates might be saved. It is possible, therefore, that Lorn, in siding with the Royalists now, had his father's secret connivance.

There can be no doubt that Argyll himself was determined to keep a toe, if not a whole foot, in the Royalist camp, though strictly "under the rose". There is an interesting letter written in this spring of 1653 by Sir Robert Moray, in the name of the Chiefs, to the King, in which Moray excuses Argyll's collaborating with the invaders on the grounds of self-preservation, and insists that he is a Royalist at heart. It is plain from this letter that Moray had had some personal talk with Argyll, and is quoting the latter's arguments. If, wrote Moray, a really effective rising took place, "he would certainly appear for the business that is now carrying on for your Majesty's service". In other words, Argyll really could not be expected to "appear" until it was clear which was going to be the winning side.

On the other hand, at this very self-same time, Argyll was considering a decision to take an active part with the English against the Royalists. He sent a servant to request a meeting with his old crony Wariston, and when they met, attempted to persuade Wariston to co-operate with him in this design. Wariston was righteously indignant; he was resolved, he said, to meddle neither with the English nor the Royalists. Argyll "told fair hopes, if I would meddle. I perceived his design, and told my continuing in old principles against associations with Malignants or Sectaries; and conjured him to repent his meddling with both, before the Lord, who had begun to reckon with his house, should make an utter end. He pressed me to keep charity with him, and we spake about the King's [proposed] match with his daughter, whereof he disclaimed the knowledge till Cassilis proposed it 8 days after the King's Coronation, except by way of sport and drink."[12]

While King Campbell thus professed his attachment to the Royalist cause on the one hand, and considered taking an active part against it on the other, King Covenant was officially and dramatically deposed. In April 1653, Cromwell had forcibly dissolved the Long Parliament which had created the New Model Army of which he was Commander-in-Chief. In July he showed the like contempt for the Long Parliament's former ally, the Kirk.

The General Assembly sat down at Edinburgh after the usual fast. For fifteen years now, this body and its Commission had ruled Scotland with an iron hand, and little did it guess that on this twentieth day of July, 1653, Nemesis was to overtake it. The Moderator, that same David Dickson who had stood rubbing his hands in glee beside the bloody scaffold after Philiphaugh, had just opened the proceedings with a prayer, when the tramp of booted feet and the ring of hooves was heard approaching the Assembly House, the door was flung open without ceremony, and there entered Lieutenant-Colonel Cotterel, followed by soldiers in the familiar red cassocks of the Commonwealth's army. Standing up on a bench, Cotterel brusquely enquired of the horrified Assembly by what authority they were sitting. Was it, he demanded, by the authority of the Commonwealth of England, or by that of the Commander-in-Chief of the English forces?

Shocked though he was, the Moderator replied with dignity, if not with truth, "that we were an ecclesiastical synod, a spiritual court of Jesus Christ, which meddled not with anything civil; that our authority was from God, and established by the laws of the land yet standing unrepealed; that, by the Solemn League and Covenant, the most of the English Army stood obliged to defend our General Assembly". Cotterel's answer was a bombshell; "in a loud voice" he informed the Assembly that, since they were not sitting by the authority of the Commonwealth or of the Commander-in-Chief, they had no right here, and he bade them be gone, adding for good measure that unless they complied he would drag them out of the room. The Moderator reiterated that they were Christ's Court, and began to embark upon one of those Protestations with which the Kirk had countered every Proclamation of Charles I. But it was not now a patient and conciliatory king with whom the Kirk had to deal. Cotterel rudely interrupted the Protestation, and ordered his soldiers to drive the reverend gentlemen out of the house.

Then did the good folk of Edinburgh witness a most notable sight. Encompassed by a troop of horse and a company of foot, the black-gowned ministers were marched, sweating and panting in the heat of that July day, out through the West Port and a mile from the town. There, bidding them form into a circle, Cotterel gave them a sermon such as they had never heard before, his text being their boldness in daring to meet without the authority of the Commonwealth. He wound up by taking away their commissions, commanding them not to venture to meet again in greater numbers than three at a time, and ordering that before eight o'clock next morning they all depart the town, under pain of being found guilty of breaking the public peace.[13]

King Covenant had fallen with ignominy; and few there were to lament him.

Chapter Three

OF all the risings in history, few can compare in feebleness with that which came to be known as Glencairn's Rising, and which gathered to a head in this summer of 1653.

Yet the circumstances were infinitely more favourable than those with which Montrose had had to struggle nine years previously. The Commonwealth of England had been established by the sword, and hence its Achilles heel was a perpetual lack of money. All the sequestrations and the fines and the taxes were inadequate to maintain the army of occupation in England; certainly there was nothing left over for that of Scotland, and Scotland herself was ruined. All through this year 1653, Lilburne kept imploring Cromwell for money for his troops. By June their arrears of pay amounted to no less than sixty thou-

sand pounds sterling, and, declared poor Lilburne, his soldiers
must live either on the country or on biscuit and cheese. (That
they preferred the former alternative is evident from the proclamations he was continually issuing against plundering.)
Money was needed also for fortifications to overawe the people;
two thousand pounds *per annum* had been assigned for these,
whereas Lilburne declared that at least five thousand a month
was needed.

The half-mutinous state of the occupying army, the difficulties
of policing a country so wild, the burning hatred of the common
people for their conquerors, and the enthusiasm of the clans for
the King's cause, all these were in favour of a successful rising.
It was ruined by three things: lack of a leader of genius, the
fatal Royalist habit of quarrelling, and the machinations of
Argyll.

On July 27th, the Royal Standard was raised at Killin, and
one of those who took part in the ceremony was Argyll's heir,
Lord Lorn. Argyll made haste to assure the English that his
son had acted in defiance of the parental authority. He sent
Lilburne a copy of the letter he had written to Lorn, in which
he was the broken-hearted father, and he assured Lilburne that
he would have come in person to give an account of his son's
conduct, had he not reason to believe that his own presence at
Inveraray would prevent his clan from joining the Royalists. "I
have taken some men into my company for defence of my person," he wrote, "which, God knows, is not worth much, but that
Christian duty in using lawful means is not to be neglected."
Little did Argyll guess that this letter to Lilburne was to be one
of the Six Famous Letters which, seven years later, was to cost
him his head.

He continued to send information of the Royalists' movements; yet despite his usefulness as a spy, and the pious language
in which all his letters were couched, the invaders remained
unconvinced of his trustworthiness, their *Diurnal of Occurrences*
referring to him as "the Old Fox". In October a circumstance
occurred which aroused the suspicions even of the trusting Lilburne. Some thirteen years previously, Argyll had invited certain Covenanting families from Renfrew and Ayrshire to come
and settle in Kintyre as his tenants. Thither at this time
marched Lorn and his cousin Kenmure, for the purpose of preventing these Covenanters from rising in the invaders' interests.
Confidently expecting help from their landlord, Argyll, the
Covenanters made a show of resistance to Lorn, taking possession
of the castle of Lochheid and garrisoning it; but no aid of any

kind coming from Argyll, and Lorn offering them excellent terms, they quickly surrendered. Argyll was ready with an excuse for doing nothing; the people of Kintyre, he assured the irritated Lilburne, would never have held out against his son. Lilburne replied curtly that Lorn's men were being transported to and fro over Loch Long by his father's clansmen, and would Argyll see to it that this was stopped.

As it happened, the presence of Lorn in the Royalist camp was proving more troublesome to them than his father's informations to the invaders. Early in September he had quarrelled with Glengarry, and with difficulty had been prevented from fighting him; and he now fell out with Kenmure because the latter had complained that Lorn had given the Kintyre Covenanters suspiciously favourable terms. Unfortunately Lorn was not the only trouble-maker; by November Glencairn and Balcarres were at loggerheads, and a special messenger had to be sent from the King to reconcile them. "The weekly prints from London," Charles wrote to a Colonel MacLeod, "which are Our constant and most particular intelligence, give Us still cause to believe that even amongst those of whose zeal and affection to Us We made no question, there is not unity enough."

Nevertheless, Lilburne's letters to Cromwell grew more and more anxious. He could get no information except from the doubtful Argyll; the country people were supplying the Royalists with horses; his men's pay was now three months in arrears and the promised supplies had not come; certain ministers were praying openly for the success of the rising, and Lilburne himself was apprehensive of an attack in force. Altogether he was beginning to panic, the spelling of his letters growing wilder and wilder. By the beginning of December he had heard that Middleton, with four ships laden with arms, was ready to sail; and on the 22nd, while congratulating Cromwell on "being called by Providence to be Lord Protector of three nations", the poor man lamented that for a long time he had not had the happiness of receiving "the least commands from your Highness, or anything to give me hopes of those supplies I often told your Highness was most necessary to be sent down hither". In all Scotland he had not more than thirteen hundred horse, and he was beginning to feel that it would be better to send someone more fit to wrestle with the situation than "your Excellency's most humble servant".

The general attack which Lilburne feared and which the Royalists should have delivered without waiting for Middleton, was never made. They occupied themselves in futile little raids,

in sending complaints to the exiled Court about the menace of
Argyll (who had just assisted Colonel Cobbett to reduce the
island of Mull and garrison Douart Castle, making all the people
there lift up their hands and swear allegiance to the Commonwealth), and in quarrelling among themselves. A Colonel Bamfield, so distrusted by the King that Charles had sent over a
warrant for his arrest, remained *persona grata* with them, and
was industriously circulating a rumour that Middleton, when
at last he came, intended to burn down the house of Glengarry.
Bamfield encouraged the jealousy of Balcarres, and egged on
Glencairn to demand from the King the earldom of Ross, which
inevitably would have created new jealousies. In January 1654,
Lorn fell out with Glencairn, high words arose, Glencairn drew
his sword, and Lorn went away in a great rage, swearing that
rather than see Glencairn command the Gordons, now the feudal
vassals of Argyll, he would lose his life. He was far readier to
lose his honour. The night after this squabble, he sent information to the English as to where they could fall upon Glencairn's
men to the best advantage, but the bearer of the letter carried
it to Kenmure. Lorn fled, and there was a rumour that he had
gone home to his father.

News that Cromwell was concluding a treaty with Holland
depressed the Royalists, since they were depending on Dutch
money and arms; and the further tidings that Middleton was
at last coming over to them did little to raise their spirits, for
he was coming almost empty-handed. "I am exceedingly
troubled," Hyde wrote him on February 13th, "and so is the
King, that you are forced to go with so lamentable supplies,
which will much discourage our friends to whom you resort."
On March 4th Lilburne reported to his superiors that Middleton
was certainly landed in Sutherlandshire with eighty soldiers:
"all the arms they brought were not many more than ten horse-
loads". But worse than lack of supplies was Middleton's failure
to unite the Royalist leaders. Lorn was back amongst them,
and was nearly killed by the young Marquis of Montrose; one,
Grahame, shot Atholl's groom through the head; Glencairn and
Sir George Munro fought a duel in which both were wounded;
and Glencairn and Atholl had to be forcibly prevented from
engaging in the like affair of honour.[14]

Argyll's active help in the subduing of Mull had dispelled Lilburne's former distrust of him, and not long before his leaving
Scotland (Monck being about to return to resume the command),
Lilburne sent the Protector a testimony of Argyll's worth as a
collaborator: "As I have all along (since the Marquis of Argyll's

coming in to the Commissioners here) observed very much fairness, and no less inclination to give real testimonies of his good affection (both in words and actions) to the Commonwealth and to your Highness, and also expressing much zeal to a firm establishment of the public peace of both Nations, I am the bolder humbly to testify thus much, according to my own observations in his Lordship's behalf. And because I have persuaded his Lordship to stay in his own country to help at this time to preserve the peace, and thereby diverted his Lordship's intended journey at this present to wait upon your Highness, I most humbly beg your Highness's favourable aspect to this bearer, Mr. Campbell, his servant, in his humble addresses to your Highness."[15]

By the end of March, both Lilburne and Argyll were in a panic, the latter for the safety of his lands, the former because there was "a worse and worse complexion" upon the common people, who were calling the Royalists their deliverers, and were only awaiting some vigorous action on their part before joining them. Argyll, who had taken such pains to ensure that he would not have the English troops quartered upon him, was now imploring Lilburne to send a strong force into his territory, assuring them ample provisions, and offering his own seat of Inveraray for the convenience of their commanders.

But on April 5th, peace was concluded between the Commonwealth and Holland, shattering all Royalist hopes of aid from the Dutch; and on the 21st, the vigorous and ruthless Monck arrived at Dalkeith. He was armed with wide civil as well as military powers. On his own authority he could suspend all magistrates, sheriffs, and ministers whom he suspected of being in sympathy with the Royalists, requisition printing-presses, administer the Oath of Allegiance to the Commonwealth to anyone he chose, reward as he should think fit those who would slay or capture any of the enemy, and impose an elaborate new system of fines.

A proclamation was issued by him prohibiting any person from travelling about the country without a pass. "By which means great sums of money were exacted from the inhabitants, by reason of the daily travel and repair, and every pass paying a shilling sterling, which was a great burden and stent through the land; for many hundreds, nay thousands, were forced to seek passes, and whoever lacked passes were taken prisoners, and declared to be enemies to the Commonwealth." Lastly, any Englishman found on good evidence to have been in arms with the Scots Royalists, could be put to death by Monck "forthwith ", and all prisoners could be transported by him on his own authority.[16]

Immediately upon his arrival, Monck reported to Cromwell that he found the extent of the rising to be far greater than he had expected, suggested that all fathers of sons engaged should be put under arrest, and brusquely demanded money for his troops, who were in a dangerously mutinous mood. Sixty-one thousand pounds he must have, and at once, besides an additional regiment of foot and horse, and six warships. It was not so much the futile and squabbling Royalists he feared, but the ordinary people. "I am still more and more confirmed," he wrote Cromwell, "that the people of this country are generally engaged in this rising, and do assist the Rebels in what they may, so far as they dare appear."

His plan of campaign was vigorous and simple. He intended to march to Stirling, and there, by the building of redoubts and by making the fords impassable for horse by "casting in some engines for that purpose", to drive the enemy northwards into the hills. Then, as soon as the snow had melted and he had grass for his horses, to force a battle. Meantime he had sent Colonel Morgan to Dingwall to watch the movements of Middleton in Sutherland. Of Argyll's zeal for the Commonwealth he was convinced; Glencairn had made an attempt to come down upon the Campbell lands, and Argyll had driven him off, taking three prisoners. Cordial letters were exchanged between Argyll and the English commander, Monck writing Cromwell that "what favour your Highness shall be pleased to bestow upon his Lordship I hope will not be ill-bestowed".

In June Monck marched from Stirling to Perth, burning the countryside as he went, and thence to the head of Loch Tay. On July 17th, he reported to Cromwell that he had driven the enemy into such inaccessible places in the hills that it was impossible to follow them; two days later Middleton came unexpectedly upon Colonel Morgan at Dalnaspidal at the head of Loch Tay. Both sides were surprised, many of Morgan's men having to fight before they could put on their boots, but Middleton made a hurried retreat, his troops scattering, and Morgan pursuing into Caithness. To all intents and purposes this most futile and ill-managed rising was over, though Middleton did not leave Scotland until April 1655, stout old Glengarry remaining with him to the last.

Considering the "disaffected" state of the common people, a policy of conciliation was necessary, though it did not meet with the approval of Monck. He solicited hard for permission

R

to execute those leaders who had fallen into his hands. "I think," he wrote Lambert, "that the taking away the lives of half a dozen or half a score of them would be a means to keep them quiet"; if this were disallowed, then he was resolved to send them as slaves to the Barbadoes. Meantime he was conferring with Argyll on what houses and cornland to burn.[17]

Among the Royalist leaders who still held out was Lord Lorn, and in September he behaved in a manner which caused the English to renew their suspicions that he had the secret connivance of his father. Argyll had asked that before the five companies of foot and four troops of horse, which were to be sent at his own request for his protection, came to Inveraray, there should be sent thither their supplies. Accordingly a vessel was dispatched with ten tons of cheese, six hundred bags of biscuit, and some ammunition. With only thirty horse at his back, Lorn surprised the guard on shore, and seized the provision ship. On Monck's hearing of the escapade, he immediately countermanded his orders for the troops to go to Inveraray, "not knowing," he wrote Cromwell, "what was intended by this, it being the Marquis's desire and advice that the provisions should be sent before the forces . . . I shall rather choose to let the country suffer than hazard the forces, the Lord Lorn not having a dozen men with him all this summer, nor could have done this without the assistance of the country, and the ship lay within half a shot of the Marquis's house, wherein was Ardkinglass with fourscore men." Argyll, of course, was all apologies and protestations of innocence, but, as one of Monck's officers wrote, "his name is Archguile".

Whatever collusion there may have been between Argyll and his heir in these public matters, there was no doubt of the personal hatred between them. In May 1655, Lorn submitted to the Commonwealth, giving five thousand pounds sterling as security for his peaceable behaviour, and went home to Inveraray, but he did not make his peace with his father. It had always been an unhappy family. Argyll had detested his own father, his stepmother and half-brother, and his feelings towards his son were as bitter. In August, Brodie visited Roseneath, where the Argyll family were living, and expressed to Lady Argyll his disapproval of her son's unsubmissive behaviour, "and also her husband's deep resenting of, and keeping in his mind, injuries, and offences, and prejudices". A few days later he wrote, "Oh, the bitterness betwixt the father and son which I observed!"[18]

There were others beside Lorn who detested the ex-dictator. "The people's great hatred," wrote Baillie at this time, "lies on him above any one man, and whatever befalls him, few does pity it; at this very time his state is very staggering." The latter was a reference to Argyll's debts. When, in November 1654, he had gone to Dalkeith to complain to Monck of Lorn's conduct, he had received "much affronts and disgraces of his creditors, who being frustrate and defrauded of their just and lawful debts, spared not, at all times as he walked, either in street or in the fields abroad [to call him], 'a false traitor'. Besides this, his horse and horse gear, and all other household stuff, were impounded in Dalkeith and at Newbattle, and brought into Edinburgh, and there compounded at the Mercat Cross for debt".[19] Argyll had succeeded in defrauding some of his creditors of their due by taking advantage of an Act made in May 1654, whereby the English Commissioners were authorized to suspend the payment of the debts of distressed persons; but he was still determined to wrest from the Commonwealth those enormous sums he alleged were owing to him, and for this purpose he went up to London in September.

At first it seemed that he had fallen out of the frying-pan into the fire. For in November one of his principal creditors, Elizabeth Maxwell, widow of the Earl of Dirleton, sued him for the debt of one thousand pounds sterling, and he was arrested. He protested against his case being dealt with by English judges, and the affair dragged on for months, the unfortunate widow being herself arrested for her "contumacy" in pressing for her money. At last the grateful Colonel Cobbett, who declared that he had owed his safety to God and Argyll during the expedition to subdue Mull in the late rising, advanced the money on security of a promise by Cromwell to Argyll of one thousand pounds yearly on the excise on wine in Scotland till the whole of the public moneys he claimed were owing to him could be filched from the taxpayers.

Argyll could afford to ignore the hatred of his compatriots, when his collaboration with the invaders of his country was bringing him such rewards.

Chapter Four

THE northern Royalists, by their pusillanimity, had failed both their King and their fellow-countrymen; the chance of a restoration of the Monarchy by Scottish arms, and of freeing Scotland from the yoke of the invader, had been thrown away, and the land was become a province of the Auld Enemy. Yet hatred continued to seethe underground, requiring only another Bruce or Montrose to bring it to the surface. In 1653, the *Diurnal of Occurrences* admitted that the people were quiet only because "they are kept so by vigilant force", and four years later Monck reported that "truly the Scots are now as malignant as ever they were since I knew Scotland, and such men as you would little believe are such".

Conquest by the Auld Enemy was hateful enough to this proud and independent people, but the manner in which it was accomplished, and the insults and the tyranny which accompanied it, inevitably increased Scotland's fury. Her forests were cut down to build ships for her conquerors. As the Covenanters had destroyed the few religious treasures which the Reformers had spared, so did the English deface the emblems of her sovereignty. On the entrance to the Parliament House and on Edinburgh Castle, "they pulled down the King's Arms, dang down the unicorn with the crown that was set upon the unicorn, and hang up the crown upon the gallows", adding insult to injury by forcing Scots hammermen and masons to do the work.[20] It had been the universal custom among this well-educated people for all public documents to be written in Latin; in May 1652, a proclamation commanded all keepers of registers, writers to the signet, and public notaries, to write henceforth in English, on pain of being discharged from their posts. There was no news save that given in the official news-sheets of the conquerors. "What the world abroad is doing," wrote Baillie in 1654, "we know no more than what the London diurnal tells us."

As early as November 1651, Nicoll had lamented that "as for justice, there was none in the land; there being no Courts of Justice, such as Secret Council, Session and Exchequer sitting for the time, all our records and registers carried off the kingdom to the Tower of London. . . . As for Edinburgh, there was no magistrate there, nor no Common Council since the fight at Dunbar; and therefore all petitions and complaints went to the Captain of Edinburgh Castle and Governor of Leith, who in effect (to speak truly) proceeded more equitably and conscientiously in justice nor our Scottish magistrates."

But it was a savage justice, and the only thing that could be said for it was that it was meted out to the English soldiers and the natives indiscriminately. In September 1650, two of the former were scourged through the streets of Edinburgh for plundering without the permission of their commander, and at the same time a Scots gardener, apprehended for giving information to the Castle, which still held out for the King, was hung up by his thumbs and lighted matches were put between his fingers till he was burnt to the bone. Nicoll admired the "great respect to justice" shown by the conquerors in their methods of punishing all kinds of crime, "by scourging, hanging, kicking, cutting off of their ears, and stigmatizing them with hot irons".

The collection called *Letters from Roundhead Officers* provides a curiously vivid picture of the occupying army. There is an almost complete lack of the religious cant and scriptural references usually associated with the Roundheads; these officers were occupied in intriguing for sequestrated estates, dunning for arrears of pay, and doing a brisk trade in "debentures". The latter were I.O.U.s given to the unfortunate privates for their arrears, and it was the custom to sell them to their officers for what the latter chose to give them in hard cash. Contempt for the country they had conquered is evident in nearly every letter; thus the officers sent to London for everything they needed, be it "good plants of cherries and apricots", "as much violet-coloured shag as will make me a gown", garden seeds, dining-room chairs, and even a housekeeper. They were not in the least averse to worldly pleasures; Lambert was continually pestering Lilburne, and later Monck, for falcons for hawking (and at last was supplied by Argyll); his officers wrote home for such things as "a good French hat of the best sort with most fashionable black bands"; and it might have been a Cavalier instead of a Roundhead officer who wrote to a friend in London: "I entreat you in the name of Mr Devevier to buy three dozen quart glass bottles of the best Canary sack in London, and that they may come in the first vessel to Leith. . . . If you effect this business well, you may be sure we shall dedicate a pottle to you and yours."

Scotland was finally incorporated with England at the end of 1652, and in the following year a Major Fitzpayne-Fisher proposed to write a history of the conquest of this ancient land. He was, he confessed, "a mere Stranger in these parts", but with quarters assigned him, with compensation for his "great journey, pains, and expenses", and an allowance from every regiment in Scotland, he was confident of "producing such a Piece as may in all points become my Pen", and deserve the patronage of the Council of State at home. Fortunately for Scotland's pride, the "Piece" was never written; she had enough to bear without such a record of her humiliations.

Glencairn's Rising increased the miseries and hardships of the common people, for both sides burnt and pillaged, and by the time it was over the country folk were almost without horses. For either these were given voluntarily to the Royalists, or were purloined by them, or were confiscated by the English. The latter occasionally paid cash, but more often gave tickets of receipt, subscribed by one John Mason, to be paid out of the public funds at some unspecified date in the future. Such worthless scraps of paper were given by the English for nearly everything they needed, including the enormous amount of coal they required for their garrisons. A typical example is that of the parish of Largo, which had to supply the garrison at Falkland with fifty-two loads each fortnight.[21]

A Catholic priest, Fr. Macbreck, thus described the state of Scotland when the futile rising was over: "I cannot express the manifold miseries of this poor land. Much burning and killing in cold blood on either side. The English have built a fort in Badenoch, and another in Lochaber. This year's crop is not very hopeful. Tertian agues are most frequent and ordinary; sundry go stark mad in every shire of the country. Our ministers rail in pulpit one against the other, he condemning him for preaching damnable doctrine, and each condemning another for dissimulation and dangerous practices; nothing here but a chaos of confusion, and withal great poverty in the land."[22]

In their obsession with their internal dissensions, the ministers had no time for the comforting of their poor people in this evil hour. The quarrel between the Protesters or Remonstrants and the Resolutioners grew more bitter every year, and in many towns there were rival synods, rival sessions, and rival preachers, one minister thundering in the kirk, the other bawling on the braeside. The Protesters, while publicly condemning the Independents, were in fact angling for their patronage, and were even copying the odd mannerisms of the English preachers. Baillie was amazed by the behaviour of one Protester in the pulpit, who affected " a strange kind of sighing, the like whereof I had never heard, as a pythonizing out of the belly of a second person ".

Since their detestation of the Resolutioners made many of the Protesters ready to collaborate with the English, the latter naturally patronized them, and this sometimes resulted in riots, for, like the General Assembly before them, the invaders forced ministers on parishes unwilling to receive them. Baillie records an instance in which a whole parish assembled to keep out the candidate chosen by the English; " the tumult begins, dry strokes are distributed; some fell upon the Sheriff's neck. The gentlemen parishioners, as soon as the Sheriff produced his English orders for the admission, did cede; but the people continued all day casting stones and crying; yet they went on with their work and thrust in the man."[23] Since the Resolutioners stood stoutly by the essential tenet of the Kirk, that Presbyterianism was the one true religion, it was natural that the "Sectaries" should have retaliated by curbing their power in every way possible; soon, lamented Baillie solemnly, he and his fellow ministers would have nothing to do " but to preach, pray, and celebrate the Sacraments ". How much misery would Scotland have been spared if her ministry had confined themselves to these duties!

But, curiously enough, the Independents who claimed liberty of conscience for all save Papists and Episcopalians, concurred with the Resolutioners in the latter's hatred of a new sect which now made its appearance in Scotland, the Quakers, though the Independents' dislike of it was due chiefly to its effect upon military discipline. A Colonel Daniel wrote frequently and with furious incoherence to Monck to complain of the contempt for authority and the neglect of duty which Quakerism was breeding among his men; his " captain-lieutenant " had joined the sect, and insisted on treating all the private soldiers as his equals. " There was one example last day when he came to St. Johnston [Perth]; he came in a more than ordinary manner to the soldiers of my company, and asking them how they did, and the men doing their duty by holding of their hats, he bade them put them on, he expected no such thing from them."[24]

The Resolutioners, on the other hand, apart from their refusal to tolerate any sect but their own, were genuinely shocked by the odd habits of the Quakers, and their dislike was increased by the fact that many of the Protesters were going over to them. " They in a furious way cry down both ministry and magistracy; some of them seem actually possessed by a devil, their fury, their irrational passions, and bodily convulsions are so great. Lieutenant Osborne, one of our first apostates to the English, and betrayers to his power of our army, for which he had great favour and rewards from Cromwell himself, is an open leader to them in the streets of Edinburgh, without any punishment. Sundry in Clydesdale, of the most zealous Remonstrant yeomen, have turned too; and their increase is feared, which is a recompense of admitting the beginnings of error."[25]   Some years later, in Richard Cromwell's Parliament, the Independents joined with the Presbyterians in getting through a motion whereby Quakers were to be whipped as vagrants.[26]

It might well have been expected that that other religious minority, the Catholics, would have suffered under the English Occupation a persecution more bitter even than that they endured under the Covenant; but in fact it was not so. They were imprisoned, of course, and fined, but though there were more priests in Scotland during this period than for many years previously, not one suffered death for his religion. It was a period notable for conversions, the reason being that the extra-ordinary variety of sects " has introduced such general confusion that many are led to prefer the immoveable firmness of the Roman Rock ".[27]   The reason for the lessening of persecution was twofold. First, whereas Cromwell had been at his most savage in his crushing of Catholic Ireland, his policy in Scotland was to curb the Kirk, and it was the Kirk which had persecuted the Catholics when it had the power. And secondly, the impecunious state of the Commonwealth, both in England and in Scotland, made the government prefer fines to any other form of punishment.

All through the English Occupation the common people of Scotland remained Royalist at heart; " they hanker still after that broken reed ", the King, indignantly declared the *Diurnal of Occurrences*. In this sentiment they were joined by the more moderate ministers, who were realizing at last what they had lost by the ruin of the Monarchy. Copies of an order prohibiting prayers for the King were affixed to every kirk door in Scotland in August 1653, but many of the Resolutioners resorted to all sorts of devices in order to continue to pray for Charles without risking the penalties for doing so openly.

Some asserted that they prayed for him under his title " only by way of distinction, as in Scotland we call any nobleman or laird that has sold his land, and has not right, yet till his death by such a title and style; and that, if they prayed not for him,

the common people would be the more stirred up and pray the
more for him, whereas now they lippen [*sic*] to the ministers'
prayers".[28]   Others, as one of them wrote to Charles, prayed
"in such terms as the people who observe might find when to
put in their shoulder, and bear you up in public prayer.   As
thus, 'Lord, remember in mercy every distressed person, and
every distressed family: and the lower their condition, and from
how much the higher station they are laid low, so much the
more remember them in mercy, and let us not be guilty, as they
who remember not the afflictions of Joseph, but remember
David, Lord, in all his troubles', or to this effect: so that you
see the duty is done in effect, the people understand it, and are
discerned to join their sighs and groans, or to give the more
silent attendance, than the rest of the prayer, though the word
of degree be not used."[29]

In the July of 1654, Baillie wrote so detailed an account of the
state of the Scottish nobility that it is worth quoting in full:

"Our nobility well nigh all are wracked.   Dukes Hamilton,
the one execute, the other slain; their estate forfault; one part
of it gifted to English soldiers; the rest will not pay the debt;
little left to the heretrix; almost the whole name undone with
debt.   Humbie execute; his sons all dead but the youngest; there
is more debt on the House than the land can pay.   Lennox is
living, as a man buried, in his house of Cobham; Douglas and
his son Angus are quiet men, of no respect.   Argyll almost
drowned in debt, in friendship with the English, but in hatred
with the country: he courts the Remonstrants, who were and
are averse from him.   Chancellor Loudoun lives like an outlaw
about Atholе, his lands comprised for debt, under a general very
great disgrace.   Marischal, Rothes, Eglinton, and his three sons,
Crawford [-Lindsay], Lauderdale, and others, prisoners in
England, and their lands all either sequestrate or forfault, and
gifted to English soldiers.   Balmerino suddenly dead, and his
son, for public debt, comprisings, and captions, keeps not the
calsie [dares not be seen upon a public road or causeway].
Wariston, having refunded much of what he got for places, lives
privily in a hard enough condition, hated by most, and neglected
by all, except the Remonstrants, to whom he is guide."

In 1655, a Council of State was set up at Edinburgh, with
supreme power over the conquered country; it was composed of
six or seven English officers, and two Scots of the kind contemptuously referred to by Baillie as "our complying gentlemen".   These were Colonel Lockhart, who just recently had
married Cromwell's niece, and had obtained the palace and park

of Falkland and the castle and park of Stirling for his collaboration with the invaders, and Colonel Sir John Swinton, who afterwards turned Quaker. This Council of State shared between
them the great offices, the Seal of Scotland, which now bore an
engraving of Cromwell on horseback, being given to Desborough.

After Cromwell's death in 1658, the remains of the Long
Parliament known as the Rump added a final insult. They
ordered that upon the Great Seal of Scotland the Arms of
England should have precedence. "I fear," wrote Wariston,
"they use us more and more as a province." Two years previously, this fanatic had been fain to admit that the ordinary
people were laying these insults and tyrannies at the right door.
"I heard," he wrote, "of the land's growing hatred of the
Covenant."[30]

Chapter Five

WHILE Scotland was reaping the bitter harvest of the
Covenant, Argyll was busy ingratiating himself with his
old ally Cromwell. His visit to London in the autumn of 1655
proved so congenial that he remained there until the summer of
1657, hopeful of obtaining the public moneys he claimed were
owing to him, and becoming a familiar figure in society. In
May 1656, he visited John Evelyn at Sayes Court, a visit which
the diarist recorded in the brief observation: "Note, the
Marquis took the turtle-doves in the aviary for owls."

In this same month of May, Argyll wrote to his old friend
Wariston, with whom he had fallen out, and who was busy in
Scotland preparing the way for the deputations of Protesters
and Resolutioners who were coming to London in the following
year to make Cromwell the adjudicator in their quarrel. It
might be possible, wrote Argyll, for him to persuade Cromwell
to give Wariston back his old post of Clerk-Register, and to pay
his debts as well. At first Wariston was righteously indignant;
he would not, he replied, take employment under invaders and
Sectaries. But on thinking it over, his greed began to loom
larger than his patriotism and his religious bigotry. "What if
the Protector wrote down," he pondered, "that he never minded
to put me out of my place, and sent down the Registers as belonging to me (as he has given Mr. R. Blair his pension again), and

would not require either my meddling in judicatories or giving any oaths or engagements, what might I do in that case?"[31]

But he still retained a distrust of Argyll, and his suspicion was strengthened by a letter from his bosom friend, a leading Protester, the Rev. James Guthrie, "wherein he writes well his suspicions of Argyll being on the design of employment, and to have me engaged to take off the reproach". Guthrie was right; Argyll's only hope of regaining some of his old power in Scotland was by making himself acceptable to the extreme Covenanters, all other parties detesting him, and to do this he was endeavouring to get Cromwell on the side of the Protesters, and to tempt Wariston, their most prominent layman, with hope of reward for which he would be obliged to Argyll.

In October the latter wrote Wariston that Cromwell was "very tender in his respect towards you and affected your condition and had appointed 300 pd. sterling yearly for you; which as it's an act of kindness from men, so (all things considered) of great mercy from the Lord, wherein I rejoice". Wariston's tortuous and greedy mind wavered still further. "This remembers me," he addressed the Lord, "of thy moving the King to favour me and give letters and orders for me even when and while in simplicity of heart and obedience to God, I was doing the things most contrary to him." His references to Cromwell in his diary took on a different tone; the "proud piece of clay" had now become the man whom the Lord had placed in power. By December Wariston was able to tell his wife that his scruples over accepting employment under an invader and Sectary were growing less and less, and a dream he had more or less clinched the matter. "I dreamed that these nations were become as a united city, and that I was appointed to be governor of it, which left an impression on me."

In January 1657, the deputations of Protesters and Resolutioners arrived in London, the former being headed by Wariston, and the latter by the Rev. James Sharp, minister of Craill, many years later, as Archbishop of St. Andrews, to be brutally murdered by the Protesters' successors, the Covenanting worthies of the reign of Charles II.

Wariston immediately tried to ruin his old professor and lifelong friend, Robert Baillie, who, though not a member of the deputation, was a leading Resolutioner, by telling Cromwell that the reason why Baillie sided with that party was "that he might keep himself in a capacity to act for the King when opportunity should offer". Baillie described this as a base libel, though after the Restoration he was to hasten to assure Lauderdale that

"I was one of those who, in my heart, and all needful expressions, adhered to the King in all his distresses. He had my continual prayers to God for his restitution, any way God pleased, even the most hard: divers know my frequent expressions of readiness to further his return to the throne, by laying down mine head on the block for it, and the utter ruin of all my worldly fortune."[32]

But the likelihood of that "restitution" was exceedingly remote in 1657, and Baillie and his Resolutioner friends were ready enough to toady to Cromwell if they could get him on their side in their bitter quarrel with the Protesters. Cromwell disappointed them. The two great bones of contention between the parties were the Act of Classes and the General Assembly of 1651 which had agreed to its repeal. To the delight of the Protesters, Cromwell revived the Act, since it ensured that no one remotely eligible for the epithet Malignant could hold office in Scotland; but he refused to pronounce a verdict on the lawfulness or otherwise of the Assembly of 1651, being shrewd enough to realize that while the Protesters and the Resolutioners were left to their bitter quarrel on the subject, there was no possibility of a revival of the power of the Kirk.

Wariston, meanwhile, had put away his last scruples in the matter of accepting employment and rewards. "Is not Cr[omwell] without the Malignants better nor Ch[arles] with them?" wrote this expert casuist. "*Reddite Caesari quae Caesar* is give to thy King or Emperor (whom ye question for usurpation) the things that belong to a King as unto God the things due to any God or given to any King and possessed and brooked by them." On June 10th he had an interview with Cromwell, and told him of "my three rights": a reward of three thousand pounds, the Clerk-Register's place, and a pension of four hundred pounds a year. Cromwell desired him to draw up the warrant for the Clerk-Registership, but in the bestowing of it there was a trifling condition. The Protector "desired me to give him from time to time full information of matters and persons their carriages in Scotland, and it should not meet me again". In other words, Wariston was to act as a spy upon his fellow-countrymen, and Cromwell would not disclose the source of his information.[33]

By the end of the month, Wariston's ambitions had soared still higher. For on the 26th, the day of Cromwell's second installation as Protector, Lilburne told Wariston that Cromwell intended to nominate five Scotsmen as peers for his "Other House", that is, the House of Lords, now revived under an ambiguous title. Four of them were to be Sutherland, Brodie, Cassilis, and Lockhart, "and he could not tell the fifth", though almost certainly it would not be Argyll. The mere possibility of its being himself made Wariston's mouth water.

Argyll, meanwhile, had returned to Scotland, and on July 15th he was one of the very few Scottish lords who consented to be present at the second proclamation of Cromwell as Protector. It was a market-day and Edinburgh was crowded, but "of 5 or 6000 Scotsmen that were present not one Scotchman open'd his mouth to say, God bless my Lord Protector".[34] But Argyll, with his prospective son-in-law, the Earl of Caithness, and four or five other Scots nobles, stood in their robes of state at the foot of the Mercat Cross which was covered with rich tapestry, while Cromwell was proclaimed "Chief Magistrate of the three nations of England, Scotland, and Ireland".[35] Having thus officially declared his allegiance to the invader of his country, Argyll returned to his Highland fastness to enjoy the monetary rewards he had obtained in England; but after Cromwell's death he reappeared in public, and went to London again to take his seat as Member for Aberdeenshire in Richard Cromwell's short-lived Parliament. If his purpose was to make sure of his income under the new Government, it succeeded. On April 16th, 1659, having already received a thousand pounds sterling, his claim for a further twelve thousand was allowed, and was charged upon the excise of Scotland.[36]

Wariston also had been doing well for himself. He had achieved his ambition of sitting in the "Other House", and he was a member of Richard's Parliament. It was a bitter disappointment to him, therefore, when Richard and his Parliament were turned out by the military, and a General Council of officers formed the Government. A new Council of State was to be chosen, however, and Wariston immediately intrigued for a place on it. "Argyll said," he wrote on May 15th, "it would be a snare to me to meddle because of their looseness in religion, and yet I thought he would fain meddle himself. Some men," he added smugly, "are using means with men and soliciting them for this employment: I solicit none but God."

His solicitations were successful, for the very next day he heard that he had been elected a member of the new Council. On the 20th, the day of his admission, he celebrated his good fortune by writing his diary in the Council Chamber. "I think it a strange change," he gloated, "in God's providence that the Protector is banished out of this house and room and that I have a call to be in it." When, in the following month, he was for a period actually President of the Council, his dream that he had been made governor of three nations seemed to be coming true. But as Argyll, who had returned to Scotland, had warned him, the times were "ticklish"; and in July Wariston was writing in a different strain: "Everyone looks upon me as ruined for meddling with these people. There is a strange contempt and hatred through the nation of this present Parliament."

The Parliament to which he referred was the old Rump which, on October 11th, was turned out yet again by the military. In the complete chaos which ensued, it soon became apparent that the attitude of one man was vital: General George Monck.

He was the only one of the military grandees strong and ruthless enough to play the part of Cromwell, and many believed that his ambition was to make himself Protector. But while busily purging the army of occupation which he commanded in Scotland, dismissing officers and men whose fidelity to himself was doubtful, Monck was writing to the Speaker in London that the firm re-establishment of a commonwealth was the only desire of his heart, and to Fleetwood that "I take God to witness that I have no further ends than the establishing of Parliamentary authority, and those good laws which our ancestors [sic] have purchased with so much blood, the settling the nations in a free Commonwealth."

On November 15th, in the Parliament House of Scotland, he met the representatives of the shires and boroughs, and in a speech again asserted his intention of restoring the Rump, commanding them to preserve the peace of Scotland during his absence. By the beginning of December he was at Berwick, and here he sat awhile, shrewdly watching the course of events in England, and having three standards made. On the first was the motto *For Magistracy and Ministry*, with a hand holding a sword; on the second *For the Gospel*, with a Bible; and on the third *For the Privileges of Parliament and Liberty and the People*. They were mottoes which all parties interpreted according to their own hopes of Monck's favour, and his conduct became the more ambiguous when, though the Rump was restored on Christmas Day, he persisted in his intention of marching to its aid. He had between six and seven thousand veteran foot and two thousand horse; and on the bitter cold morning of January 1st, 1660, he began to march slowly but inexorably south.

In London the three main parties in this time of chaos, the Rump, the military grandees, and the Presbyterian City, speculated furiously upon his intentions, and sent deputations hasting to meet him on his march. Wariston caught the general panic, and, as usual in such circumstances, "cast the lot" to discover from the Lord whether he should remain where he was when Monck arrived, or go into hiding; also as usual it fell upon the side of safety first. With five hundred pounds purloined from the Exchequer in his pocket, he took refuge in the house of a poor pewterer, trembling when he heard that Monck was calling him an "incendiary" and the cause of the long strife between Protesters and Resolutioners.

"Whereas I thought I was following the call of God's providence," he wrote in one of his rare moments of honesty, "the truth is I followed the call of providence when it agreed with my humour and pleased my idol [himself] and seemed to tend to my honour and advantage, but if that same providence had called me to quit my better places and take me to meaner places or none at all, I had not so hastily and contentedly followed it." Yet while acknowledging at last his own avarice and self-deception, and his selling of places when he was Clerk-Register in the reign of King Covenant, he could not help boasting even now to the pewterer with whom he lodged, of the great welcome he had received from both Houses on his entry into London in 1643, the year of the Solemn League and Covenant, of the commissioners and the coaches which had been sent out to meet him, "wherein," he admitted sadly in his diary, "coaches was an addition."

Finding that Monck on his arrival in London would not so much as speak to him, Wariston set out for Scotland on March 27th, "hated of all sort of the people of this kingdom, for being president in England of the Committee of Safety, and for his great oppression in Scotland, in raising the prices of all writs and evidences, and great extortion of the subjects".[37] Even his closest friend among the Protesters, the Rev. James Guthrie, had turned against him, and he was greeted on his arrival by copies of letters written by Guthrie to him in 1654 and 1656 against accepting posts under Independents and invaders, which copies Guthrie had placed, without comment, in his old friend's study. But far worse than this was Monck's attitude. "I have heard," wrote Wariston on May 1st, "of General Monck's saying that he had letters under my hand that would take off my head."

For Monck had declared himself at long last; he had acceded (at precisely the right moment for himself) to the universal demand for a freely elected parliament which could mean one thing only: an invitation to the King to come home. The declaration of this Convention Parliament that the government consisted by law in King, Lords, and Commons, arrived in Edinburgh on May 7th. Wariston saw it next day, and noted that the clause giving indemnity to all save the surviving regicides, and those whom Parliament should choose to except, did not apply to Scotland. Since Loudoun had just informed him that he and Argyll were the two most hated men in their own country, Wariston's terror must have increased; but he remained hoping against hope until July, when a warrant was issued for his arrest. He went into hiding, and later fled to Holland.

On Monday, May 14th, King Charles II was proclaimed at the Mercat Cross of Edinburgh. There had been rejoicing enough at that other proclaiming of him, eleven years before, after his father's murder; but on this early summer's day of 1660, the whole of Edinburgh went mad with joy. Bells pealed, trumpets brazened, drums "touked", cannon thundered, the spouts of the conduits ran wine, folk danced round bonfires, and the Provost and bailies, after drinking the King's health, smashed their glasses in reckless extravagance. On June 19th there was another celebration, even more costly, the magistrates feasting at a table set up at the Cross and smashing no less than three hundred dozen wine-glasses in an excess of loyalty. As a grand finale, the Devil was set up on one pole and an effigy of Cromwell on another at the Castlehill, where "it was ordered by firework, engine, and train, the Devil did chase that traitor, and pursued him still, till he blew him into the air".

Nicoll, the humble diarist who had recorded the miseries of his country throughout the English Occupation, painted an inimitable picture of her joy when at last she was freed from King Covenant and foreign invader alike:

"At this time, our gentry of Scotland did look with such gallant and joyful countenance, as if they had been the sons of princes . . . and it was the joy of this nation to behold the flower of the kingdom, which for so many years had been overclouded, and now to see them upon brave horses, prancing in their accustomed places, in tilting, running of races, and such like. . . . The poor swans, also, whose wonted habitation was the Loch at the north end of Linlithgow, took banishment upon them at the incoming of these English usurpers, and did seek another domicile, by the space of ten years, and never returned till the King's Majesty returned to England, and was proclaimed King.

"Another thing observable is this, these English usurpers built a strong citadel in the town of Perth, and upon the port thereof were placed the Arms of the pretended Commonwealth. Out of the same part of the wall where the 'scutcheon was fixed, there did in April last, 1660, a thistle come forth, which before the middle of May thereafter did overgrow these Arms of the Commonwealth."

THE RECKONING
1660-1661

I

THE worst enemies of King Charles II could not include vindictiveness among his faults, and when, after fifteen years of exile, he was restored to his father's throne, his own inclination was to forgive and forget all the treasons and betrayals and rebellions of those bitter years. Robert Baillie, whom the King made Principal of the University of Glasgow, while being "wounded to the heart" by the news that the Prayer Book was being used in the Chapel Royal at Whitehall, paid a generous tribute to Charles's attitude when he returned to his native land:

"The King, in wisdom, moderation, piety, and grave carriage, giving huge satisfaction to all. . . . He endeavoured carefully to relieve all that had been sufferers for him and his father. He pressed the Houses to haste the Bill of Indemnity. They excepted a very few from it; scarce a dozen execute; in which the people had much more satisfaction than he, for he could have been induced to pardon all. But it was the justice of God that brought Peters, Harrison, and others [of the regicides] to a shameful death; to hang up the bones of Oliver, Bradshaw, Ireton, Pride, on the gibbet at Tyburn; and to disgrace the two Goodwins, blind Milton, Owen, Skerrie, Lockier, and others of that malignant crew."[1] By "malignant crew" Baillie meant, of course, the Covenant's old allies, the rebels of England.

If Charles had excuse enough to have avenged himself upon English rebels, he had an even greater one for punishing the Scots whose treasons against his father had begun the Civil War, whose aid to the English rebels had enabled them to win it, who had sold Charles I after promising him protection, and who had persecuted and butchered the most faithful adherents of both kings. The lack of an indemnity for Scotland would have enabled him, had he so desired, to have taken the lives of those prime mischief-makers, the ringleaders of the Protesters, who

275

even now were plotting fresh rebellion; and had he done so, Scotland might well have escaped the troubles caused by these fanatics during his reign and that of his successor.

Instead, four men and four only, paid the supreme penalty: Argyll, Wariston, the Rev. James Guthrie, and an obscure person named Govane.

If there was one man above all others whose conduct had shown that while he lived his country would suffer from his intrigues and treacheries, that man was Archibald Campbell, Marquis of Argyll. Yet even he, had he remained in retirement at home, as he had done during the chaotic months which had preceded the Restoration, would not have paid the extreme penalty, even though he might have lost his estates. But his lust for power and his insatiable greed prevented him from taking this sensible course; and in the summer of 1660 he was guilty of the incredible impudence which was to bring him to his death.

As a Highlander, and therefore superstitious, he should have known better, for the heavens had been most lavish with omens and warnings. Years before, his sister, Lady Kenmure, had told the Rev. Samuel Rutherford that her skill in the art of physiognomy enabled her to predict that her brother "would die in blood". On the day the King landed in England, Baillie's daughter and son-in-law were at Roseneath, and observed that "all the dogs that day did take a strange yowling and glowering up to my lord's chamber for some hours together". On his last visit to Kintyre, Argyll was playing "at the bullets" with some gentlemen, and when he stooped to lift a bullet, one of these friends of his turned pale, and exclaimed: "Bless me, what is that I see? My lord with his head off, and all his shoulder full of blood." Finally, when Argyll was starting off on his fatal journey to London in this summer of 1660, the friends who were seeing him off were waylaid by a dumb man, who laid his staff on the ground, and lying down with his neck on the staff, smote the back of his neck with his hand, afterwards pointing to Argyll in his galley.[2]

But apart from such supernatural warnings, it is difficult to understand why Argyll was so mad as to believe that he would have a good reception from the King; possibly he relied upon Charles's well-known clemency, yet even so to intrude himself into the royal presence was the very height of presumption and stupidity. From the Argyll Papers and from Baillie, it would appear that it was Lord Lorn, then in London and in favour at Court, who advised his father to come up; but here again it is hard to understand why Argyll should have trusted his hated heir in so important a matter.

He arrived in London early in July, and on the 8th he called several times at the lodging of the Lord Chancellor, Clarendon, to arrange for an audience with the King. Clarendon refused to see him, but Argyll hung about outside, and when the Chancellor, in company with Lorn, came out to enter his coach and drive to Whitehall, Argyll caught him by the sleeve. Brushing away his hand, Clarendon exclaimed curtly, "Not a word, my lord!" Even after this rebuff, Argyll remained so sure of himself that he went by water to Whitehall, arriving there before Clarendon and Lorn. As these two passed through the ante-room to the King's Chamber of Presence, Argyll waylaid his son and sent him in with a message to his Majesty; he was waiting, said the ex-dictator of Scotland, to kiss the royal hand.

Such impudence could have only one result. Charles sent for Secretary Nicholas and instructed him to order Garter King at Arms to arrest Argyll on a charge of high treason. The arrest was made in the crowded ante-chamber; and while the "gley-eyed Marquis" was being driven to the Tower, the King was being congratulated on having secured the most dangerous man in Scotland, against whose malice Argyll's father had warned his own.

During the remainder of his time on earth, Argyll must surely have remembered his own treatment of Montrose when at last he had got that mortal enemy into his power, and have contrasted it with that which he was accorded now. He was allowed every privilege of a State prisoner, he was to have a fair trial by his peers, writing materials were supplied to him, and his wife was allowed to share his quarters. He employed his time in writing his last instructions to the heir whom he had hated so bitterly. As a literary effort it was not distinguished, and even Argyll's biographer, Mr. Willcock, betrays some disappointment with his hero's instructions to his son on the subject of courage: "Those who know of the want of courage which has been brought against the Marquess, will naturally turn with some curiosity to see what he has to say about that virtue. They will not, however, find much that is interesting in the chapter, as the ideas and the terms in which they are couched are quite commonplace."

But there was one maxim which, coming from Argyll, was sufficiently startling: "'Tis better to trust in valour than in policy."

II

On November 30th the order was given to the Lieutenant of the Tower to deliver Argyll into the custody of the Earl of Middleton, formerly Sir John Middleton, who had just been appointed Royal Commissioner for Scotland. A week later the prisoner was sent home on board the *Eagle* man-of-war, accompanied by his old colleague, Colonel Sir John Swinton, who, charged with taking office under Cromwell, had been arrested at the Restoration and sent to Newgate. Argyll cannot have found Swinton a congenial companion, for the latter, excommunicated by the Kirk in 1651, had now turned Quaker. The voyage lasted a fortnight, the weather being so stormy that the sea very nearly anticipated the headsman's work.

As Argyll and Swinton were brought from Leith to Edinburgh, "many thousands did gaze and exclaim against them as they came up the street, calling them traitors and such like "[3]; but while he was the principal object of the people's hate, Argyll could congratulate himself on the fact that, with his head covered, he was escorted to the comparative comfort of the Castle, whereas the excommunicated Swinton was hustled bareheaded to the common jail. Swinton, however, was destined to have the last laugh, for although he could have been hanged without trial, since he had been condemned for treason ten years previously, he was pardoned.

Scotland, meanwhile, was about to witness the outward and visible signs of her restoration as a sovereign State. On January 1st, 1661, there was a particularly magnificent Riding of the Parliament which Middleton had come to open; it was marked by the production of the Honours, the Crown, Sceptre, and Sword, which the Earl Marischal and his brother had managed to conceal from the invaders throughout the English Occupation. On the 4th, a royal Proclamation was read, ordering Montrose's remains to be collected for a splendid reinterment at the King's expense. Accordingly the trunk was dug up from the felons' pit in the Boroughmuir, the hands and limbs were fetched from the towns upon the gates of which they had mouldered for eleven years, and workmen set up a large scaffold against the Tolbooth, so that officials could take down from its highest prick the head of the Royalist champion.

The Estates then got down to business. The Oaths of Allegiance and Supremacy were tendered, the latter containing the words, "The King is supreme Governor over all persons and in all causes". There were some scruples in Presbyterian bosoms over this, but the moderates were satisfied when Middleton and Chancellor Glencairn gave assurance that the words did not imply a power over the internal affairs of the Kirk. The few extremists remained unsatisfied, demanding to have the word "civil" inserted between those of "supreme Governor", and refusing to take the oath unless this was done. "At this I was very sorry," wrote Baillie, "for I feared it should occasion trouble, and a new schism, without great cause. . . . For myself, I took the Oath of Allegiance and Supremacy thirty-four years ago, when I entered regent [at Glasgow University], and yet never scrupled it."

The Acts of all the illegal parliaments which had sat without royal warrant since 1638 were then annulled; and at the end of the month, the Estates, according to ancient Scots law, formed themselves into a judicial court for the trial of Argyll. On the 31st, a herald went to the Castle, formally summoning the prisoner to attend in the Parliament House, that House where for so many years he had reigned as dictator, and where now he must answer a charge of high treason. He desired the Estates to instruct Sir John Nisbet, a distinguished advocate, to undertake his defence, but Nisbet refusing, the Estates appointed six others, including Sir George Mackenzie, later Lord Advocate of Scotland. Baillie admits that in the forthcoming trial "there was no lack of full hearing and debates to the uttermost", and all the accounts confirm this statement.*

Argyll was brought to the Parliament House by coach on February 13th, and here he and his six counsel were accommodated upon a special platform erected near the entrance doors. The prisoner's demand to harangue his judges before the reading of the indictment being refused, this immensely long document, containing fourteen articles of treason, was read by the Lord Advocate, Sir John Fletcher.

The charges fell under three main heads. First there were those connected with Argyll's conduct during the Civil Wars: the invasion of England in 1644, the delivering of Charles I to the English in 1647, the prisoner's opposition to the Engagement in the following year, the part he had taken in the Whiggamore Raid, his reception of Cromwell after the defeat of the Engage-

---

* The formal record of the trial, with details of the day-to-day proceedings, has disappeared. The account given here is taken from Howell's State Trials, Burton's History, Wodrow's History, Lamont's Diary, and the Life of Robert Blair.

ment, and the executions of Huntly and Montrose. Under the second head were various barbarous murders perpetrated by those under his command during and after the Civil Wars. Lastly, he was charged with concurring in the usurpation of Cromwell, with opposing Middleton and Glencairn in the Royalist rising of 1653-4, with being officially present at the proclamation of the second Protectorate of Cromwell in Edinburgh, and with sitting in the Parliament of Richard Cromwell. To these charges was added afterwards one other: that when Oliver Cromwell had been in Edinburgh at his invitation in the autumn of 1648, Argyll had planned with him the execution of the King.

The prisoner's best chance of escape lay in the clemency of Charles II, and, hoping that the King would send down a pardon, he played for time. He pretended that he had not been given sufficient opportunity to consult with his counsel anent the process, and the Estates immediately gave him until February 26th to prepare his defence with their help. When, on that day, he again begged for further time, he was again allowed a respite, being ordered to appear on March 5th. His defence, when at last he was forced to produce it, was a masterpiece of prevarication.

He answered in general to the first set of charges that the responsibility for the acts of which he was accused belonged, in fact, to the Estates or their Committee. As for the selling of the King, he had been in Ireland when Charles arrived at the Scots camp at Newark, and later he had gone to London for the express purpose of sounding two prominent English Royalists, the Duke of Richmond and the Marquis of Hertford, on the advisibility of the Scots army declaring for the King. For this there is Argyll's bare word; and it will be remembered that during that visit to London in 1646, he had announced to the Parliament his entire approval of the Propositions which would have destroyed the Monarchy in everything except name, and had expressed his hope of an incorporation of Scotland with the Auld Enemy.

For the second set of charges he again shelved all responsibility. He could not be called to account, he declared, for acts committed by his officers and vassals unless they were done by his express orders. He denied taking any man's life except in conflict, "or by order of law for notorious crimes, according to standing Acts of Parliament". As for his being in arms at Stirling after the defeat of Hamilton in 1648, "the defender was pursuing no forces, but coming to meet with the Committee . . .

being to consult what was best, fearing no harm, being at Stirling, was invaded by George Munro and others, and some of his
friends who were with him were killed and others taken
prisoners".

In the matter of Glencairn's Rising, he had the impudence to
declare that his failure to join it was due solely to the fact that
he had received no summons either from Middleton or Glencairn to join with them, and that he did not know they had the
King's commission. For his collaboration with the English, he
had been, he asserted, one of the very last to submit to them.
His invitation to Cromwell to come to Scotland he flatly denied;
and as for Cromwell's being entertained by him in Edinburgh
Castle, he was not, said Argyll blandly, the keeper of that
fortress.

His presence at the proclamation of the Second Protectorate
had been quite accidental; he had just happened to be there on
his private concerns. (He did not condescend to explain how it
was that he had appeared on the steps of the Mercat Cross in
his robes of state.) He excused his sitting in Richard's Parliament by saying that it was the only visible power and authority
in the two kingdoms, that he had been obliged to safeguard his
own just rights, and to secure the laws and religion of his
country. His hopes of being able to do something towards pro-
moting the interests of his lawful King had, he added solemnly,
"weighed also with him".

III

The trial had proceeded so far when the King sent an order
which increased Argyll's hopes that the King's clemency would
save him. All charges against the prisoner connected with crimes
committed before 1651 were to be dropped, save that of having
connived with Cromwell in the execution of the late King. In
his reluctance to shed blood, Charles desired to go even further;
he asked that, when the trial was concluded, the whole record of
it should be sent to him, and that sentence should not be pronounced until he had read and considered it. But Middleton
protested so strongly that such a favour to Argyll would be
resented by the Estates as a breach of their privileges, that the
King abandoned it.

There remained, therefore, only the third set of charges
against the prisoner, those which concerned his collaborating
with the English invaders and his opposition to Glencairn's

Rising, and the accusation of concurring in the late King's death. The latter charge ran thus:

"That your monstrous and execrable treason may appear to all the world, it is of verity, that in the year 1648, at a private conference betwixt you, Oliver Cromwell, and Colonel Ireton, the said Oliver complaining of the many difficulties that attended their affairs, by reason of the divers designs which his Majesty had on foot from time to time against them: you, the said Marquis, made answer, 'That their danger was great indeed, in regard that if any of these designs should take effect, they were all ruined.' And therefore gave your positive answer, that they should proceed to the questioning of the King for his life; assuring them that they would never be safe until they had taken away his Majesty's life. At least you did know of the horrible and treasonable design of murdering his said Majesty; and did most treasonably conceal, and not reveal the same till after the said horrid deed was committed, and so past prevention or remedy."

The votes of the Estates were then taken as to whether Argyll was guilty or not guilty of this charge; there being no witnesses to prove it, he was acquitted. For the remaining charges, he offered not a defence but a submission, throwing himself upon the royal mercy. This was, he declared, of such depth, "that having swallowed and passed by not only personal but national guiltiness, of much more a deeper dye than any the petitioner can be charged with . . . so will not strain to pass by and pardon the faults and failings of a person, who never acted but in a public joint way, without any sinister or treasonable design against his Majesty and his royal father". But the Estates would have none of this, and ordered the prisoner to prepare a proper defence against the remaining set of charges.

Almost every day throughout March and April, he was brought to the Parliament House, using as weapons in his fight for his life fawning compliments to Middleton ("whose unspotted loyalty to his Majesty we all can witness"), biblical allusions, bare-faced lying, and reiterated appeals to "that transcendent and princely clemency wherewith his Majesty is so admirably delighted", and which would prove, he said solemnly, "one effectual cement to conciliate the most anti-monarchical and disaffected persons (excepting some of those barbarous fanatics)". Then he would lapse into self-pity; great men like himself, he lamented, were ever subject to the envy and rancour of "the inconsiderable multitude". Disregarding the fact that all charges against him prior to 1651 had been dropped, he sought to justify himself in regard to them. He had met Cromwell, "that monstrous usurper", only to prevent his coming to Scotland in 1648. Hamilton he had regarded as "a truly noble and worthy person"; Huntly he had done his utmost to preserve; and as for Montrose, not only was he innocent of taking any part in his death, but he had done his best to bring about a treaty with him in 1645.

He wearied his judges with the collection of Hebrew prophets and pagan philosophers to whom he appealed to prove his point that when a usurper was in possession, "the safety of the people is the supreme law". He asserted again and again that he had not collaborated with the English invaders, except in so far as he was forced to it by having troops quartered upon him, and (rather strangely) by a great sickness with which the Lord had been pleased to visit him at that time. He had been, he said, "like a forced chaste virgin", obliged to submit to irresistible force. A gasp must have run round the House when he calmly declared that he had done his best to persuade his neighbours to join Glencairn's Rising, he who had given information against his own son for doing so. He ended by asserting that it was an essential part of the King's Prerogative (which he himself had sought to destroy) to dispense with the severity of the laws, and he begged the intercession of the Estates on his behalf. It cannot have been a very pleasant exhibition: this man, who never in his life had shown mercy, now grovelling for it in the scene of his former tyrannies.

But notorious though his collaboration with the English had been, it was difficult to prove, and this fact, together with the King's known clemency, made Argyll's case look so hopeful that his second son, Lord Neil Campbell, made a trip to London, for the purpose apparently of bragging about the certainty of his father's acquittal. There can be no doubt that such boasts reached the ears of one who had found Argyll exceedingly useful during the English Occupation, but who now was anxious only to show his own complete conversion to Royalist principles. They were the ears of that most cunning old trimmer, General George Monck.

IV

However favourable his case looked, either Argyll's guilty conscience or his well-known cowardice induced him to form a plot for his escape from the Castle. Perhaps he remembered the escape of Lord Ogilvy, which had so enraged him in 1646; at any rate he attempted to copy that young Royalist's method. During an interval in his trial he kept his bed, pretending one of those convenient sicknesses with which the Lord was pleased to visit him at awkward moments. During this period his wife, who was still allowed free access to him, came and went in a covered sedan-chair. But the very cowardice which impelled him to flee as he had fled from so many battle-fields, prevented him from going through with the enterprise. On the day arranged for his escape, he put on his wife's clothes, and was in the very act of stepping into the chair, when, as his biographer discreetly puts it, " the constitutional timidity with which many credited him shook his resolution ".

The final stages of the trial arrived. The Estates had shown enormous patience, but it was now drawing towards the end of May, and having heard all the evidence, such as it was, for and against the charge of collaboration with the English, the House was about to vote on Argyll's guilt or innocence, when there occurred a most dramatic interruption. A gentleman entered in haste, bearing a sealed packet which he presented to the Royal Commissioner. It was bitterly ironical that this gentleman's name should have been Campbell, for the packet contained that which amounted to the death-warrant of MacCalein Mhor: the Six Famous Letters.

They were letters written by Argyll to Lilburne and to Monck during the English Occupation; and they proved without the shadow of a doubt that the prisoner had been an active and willing collaborator with the invaders of his country. It was there in black and white; he did not, and indeed could not, deny it. By his own hand he was condemned.

Many writers have blamed Monck severely for his action in sending these letters. Burnet called it "a betraying the confidence that they then lived in ". But such a charge overlooks the fact that the letters were official, and not private; they were the letters of a man who, of his own free will and for his own selfish ends, was giving information against his King's faithful subjects, and in return for favours was fawning upon the invaders of his native land. No doubt Monck's action in sending these letters which inevitably would condemn an old ally was a mean one; but then Monck was not a pleasant character, and the fact which must have counted with him was that he had turned his coat at precisely the right moment, whereas Argyll, though notorious for his cunning, had not. And even a better man than Monck was might have succumbed to the temptation of sending proof

positive, which he alone could supply, against a criminal who
was about to cheat the headsman for lack of it.

The letters swept away the prisoner's lame defence, and the
verdict of Guilty was carried unanimously, the young Marquis
of Montrose alone refraining from giving his vote, on the
grounds that he had too deep a personal resentment against the
prisoner to act as an impartial judge. Next day, May 25th,
Argyll was brought to the bar to hear his sentence which, in
the absence of the Commissioner, was pronounced by his old
rival for the leadership of the Covenant, Crawford-Lindsay:
"That you are found guilty of high treason, and adjudged to
be executed to the death as a traitor, your head to be severed
from your body at the Cross of Edinburgh, upon Monday, the
27th instant, and affixed in the same place where the Marquis
of Montrose's head was formerly, and your Arms torn before
the Parliament and at the Cross." After pleading in vain for a
respite of ten days so that the King might be acquainted with
his sentence, Argyll was removed to the Tolbooth, seeing as he
went the preparations for celebrating the first anniversary of
the Restoration, just ordered to be kept for ever as a public
holiday.

While he had been in the Castle he had heard the sounds of
a more solemn occasion. He had heard the tolling of kirk bells
and the beat of muffled drums, as the long procession following
the remains of Montrose had wound its way from Holyroodhouse to St. Giles. Surely he must have contrasted then his own
conditions, the fair trial, the privileges of a State prisoner, with
those he had accorded his fallen enemy eleven years before. He
must have seen in memory that wounded and fever-racked
captive bound on the hangman's cart, the haggard eyes which
had abashed his own as he had squinted between the shutters,
the thirty-foot gallows, the hideous butchery, the exhibition of
the mangled limbs, the trunk buried in the felons' pit. Above
all he must have recalled his own final piece of petty spite, his
refusal of Montrose's request for a razor, the request of one who
would appear decent and comely at his death.

And now, during his own last hours, Argyll had his wife, his
friends, and his physician with him; his favourite minister, that
same David Dickson who had invented the hideous proverb,
"The wark gangs bonnily on", slept with him in his cell. His
servants attended to his wants; the list of those whom he desired
to be with him on the scaffold was allowed. His execution was
timed for two o'clock on Monday afternoon, and with a delicacy
most striking in that rough age, the authorities ordered that the

clock of the Tolbooth be stopped at one, so that the prisoner should not hear the ominous next three quarters chiming.

He dined at noon, called for wine, and afterwards, according to his invariable custom, took a short sleep. His sons-in-law, the Earls of Lothian and Caithness, his kinsmen, the Earl of Loudoun and Montgomery of Skelmorie, three ministers, including his chaplain, Robert Trail, and his physician, Mr. Cunningham, all in deep mourning as was the prisoner, made up the little procession which walked the short distance from the Tolbooth to the Mercat Cross, beside which was the scaffold with the Maiden upon it. As a last and unheard-of privilege, the prisoner was permitted to wear his hat.

It was inevitable that Argyll's reputation for cowardice should have made friend and foe alike almost indecently curious as to how he would behave himself in this dread hour. Sharp eyes noticed that, during his speech, he played continually with the buttons of his doublet, nervously unfastening and fastening them again, and that he moved from one corner of the scaffold to another all the time he spoke. But, wrote Sir George Mackenzie, who had visited him in jail, "I remember that I having told him, a little before his death, that the people believ'd he was a coward and expected he would die timorously, he said to me that he would not die as a Roman braving death, but he would die as a Christian without being affrighted". Of Montrose's death Argyll had written to Lothian: "He got some resolution after he came here, how to go out of this world, but nothing at all how to enter into another." Those words, with far more justice, might have been written of Argyll himself.

For his speech was a lecture, and a justification of himself; there was no word of repentance for sin, either private or public. It was the speech of a good Covenanter and a bad Christian.

If there were any present, he began, who expected him to justify himself, he must disappoint them; he then proceeded to justify himself for the space of half an hour. He had not entered upon " the work of reformation " with any design of advantaging himself or to the prejudice of the royal authority. He had never, he declared (having forgotten, it would seem, the Six Famous Letters), collaborated with the English invaders, and he had done everything in his power to advance the King's cause.

There were, he went on, three sorts of people in the kingdom at this time. The first were the openly profane, "and truly I may say, though I have been a prisoner, I have not had mine ears shut; I hear assuredly that drinking, swearing, whoring were never more common, never more countenanced than now they are ". The second sort were those "who care not whether the Church of God sink or swim ". All he had to say to them was, remember that they and their posterity were pledged to uphold the two Covenants. Lastly there were the Elect. For them he feared that there was suffering ahead, and Christians must make their choice either to sin or suffer, though those who chose to sin would not escape suffering. It might not be the kind which he was now to endure, he said, pointing to the Maiden, but very much worse. "Mine," he concluded happily, "is but temporal, theirs shall be eternal. When I shall be singing, they shall be howling."

After most solemnly affirming once again that he was innocent of all connivance with Cromwell in the murder of Charles I, he took off his doublet and prayed with one of the ministers. He then gave the hangman a napkin containing money, his watch to the Earl of Caithness, a double-ducat to Lothian, and a silver pen to Loudoun. His behaviour so far had been decent if uninspired, but now that the fatal moment had arrived, his friends became uncomfortably expectant of a display of cowardice. "Now, my lord, hold your grip sicker," tactlessly implored the Rev. Hutcheson, or, in modern parlance, "Take a firm grip of yourself". "Mr. Hutcheson," Argyll rebuked him, "you know what I said to you in the chamber. I am not afraid to be surprised with fear." Cunningham, the physician, took hold of the victim's wrist as the red head was laid on the wooden bar between the two uprights of the Maiden, and later told Burnet the surprising fact that he found the pulse beating at its usual rate.

After a decent interval for private prayer, the signal was given, the knife fell, and the head of the most dangerous man in Scotland rolled into the basket. It was set upon that spike of the Tolbooth where for so many years a nobler head had mouldered; three years later, by order of the King, it was taken down and buried with the body in the family vault at Kilcum.*

v

Soon after the Restoration, warrants had been issued for the arrest of Sir James Stewart, the former Provost of Edinburgh, who had presented the Western Remonstrance to the Estates

* On May 27th, 1895, a sumptuous memorial to Argyll was unveiled in St. Giles. One cannot help wondering what he would have thought of the present aspect of that kirk, with its cross and its organ.

with such studied insolence that he had refrained from bowing to the King; of Sir John Chiesley; Colonels Barclay and Ker; two leading lights of the Protesters, James Guthrie and Patrick Gillespie; and a man named Govane. Of these, Stewart, Chiesley, Barclay, and Gillespie, were all pardoned; Ker, like Wariston, fled to Holland; and Govane, convicted of fighting against his native country in 1651, was hanged. "But so inconsiderable a person had not died, if he had not been suspected to have been upon the scaffold when King Charles the First was murthered; though he purged himself of this when he died, and his guilt was that he brought to Scotland the first news of it, and seemed to be well satisfied with it."[4]

The Rev. James Guthrie met a well-deserved death by hanging at the Mercat Cross of Edinburgh on June 1st, a few days after Argyll. He had been the author of both the West Kirk Declaration and the Western Remonstrance, which had demanded a disowning of the King's cause and a treaty with the invader, and also of a tract, *The Causes of God's Wrath*, in which he had charged Charles I and his successor with all the blood which had been shed in the three kingdoms. But the King's clemency was such that even so hardened a rebel would have been pardoned had he not persisted in defying the royal authority after the Restoration. In August 1660, he presented a "Supplication", in which he demanded the imposing of the extreme Presbyterianism of the Protesters upon the three kingdoms, and the abolition of the Episcopal form of worship even in the King's Chapel Royal. It was reported of him that after his condemnation, "he would willingly have redeem'd his life by a submission, but that the multitude of ladies upbraided him with the very report of what would strike at the root of religion, and so thrust him violently upon his death".[5] It was this species of "lady", these "holy sisters", who, some years later, were to shelter the murderers of old Archbishop Sharp.

There remained the high priest of King Covenant, Sir Archibald Johnston of Wariston.

For some while after his flight, he lived securely in Holland and in Germany, but in 1662 he moved to France, where he was recognized, arrested, and extradited. He was brought to London in the January of the following year, and kept in the Tower until June, when he was sent down to Scotland and confined in the Edinburgh Tolbooth. He had already been condemned in his absence for having accepted office under Cromwell, but he was brought before the Council to say what he could in his own defence. Instead, he fell upon his face, "roaring, and with tears entreated they would pity a poor creature"; he swore that he had lost his memory, and could remember "neither matter of law nor matter of fact, nor a word of the Bible".

The Council acceded to his entreaties for physicians and ministers to attend to the health of his body and soul, and gave him a fortnight in which to benefit from their ministrations. But at the end of that time, when he was brought before the Council again, he made an even more revolting exhibition of himself. "I have often heard," Lauderdale wrote to Sir Robert Moray, "of a man feared out of his wits, but never saw it before." He pretended that the unskilfulness of his physicians in bleeding him had unhinged his mind, and he "run up and down upon his knees, begging mercy". The Council put a stop to the spectacle by ordering his former sentence to be executed upon him.[6]

On July 23rd, he was brought to the gallows at the Mercat Cross. Exactly opposite that spot stood his town house, from the windows of which he had watched so much of the drama of the past twenty-five years. There by the Cross had stood the grisly scaffold, "the Altar of Argyll and the ministers", on which the bloody sacrifices in which King Covenant had delighted had been offered; there poor swooning Ladywell, sick old Huntly, gallant Montrose, and so many other victims had met an unjust death. And now he who, after Argyll, had been King Covenant's chief henchman, was being called upon to pay the reckoning.

He had recovered some measure of composure, a fact which, wrote Sir George Mackenzie, "his friends ascribed to God's miraculous kindness to him; but others thought that he had only formerly put on this disguise of madness, to escape death in it". He made a long speech, described by Lauderdale as "stark staring nought", reading it from a paper; in its extraordinary style it resembled those diaries in which he had recorded so many "castings of the lot", so many divine revelations which had proved to be but his own fancy, such startling casuistry when his conscience and his ambition were at war.

Unlike Argyll, he had the grace to confess to some of his crimes. He admitted his compliance with the English invaders, "through the power of temptations, and too much fear anent the straits that my numerous family might be brought into"; and he confessed that, in following what he called the Lord's work, he had not been altogether free from self-seeking. The rest of his speech was an obscure account of how the Lord had vouchsafed him a last revelation: that the cause of the Covenant

T

would be revived. He prayed that the eyes of those who were the enemies of himself and the Lord might be opened, and he concluded in his own peculiar style:

"I do here submit and commit my soul and body, wife and children, and their children's children from generation to generation for all, and all others Our Lord's friends and followers, and all His doing, suffering, witnessing and sympathizing ones, unto the Lord's choicest mercies, graces, favours, services, employments, empowerments, enjoyments, improvements, and inheritments in earth and in Heaven, in time and in Eternity; All which suits, with all others which He hath at any time by His Spirit moved and assisted me to make and put up according to His will, I leave before the Throne, and upon the Father's merciful bowels, and the Son's mediating merits, and the Holy Spirit's compassionate groans, for now and ever more."

According to an admirer who wrote an account of his end, Wariston read this long rigmarole twice; his last words were of his assurance of "being clothed in a long white robe before night"; and on being turned off the ladder he "peaceably slept away into glory, with his precious hands upraised in prayer and no convulsions of any kind".

REFERENCES AND NOTES

REFERENCES AND NOTES

PROLOGUE

1. Balfour, IV, 371-2.
2. Fuller's *Church History*, X, 218.
3. Spalding, I, 34, 35.
4. Heylyn, 149.

PART ONE

1. Mathieson, I, 29.
2. Heylyn, 149-50.
3. Burnet, *Dukes of Hamilton*, 35-6.
4. Burnet, *His. of My Own Times*, 56-7.
5. Bramhall, 25.
6. Ibid., 19-20.
7. Ibid., 13-15.
8. Guthrie, 8.
9. Mathieson, I, 360.
10. *Large Declaration*, 16.
11. Monteth, 6.
12. Row, 174.
13. Mathieson, I, 350-1.
14. *Large Declaration*, 9.
15. Burnet, *His. of My Own Times*, 34. Hamond L'Estrange, 130.
16. Sanderson, 200. Baillie, I, Appendix, 476-7. Balfour, I, 219-20. Hamond L'Estrange, 139-40. *Large Declaration*, 12-15.
17. *Large Declaration*, 45.
18. *Scots Affairs*, I, 6-7.
19. Monteth, 19. *Large Declaration*, 19-22.
20. Introduction to Spottiswoode's *History*, CVII.
21. Hope, 64. Baillie, I, 18. *Scots Affairs*, II, 7-8. *A Brief and True Relation of what fell out on the Lord's Day, the 23rd of July, 1637*.
22. Guthrie, 20.
23. *Dukes of Hamilton*, 39-41. *Scots Affairs*, II, 11. Spalding, I, 79-80.

24. Baillie, I, 21.
25. Ibid., 21, 24-5.
26. Rothes, 26-7.
27. Baillie, I, 39-40.
28. *Scots Affairs*, I, 30.
29. Rothes, 56-7.
30. *Scots Affairs*, I, 33; N.
31. Wariston's Diary, 1634-39, 321.
32. Rothes, 79-92.
33. Wariston's Diary, 1634-39, 327.
34. Ibid., 331.
35. *Scots Affairs*, I, 45.
36. Rothes, 107, 109.
37. Spalding, I, 87; N.
38. Hailes, II, 25-6.
39. Baillie, I, Appendix, 463-4.
40. Baillie, I, 67-8.
41. *Staggering State*, 96.
42. *Scots Affairs*, I, 50. Guthrie, 101. D'Israeli, IV, 5-7.
43. Warwick, 111-13.
44. Clarendon, II, 55.
45. *Britane's Distemper*, 56-7.
46. Wodrow, *Analecta*, I, 22.
47. Burnet, *His. of My Own Times*, 43.
48. *The Great Marquess*, 336.
49. *Scots Affairs*, I, 68-9.
50. Balfour, II, 265. *Scots Affairs*, I, 72.
51. Guthrie, 34-5. Montrose himself told Guthrie this.
52. Baillie, I, 85.
53. Rothes, 122.
54. *Dukes of Hamilton*, 91.
55. Balfour, II, 289-91. *Large Declaration*, 154-5. Spalding, I,
    107.
56. *Large Declaration*, 183.
57. *Scots Affairs*, I, 132.
58. Mathieson, I, 396-7. *Dukes of Hamilton*, 108-111. Spalding,
    I, 110-111.
59. Spalding, I, 108-9.

PART TWO

1. *Scots Affairs*, I, 104. Guthrie, 39. Hamond L'Estrange, 162.
Burnet, *His. of My Own Times*, 53.

2. *Memoirs of Scots Catholics*, I, 202-3. *Dukes of Hamilton*, 106.
3. Spalding, I, 116. Guthrie, 39-40.
4. Baillie, I, 105-7.
5. *Hamilton Papers*, 59. *Scots Affairs*, I, 157. *Dukes of Hamilton*, 125. Baillie, I, 124.
6. *Scots Affairs*, I, 152. Baillie, I, 133.
7. *Scots Affairs*, I, 170.
8. *Large Declaration*, 281-4. *Scots Affairs*, I, 187. Wariston's Diary 1634-9, 377.
9. *Scots Affairs*, I, 191-2.
10. Baillie, I, 158.
11. Monteth, 34.
12. *Scots Affairs*, II, 148.
13. Ibid., 165.
14. Wishart, 291. Baillie, I, 112.
15. *Scots Affairs*, II, 171-2. Guthrie, 41. Baillie, I, Appendix, 485.
16. Stevenson, *His. of the Church of Scotland*, II, 676.
17. Turner, 16.
18. *Scots Affairs*, II, 222.
19. *Britane's Distemper*, 229.
20. Spalding, I, 165.
21. *The Marquess of Huntly his Reply to Certain Noblemen.*
22. *Scots Affairs*, II, 218, N., 249. Spalding, I, 181. *Dukes of Hamilton*, 176.
23. *Dukes of Hamilton*, 178-9.
24. Lang, III, 76-7. Burnet, *His. of My Own Times*, 42-4.
25. Warwick, 139.
26. D'Israeli, IV, 68.
27. Baillie, I, Appendix, 484. *Memoirs of Scots Catholics*, II, 64. Spalding, I, 258.
28. Guthrie, 59. D'Israeli, IV, 351.
29. Sanderson, 194.
30. Spalding, I, 252, 264-5.
31. Baillie, I, 226.
32. *The Great Marquess*, 101.
33. *Scots Affairs*, III, 182.
34. Ibid., 165. *C.S.P.D.* 1640-1, 53. Balfour, II, 390.
35. *His. MSS. Com.*, VI, 616.
36. *Scots Affairs*, III, 165-6.
37. *Acts of the Parliament of Scotland*, V, 399.
38. Baillie, I, 262.
39. Ibid., 278-83, 301-2, 316, 353.

40. Napier, *Memoirs of Montrose*, I, 261. From original in the Montrose charter-chest.
41. Baillie, II, Appendix, 468.
42. *Argyll Letters*, 36-7.
43. This paper was found by Mark Napier in the Montrose charter-chest. The shameful way in which Captain Stewart's evidence was twisted is given at length in the same author's *Memoirs of Montrose*, I, 319 *et passim*, from the original MSS in the Advocates' Library.
44. Baillie, I, 378.
45. Guthrie, 80-1.
46. Baillie, I, 388.
47. Carte, *Ormonde Papers*, I, 4.
48. Baillie, I, 385-6.
49. Balfour, III, 42.
50. Ibid., 69-72.
51. Ibid., 65.
52. *Nicholas Papers*, I., 25.
53. Balfour, III, 95-130. Hope, 153. Baillie, I, 391-4. Spalding, II, 77-80. *Dukes of Hamilton*, 236-9. The exceedingly obscure and contradictory depositions may be read in *His. MSS. Com.*, IV, 163-70.
54. *Staggering State*, 125.
55. Peterkin, 313.
56. *Britane's Distemper*, 57.
57. Peterkin, 317.
58. Spalding, II, 173.
59. Baillie, II, 55-6.
60. *Dukes of Hamilton*, 261.
61. Guthrie, 111-12.
62. Baillie, II, 75-6.
63. Wishart, 39.
64. Spalding, II, 261-2.
65. Warwick, 164-5.
66. Spalding reproduces it in full, II, 263-6.
67. Baillie, III, 99.
68. Spalding, II, 285.
69. Montereul, II, 542, 556.
70. *Britane's Distemper*, 46.
71. Spalding, II, 355-6.
72. Ibid., 376.
73. Balfour, III, 183.

INTERLUDE

1. Balfour, III, 245.
2. *Dukes of Hamilton*, 260.
3. Napier, *Memoirs of Montrose*, II, 423-4; N.
4. Wishart, 84. See the ratification of his pardon by the Covenanters for the three murders, Napier, *Memoirs of Montrose*, I, Appendix VI.
5. Baillie, II, Appendix, 417-24.
6. *Memoirs of Scots Catholics*, I, 305-6.
7. *Britane's Distemper*, 96.
8. Wishart, 110-11.
9. Balfour, III, 256.
10. *Britane's Distemper*, 100-1. *Memoirs of Scots Catholics*, I, 321-4. Wishart, 110-12. Guthrie, 141. Balfour, III, 272-3.
11. Wishart, 159.
12. Guthrie, 154. Wishart, 170-1. *Memoirs of Scots Catholics*, I, 348-9.
13. Guthrie, 162. *Memoirs of Scots Catholics*, I, 356. Burnet, *His. of My Own Times*, 66-7.
14. Wishart, 201. Mackenzie's *Works*, II, 384. *Britane's Distemper*, 209.
15. Guthrie, 166.
16. Burnet, *His. of My Own Times*, 66-7. Balfour, III, 325.
17. *Staggering State*, 76 and N. Wishart, 242.
18. Balfour, III, 341, 346-7.
19. Wishart, 249.

PART THREE

1. Lamont, 4.
2. Spalding, II, 691, 383.
3. Nicoll, 70.
4. *Blairs Papers*, 225, 226.
5. Nicoll, 4.
6. *Charles II and Scotland*, 136. Carlyle's *Cromwell*, Letter CXLIX.
7. Nicoll, 8. Lamont, 10.
8. Mathieson, I, 194. Dalyell, 618, 624-5.
9. Balfour, III, 437.
10. Dalyell, 623, 642.

11. *Diurnal of Occurrences.*
12. *Memoirs of Scots Catholics,* I, 191, 210-18.
13. Guthrie, 203-4.
14. Wariston's Diary, 1634-9, 380.
15. *Letters from Roundhead Officers,* 37.
16. Spalding, I, 358.
17. Montereul, I, 17.
18. Ibid., 109.
19. Ibid., 126.
20. *Charles I in 1646,* 19, 20.
21. Montereul, I, 177.   Warwick, 327.
22. *Charles I in 1646,* 32.
23. Ibid., 37-9.
24. Baillie, II, 367.
25. Examination of Dr. Michael Hudson.   Peck's *Des. Cur.,*
    XXV.
26. Hailes, II, 170.
27. *Dukes of Hamilton,* 356.   Sir Philip Warwick also bore
    testimony to the King's "great ability and knowledge, when
    he was destitute of all aids".   Warwick, 324.
28. *Charles I in 1646,* 45, 46.
29. Guthrie, 171-2.   Wishart, 234.
30. *The Great Marquess,* 193.
31. *Journal of the House of Lords,* VIII, 392-3.
32. Warwick, 324-5.
33. Montereul, I, 244.
34. *History of Independency,* 81.   Guthrie, 197.
35. *Dukes of Hamilton,* 394.
36. Montereul, I, 445.
37. *Nicholas Papers,* I, 73.
38. Echard, 629.

PART FOUR

1. Montereul, II, 82-93.
2. Turner, 46.   Montereul gives the number of the massacred
   as 400, and the *Acts of the Parliament of Scotland* (VII, 338)
   as 500.
3. Guthrie, 199.   Turner, 47.
4. Montereul, II, 140, 142.
5. Turner, 50.   Baillie, III, 18.
6. Montereul, II, 331.
7. *Argyll Letters,* 40.

8. Rushworth, I, Part IV, 982.
9. Montereul, II, 407-8.
10. Ibid., 409.
11. Ibid., 420-1.
12. *General Assembly Commission Records*, 1646-7, 393, 412. Guthrie, 214-15. Baillie, III, 36. Balfour, III, 395-6.
13. Guthrie, 218.
14. Ibid., 223.
15. Burnet, *His. of My Own Times*, 72.
16. *Hamilton Papers*, 177, 190, 196.
17. Baillie, III, 38, 48-9. Turner, 242.
18. Baillie, III, 54.
19. *Dukes of Hamilton*, 461. Quoting from the Articles of Surrender.
20. Guthrie, 241. *Dukes of Hamilton*, 471-2. Wishart, 320-1.
21. Wishart, 318-19.
22. *Dukes of Hamilton*, 480.
23. Monteth, 401-3.
24. *Britane's Distemper*, 212, 213.
25. Turner, Guthrie, Echard, Wishart, and Clarendon, the latter in a letter to Lord Jermyn, all either hint or state plainly that this was so.
26. *Life of Robert Blair*, 210.
27. Echard, 645-6.

PART FIVE

1. Baillie, III, 383-5. Guthrie, 254.
2. Balfour, III, 386.
3. Baillie, III, Appendix, 458-9, 460-1.
4. Baillie, III, 75-81.
5. *History of Independency*, 131-2.
6. *Dukes of Hamilton*, 483.
7. Ibid., 510.
8. *Britane's Distemper*, 224.
9. Monteth, 507.
10. Baillie, III, 99-100.
11. *His. MSS. Com.*, VI, 612. Baillie, III, Appendix, 523.
12. Echard, 674.
13. *Letters of King Charles II*, 14.
14. *Charles II and Scotland*, 126.
15. Ibid. Introduction, XXII.

16. *Memoirs of Montrose*, II, 770-1, 789. From originals in the Montrose charter-chest. The whole question of Charles's conduct in regard to Montrose is discussed exhaustively by Andrew Lang, *His. of Scotland*, III, 221-6.
17. *The Marquis of Montrose*, 249.
18. Whitelock's *Memorials*, May 20th.
19. *Genealogy of the Stewarts of Allanton and Coltness*.
20. Argyll's biographer, Mr. Willcock, has sought to discredit this story on the grounds that there is no evidence whatever of Lady Haddington's immorality. But an account of her death in 1685, written by a Fr. Macbreck, provides ample evidence. See *Blairs Papers*, 87.
21. Letter from M. de Graymond, French Resident in Edinburgh. Quoted by Napier, *Memoirs of Montrose*, II, 781. *Wigton Papers*, 316, 369; N. Wishart, 404-5.
22. Wishart, 405.
23. *Memoirs of Scots Catholics*, II, 51. Skinner's *Ecclesiastical History*, 417.
24. Jaffray, 32.
25. Nicoll, 16-17.
26. Ed. Walker, 161. Carnwath was later imprisoned in the Tolbooth.
27. *Personal History of Charles II*, 134.
28. *Brief Relation*, June 4th.
29. Note by Lord Dartmouth, Colonel Legge's descendant, in Burnet's *His. of My Own Times*, 1823 Ed., I, 150.
30. Ibid.
31. Clarendon, XIII, 795.
32. Balfour, IV, 86.
33. Nicoll, 21-2.
34. Ed. Walker, 165.
35. Ibid., 162.
36. Monteth, 509.
37. *Nicholas Papers*, I, 194-5.
38. *His. MSS. Com.*, VI, 613.
39. Ed. Walker, 180-1.
40. Balfour, IV, 99-100.
41. Guthrie, 129.
42. *His. MSS. Com.*, VI, 606.
43. Ed. Walker, 187.
44. It is reproduced in Balfour, IV, 141.
45. Baillie, III, 109.
46. *A Discovery after some Search of the Sins of the Ministers*, 1651.

47. Nicoll, 38-9.
48. *Analecta*, I, 67.
49. Balfour, IV, 306.
50. Clarendon, XIII, 809.

PART SIX

1. Nicoll, 56. Balfour, IV, 314.
2. *Blairs Papers*, 43; N.
3. Nicoll, 61.
4. Balfour, IV, 314-16. Nicoll, 58. Lamont, 35.
5. *Scotland and the Commonwealth*, Appendix XVI.
6. Ibid., 34. *Letters from Roundhead Officers*, 47.
7. *Scotland and the Commonwealth*, 48, 50, and N.
8. *Scotland and the Protectorate*, Appendix IX.
9. *Consult of Ministers*, I, 49-50.
10. Lamont, 44. Appendix to *Scots Affairs*, LVII-VIII.
11. Nicoll, 60-1.
12. Wariston's Diary 1650-54, 218.
13. Baillie, III, 225-6. *Mercurius Politicus*, July 21st-28th. Lamont, 56-7.
14. *Scotland and the Protectorate*, 89. *Diurnal of Occurrences*.
15. *Scotland and the Protectorate*, 61-2.
16. Ibid., 76-80. Nicoll, 124.
17. Baillie, III, 259. *Scotland and the Protectorate*, 244, 261.
18. Brodie, 147, 150.
19. Nicoll, 140.
20. Ibid., 81.
21. Lamont, 64, 83.
22. *Blairs Papers*, 51.
23. Baillie, III, 258.
24. *Scotland and the Protectorate*, 363.
25. Baillie, III, 323.
26. Burton, IV, 440.
27. *Memoirs of Scots Catholics*, II, 65.
28. Wariston's Diary, 1650-54, 257.
29. *Scotland and the Protectorate*, 322-3.
30. Wariston's Diary, 1650-54, 257.
31. Ibid., 1655-60, 33.
32. Baillie, III, 405.
33. Wariston's Diary, 1655-60, 91, 93.
34. *Scotland and the Protectorate*, 362.
35. Nicoll, 200. Lamont, 99.

36. Burton, IV, 447, 448.
37. Nicoll, 279.

EPILOGUE

1. Baillie, III, 42-3.
2. Ibid., 466-7.　*Analecta*, I, 73.　Law's *Memorialls*, 116.
3. Lamont, 129.
4. Mackenzie, 51.
5. Ibid., 50.
6. Ibid.　*Lauderdale Papers*, I, 155-6.

BIBLIOGRAPHY

BIBLIOGRAPHY

A Collection of Letters written to his Excellency, General George Monck. 1714.

A Compleat History of the Life and Reigne of King Charles. William Sanderson. 1658.

A Fair Warning to take heed of the Scotish Discipline. Dr. John Bramhall. 1649.

A Large Declaration concerning the late Tumults in Scotland. 1639.

A Peaceable Warning to the Subjects in Scotland. Dr. John Forbes. 1638.

A Relation of the Proceedings concerning the Affairs of the Kirk of Scotland. John, Earl of Rothes. (Bannatyne Club.)

A Short Abridgement of Britane's Distemper. Patrick Gordon.

Acts of the Parliament of Scotland.

An Ecclesiastical History of Scotland. John Skinner. 1788.

Analecta. Robert Wodrow. (Maitland Club.)

Biographical Collections. Ibid. (New Spalding Club.)

Blairs Papers, 1603-1660. Ed. Malcolm V. Hay.

Calendar of State Papers, Domestic.

Charles I in 1646. (Camden Society.)

Charles I in the Isle of Wight. George Hillier.

Clarendon State Papers.

Commentaries on the Life and Reign of Charles I. I. D'Israeli. 1830.

Correspondence of Sir Robert Ker, first Earl of Ancram, and his son William, third Earl of Lothian.

Cromwell's Scotch Campaign, 1650-51. W. S. Douglas. 1898.

Cyprianus Anglicus: or the History of the Life and Death of William Laud. P. Heylyn, D.D. 1719 edition.

Desiderata Curiosa. Francis Peck. 1779.

Diary of Alexander Brodie of Brodie. (Spalding Club.)

Diary of Thomas Burton. Vol. IV.

Diary of Sir Thomas Hope of Craighall, 1633-45. (Bannatyne Club.)

Diary of Alexander Jaffray. 1834 edition.

Diary of Johnston of Wariston, 1634-39, 1650-54, 1655-60.

Diary of Mr. John Lamont of Newton, 1649-71.

Diary of Public Transactions and other Occurrences. John Nicoll. (Bannatyne Club.)

Domestic Life in Scotland, 1488-1688. John Warrack. 1920.

Early Travellers in Scotland. P. Hume Brown. 1891.

General Assembly Commission Records.

Hamilton Papers. (Camden Society.)

Hardwicke Collection of State Papers.

Highlanders of Scotland. W. F. Skene.

Historical Collections. John Rushworth.

Historical Discourses. Sir Edward Walker. 1705.

Historical Manuscripts Commission Reports.

Historical Works of Sir James Balfour.

History of England. Laurence Echard. 1720.

History of My Own Times. Gilbert Burnet. 1897 edition.

History of St. Andrews. Rev. C. J. Lyon.

History of Scotland. Andrew Lang. 1904.

History of Scots Affairs. James Gordon.

History of the Church of Scotland during the Commonwealth. Rev. James Beattie. 1842.

History of the Church of Scotland. Archbishop Spottiswoode.

History of the Commonwealth and Protectorate. Samuel Rawson Gardiner.

History of the Great Civil War. Ibid.

History of the Kirk of Scotland from the year 1550 to August, 1637. John Row.

History of the Rebellion and Civil Wars in England. Edward, Earl of Clarendon. 1839 edition. (In this edition the original MS. in the Bodleian is followed, and passages suppressed in other editions are restored.)

History of the Sufferings of the Church of Scotland. Robert Wodrow.

History of the Troubles of Great Britain. Robert Monteth. Eng. translation by Capt. James Ogilvie. 1735.

Johnston of Wariston. William Morison. (Famous Scots Series.)

Journals of the House of Commons.

Journals of the House of Lords.

Lauderdale Papers. (Camden Society.)

Letters and Journals of Robert Baillie. (Bannatyne Club.)

Letters and Papers illustrating the Relations between Charles the Second and Scotland in 1650. Samuel Rawson Gardiner. 1894.

Letters from Roundhead Officers written from Scotland, 1650-1659. (Bannatyne Club.)

Letters of King Charles II. Ed. Arthur Bryant.

Letters to the Argyll Family. (Maitland Club.)

Life and Campaigns of Alexander Leslie. Charles Sanford Terry. 1899.

Life of James Butler, Duke of Ormonde, with a Collection of Letters. T. Carte.

Lives and Characters of the Officers of the Crown and State of Scotland. George Crawfurd. 1726.

Memorials and Letters relating to the History of Great Britain in the Reign of Charles the First. Ed. Lord Hailes.

Memorials of Montrose and his Times. Mark Napier. 1850.

Memorials of the English Affairs, 1625-60. Bulstrode White-locke.

Memorialls of the Trubles in Scotland and England. John Spalding. (Spalding Club.)

Memoirs of Henry Guthrie, late Bishop of Dunkeld. 1702.

Memoirs of John Gwynne. Ed. Sir Walter Scott. 1822.

Memoirs of his own Life and Times. Sir James Turner.

Memoirs of Montrose. Dr. George Wishart. 1819 edition.

Memoirs of the Affairs of Scotland from the Restoration of King Charles II. Sir George Mackenzie. 1821 edition.

Memoirs of the Dukes of Hamilton. Gilbert Burnet. 1852 edition.

Memoirs of the Life of Mr. Robert Blair. 1754.

Memoirs of the Marquis of Montrose. Mark Napier. 1856.

Memoirs of the Reign of King Charles I. Sir Philip Warwick. 1702.

Memoirs of the Scottish Catholics during the XVIIth and XVIIIth Centuries. W. Forbes Leith, S.J.

Nicholas Papers. (Camden Society.)

Old Church Life in Scotland. Lectures on Kirk-sessions and Presbytery Records. Dr. Andrew Edgar. 1886.

Politics and Religion. W. Law Mathieson.

Records of the Kirk of Scotland. Alexander Peterkin. 1838.

Records of the Presbytery of St. Andrews. (Abbotsford Club.)

Records of the Scottish Privy Council.

Register of the Consultations of the Ministers of Edinburgh. (Scottish History Society.)

Relations and Observations. Clement Walker. 1648.

Scotland and the Commonwealth. Ed. C. H. Firth. 1895.

Scotland and the Protectorate. Ibid. 1899.

Scotland before 1700 from Contemporary Documents. P. Hume Brown. 1893.

Spottiswoode Miscellany. Vol. II.

The Argyll Papers. Ed. J. Maidment. 1834.

The Clan Campbell. Ed. Rev. Henry Paton. 1913.

The Cromwellian Union. (Scottish History Society.)

The Darker Superstitions of Scotland. John Graham Dalyell. 1834.

The Diplomatic Correspondence of Jean de Montereul. (Scottish History Society.)

The Great Marquess. John Willcock. 1903.

The Heraldry of the Campbells. G. Harvey Johnson. 1920.

The House of Argyll and the Collateral Branches of Clan Campbell. 1871.

The Last Discourse of the Right Honble. the Lord Warestoune. By a Favourer of the Covenant and Work of Reformation. 1664.

The Macdonald Bards. Keith Norman Macdonald. 1900.

The Marquis of Montrose. John Buchan. 1913.

The Pennyles Pilgrimage of John Taylor. 1618.

The Reign of King Charles. An History, disposed into Annals. Hamond L'Estrange. 1656.

The Staggering State of Scots Statesmen. Sir John Scot of Scotstarvet. 1754.

Wigton Papers. (Maitland Club Miscellany.)

INDEX

INDEX

Aberdeen, opponents of the Covenant at, 47; forced to sign the Covenant, 79; captured by Montrose, 132-3; surrenders to the English, 240

Abernethy, Thomas, 64

Aboyne, Lord, 2nd son of 2nd Marquis of Huntly, 80-1, 89, 121, 127, 132, 139-40, 142-3, 180, 209

Act of Classes, 201-3, 205, 234, 237, 268

Act of Ratification, 18

Act of Revocation, 31-2, 60

Airlie, Earl of, 90, 129, 142, 229

Airth, Earl of, 59

Almond, Lord (later Earl of Callander, q.v.), 97, 106, 134

Angus, Earl of. *See* Douglas, Marquis of

Annandale, Earl of, 31, 143

Antrim, Earl of, 125, 130

Argyll, Archibald Campbell, 7th Earl of, 52, 54

Argyll, Archibald Campbell, 8th Earl and 1st Marquis of (formerly Lord Lorn, q.v.), 85, 93, 117, 119, 155, 176, 230, 261; and the General Assembly of 1638, 68-70, 75; and the Pacification of Berwick, 81; insults Charles I, 82; dismissed from office of Justiciary of the Isles, 87; his power over the Covenanters, 88-9; his Commission of Fire and Sword against Stewarts of Atholl and Ogilvies of Airlie, 89-92; conflict with Montrose, 95-102; and Charles I's visit of 1641 to Scotland, 104-6; and 'The Incident', 106-11; created a marquis, 110; dominates General Assembly of 1642, 112; calls a Convention in 1643, 113; offers Montrose the Lieutenant-Generalship, 114-15; and Huntly's rising of 1644, 121-3; and Colkitto's rising, 126; spurns Montrose's appeal to return to the King's allegiance, 130-1; and Montrose's capture of Aberdeen, 132-3; offers prize for capture of Montrose, 133; his forces repelled by Montrose at the Ythan River, 133-4; lays down his commission, 134-5; flies alone to Roseneath, 135-6; defeated by Montrose at Inverlochy, 136-8; and Montrose's victory at Kilsyth, 141-2; in Ireland and London, 171-2; receives payment for betrayal of Charles I, 175; presses for his pension, 179-80; and the sack of Dunavertie, 180-1; and the Engagement, 185-6; challenges Crawford-Lindsay, 188-9; negotiates with Cromwell, 189-90; Hamilton's weakness towards, 191-3; recovers his power, 196-8; welcomes Cromwell to Edinburgh, 198-200; and the Act of Classes, 201-3; refuses to intervene on Hamilton's behalf, 207; insists on Huntly's execution, 208-9; does not desire Charles II in Scotland, 209-10, 214; insists on Montrose being hanged, 215; wishes Charles II to marry his daughter, 219-20; and Charles II's household, 222; promised honours by Charles II, 228; alleged intrigue with Cromwell, 230-1; and Charles II's coronation, 235; growing feeling against, 237-8; his agreement with the Commonwealth, 241-6; informs on Glengarry, and his double-dealing, 250-1; and Glencairn's Rising, 253; continues to send information to the English, 253-8; dislikes his son, 258; his debts, 259; ingratiates himself with Cromwell, 266-7; officially declares his allegiance to Cromwell, 269; much hated, 272; journey to London at the Restoration, 276-7; arrested, 277; taken to Scotland, 278-9; trial of, 279-85; plans escape, 283-4; sentenced and executed, 285-7

Arminianism, 71
Articles of Perth. *See* Five Articles of Perth
Ashburnham, Mr., 166, 169
Ashurst, Mr., 187
Assembly of Divines, 118, 131-2, 158, 172
Astley, Sir Jacob, 93
Atholl, Earl of, 89

Baillie, Robert, 39-40, 43, 48, 56-8, 64-5, 71, 81, 88, 94-5, 102, 104, 109, 115-19, 132-3, 153, 156-7, 159-60, 169, 174-6, 182, 188, 193, 201, 230-3, 236, 249, 258, 260-3, 265, 267-8, 275-6
Baillie, Sir William, 134
Baillie, William, 134-5, 137-41, 190, 225
Balcanquhal, Dean, 83
Balcarres, Earl of, 141, 240, 254
Balfour, Sir James, 13, 17, 153, 219
Balfour, Nicholas, 38
Balmerino, first Lord, 33-4, 101
Balmerino, John Elphinstone, 2nd Lord, 33-4, 105, 184
Bamfield, Colonel, 255
Barclay, Colonel, 288
Barclay, Robert, 222
Baynes, Cornet, 157
Beaton, Cardinal, 37
Bellasis, Lord, 168
Bellièvre, President, French Ambassador in England, 173-4, 177
Bellièvre, junior, brother of French Ambassador to England, 174-6
Bennet, David, 235
Birch, Colonel, 187
Bishop's War, First, 77
Blackmore, Colonel, 243
Blair, Rev. Robert, 146, 155-6, 200, 247
Blake, David, 26
Boisivon, French agent, 154
Book of Canons, 35, 40, 58
Book of Discipline, 63
Boyd, Lord, 97
Brayne, Colonel, 241
Brechin, Presbytery of, 65
Brereton, Sir William, 21
Brienne, French Secretary of State, 119
Brodie, Alexander, 155, 218, 258, 269
Buchan, Earl of, 16
Buchan, John, 214
Buckingham, Duke of, 219, 229

Burleigh, Lord, 88, 104-5, 121-2, 131-2, 202
Burnet, Gilbert, Bishop of Salisbury, 25, 29, 38, 50, 55, 78, 119, 169, 172
Byron, John, 1st Lord, 191-2

Caithness, Earl of, 269, 286-7
Callander, Earl, 186, 190, 193-4
Calvin, 28, 150
Calvinism, in Scotland, 24
Camerons of Lochaber, 91
Campbell, Argyll's steward, 242
Campbell, Lady Anne, 219
Campbell, Sir Donald, of Auchinbreck, 137
Campbell, Sergeant Dugald, 90-1
Campbell, Lord Neil, 2nd son of Marquis of Argyll, 283
Campbell Clan, 51
Capel, Lord, 207
Carbisdale, Montrose defeated at, 213
Carmichael, Rev. Frederick, 131, 226
Carmichael, Sir James, 41
Carnegie, Lord, of Kinross, 65-6
Carnwath, Robert Dalyell, 2nd Earl of, 107-8, 114, 219
Cassilis, Earl of, 50, 96, 112, 141, 172, 189-90, 202-3, 269
Catholics, oppressed by the Reformed Church, 154-5; under the Commonwealth, 264
Causes of God's Wrath, The (Rev. James Guthrie), 288
Chambres, Abbé, 85
Charles I, 98, 200; crowned at Edinburgh, 13-17; at ceremony of the Riding of Parliament, 18-19; ignorance of Scotland, 29-30; and the endowment of the Church of Scotland, 31-3; and Lord Balmerino, 33-4; and the Scottish Service Book, 34-9; his Declaration, 41-2, 45; reliance upon Hamilton, 49-50; pardons 7th Earl of Argyll, 52; favours Lord Lorn, 53-4; his proclamation, 55-61; republishes Confession of Faith, 58; orders General Assembly of 1638 to dissolve, 64-5; on the General Assembly, 74; sends Hamilton into Scotland, 78, 80; opens peace negotiations with Covenanters, 81; insulted by Argyll, 82; and the Covenanter invasion of England, 93-5; visit of 1641 to Scot-

land, 103-6; and 'The Incident', 106-8; and Montrose, 127; his strategy upset by Covenanter invasion of 1644, 128-9; and Jean de Montereul, 161-6; anxiety for safety of Montrose, 163; meets the Covenanters, 166-71; and the Nineteen Propositions, 171-3; betrayed by Covenanters to the English, 174-8; imprisoned in Carisbrooke Castle, 185; concludes secret treaty (the Engagement) with Covenanters, 185-190; execution of, 203

Charles II: Proclaimed in Edinburgh, 203-4; Covenanters' attempt to subvert, 204-6; and Montrose's proposed invasion of Scotland, 211-13; concludes Treaty of Breda, 213; attempts to safeguard Montrose, 213-14; arrives in Scotland, and signs both Covenants, 217-19; and his proposed marriage to Argyll's daughter, 219-20; insulted by Covenanters, 222-4; and the battle of Dunbar, 225, 227; promises dukedom, etc., for Argyll, 228; and The Start, 229-30; prepares to invade England, 233-7; crowned at Edinburgh, 234-5; defeated at Worcester, 240; returns to exile, 249; and Glencairn's Rising, 254; Restoration of, 272-3; orders arrest of Argyll, 277; and the trial of Argyll, 281

Civil War: beginning of hostilities, 111; Marston Moor, 125; position in 1645, 161-2; position in 1646, 162-4

Charteris, Captain Alexander, 217

Chiesley, Sir John, 200, 219, 229, 288

Church of Scotland. See Scotland, Church of

Clandestine Band, 32, 70, 87

Clarendon, Edward Hyde, Earl of, 32, 42, 50, 55, 82, 93, 110, 220, 277

Cobbett, Colonel, 255, 259

Cobbett, Mr., 115

Cochrane, Colonel, 103, 105, 108

Colkitto (Alastair MacDonald), 125-6, 130-1, 133, 136, 142-4, 170, 180-1

Commission of Fire and Sword, 89-92

Commonwealth and Protectorate: victory over the Covenanters at Dunbar, 224-7; conquer Scotland, 239-41; agreement with Argyll, 241-6; imposition of the Oath of Allegi-

ance upon Scotland, 242, 246-7; and the Church of Scotland, 247-9; dismisses the Church's General Assembly of 1653, 251-2; and Glencairn's Rising, 252-9; treaty with Holland, 255-6; social condition of Scotland under, 260-5; set up Council of State for Scotland, 265-6; and the Protesters and Remonstrants, 266-8; the Rump Parliament, 270-1

Confession of Faith, 44-5, 58, 223

Conway, Lord, 93

Cornwallis, Anne, 52

Cotterel, Lieutenant-Colonel, 251-2

Court of High Commission, 27-8, 40, 58, 71

Covenant, National: origins, 43-8

Covenanters: at war with Charles I, 76-8; send Montrose against Huntly, 78-9; angered by Montrose's terms to Huntly, 79-80; and the Pacification of Berwick, 81-2; continued hostility to Charles I, 82-5; accept aid from France, 85-6; prepare for renewal of war, 87; Argyll's power over, 88-9; and Argyll's Commission of Fire and Sword, 89-92; invade England, 92-4; and the Treaty of Ripon, 94; and the trial of Strafford, 94-5; the Argyll-Montrose feud, 95-102; and 'The Incident', 106-11; seek to impose their creed on English Church, 111-12; the Convention of 1643, 113-15; and the Solemn League and Covenant, 115-19; invasion of England in 1644, 119-20; Colkitto's fight against, 125-6; and Montrose's march on Perth, 131-2; Argyll's and Montrose's forces in conflict, 132-4; William Baillie replaces Argyll as army commander, 134-5; Montrose's victories over, 135-43; Leslie defeats Montrose at Philiphaugh, 143-8; their oppressive rule, 149-55; fanaticism, 155-6; friction with English Parliamentarians, 158-60; and the French mission of Jean de Montereul, 161-6; urge Charles I to sign the Covenant, 166-71; and the Nineteen Propositions, 171-3; betray Charles I to the English, 174-8; emergence of two distinct parties, 179-84; and the secret treaty (the

Engagement) with Charles I, 184-90; Hamilton's weakness towards Argyll, 191-3; defeat of the Engagers, 193-5; Argyll recovers his power, 196-8; and Cromwell's visit to Edinburgh, 198-200; and the Act of Classes, 201-3; attempt to subvert Charles II, 204-6; and the execution of Hamilton and Huntly, 206-9; conclude Treaty of Breda with Charles II, 209-13; agreement with Charles II regarding Montrose, 213-14; and the hanging of Montrose and his followers, 214-17; and Charles II's signature of both Covenants, 217-19; and Cromwell's invasion of Scotland, 220-4; defeated at Dunbar, 224-7; divisions and dissensions after Dunbar, 227-33; and Charles II's preparations for invading England, 233-8; and the English conquest of Scotland, 239-41; Argyll's agreement with the Commonwealth, 241-6; and the rule of the Commonwealth, 246-52

Crawford, Ludovic Lindsay, 16th Earl of, 107-9, 127, 135, 139, 142

Crawford-Lindsay (Lord Lindsay of the Byres, q.v.), 141, 172, 188-9, 202, 285

Cromwell, Oliver, 188, 201-3, 215, 236-7; and Marston Moor, 125-6; and Lord Manchester, 159; Argyll sends emissary to, 190; visits Edinburgh, 199-200; attempts to wring Engagers' names from Hamilton, 207, 208; in Ireland, 210-11; invades Scotland, 221-4; defeats Covenanters at Dunbar, 224-7; master of south Scotland, 231-3; victory over Charles II at Worcester, 239-40; concludes treaty with Holland, 255; curbs the Church of Scotland, 264; and the Protesters and Remonstrants, 266-8; revives Act of Classes, 268

Cromwell, Richard, 172, 262, 269
Cumbernauld Band, 97, 106
Cunningham, Mr., 286-7

Daniel, Colonel, 263
Deane, Major-General Richard, 241, 243-6
Derby, Lord, 114

Dick, William, 107-8
Dickson, Rev. David, 27, 44, 146, 175, 196, 202, 251, 285
Diodati, John, 74
Dirleton, Earl of, 259
Dispute against the English Popish Ceremonies . . ., 38-9
Diurnal of Occurrences, 264
Douglas, Lady Anne, 52
Douglas, Sir Joseph, 204
Douglas, Marquis of, 143-4
Douglas, Marchioness of, 208
Douglas, Rev. Robert, 235
Drummond, Lady, 208
Dun, Erskine of, 66
Dunavertie, sack of, 181
Dunbar, battle of, 224-7
Dundas, Governor of Edinburgh Castle, 233
Dunfermline, Earl of, 133
Durham, Rev. Robert, 226
Durie, 101

Earl Marischal, 126, 278
Echard, Laurence, 32
Edinburgh Castle, surrendered to the English, 233
Eglinton, Earl of, 187, 190, 196, 202, 224
Elcho, Lord, 121-2, 131, 199, 226
Elgin, opponents of the Covenant at, 47
Elizabeth I, 24, 26, 115
Elizabeth, Princess, 2nd daughter of Charles I, 157
Elphinstone, Sir George, Justice Clerk, 14
Engagement, the, 185-90
Engagers, the, 191-221 passim
Erskine, Arthur, of Scotscraig, 218
Estrades, Count D', 85
Evelyn, John, 266

Fairfax, Lord, 163
Fanaticism, of Covenanters, 155-7
Fishing, forbidden on Sunday, 151
Fitzpayne-Fisher, Major, 262
Five Articles of Perth, 28-9, 35, 58, 71
Fleming, Sir William, 213
Fletcher, Sir John, 279
Forbes, William, Bishop of Edinburgh, 28

France: seeks English neutrality, 85-6; seeks to prevent alliance of Covenanters and English rebels, 119-20; de Montereul's mission to Charles I and the Covenanters, 161-6

Fraser, James, 216

Galloway, Bishop of, 39
Gardiner, S. R., 213
Gibson, Sir Alexander, of Durie, 109, 202
Gillespie, Rev. George, 159, 187
Gillespie, Patrick, 288
Glasgow, opponents of the Covenant at, 48
Glencairn, Earl of, 50, 109, 141, 187
Glencairn's Rising, 252-9, 262, 281, 283
Glengarry, Highland chief, 249-50
Gloucester, Duke of, youngest son of Charles I, 163
Gordon, Alexander, Laird of Earlstoun, 54-5
Gordon, James, 32, 38, 71, 73
Gordon, Sir John, of Haddo, 122, 126
Gordon, Lord, heir of 2nd Marquis of Huntly, 80, 88-9, 96, 122, 138, 250
Gordon, Lady Mary, 121
Gordon, Nathaniel, 147
Gordon, Patrick, 78
Gordon of Newton, 184
Govane, a Covenanter, 276, 288
Grahame, John, of Auchterarder, 98-9
Grahame, Lord, 139
Grahame, Patrick, of Inchbrakie, 130
Green Tables. See Tables
Gun, Colonel, 81
Guthrie, Andrew, 147
Guthrie, Henry, Bishop of Dunkeld, 38, 86, 102, 202
Guthrie, Rev. James, 235, 267, 271, 288

Haddington, Earl of, Lord Privy Seal, 14
Haddington, Countess of, 208, 215-16
Haig, lawyer, 33
Hamilton, James, third Marquis (later first Duke) of, 14, 79, 82, 228, 237; character, 49-50; and Charles I's proclamation, 55-60; and the General Assembly of 1638, 64-8; in secret communication with Covenanters, 80; and 'The Incident', 106-11; his divided loyalties, 112-13; created a duke, and goes to England, 114; his double dealing, 127; urges Charles I to sign the Nineteen Propositions, 172-3; receives payment for Charles I's betrayal, 175; struggle for power with Argyll, 179-84; and the Engagement, 185-90; fails to march immediately to Charles I's aid, 191; his weakness towards Argyll, 191-3; and the defeat of the Engagers, 193-5; trial and execution, 206-8
Hamilton, William, 2nd Duke of (formerly Earl of Lanerick, q.v.), 218, 240
Hammond, Robert, 185
Hanna, James, Dean of St. Giles, 36
Hartfell, Earl of, 130, 143, 147
Hay, Sir Francis, of Dalgetty, 217
Hay, Sir John, Clerk-Register, 14, 40
Henderson, Alexander, 44, 103-4, 111-12, 127, 169
Henrietta Maria, Queen, 113-14
Hepburn, Sir Adam, 101
Hertford, Marquis of, 280
Holbourn, Major-General, 199, 225-6, 239
Home, Earl of, 119, 143
Hope, Sir Alexander, 235
Hope, Sir Thomas, 14, 38, 40-1, 107, 113, 155-6
Hopton, Lord, 163
Hudson, Dr. Michael, 167-8, 170
Hume, Major, 141
Huntly, George, 2nd Marquis of, 43, 91, 145, 250; 'the Cock o' the North', 77-8; appointed Royal Lieutenant of the North, 78; Montrose sent to oppose him, 78-9; imprisoned in Edinburgh Castle, 80; released from imprisonment, 89; his abortive rising of 1644, 120-1; attitude to Montrose, 129; his strongholds captured, 180-1; imprisoned, 185, 193, 203; executed, 208-9
Huntly, Lewis, 3rd Marquis of, 209, 240
Hurry, Major-General Sir John, 138, 217
Hutcheson, Rev., 287
Hyde, Sir Edward (later Earl of Clarendon, q.v.), 205, 249, 255

Immorality, punishments for, 151
Independents, 116, 159, 163, 198-9, 210, 222, 249, 263
Ingoldsby, Colonel, 247
Innes, Major, 188
Inverlochy, Montrose's victory at, 136-8
Irving, Sir Alexander, 121
Irving, Lady, 121
Irving the younger, of Drum, 122

Jaffray, Alexander, 218
James I (James VI of Scotland and I of England), 18, 24, 26-7, 29-31, 34, 37, 40, 49, 63, 78, 149-50
James IV of Scotland, 18
'John de Maria,' 47
Johnston, Archibald. See Wariston

Kenmure, Lady, 276
Ker, Colonel, 232-3
Kilpont, Lord, 132
Kilsyth, Montrose's victory at, 138-43
Kinnoul, Earl of, 14, 18-19, 54
Kinnoul, 2nd Earl of, 114, 127
Kirk, the. See Scotland, Church of
Knox, John, 23-4, 37, 44, 149-50

Lachlan, Major, 146
Lambert, Major-General George, 193, 232, 239, 261
Lamont, John, 151-2
Lanerick, Earl of (later 2nd Duke of Hamilton, q.v.), 106-7, 113, 141, 143, 179, 185, 192, 202, 218
Lang, Andrew, 42, 46
Langdale, Sir Marmaduke, 191
Langton, 104
Large Declaration, 75
Laud, William, Archbishop of Canterbury, 14, 31, 38, 87-8
Lauderdale, Earl of, 185, 212, 267, 289
Law, Mungo, 137
Legge, Colonel, 220
Leith, Patrick, 184
Leslie, Alexander (later Lord Leven, q.v.), 76, 79, 86, 89, 93, 96, 103, 109, 118
Leslie, David, 118, 143-8, 180-1, 186, 190, 197, 224-5, 228, 233
Leslie, Fr. George, 209 n.
L'Estrange, Hamond, 96

Letters from Roundhead Officers, 261
Levellers, 191
Leven, Lord (formerly Alexander Leslie, q.v.), 118-20, 126, 128, 186, 190, 239
Lewis, Lord (later 3rd Marquis of Huntly, q.v.), 121, 182, 209
Libberton, Charles Winram of, 210-11, 218
Lilburne, Colonel Robert, 246, 249-50, 252-5, 261, 268, 284
Lindsay, David, Bishop of Brechin (later Bishop of Edinburgh), 17, 36-7, 39, 72
Lindsay of the Byres, Lord, 50, 67, 109, 138-9 (for later references see Crawford-Lindsay)
Linton, Lord, son of the Earl of Traquair, 143-4
Lockhart, Colonel, 265-6, 269
Logie, John, 126
Lom, Iain, 136-7
Long, Robert, 213
Lords of Erection, 30-2
Lorn, Lord (later 8th Earl, and first Marquis of Argyll), 49; antecedents, 51-2; marriage, and family quarrels, 52-3; favoured by Charles I, 53-4; character, 54-5. (For subsequent career see Argyll.)
Lorn, Lord (heir of Marquis of Argyll), 110, 215-16, 219, 250, 253-5, 258, 267-7
Lothian, Earl of, 168, 188, 202, 210, 219, 230, 236, 286-7
Londoun, John Campbell, Earl of, 41, 67, 85-7, 105-6, 110, 126, 141, 164, 173, 179, 185, 194, 196, 201, 214, 235-6, 241-2, 272
Louis XIII, 85
Lumsden, Robert, 240

Macaulay, James, 152
Macbreck, Fr. James, 154-5, 262
MacDonald, Alastair, 122-3. See also Colkitto
MacDonalds of Keppoch, 91-2
Mackenzie, Sir George, 279, 286, 289
MacLeod, Colonel, 254
Manchester, Lord, 159
Manifesto to all good Christians . . ., 76
Mar, Earl of, 86, 196
Marshall, Stephen, 187

Marston Moor, battle of, 125, 128, 130
Mary, Princess Royal of England (later Princess of Orange), 18
Mary Queen of Scots, 37
Mason, John, 262
Mauchline - moor, Engagers defeat Covenanters at, 193
Maurice, Prince, 166
Maxwell, Lord (later Earl of Niths-dale, q.v.), 31
Maxwell, Elizabeth, 259
Mazarin, Cardinal, 161-2, 164, 170, 180
Mercurius Politicus, 241
Michelson, 'she prophetess', 59
Middleton, Sir John (later Earl of Middleton), 181, 193, 249, 254-5, 278, 281-2
Mildmay, Sir Henry, 175
Mitchell, Rev. David, 47
Monck, George, 239-42, 247, 255-9, 260-1, 270-2, 283-5
Montgomery, Colonel Robert, 229, 232
Montgomery of Skelmorie, 86, 286
Montrose, James Grahame, 5th Earl (later first Marquis) of, 49, 56, 65, 89, 163, 170, 194, 223, 252; and Charles I's Declaration, 43; opposes Carnegie's election, 66; sent by Covenanters to oppose Huntly, 78-9; grants terms to Huntly, 79; conflict with Argyll, 95-102; and 'The Incident', 108-11; and Henrietta Maria, 114; offered the Lieutenant-Generalship, 114-15; resolves to support Charles I, 127-9; returns in disguise to Scotland, 129-30; appeals to Argyll to return to the King's allegiance, 130-1; marches on Perth, 131-2; captures Aberdeen, 132-3; repels Argyll's force at the Ythan River, 133-4; defeats Argyll's forces in Argyllshire, 135-6; defeats Argyll's forces at Inverlochy, 136-8; his victory at Kilsyth, 138-43; prepares to help Royalists in England, 143-4; defeated by David Leslie at Philiphaugh, 144-8; escapes from Scotland, 180; in exile, 203; desires to overthrow Argyll's government, 211; defeated at Carbisdale, 213; Charles II's attempt to safeguard, 213-14; captured and hanged, 214-17

Montrose, James Grahame, 2nd Marquis of, 255
Montereul, Jean de, 161-70, 173, 177, 179-80, 182-3, 186-7, 194
Moray, Bishop of, Great Almoner, 17, 19
Moray, Sir Robert, 186, 250
Morgan, Colonel, 257
Morton, Regent, 23, 69
Morton, William, 7th Earl of, Lord Treasurer, 14, 52-3, 104-5, 114, 130
Munro, Sir George, 196-7, 255
Munro, Major, 103, 105
Murray, William, Groom of the Bedchamber to Charles I, 49, 109, 214
Murray, William, brother of the Earl of Tullibardine, 147

Napier, Lord, 100, 115, 139, 171
Naseby, 140
National Covenant. See Covenant, National
Nevoy, John, 181
New Model Army, 159, 162, 179, 182, 185, 191, 195, 251
Newcastle, Lord, 128
Nicholas, Secretary, 32, 106, 166, 223, 230, 235, 277
Nicoll, John, 151-2, 260-1
Nineteen Propositions, the, 171-3
Nisbet, Sir John, 279
Nisbet, Sir Philip, 146
Nithsdale, Earl of (formerly Lord Maxwell, q.v.), 127, 129-30
Northumberland, Earl of, 163
Norwich, Earl of, 207

Oath of Allegiance, to Commonwealth, 242
Ogilvies of Airlie, oppose the Covenant, 89
Ogilvy, Alexander, 146
Ogilvy, Lord, son of the Earl of Airlie, 90, 115, 127, 142, 284
Ogilvy, Lady, 91
O'Kean, Colonel, 146
Orkney, Bishop of, 72
Ormonde, Duke of, 103, 200, 205, 210-11
Osborne, Lieutenant, 264
Overton, Colonel, 243
Owen, Sir John, 207

Pacification of Berwick, 81-2

Panter, Dr., Professor of Divinity at St. Andrews, 71

Philiphaugh, Montrose defeated at, 144-8

Pierson, Major, 241

Poverty, in Covenanting Scotland, 155

Prince of Orange, 209

Prince of Wales (later Charles II, *q.v.*), 18, 163, 183

Protectorate. *See* Commonwealth and Protectorate

Protesters, the, 262-4, 267-71, 275

Quakerism, 263-4

Ramsay, Rev. Robert, 248

Reformation, in Scotland, 23-6

Reid, Colonel, 243

Remonstrants, the, 230-2, 237. *See also* Protesters

Resolutioners, the, 248-9, 262-4, 267-71

Retz, Cardinal de, 161

Richelieu, Cardinal, 85

Richmond, Duke of, 280

Riding of the Parliament, ceremony of, 18-19

Rollo, Sir James, 115, 127, 137, 146

Rollo, Sir William, 145-6

Ross, Bishop of, 34

Rothes, Earl of, 16, 42-6, 85-6, 110, 216

Roxburgh, Earl of, 37, 41, 43, 143-4, 202

Rump Parliament, 270-1

Rupert, Prince, 115, 126, 130, 166

Rutherford, Rev. Samuel, 276

Ruthven, General, 87

Ruthven, Sir Thomas, 202

Savile, Lord, 84-5

Scotland: social conditions under Covenanter rule, 149-57; invasion of, under Cromwell, 221-4; Oath of Allegiance to Commonwealth imposed upon, 242, 246-7; social conditions under Commonwealth rule, 260-5; fully incorporated with England in 1652, 262; state of the nobility under the Commonwealth, 265; Council of State set up by Commonwealth, 265-6; and the Restoration, 271-3

Scotland, Church of: establishment of, 26-7; the Court of High Commission, 27-8; the Five Articles, 28-9; endowment, and the Lords of Erection, 30-3; outcry against the Service Book, 34-9; outcry against the bishops, 40-8; and Charles I's Declaration, 41-3; origins of the Covenant, 43-8; the Confession of Faith, 44-5; Charles I's proclamation regarding the Covenant, 55-61; Charles I's republication of the Confession of Faith, 58; General Assembly disobeys Charles I's order to dissolve, 63-9; the Assembly's excommunication of the bishops, 69-75; its oppressive code, 149-55; fanaticism, 155-7; and the battle of Dunbar, 225, 227; postpones Charles II's coronation, 234; attempts to usurp Charles II's authority, 236-7; under the Commonwealth, 247-9; Lieut.-Col. Cotterel's dismissal of General Assembly of 1653, 251-2; quarrel between Protesters and Resolutioners, 262-4; curbed by Cromwell, 264

Scott, Sir John, 199

Seaforth, Covenanter army leader, 136-7

Secret Council, Lords of, 33

Service Book, 34-9, 42, 64, 71, 150

Seton, Lady, 208

Sharp, Rev. James, 267

Short Parliament, 87

Sibbald, Colonel, 90, 134, 217

Sinclair, Lord, 100, 103, 105, 122

Six Famous Letters, 253, 284, 286

Skippon, Philip, 176

Smythe, Adjutant-General, 244-5

Social conditions, under the Covenanters, 149-55; under the Commonwealth, 260-5

Solemn League and Covenant, 116-19, 229

Spalding, John, 32, 103

Spang, cousin of Robert Baillie, 48

Spottiswoode, Archbishop, 14-17, 28, 36-7, 54, 72

Spottiswoode, Sir John, 216-17

Spottiswoode, Sir Robert, 147

Start, The, 229-31

Stewart, Rev. Gavin, 152

Stewart, James, of Ardvoirloch, 132

Stewart, Sir James, of Coltness, 215, 287-8

Stewart, John, of Ladywell, 90, 96, 99, 101-2

Stewart, Lady Mary, 215

Stewart, Sir Thomas, of Grandtully, 96

Stewart, Captain Walter, 99-101

Stewart of Blackhall, 100

Stewarts of Atholl, oppose the Covenant, 89

Stirling, Viscount, Secretary, 14, 106

Stirling of Keir, 100

Strachan, Major (later Colonel), 190, 214, 228-9, 232-3

Strafford, Earl of, 84-5, 93-4

Strange, Dr., Principal of Glasgow University, 67

Stuart, Montrose's Adjutant, 145, 147

Sutherland, Earl of, 269

Swinton, Sir John, 233, 266, 278

Sydserf, Thomas, Bishop of Galloway, 54

Tables, the, 40-8 *passim*, 63, 65

Taxation, 155

Taylor, John, the Water Poet, 22

Tiend Commission, 32

Trail, Robert, 286

Transportation of ministers, 152-3

Traquair, Earl of, 14, 39, 42, 82-4, 99, 130, 143-5, 185

Treaty of Breda, 213, 217, 230

Treaty of Ripon, 94, 103

Tullibardine, Earl of, 147

Turner, Sir James, 50, 76-7, 168, 181, 186

Walker, Clement, 50, 206

Walker, Sir Edward, 218

Walsh, preacher, 26

Walton, Colonel Valentine, 125

Wariston, Archibald Johnston of, 44, 71, 85, 189, 210, 215, 276; and the Proclamation of Charles I, 57, 60; and Dun's commission, 66; appointed censor, 74; a tool of Argyll, 110; presses for vengeance on Montrose's followers, 146; his fanaticism, 155-7; receives payment for betraying Charles I, 175; and the Act of Classes, 201-2; his order for the hanging of Carnwath, 219; and Charles I, 221; and the Independents, 222; meets Cromwell, 235-6; and terms for Charles I, 237; refusal to negotiate with Royalists, 250-1; and the Protesters and Resolutionists, 266-8; ambitions to sit in House of Lords, 268-9; secures place on Council of State, 269-70; panics at prospect of Restoration, 271-2; flies to Holland, 272; trial and execution, 288-90

Warwick, Sir Philip, 33, 50, 117

Western Remonstrance, 229-31

Whalley, Colonel, 247

Whiggamore Raid, 196

Wigton, Earl of, 39, 97

Willcock, John, 55, 88, 171, 277

Wilmot, Lord, 93

Winram, Charles, of Libberton. *See* Libberton

Wishart, Dr. George, 115, 197

Witchcraft, 153-4

Wodrow, Robert, 55

Vane, Sir Harry, 106, 116

Yeomen of the Guard, 14-15

Ythan River, clash of Argyll's and Montrose's forces at, 133-4